New General Mathematics

for Junior Secondary Schools 1
UBE Edition

M F Macrae
A O Kalejaiye
Z I Chima
G U Garba
J B Channon
A McLeish Smith
H C Head

New General Mathematics

for Junior Secondary Schools 1
UBE Edition

M F Macrae
A O Kalejaiye
Z I Chima
G U Garba
J B Channon
A McLeish Smith
H C Head

Pearson Education Limited
Edinburgh Gate
Harlow
Essex
CM20 2JE
England and Associated Companies throughout the
World.

© Pearson Education Limited 2007

The right of M F Macrae, Z I Chima, G U Garba,
A O Kalejaiye, J B Channon, A McLeish Smith and
H C Head to be identified as the authors of the Work
has been asserted by them in accordance with the
Copyright, Designs and Patents Act of 1988.

All rights reserved. No part of this publication may be
reproduced, stored in a retrieval system, or transmitted
in any form or by any means, electronic, mechanical,
photocopying, recording, or otherwise without the
prior written permission of the Publishers or a licence
permitting restricted copying in the United Kingdom
issued by the Copyright Licensing Agency Ltd, 90
Tottenham Court Road, London, W1P 0LP.

ISBN: 978-1-4058-6998-0

First published 2000
This edition 2007
Printed in Malaysia (CTP-VVP)

20 19 18 17 16 15 14 13 12
IMP 15 14 13 12 11 10 9

Preface

New General Mathematics

This widely popular series has been revised to reflect the 2007 Nigerian Educational Research and Development Council (NERDC) National Mathematics Curriculum for upper basic level.[1]

A survey of schools indicated that, in addition to coverage of the NERDC mathematics curriculum and general updating, the inclusion of chapter objectives and suggestions for teaching and learning materials would strengthen the series. We have also used the opportunity to ensure that examples and exercises contain, where appropriate, references to emerging issues such as information and communications technology, social awareness, the environment and health. Exercises have now been graded into three levels of difficulty. In addition, at various places within the books, there are challenges and puzzle boxes to encourage non-routine problem solving. While making these revisions, care has been taken to retain the style and rigour of the previous *New General Mathematics* course books.

The authors wish to express their appreciation to the many students and teachers who have corresponded with them over the years. In addition we would like to acknowledge our debt to Dotun Kalejaiye, John Channon, Alex McLeish Smith and Henry Head, whose inputs to earlier versions helped to create such a sound foundation for this highly respected series.

MFM, ZIC, GUG
Lagos 2007

---

[1] The National Curriculum covers the 9-year Universal Basic Education cycle. The Upper Basic level is the last three years of this cycle, and is equivalent to the 3-year Junior Secondary phase. The NGM course covers the mathematics component of Junior Secondary/Upper Basic schooling.

Using this book

Each chapter contains the following:

- **Chapter objectives**
  This tells you what you will be able to do if you work carefully through the chapter.

- **Teaching and learning materials**
  This section gives suggestions on what the teacher and student should bring to the lesson. We appreciate that it will not always be possible to provide everything that is listed. However, we wish to stress that mathematics is a 'doing' subject. Therefore every student will need at least an exercise book, a pen, a mathematical set and, when appropriate, graph paper.

- **Worked examples**
  These provide guidelines and models for setting out mathematical work.

- **Graded exercises**
  For the new edition we have graded the exercises by writing the question numbers in three different ways:
  - ① You must do all of these questions if you are to understand the topic.
  - ② You should do these questions if possible.
  - ③ If you want a challenge, then you could do these questions.

  Where you see *QR* beside an exercise or a question, this stands for *Quantitative Reasoning*. You should do and discuss these questions with your teacher and class-mates. They give special practice at improving your number-work and your ability to calculate.

- **Chapter summary**
  This appears at the end of the chapter and lists the main learning outcomes.

- **Puzzle corners**
  Throughout this book you will find occasional puzzle corners. Try the puzzles in your spare time. To keep you guessing, we have deliberately *not* included answers!

PUZZLE CORNER

Trading

A trader bought an item for ₦ 1500 and then sold it for ₦ 2000. She then bought it back for ₦ 2500 and finally sold it for ₦ 3000

How much did she gain or lose on this trading?

PUZZLE CORNER

Regular Polygons

Can you see any regular polygons in this pattern?

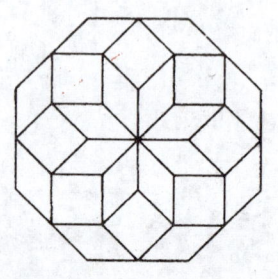

How many of each kind?

Contents

Curriculum Matching Chart viii

Preliminary chapter
Basic operations; the SI system 1
  P-1 Basic operations 1
  P-2 The SI system of units 8

Chapter 1
Development of number systems 11
  1-1 Counting 11
  1-2 Symbols for numbers 13
  1-3 The place-value system 17

Chapter 2
Large and small numbers 19
  2-1 Large numbers 19
  2-2 Reading and writing large numbers 20
  2-3 Small numbers 21

Chapter 3
Factors and multiples 23
  3-1 Factors 23
  3-2 Highest common factor (HCF) 25
  3-3 Multiples 26
  3-4 Lowest common multiple (LCM) 27

Chapter 4
Fractions 1:
Fractions and percentages 29
  4-1 Common fractions 29
  4-2 Equivalent fractions 30
  4-3 Basic operations on fractions 32
  4-4 Percentages 36

Chapter 5
Use of symbols 1:
Letters for numbers 40
  5-1 Open sentences 40
  5-2 Letters for numbers 41

Chapter 6
Solids 1: Properties 44
  6-1 Three-dimensional shapes 44
  6-2 Cuboids and cubes 45
  6-3 Cylinders and prisms 49
  6-4 Cones and pyramids 51
  6-5 Spheres 53
  6-6 Naming vertices, edges and faces 54

Chapter 7
Algebraic simplification 1: Grouping 56
  7-1 Coefficients 56
  7-2 Grouping positive and negative terms 57
  7-3 Grouping like and unlike terms 58

Chapter 8
Angles 1: Measurement 61
  8-1 Angle as rotation 61
  8-2 Angles between lines 61
  8-3 Measuring angles 64
  8-4 Constructing angles 67

Revision exercises and tests
Chapters 1–8 69

Chapter 9
Fractions 2:
Decimals and percentages 73
  9-1 Decimals 73
  9-2 Addition and subtraction 73
  9-3 Multiplication and division 74
  9-4 Conversion 78
  9-5 Decimals and percentages 79

Chapter 10
Use of symbols 2: Word problems 81
  10-1 Algebra from words 81

Chapter 11
Plane shapes 1: Properties 85
  11-1 Rectangles and squares 85

11-2	Triangles	86
11-3	Polygons	88
11-4	Circles	89

Chapter 12
Directed numbers:
Addition and subtraction — 92
12-1	The number line	92
12-2	Directed numbers	96
12-3	Adding and subtracting positive numbers	97
12-4	Adding and subtracting negative numbers	99

Chapter 13
Plane shapes 2: Perimeter — 102
13-1	Measuring perimeters	102
13-2	Using formulae to calculate perimeters	104
13-3	Perimeter of circles	107

Chapter 14
Plane shapes 3: Area — 112
14-1	Area	112
14-2	Area of rectangles and squares	113
14-3	Area of parallelograms	116
14-4	Area of triangles and trapeziums	118
14-5	Area of circles	121

Chapter 15
Algebraic simplification 2: Brackets — 124
15-1	Multiplying and dividing algebraic terms	124
15-2	Order of operations	126
15-3	Removing brackets	127

Chapter 16
Solids 2: Volume — 130
16-1	Volume	130
16-2	Volume of cuboids and cubes	131
16-3	Capacity of containers	132
16-4	Volume of right-angled triangular prism	133

Revision exercises and tests
Chapters 9–16 — 135

Chapter 17
Statistics 1:
Purpose and data collection — 139
17-1	The need for statistics	139
17-2	Data collection	141

Chapter 18
Statistics 2: Presentation of data — 144
18-1	Types of presentation	144
18-2	Lists and tables	144
18-3	Graphical presentation	144

Chapter 19
Simple equations — 150
19-1	Equations	150
19-2	Solution of an equation	151

Chapter 20
Angles 2: Angles between lines;
angles in a triangle — 156
20-1	Angles between lines	156
20-2	Calculating the sizes of angles	157
20-3	Parallel lines	160
20-4	Angles in a triangle	162

Chapter 21
Construction:
Parallel and perpendicular lines — 166
21-1	Construction	166
21-2	Construction of parallel lines	166
21-3	Constructing perpendiculars	167

Chapter 22
Statistics 3: Averages — 171
22-1	Averages	171
22-2	The mean	171
22-3	The median	172
22-4	The mode	173

Chapter 23
Estimation and approximation — 176
23-1	Estimation	176
23-2	Rounding off numbers	178
23-3	Approximation	179

Chapter 24
Base two arithmetic — 183
24-1	Number bases	183

24-2 Binary numbers 184
24-3 Operations with binary numbers 186

**Revision exercises and tests
Chapters 17–24** 189

Tables 194

Answers 197

Index 231

CURRICULUM MATCHING CHART

Chapter	Chapter Title	NERDC Curriculum Themes and Topics	NERDC Performance Objectives
Preliminary	Basic operations; the SI system	*Basic Operations, p 8* *Topic 1: Addition and Subtraction*	Add, subtract numbers correctly
1	Development of number systems	*Basic Operations, p 8* *Topic 1: Addition and Subtraction*	State the place value of numbers
2	Large and small numbers	*Number & Numeration, p 1* *Topic 1: Whole Numbers*	Count and write in millions, billions, trillions Count, write and read large quantities Develop QR with large numbers
3	Factors and multiples	*Number & Numeration, pp 3 and 4* *Topics 3 and 4: LCM, 4HCF*	Find LCM and HCF of whole numbers Develop QR with LCM and HCF
4	Fractions 1: Fractions and percentages	*Number & Numeration, pp 1 and 2* *Topic: 2 Fractions* *Basic Operations, p 9* *Topic 1: Addition and subtraction*	Identify and use equivalent fractions Arrange fractions in ascending and descending order Add and subtract fractions
5	Use of symbols 1: Letters for numbers	*Algebraic Processes, p 10* *Topic 1: Use of symbols*	Solve problems with open sentences Add, subtract, multiply, divide in open sentences Use letters to represent symbols in open sentences
6	Solids 1: Properties	*Geometry and Mensuration, p 16* *Topic 2 Three-dimensional figures*	Identify the properties of cubes, cuboids, pyramids, cones, cylinders and spheres
7	Algebraic simplification 1: Grouping	*Algebraic Processes, p 12* *Topic 2: Simplification of algebraic expressions*	Identify positive and negative coefficients of terms Add and subtract like terms Collect and simplify like terms
8	Angles 1: Measurement	*Geometry and Mensuration, p 17* *Topic 4: Angles*	Measure angles
9	Fractions 2: Decimals and percentages	*Number & Numeration, p 2* *Topic 2: Fractions* *Basic Operations, p 9* *Topic 1: Addition and subtraction*	Convert fractions to decimals Convert decimals to fractions Convert fractions to percentages Convert percentages to fractions Add and subtract decimal fractions Develop QR in problems with fractions
10	Use of symbols 2: Word problems	*Algebraic Processes, p 11* *Topic 1: Use of symbols* *Algebraic Processes, p 14* *Topic 2: Simplification of algebraic expressions*	Solve open sentences involving two arithmetic operations Solve word problems involving use of symbols Write word problems in symbolic terms

Chapter	Chapter Title	NERDC Curriculum Themes and Topics	NERDC Performance Objectives
11	Plane shapes 1: Properties	*Geometry and Mensuration, p 15* *Topic 1: Plane shapes*	Identify various plane shapes by name and property
12	Directed numbers: Addition and subtraction	*Basic Operations, pp 8 – 9* *Topic 1: Addition and subtraction*	Draw and use the number line to illustrate directed numbers Relate negative numbers to everyday activities Add and subtract positive and negative numbers
13	Plane shapes 2: Perimeter	*Geometry and Mensuration, p 15* *Topic 1: Plane shapes*	Find the perimeter of regular polygons (square, rectangle, triangle, trapezium, parallelogram and circle) Find the perimeter of irregular shapes Relate perimeter to real-life situations
14	Plane shapes 3: Area	*Geometry and Mensuration, p 15* *Topic 1: Plane shapes*	Find the area of regular and irregular shapes (square, rectangle, triangle, trapezium, parallelogram and circle) Find the perimeter of irregular shapes Relate finding area to real-life situations
15	Algebraic simplification 2: Brackets	*Algebraic Processes, pp 13 – 14* *Topic 2: Simplification of algebraic expressions*	Insert/remove brackets Simplify algebraic expressions Write word problems in symbolic terms Develop QR in problems involving brackets
16	Solids 2: Volume	*Geometry and Mensuration, p 16* *Topic 2: Three-dimensional figures*	Find the volume of cubes, cuboids
17	Statistics 1: Purpose and data collection	*Everyday Statistics, pp 18 – 19* *Topic 1: Need for statistics* *Topic 2: Data collection*	List purposes of statistics Use statistics for planning, analysis and prediction Collect statistical data
18	Statistics 2: Presentation of data	*Everyday Statistics, p 19* *Topic 3: Data presentation*	Present statistical data in lists, tables and graphs
19	Simple equations	*Algebraic Processes, p 11 and 14* *Topic 1: Use of symbols* *Topic 3: Simple equations*	Solve open sentences involving two operations Define simple equations Solve simple equations Check the solution of an equation
20	Angles 2: Angles between lines; angles in a triangle	*Geometry and Mensuration, p 17* *Topic 4: Angles*	Identify and recall the properties of vertically opposite angles, angles at a point, angles on a straight line, adjacent angles, alternate angles, corresponding angles Find the sum of the angles of a triangle Relate angles to real situations

xi

Chapter	Chapter Title	NERDC Curriculum Themes and Topics	NERDC Performance Objectives
21	Construction: Parallel and perpendicular lines	*Geometry and Mensuration, p 17* *Topic 3: Construction*	Construct parallel lines Construct perpendicular lines
22	Statistics 3: Averages	*Everyday Statistics, pp 18 and 19* *Topic: Averages*	Determine the mean, median and mode of a set of data
23	Estimation and approximation	*Number & Numeration, pp 5 and 6* *Topic 5: Estimation* *Topic 6: Approximation*	Estimate lengths, distances, capacity and mass of various objects Approximate answers to addition, subtraction, multiplication and division problems Round off numbers to various degrees of accuracy Develop QR in estimation and approximation
24	Base two arithmetic	*Number & Numeration, p 7* *Topics 7–10: Operations with base two numerals*	Convert numbers between bases ten and two Count and group objects in twos Add, subtract, multiply with binary numbers up to 3-digits Develop QR in number base conversion and base two arithmetic

Note: QR means *Quantitative Reasoning* (ability to cope with numbers and calculation)

Preliminary chapter
Basic operations; the SI system

OBJECTIVES

You should be able to:
1. Add, subtract, multiply and divide whole numbers
2. Add, subtract, multiply, divide and simplify elementary fractions and decimals
3. State and apply the basic units of length, mass, capacity and time
4. Convert measurements from one unit to another.

Teaching and learning materials

Teacher: Addition and multiplication wall charts; metre rule, measuring tape, 1 kg mass, 1-litre container (e.g. empty juice packet or bottle), clock

P-1 Basic operations

You must be able to add, subtract, multiply and divide whole numbers. These skills will help you in **quantitative reasoning** [QR] and will be useful throughout school and in later life.

This chapter contains tests to give you practice in the basic number skills. There are tests in each of the following:

addition skills	(Tests A–J, page 3)
subtraction skills	(Tests A–J, page 4)
multiplication skills	(Tests A–J, page 5)
division skills	(Tests A–J, page 6)
fractions and decimals	(Tests A–J, page 7)

Each test is in the column under the test heading. Do each test as follows.

a Allow 10 minutes to do each test.
b Try to do every item.
c Use the answers in the back of the book to correct the test.
d If you get an item wrong, find the line that the item was in. Then do all the items in that line right across the page. For example, suppose you get item 6 wrong in Test B. Do all the items 6 in Tests A, B, C, D, and E.
e If you still get these items wrong, see your teacher for assistance.

There are many different methods of adding, subtracting, multiplying and dividing. Use the method you already know. If you find that you make too many mistakes, your teacher may show you another method.

Do *not* do all the tests at once. There are enough tests to do one every week of the school year. Your teacher will tell you when to do the tests.

You will find the following useful when doing this chapter. Try to memorise the following facts.

Addition

+	1	2	3	4	5	6	7	8	9	10
1	2	3	4	5	6	7	8	9	10	11
2	3	4	5	6	7	8	9	10	11	12
3	4	5	6	7	8	9	10	11	12	13
4	5	6	7	8	9	10	11	12	13	14
5	6	7	8	9	10	11	12	13	14	15
6	7	8	9	10	11	12	13	14	15	16
7	8	9	10	11	12	13	14	15	16	17
8	9	10	11	12	13	14	15	16	17	18
9	10	11	12	13	14	15	16	17	18	19
10	11	12	13	14	15	16	17	18	19	20

Your teacher will show you how to use this table for simple subtraction facts.

Multiplication

×	1	2	3	4	5	6	7	8	9	10
1	1	2	3	4	5	6	7	8	9	10
2	2	4	6	8	10	12	14	16	18	20
3	3	6	9	12	15	18	21	24	27	30
4	4	8	12	16	20	24	28	32	36	40
5	5	10	15	20	25	30	35	40	45	50
6	6	12	18	24	30	36	42	48	54	60
7	7	14	21	28	35	42	49	56	63	70
8	8	16	24	32	40	48	56	64	72	80
9	9	18	27	36	45	54	63	72	81	90
10	10	20	30	40	50	60	70	80	90	100

Your teacher will show you how to use this table for division facts.

Fractions, decimals, percentages

Equivalence: e.g. (a) $56\% = \dfrac{56}{100} = 0\cdot 56$

(b) $\dfrac{56}{100} = \dfrac{14}{25}$ (lowest terms)

Conversion: e.g. (c) $\dfrac{3}{4} = \dfrac{3\cdot 00}{4} = 0\cdot 75 = \dfrac{75}{100}$

$= 75\%$

Addition: Revision and practice

	Test A [QR]	Test B [QR]	Test C [QR]	Test D [QR]	Test E [QR]
1	5 + 3	2 + 7	5 + 4	3 + 4	3 + 2
2	11 + 6	3 + 13	10 + 9	12 + 7	4 + 14
3	7 + 8	9 + 4	6 + 7	2 + 9	5 + 7
4	44 + 4	6 + 31	43 + 2	1 + 76	81 + 8
5	3 + 9 + 1	3 + 5 + 7	2 + 8 + 9	5 + 8 + 5	9 + 6 + 1
6	48 + 3	9 + 28	66 + 5	7 + 83	35 + 5
7	23 + 41	82 + 17	49 + 40	64 + 34	22 + 26
8	28 + 26	53 + 64	47 + 33	36 + 55	81 + 65
9	75 + 58	27 + 93	45 + 59	68 + 68	82 + 49
10	445 + 386	383 + 750	939 + 859	637 + 295	486 + 485
11	423 + 397	544 + 961	246 + 255	680 + 361	874 + 727
12	312 + 89 + 651	629 + 502 + 143 + 817	153 + 153 + 75 + 9	374 + 1280 + 6400	378 + 344 + 206

	Test F [QR]	Test G [QR]	Test H [QR]	Test I [QR]	Test J [QR]
1	1 + 8	7 + 3	0 + 2	6 + 3	1 + 9
2	15 + 2	4 + 12	7 + 11	18 + 2	3 + 16
3	8 + 6	8 + 9	8 + 3	4 + 7	4 + 8
4	6 + 90	75 + 4	5 + 62	50 + 9	7 + 22
5	7 + 5 + 5	7 + 8 + 3	6 + 4 + 6	8 + 9 + 2	4 + 5 + 6
6	4 + 59	46 + 6	7 + 74	55 + 8	6 + 39
7	55 + 23	34 + 43	53 + 36	23 + 71	30 + 28
8	34 + 70	92 + 76	39 + 49	94 + 25	36 + 57
9	36 + 64	79 + 39	72 + 68	83 + 38	94 + 97
10	471 + 963	704 + 727	491 + 654	736 + 819	356 + 357
11	385 + 315	608 + 405	546 + 556	435 + 367	809 + 195
12	961 + 86 + 422	256 + 165 + 54 + 32	434 + 504 + 614 + 24	34 + 85 + 75 + 26	693 + 631 + 676

Subtraction: Revision and practice

	Test A [QR]	Test B [QR]	Test C [QR]	Test D [QR]	Test E [QR]
1	6 − 2	7 − 4	9 − 5	8 − 0	3 − 1
2	18 − 5	14 − 11	15 − 3	19 − 15	16 − 6
3	10 − 3	20 − 5	10 − 8	20 − 11	10 − 5
4	14 − 6	11 − 7	18 − 9	13 − 5	12 − 3
5	28 − 4	99 − 8	35 − 1	47 − 3	65 − 2
6	49 − 23	56 − 42	28 − 17	85 − 32	78 − 15
7	62 − 58	73 − 65	36 − 28	95 − 87	28 − 19
8	33 − 17	85 − 36	72 − 47	96 − 29	64 − 37
9	271 − 93	314 − 46	850 − 83	426 − 58	537 − 39
10	523 − 265	635 − 577	748 − 258	571 − 374	854 − 548
11	204 − 146	402 − 273	500 − 156	603 − 405	307 − 128
12	2037 − 849	3503 − 1597	5662 − 5074	4080 − 1976	2005 − 1229

	Test F [QR]	Test G [QR]	Test H [QR]	Test I [QR]	Test J [QR]
1	5 − 4	8 − 3	7 − 5	3 − 3	9 − 3
2	17 − 10	13 − 1	16 − 13	19 − 4	18 − 11
3	20 − 6	10 − 9	20 − 12	10 − 7	20 − 17
4	15 − 8	17 − 8	16 − 7	14 − 9	13 − 6
5	61 − 0	42 − 2	88 − 6	76 − 3	37 − 2
6	99 − 65	36 − 14	59 − 44	64 − 24	84 − 53
7	51 − 49	84 − 75	47 − 39	41 − 32	35 − 26
8	45 − 29	60 − 26	93 − 68	61 − 46	82 − 59
9	763 − 76	625 − 86	211 − 72	142 − 57	374 − 95
10	982 − 298	614 − 219	433 − 224	641 − 368	770 − 482
11	405 − 198	708 − 539	201 − 165	306 − 287	502 − 396
12	5231 − 506	6814 − 5807	7486 − 2979	3113 − 2066	6104 − 825

Multiplication: Revision and practice

	Test A [QR]	Test B [QR]	Test C [QR]	Test D [QR]	Test E [QR]
1	6 × 7	9 × 8	6 × 9	7 × 4	7 × 8
2	2 × 8 × 2	5 × 2 × 6	2 × 4 × 8	2 × 8 × 5	9 × 2 × 2
3	4 × 21	43 × 2	5 × 11	61 × 1	3 × 12
4	9 × 13	6 × 14	2 × 17	8 × 16	5 × 18
5	39 × 8	78 × 4	63 × 7	69 × 5	26 × 9
6	36 × 100	1000 × 52	860 × 10	100 × 4	7 × 1000
7	428 × 7	8431 × 5	325 × 9	3781 × 3	472 × 6
8	3126 × 4	335 × 6	7735 × 3	172 × 7	8549 × 2
9	5 × 2 × 34	4 × 5 × 19	26 × 6 × 5	8 × 65 × 5	5 × 54 × 12
10	80 × 59	57 × 30	70 × 82	78 × 40	90 × 61
11	43 × 52	254 × 57	74 × 61	820 × 29	93 × 17
12	562 × 308	425 × 409	257 × 830	621 × 341	542 × 209

	Test F [QR]	Test G [QR]	Test H [QR]	Test I [QR]	Test J [QR]
1	9 × 4	6 × 8	9 × 7	7 × 7	9 × 9
2	3 × 8 × 2	3 × 7 × 3	4 × 6 × 2	3 × 3 × 5	2 × 3 × 7
3	53 × 0	2 × 23	30 × 3	4 × 22	3 × 23
4	7 × 16	4 × 14	3 × 15	6 × 19	7 × 13
5	48 × 3	28 × 7	83 × 6	24 × 9	37 × 4
6	10 × 60	508 × 100	1000 × 90	10 × 1000	100 × 300
7	8307 × 2	904 × 8	3941 × 4	861 × 8	6275 × 5
8	156 × 9	2369 × 3	138 × 8	6141 × 5	346 × 8
9	5 × 78 × 6	25 × 67 × 2	3 × 19 × 10	5 × 58 × 8	15 × 37 × 4
10	30 × 62	29 × 80	50 × 38	87 × 60	20 × 93
11	713 × 35	87 × 71	389 × 17	62 × 36	105 × 47
12	485 × 168	647 × 392	705 × 516	470 × 288	452 × 219

Division: Revision and practice

Note: 12 ÷ 6, $\frac{1}{6}$ of 12, $\frac{12}{6}$, $6\overline{)12}$ are different ways of writing 12 divided by 6.

	Test A [QR]	Test B [QR]	Test C [QR]	Test D [QR]	Test E [QR]
①	9 ÷ 3	$\frac{1}{4}$ of 8	$\frac{8}{2}$	$3\overline{)6}$	6 ÷ 2
②	$\frac{64}{8}$	$3\overline{)24}$	42 ÷ 6	$\frac{1}{8}$ of 72	$\frac{54}{9}$
③	$\frac{1}{2}$ of 72	$\frac{80}{2}$	$2\overline{)90}$	52 ÷ 2	$\frac{1}{2}$ of 86
④	$5\overline{)65}$	56 ÷ 4	$\frac{1}{6}$ of 72	$\frac{91}{7}$	$3\overline{)51}$
⑤	196 ÷ 7	$\frac{1}{6}$ of 150	$\frac{154}{7}$	$8\overline{)184}$	162 ÷ 6
⑥	$\frac{62\,000}{100}$	$\frac{1}{10}$ of 440	$\frac{50\,000}{1\,000}$	600 ÷ 100	$10\overline{)8\,000}$
⑦	$\frac{1}{6}$ of 258	$\frac{455}{7}$	$5\overline{)690}$	3 828 ÷ 4	$\frac{1}{8}$ of 464
⑧	$8\overline{)1\,624}$	$3\overline{)927}$	$4\overline{)2\,032}$	$5\overline{)535}$	$4\overline{)2\,408}$
⑨	1 072 ÷ 8	$5\overline{)6\,005}$	5 202 ÷ 9	$4\overline{)4\,008}$	7 206 ÷ 2
⑩	$31\overline{)3\,162}$	$25\overline{)7\,525}$	$44\overline{)9\,108}$	$30\overline{)1\,680}$	$45\overline{)9\,135}$
⑪	$43\overline{)1\,247}$	$59\overline{)18\,054}$	$32\overline{)2\,752}$	$92\overline{)10\,580}$	$57\overline{)3\,591}$
⑫	$49\overline{)15\,043}$	$37\overline{)30\,451}$	$90\overline{)26\,100}$	$33\overline{)25\,971}$	$69\overline{)57\,822}$

	Test F [QR]	Test G [QR]	Test H [QR]	Test I [QR]	Test J [QR]
①	7 ÷ 7	5 ÷ 1	$\frac{4}{2}$	$\frac{1}{3}$ of 3	0 ÷ 2
②	$9\overline{)45}$	63 ÷ 7	$\frac{1}{7}$ of 49	$\frac{48}{8}$	$7\overline{)70}$
③	$\frac{58}{2}$	$2\overline{)98}$	36 ÷ 2	$\frac{1}{2}$ of 76	$\frac{34}{2}$
④	84 ÷ 6	$\frac{1}{8}$ of 96	$\frac{117}{9}$	$4\overline{)68}$	128 ÷ 8
⑤	$\frac{1}{8}$ of 192	$\frac{189}{9}$	$5\overline{)135}$	234 ÷ 9	$\frac{1}{4}$ of 116
⑥	$\frac{405\,000}{1\,000}$	$\frac{1}{100}$ of 1000	$10\overline{)62\,000}$	$\frac{1\,000}{1\,000}$	$\frac{70\,000}{100}$
⑦	$\frac{2\,227}{3}$	$4\overline{)2\,268}$	894 ÷ 6	$\frac{1}{5}$ of 1 165	$\frac{4\,566}{6}$
⑧	$7\overline{)910}$	$6\overline{)6\,012}$	$3\overline{)618}$	$6\overline{)4\,224}$	$9\overline{)972}$
⑨	1 827 ÷ 9	$6\overline{)1\,806}$	4 004 ÷ 7	$5\overline{)7\,700}$	8 007 ÷ 3
⑩	$76\overline{)8\,056}$	$80\overline{)24\,560}$	$55\overline{)16\,940}$	$41\overline{)12\,505}$	$66\overline{)6\,798}$
⑪	$54\overline{)11\,232}$	$35\overline{)7\,455}$	$48\overline{)41\,952}$	$37\overline{)3\,478}$	$23\overline{)11\,661}$
⑫	$21\overline{)20\,265}$	$72\overline{)58\,176}$	$57\overline{)52\,155}$	$45\overline{)32\,625}$	$18\overline{)16\,344}$

Fractions and decimals: Revision and practice

		Test A [QR]	Test B [QR]	Test C [QR]	Test D [QR]	Test E [QR]
1	Reduce to lowest terms	$\frac{12}{24}$	$\frac{27}{36}$	$\frac{66}{99}$	$\frac{5}{20}$	$\frac{21}{28}$
2	Which is bigger?	$\frac{1}{4}$ or $\frac{1}{5}$	$\frac{3}{4}$ or $\frac{7}{8}$	$\frac{1}{2}$ or $\frac{18}{38}$	$\frac{7}{12}$ or $\frac{2}{3}$	$\frac{1}{7}$ or $\frac{5}{28}$
3	Arrange in ascending order	$\frac{9}{10}, \frac{19}{20}, \frac{4}{5}$	$\frac{4}{9}, \frac{2}{3}, \frac{7}{15}$	$\frac{5}{6}, \frac{6}{5}, \frac{4}{5}$	$\frac{3}{8}, \frac{5}{12}, \frac{1}{3}$	$\frac{13}{36}, \frac{11}{36}, \frac{1}{3}$
4	Change to a decimal	$\frac{3}{4}$	$\frac{1}{5}$	$\frac{1}{10}$	$\frac{1}{2}$	$\frac{2}{5}$
5	Change to a fraction	0·7	65%	0·18	40%	32%
6	Change to a percentage	$\frac{1}{4}$	0·55	$\frac{9}{10}$	0·62	0·51
7	Add	$\frac{1}{2} + \frac{1}{3}$	0·29 + 0·37	$\frac{1}{4} + \frac{1}{8}$	33% + 42%	0·55 + 0·73
8	Subtract	$\frac{5}{8} - \frac{1}{4}$	2·82 − 1·71	$\frac{1}{2} - \frac{3}{10}$	9·31 − 4·88	7·89 − 3·51
9	Multiply	$\frac{1}{5} \times \frac{2}{3}$	0·4 × 0·4	$\frac{5}{9} \times \frac{3}{4}$	0·21 × 0·04	0·3 × 0·8
10	Divide	$\frac{1}{8} \div \frac{1}{2}$	0·9 ÷ 0·45	$\frac{2}{3} \div \frac{4}{5}$	2·7 ÷ 0·18	0·45 ÷ 0·5
11	Simplify	$\frac{3}{4}$ of 80%	(1·1 + 0·3) ÷ 0·7	$\frac{4}{5} \times \frac{1}{2} - \frac{1}{10}$	0·2 × 5·5 − 0·07	25% of (2·1 + 1·5)
12	Simplify	$\frac{9}{10} \div (\frac{3}{10} - \frac{1}{5})$	0·8 ÷ (0·17 − 0·09)	60% of $\frac{1}{4}$	6·3 + 0·5 × 4·8	0·64 ÷ (0·27 − 0·11)

		Test F [QR]	Test G [QR]	Test H [QR]	Test I [QR]	Test J [QR]
1	Reduce to lowest terms	$\frac{6}{12}$	$\frac{3}{24}$	$\frac{17}{51}$	$\frac{7}{21}$	$\frac{63}{84}$
2	Which is bigger?	$\frac{11}{12}$ or $\frac{2}{3}$	$\frac{11}{24}$ or $\frac{11}{25}$	$\frac{2}{3}$ or $\frac{3}{4}$	$\frac{1}{2}$ or $\frac{3}{7}$	$\frac{2}{9}$ or $\frac{1}{5}$
3	Arrange in ascending order	$\frac{1}{2}, \frac{1}{4}, \frac{1}{3}$	$\frac{7}{11}, \frac{7}{10}, \frac{7}{12}$	$\frac{5}{2}, \frac{2}{5}, \frac{5}{4}$	$\frac{2}{5}, \frac{3}{10}, \frac{1}{3}$	$\frac{3}{2}, \frac{3}{4}, \frac{4}{3}$
4	Change to a decimal	$\frac{1}{4}$	$\frac{3}{20}$	$\frac{3}{100}$	$\frac{4}{5}$	$\frac{17}{20}$
5	Change to a fraction	0·44	15%	0·84	27%	0·25
6	Change to a percentage	$\frac{1}{5}$	0·25	$\frac{1}{2}$	0·09	$\frac{3}{4}$
7	Add	$\frac{1}{8} + \frac{1}{2}$	68% + 7%	$\frac{1}{10} + \frac{1}{2} + \frac{2}{5}$	0·92 + 0·18	$\frac{2}{3} + \frac{1}{9}$
8	Subtract	$\frac{1}{2} - \frac{1}{4}$	4·11 − 3·78	$\frac{1}{3} - \frac{1}{4}$	2·12 − 1·62	$\frac{3}{4} - \frac{3}{8}$
9	Multiply	$\frac{1}{10} \times \frac{5}{6}$	0·09 × 0·73	$\frac{3}{4} \times \frac{3}{4}$	0·1 × 0·9	$\frac{1}{2} \times \frac{3}{7}$
10	Divide	$\frac{1}{10} \div \frac{1}{3}$	5·1 ÷ 0·17	$\frac{5}{8} \div \frac{15}{2}$	6·3 ÷ 0·9	$\frac{4}{5} \div \frac{1}{10}$
11	Simplify	$\frac{3}{4} \times \frac{1}{2}$ of 40%	5% of $\frac{2}{3}$	70% of (7·2 ÷ 0·8)	$\frac{2}{3}$ of (10·2 − 0·6)	40% of $(\frac{5}{8} + \frac{1}{8})$
12	Simplify	$\frac{5}{9} \div (\frac{2}{3} - \frac{1}{2})$	$\frac{7}{8} \times \frac{2}{3} - \frac{1}{4}$	0·4 × 0·6 − 0·13	$(\frac{1}{7} \div \frac{4}{3}) \times \frac{7}{9}$	0·11 × (0·9 ÷ 0·1)

P-2 The SI system of units

The **SI system of units** is an internationally agreed method of measuring quantities such as length, mass, capacity and time. SI is short for *Système International d'Unités* (International System of Units). Nearly every country in the world uses the SI system.

Except for the measurement of time, the SI system uses decimal multiples to build up tables connecting the units for each quantity. The basic quantities are length, mass, capacity and time. Other quantities, such as area, volume, speed and density, can be expressed in terms of the basic quantities.

Full SI units are given on pages 194 to 195.

Length

The **metre** is the basic unit of length. The metre was first taken as one ten-millionth part of the distance between the North Pole and the Equator. In Table P.1, Greek prefixes are used for multiples of a metre (distances greater than a metre). Latin prefixes are used for sub-multiples of a metre (distances less than a metre).

Notice from the table on page 194 that the value of each unit is ten times that of the unit just below it. 1 km = 10 hm, 1 cm = 10 mm, etc. This is the same as the decimal place-value system in which digits increase in value by ten times as they move one place to the left.

The hectometre, decametre and decimetre are not used very often. The centimetre is useful for measuring short lengths but industry prefers to give such lengths in millimetres. This leaves the kilometre, the metre and the millimetre.
1 km = 1 000 m and 1 m = 1 000 mm.
Table P.1 gives the common units for length.

length	abbreviation	relationship to basic unit
1 *kilo*metre	1 km	1000 m
1 metre	1 m	1 m
1 *centi*metre	1 cm	0·01 m
1 *milli*metre	1 mm	0·001 m

Table P.1

☞ *Optional:* Do Exercise 5 of your Students' Practice Book.

Mass

The **gramme** is the basic unit of mass. A gramme is the mass of 1 cubic centimetre of water at a temperature of 4 °C. This is a very small unit. For this reason, the kilogramme (1 000 grammes) has become the standard unit of mass.

The prefixes are the same as those for lengths. The abbreviations follow those for length but are based on g, the abbreviation of gramme.

The kilogramme, the gramme and the milligramme are the only units used for practical purposes. A further unit is used for large masses, the **tonne** (t). 1 tonne = 1 000 kg, 1 kg = 1 000 g and 1 g = 1 000 mg.

Table P.2 gives the common units for mass:

mass	abbreviation	relationship to basic unit
1 tonne	1 t	1 000 000 g = 1 000 kg
1 kilogramme	1 kg	1000 g
1 gramme	1 g	1 g
1 milligramme	1 mg	0·001 g

Table P.2

Capacity

The **litre** is the basic unit of capacity. A litre is the space occupied by 1 kg of water at standard temperature and pressure. Only the kilolitre, litre and millilitre are used for practical and scientific purposes (Table P.3).

capacity	abbreviation	relationship to basic unit
1 kilolitre	1 kℓ	1 000 ℓ
1 litre	1 ℓ	1 ℓ
1 millilitre	1 mℓ	0·001 ℓ

Table P.3

Time

The **second** is the basic unit of time. Units of time do not follow the decimal system (Table P.4).

time	abbreviation	relationship to basic unit
1 second	1 s	1 s
1 minute	1 min	60 s
1 hour	1 h	3600 s = 60 min

Table P.4

Money

Many countries in the world use a decimal system for money. For example, in Nigeria the basic unit, the naira (₦), is divided into 100 kobo (k):

1 naira (₦) = 100 kobo (k)

At present the kobo is seldom used. In some countries the smaller units are commonly used, for example,

In the USA, 1 dollar ($) = 100 cents (c)
In Europe, 1 euro (€) = 100 cents (c)
(Note: not all of the countries in Europe use euros.)
In the UK, 1 pound (£) = 100 pence (p)

Many countries have undivided currencies, e.g. in French-speaking countries in West Africa the franc (CFA) is undivided.

The tables on page 195 give further examples of divided and undivided currencies.

In this course, some questions will be set in $, € and £ to give practice with divided currencies. However, most questions will be set in naira.

The SI units for area and volume appear in Chapters 14 and 16.

In a decimal system it is easy to write down compound quantities as decimals without doing any calculation. For example:

a 1 metre and 67 centimetres = 1·67 m
= 167 cm
= 1670 mm

b 34 euro and 75 cents = €34.75
= 3475 c

c 14 kilolitres and 3 litres = 14·003 kℓ
= 14 003 ℓ
= 14 003 000 mℓ

Exercise Pa [Oral/QR]

1. Express the following in metres.
   a 3 km   b 5 km   c 8 km
   d 2 km   e 6 km   f 10 km
   g 9 km   h 13 km i 7 km
   j 4 km   k 3·5 km l 4·2 km
   m 6·8 km n 8·1 km o 5·9 km
   p 10·4 km q 2·7 km r 9·3 km

2. Express the following in metres.
   a 3·85 km   b 2·44 km
   c 8·39 km   d 6·05 km
   e 9·14 km   f 1·07 km
   g 4·124 km h 2·993 km
   i 7·625 km j 5·704 km
   k 3·009 km l 2·058 km
   m 9 km and 400 m n 4 km and 620 m
   o 3 km and 315 m p 1 km and 82 m
   q 5 km and 50 m   r 6 km and 108 m
   s 7 km and 8 m   t 1 km and 4 m

3. Express the following in kilometres.
   a 5000 m   b 8000 m
   c 10 000 m d 1500 m
   e 2400 m   f 9500 m
   g 6520 m   h 4350 m
   i 7330 m   j 3748 m
   k 1375 m   l 5822 m
   m 2056 m   n 9040 m
   o 4007 m   p 3 km and 416 m
   q 7 km and 502 m r 6 km and 847 m
   s 10 km and 500 m t 8 km and 420 m
   u 1 km and 440 m v 9 km and 25 m
   w 5 km and 5 m   x 2 km and 9 m

4. Express the following in metres.
   a 173 cm   b 458 cm   c 843 cm
   d 150 cm   e 105 cm   f 280 cm
   g 101 cm   h 100 cm   i 99 cm
   j 53 cm   k 40 cm   l 8 cm
   m 19 cm   n 5 cm   o 50 cm

5 Express the following in metres.
  a 1 000 mm   b 2 000 mm
  c 7 000 mm   d 6 800 mm
  e 4 100 mm   f 1 400 mm
  g 3 726 mm   h 9 504 mm
  i 8 119 mm   j 600 mm
  k 300 mm   l 200 mm
  m 51 mm   n 60 mm
  o 3 mm

Exercise Pb

1 Add the following and give the answers in kg.
  a 2·3 kg, 5·8 kg, 2·1 kg
  b 785 g, 97 g, 605 g
  c 574 g, 1·706 kg, 605 g
  d 2·8 t, 450 kg, 1·37 t

2 Add the following and give the answers in litres (ℓ).
  a 3·7ℓ, 2·4ℓ, 1·8ℓ
  b 400 mℓ, 800 mℓ, 80 mℓ
  c 1·588ℓ, 475 mℓ, 2·014ℓ
  d 2 kℓ, 2·3 kℓ, 850ℓ

3 Add the following and give the answers in naira.
  a ₦420, ₦360, ₦2 200
  b ₦950, ₦1 875, ₦350
  c ₦77, ₦125, ₦505
  d ₦15, ₦35, ₦825

4 Add the following and give the answers
  i) in dollars,
  ii) in cents.
  a 84c, 36c, 19c
  b 77c, $1.23, 50c
  c $14.99, $3.65, 89c
  d $5.55, $9.99, $2.22

5 How many minutes in
  a $2\frac{1}{2}$h   b $1\frac{1}{4}$h   c $1\frac{2}{3}$h   d 180 s   e 150 s?

6 How many seconds in
  a 5 min   b $1\frac{1}{3}$ min   c $\frac{1}{4}$h   d $\frac{1}{2}$h   e 3 h?

☞ *Optional:* Do Exercise 6 of your Students' Practice Book.

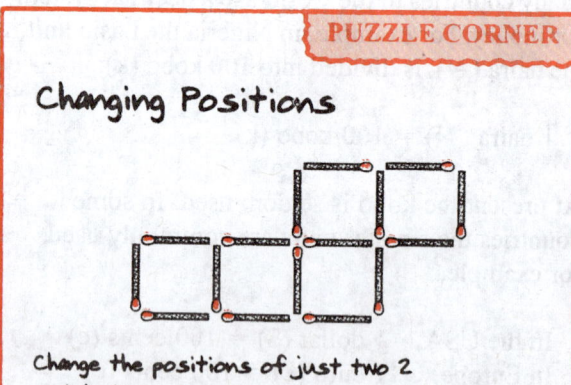

PUZZLE CORNER

Changing Positions

Change the positions of just two 2 matchsticks to reduce the number of squares from five to four.

PUZZLE CORNER

Stick a 1 in front ...

Start with 2 and stick a 1 in front — you get 12, which is exactly 6 times the number you started with.

Can you find a number so that when you stick a 1 in front you get
... 3 times the starting number?
... 5 times the starting number?
... 9 times the starting number?

Is there only one correct answer to each of these questions?

1 Development of number systems

OBJECTIVES

You should be able to

1 Count in tens and other number groupings (e.g. twenties, sevens, sixties)
2 Write Roman and Hindu-Arabic numerals
3 Use simple number codes for phrases and sentences
4 Add and subtract numbers using a simple paper counting board
5 State the place values of digits in whole numbers and decimal fractions

Teaching and learning materials

Teacher: Teacher: Counters (e.g. smooth stones or pebbles, large seeds, bottle tops); sheet of large plain paper (e.g. A4); an abacus or counting frame (if possible)

Students: Counters (e.g. smooth stones or pebbles, large seeds, bottle tops)

1-1 Counting

It is most likely that mathematics began when people started to count and measure. Counting and measuring are part of everyday life. Nearly every language in the world contains words for numbers and measures.

People have always used their fingers to help them when counting. This led them to collect numbers in groups: sometimes fives (fingers of one hand), sometimes tens (both hands) and even in groups of twenty (hands and feet). For example, someone with 23 sheep might say, 'I have four fives and three' sheep or 'two tens and three' sheep or 'one twenty and three' sheep. It would depend on local custom and language. In every case, the number of sheep would be the same.

When people group numbers in fives we say that they are using a **base five** method of counting. Most people use **base ten** when counting. For this reason, base ten is used internationally.

Exercise 1a   (Oral/Discussion/QR)

1 Say the numbers from 1 to 30 in your mother tongue.
2 What is the base of counting of your mother tongue?
3 Do you know of any other bases of counting?
4 Why are bases five, ten and twenty most common?

Table 1.1 gives the words for the numbers 1 to 20 in the Hausa, Igbo and Yoruba languages. Use Table 1.1 for questions 5 and 6.

	Hausa	Igbo	Yorùbá
1	ɗaya	otu	oókan
2	biyu	abụo	eéjì
3	uku	ato	ẹẹ́ta
4	huɗu	ano	ẹẹ́rin
5	biyar	ise	aárùn-ún
6	shida	isii	ẹẹ́fà
7	bakwai	asaa	eéje
8	takwas	asato	ẹẹ́jo
9	tara	iteghete	ẹẹ́sàn-án
10	goma	iri	ẹẹ́wàá
11	goma sha ɗaya	iri na otu	oókànlá
12	goma sha biyu	iri na abụo	eéjìlá
13	goma sha uku	iri na ato	ẹẹ́tàlá
14	goma sha huɗu	iri na ano	ẹẹ́rìnlá
15	goma sha biyar	iri na ise	ẹẹ́ẹ̀dógún
16	goma sha shida	iri na isii	ẹẹ́rìndínlógún
17	goma sha bakwai	iri na asaa	ẹẹ́tàdínlógún
18	goma sha takwas	iri na asato	eéjìdínlógún
19	goma sha tara	iri na iteghete	oókàndínlógún
20	ashirin	iri abụo	ogún

Table 1.1

5. **a** What base of counting do you think the Hausa language is in?
   b What do you think is the Hausa word for 'and'?

6. **a** What base of counting do you think the Igbo language is in?
   b What do you think is the Igbo word for 'and'?

7. In English the word 'score' means twenty. If a person reaches the age of three score and ten, how old do you think he or she is?

8. It is said that the Yoruba system of counting is in base twenty.
   a Look at the words for 4, 20 and 16. How is the word for 16 made from the words for 4 and 20?
   b Look at the Yoruba words for 1, 2, 3, 4 and then 11, 12, 13, 14. Does each set of words have something in common?
   c If possible, find the Yoruba words for 30, 40, 50, 60, 70, 80, 90, 100. Also try to find the Yoruba words for 200, 300, 400, 500, 600, 700, 1000.
   d Is it true that the Yoruba system of counting is in base twenty?

Other bases of counting: seven and sixty

There are seven days in a week. Suppose that a baby is 2 weeks and 5 days old. This means that it is 2 lots of 7 days and 5 days old, 19 days altogether.

Example 1

Find the total of 1 week 5 days, 6 days *and* 3 weeks 4 days. *Give the answer* **a** *in weeks and* days, **b** *in days.*

a wk d   Method in days column:
       1   5   5 + 6 + 4 = 15 days
           6   = 2 × 7 days + 1 day
       3   4   = 2 weeks + 1 day
       ─────
       6   1   write down 1 day and carry
                 2 weeks
                 answer: **a** 6 weeks and 1 day

b 6 wk 1 d = 6 × 7 days + 1 day
              = 42 days + 1 day
              = 43 days

Example 2

Today is Wednesday. What day of the week will it be in 160 *days time?*

Change 160 days to weeks and days.
160 d = 160 ÷ 7 wk = 22 wk 6 d
After 22 weeks it will be Wednesday again.
Count a further 6 days on from Wednesday:
Thursday, Friday, Saturday, Sunday, Monday, **Tuesday**. It will be Tuesday in 160 days time.

There are 60 seconds in a minute and 60 minutes in an hour.

Example 3

Find the number of seconds in 3 min 49 s.
Number of seconds in 3 min = 3 × 60 s = 180 s
Number of seconds in 3 min 49 s = 180 s + 49 s
                                = 229 s

Example 4

Add the following times together. Give the answers in hours and minutes.
3 h 40 min, 2 h 25 min, 28 min, 1 h 35 min

h   min   Method in minutes column:
3   40   40 + 25 + 28 + 35 = 128 min
2   25   = 2 × 60 min + 8 min
    28   = 2 h 8 min
1   35   write down 8 min and carry 2 h
───────
8   8   **answer:** 8 h 8 min

Exercise 1b

1. A baby is 3 weeks and 4 days old. What is its age in days?

2. During a dry season it did not rain for 128 days. How many weeks and days is this?

3. Add the following.

   a wk d   **b** wk d
        4   4   1   5
        1   2   2   6

c	wk	d		d	wk	d
	1	4			3	1
	1	4			2	6

4 Suppose today is Thursday. What day of the week will it be after
  a 20 days,   **b** 50 days,
  c 70 days,   **d** 100 days?

5 Find the number of seconds in the following times.
  a 2 min   **b** 10 min 54 s
  c 3 min 22 s   **d** 1 h

6 Find the number of minutes in the following.
  a 240 s   **b** 5 h
  c 2 h 34 min   **d** 1 day

7 Add the following.

a	min	s		b	min	s
	1	42			24	5
	3	7			5	55

c	h	min		d	h	min	s
	2	12			1	34	28
	1	49				45	50

8 Find out why there are 7 days in a week and why base 60 is used for minutes and hours.

In Chapter 24, we will meet another important counting base.

1-2 Symbols for numbers

As civilisations developed, spoken languages were written down using **symbols**. Symbols are letters and marks which represent sounds and ideas. Thus the words on this page are symbols for spoken words. Numbers were also written down. We use the word **numerals** for number symbols. For example, ᴎ and ☰ are the numerals for two in Arabic and Chinese. We use the numeral 2 for two.

Tally system

The first numerals were probably tally marks. People who looked after cattle made tally marks to represent the number of animals they had.

The tally marks were scratched on stones or sometimes cut on sticks (Fig. 1.1).

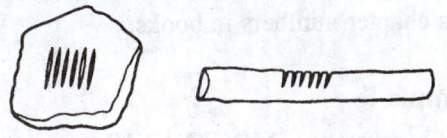

Fig. 1.1

We still use the tally system; it is very useful when counting a large number of objects. We usually group tally marks in fives; thus ⊮⊮⊮ ⊮⊮⊮ ⊮⊮⊮ || means three fives and two, or seventeen. Notice that in each group of five, the fifth tally is marked across the other four:
|||| = 4; ⊮⊮⊮ = 5.

Exercise 1c   (Oral/QR)
What numbers do the following tally marks represent?

1 ⊮⊮⊮ ⊮⊮⊮ ||||
2 ⊮⊮⊮ |||
3 ⊮⊮⊮ ⊮⊮⊮ ⊮⊮⊮ |
4 ⊮⊮⊮ ⊮⊮⊮ ⊮⊮⊮ ⊮⊮⊮
5 ⊮⊮⊮ ⊮⊮⊮ ⊮⊮⊮ ⊮⊮⊮ ⊮⊮⊮ ||
6 ⊮⊮⊮ ⊮⊮⊮ || ⊮⊮⊮ ⊮⊮⊮
7 ⊮⊮⊮ ⊮⊮⊮ ⊮⊮⊮ ⊮⊮⊮ ⊮⊮⊮ ⊮⊮⊮ ⊮⊮⊮ ⊮⊮⊮ ⊮⊮⊮ |||
8 ⊮⊮⊮ ⊮⊮⊮ ⊮⊮⊮ ⊮⊮⊮ ⊮⊮⊮ ⊮⊮⊮ ⊮⊮⊮
9 ⊮⊮⊮ ⊮⊮⊮ ⊮⊮⊮ ⊮⊮⊮ ⊮⊮⊮ |||| ⊮⊮⊮ ⊮⊮⊮ ⊮⊮⊮ ⊮⊮⊮ ⊮⊮⊮
10 ||||

Roman system

There were many ancient methods of writing numbers. The Roman system is still used today.

The Romans used capital letters of the alphabet for numerals. In the Roman system I's stand for units, X's stand for tens and C's stand for hundreds. Other letters stand for 5's, 50's and 500's. Table 1.2 shows how the letters were used.

1	I	20	XX
2	II	40	XL
3	III	50	L
4	IIII or IV	60	LX
5	V	90	XC
6	VI	100	C
7	VII	400	CD
8	VIII	500	D
9	VIIII or IX	900	CM
10	X	1000	M

Table 1.2

Roman numerals were first used about 2500 years ago. They are still in use today. You sometimes find Roman numerals on clockfaces and as chapter numbers in books.

Example 5

What number does MDCLXXVIII represent?

Work from the left:

$$\begin{aligned} M &= 1000 \\ D &= 500 \\ C &= 100 \\ L &= 50 \\ \text{(two tens)} \quad XX &= 20 \\ V &= 5 \\ \text{(three units)} \quad III &= 3 \end{aligned}$$

Adding: MDCLXXVIII = 1678

In Table 1.2, look at the numerals for 4, 40 and 400. Also look at 9, 90 and 900. 40 is XL; XL is X before L, i.e. 10 before 50. In the same way, 9 is IX or 1 before 10. Therefore the order of writing the symbols is important.

Example 6

What number does CCXC represent?

Working from the left:

$$\begin{aligned} \text{(two hundreds)} \quad CC &= 200 \\ \text{(10 before 100)} \quad XC &= 90 \end{aligned}$$

Adding: CCXC = 290

Example 7

Write the number 1934 in Roman numerals.

Working from the left:

$$\begin{aligned} 1000 &= M \\ 900 &= CM \quad \text{(100 before 1000)} \\ 30 &= XXX \quad \text{(three tens)} \\ 4 &= IV \quad \text{(1 before 5)} \end{aligned}$$

Adding: 1934 = MCMXXXIV

Exercise 1d

1. Find the numbers that the following Roman numerals represent.

   a XXV   b XXVI
   c XXIV   d LVII
   e XLVII   f CCXCVIII
   g DCCV   h MCCCXII
   i MCDLXXI j MDCCCXLIV
   k MCM   l MCMLXXXIV

2. Write the following numbers in Roman numerals.

   a 12   b 18   c 19   d 26
   e 39   f 41   g 200   h 175
   i 294   j 512   k 1422 l 1999

A simple code

The Romans used letters of the alphabet to stand for numbers. We can use numbers to stand for letters of the alphabet. This gives a simple code as shown in Table 1.3.

A	B	C	D	E	F	G	H	I	J	K	L	M
1	2	3	4	5	6	7	8	9	10	11	12	13
N	O	P	Q	R	S	T	U	V	W	X	Y	Z
14	15	16	17	18	19	20	21	22	23	24	25	26

Table 1.3

Example 8

What does (6, 1, 20)(2, 15, 25) mean in the code in Table 1.3?

From the table,
6 = F, 1 = A, 20 = T
(6, 1, 20) = FAT
2 = B, 15 = O, 25 = Y
(2, 15, 25) = BOY
Thus (6, 1, 20)(2, 15, 25) means FAT BOY.

Example 9

Translate I LOVE YOU into simple code using Table 1.3.

From Table 1.3,
I = (9)
L = 12, O = 15, V = 22, E = 5
LOVE = (12, 15, 22, 5)
Y = 25, O = 15, U = 21
YOU = (25, 15, 21)
I LOVE YOU = (9)(12, 15, 22, 5)(25, 15, 21)

Exercise 1e

1. Use the code in Table 1.3 to translate the following.
   a (14, 9, 7, 5, 18, 9, 1)
   b (1, 2, 21, 10, 1)
   c (20, 8, 5)(13, 1, 18, 11, 5, 20)
   d (13, 5, 5, 20)(13, 5)(20, 15, 13, 15, 18, 18, 15, 23)
   e (1, 12, 12)(9, 19)(23, 5, 12, 12)
   f (8, 1, 12, 6)(16, 1, 19, 20)(19, 5, 22, 5, 14)

2. Write your own name in code.

3. Translate the following into code.
   a SAVE FUEL
   b GO TO BENIN
   c HELP NEEDED
   d LEAVING TONIGHT
   e NOTHING IS PERMANENT
   f FIVE O CLOCK

4. In another code, (8, 1, 22, 7, 12)(14, 1, 17)(19, 14, 22, 7, 21) stands for UNITY AND FAITH. Find what the following stand for in this code.
   a (14)(19, 8, 1, 1, 12)(17, 14, 12)
   b (21, 14, 1, 17)(22, 7)(22, 1)
   c (17, 8, 7, 12)(17, 14, 12)
   d (22, 1, 19, 22, 1, 22, 7, 12)
   e (7, 22, 1)(21, 14, 7)

☞ *Optional:* Do Exercise 2 of your Students' Practice Book.

The Roman system made it difficult to add and subtract numbers. Paper and pencil calculations took a long time. Traders and bankers used simple calculating machines. The counting board and the abacus were early examples of these.

The counting board

A counting board was a block of stone or wood ruled in columns. Loose counters, stones or seeds were placed in the columns to show the value of the numbers in the columns (Fig. 1.2).

Counters in the right-hand column (U) represented units, counters in the next column (T) represented tens, and so on. In Fig. 1.2 the counters show the number 154. Usually the columns were not labelled. Small crosses were used to mark every three columns. We still group digits in threes when writing large numbers, e.g. 6 452 308.

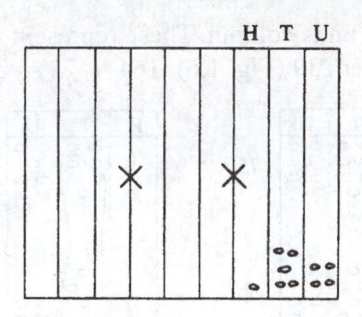

Fig. 1.2

It is easy to make a paper counting board; look at Fig. 1.3. Use the paper counting board to work through Examples 10 and 11 below and in Exercise 1f.

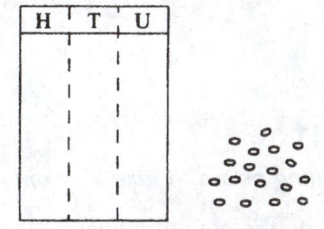

Fig. 1.3 Rule or fold a sheet of paper into three columns. Use small stones or seeds as counters.

Example 10

Show the addition 164 + 75 on a counting board.

a Put 1 stone in the hundreds column, 6 stones in the tens column and 4 stones in the units column to represent 164. Add 7 stones to the tens column and 5 stones to the units column. This adds 75 to 164 (Fig. 1.4).

b There are now 9 stones in the units column and 13 stones in the tens column. Ten tens make one hundred. Remove 10 stones from the tens column and put 1 stone in the hundreds column (Fig. 1.5).

c This leaves 2 stones in the hundreds column, 3 stones in the tens column and 9 stones in the units column. These represent the number 239 (Fig. 1.6). 164 + 75 = 239.

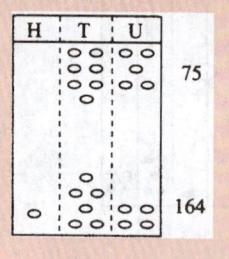

Fig. 1.4

Fig. 1.5

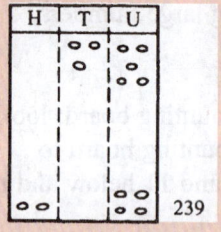

Fig. 1.6

Example 11

Use a counting board to take 17 from 42.

a Enter 42 on the counting board (Fig. 1.7).

b In the units column, it is impossible to take 7 stones from 2 stones. Each stone in the tens column represents ten units. Remove 1 stone from the tens column and put 10 stones in the units column. We have now changed 42 from 4 tens and two to 3 tens and twelve (Fig. 1.8). Subtract 17 by taking 1 stone from the tens column and 7 stones from the units column (Fig. 1.9).

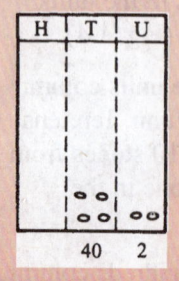

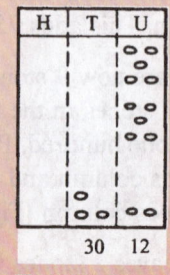

Fig. 1.7

Fig. 1.8

c This leaves 2 stones in the tens column and 5 stones in the units column. These represent the number 25 (Fig. 1.10). 42 − 17 = 25.

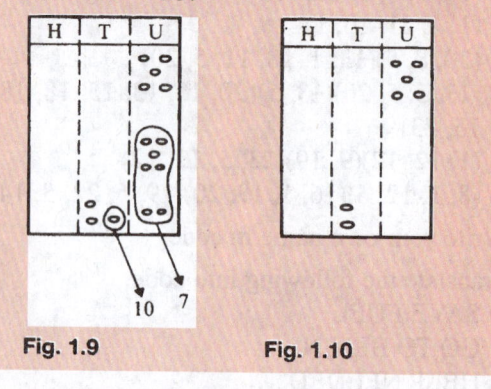

Fig. 1.9

Fig. 1.10

The abacus

The abacus is similar to the counting board. An abacus has wires and beads instead of columns and counters. The wires are mounted on a frame, as shown in Fig. 1.11. To record numbers, the beads are moved from the top of the frame to the bottom. In Fig. 1.11, the abacus shows the number 625.

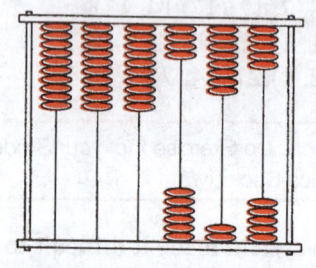

Fig. 1.11 An abacus showing the number 625.

Exercise 1f

Use a paper counting board and stones, or an abacus, to calculate the following.

1. 135 + 243
2. 671 + 28
3. 438 + 26
4. 273 + 485
5. 166 + 257
6. 187 + 187
7. 488 − 235
8. 693 − 122
9. 45 − 19
10. 67 − 25
11. 245 − 162
12. 314 − 136

☞ *Optional:* Do Exercise 1 of your Students' Practice Book.

16

1-3 The place-value system

People who used the abacus began to notice the importance of the different values of the columns. For example, six beads in the hundreds column were ten times greater in value than six beads in the tens column. This led to one of the most important discoveries in the history of numbers: the **place-value system** of numeration.

In a place-value system, the numbers of units, tens, hundreds, ..., are each represented by a single numeral. However, each numeral must be written in a special position or place. Thus, for any whole number, the **units place** is at the right-hand end of the number, the **tens place** is next to the units place on the left, and so on. For example, the number 3902 means 3 **thousands**, 9 **hundreds**, 0 **tens** and 2 **units** (Fig. 1.12).

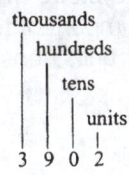

```
      thousands
        hundreds
          tens
            units
        3 9 0 2
```
Fig. 1.12

In the Roman system the same number is MMMCMII.

Notice the following.
a The place-value system takes up less space.
b With a tally system, we need to make new symbols as numbers grow. It can be difficult to remember all the symbols. For example, the Roman numeral for ten thousand is CCIƆƆ.
c The base ten place-value system uses only ten symbols. As numbers grow we use more places. We use one of the symbols, 0, to show that a place is empty. Thus ten thousand is 10000, using two symbols and five places.

The Hindu–Arabic system

The Hindus of India were the first people to develop the place-value system. They used symbols for the numbers one to nine and a special symbol for the number zero. The symbol for zero was especially important. A zero made it possible to show that a place was empty.

About a thousand years ago, Arab traders took the Hindu system to Europe. The place-value system made it possible to do calculations without using an abacus. As a result it became popular in most countries of the world.

In time, the shapes of the ten symbols changed but the idea of place value stayed the same. The ten symbols are sometimes called **digits**. *Digit* is Latin for finger. For historical reasons, our present number system is called the Hindu–Arabic system. The digits we use are quite different from those used in Arabic countries (Table 1.4).

Hindu–Arabic (International)	0 1 2 3 4 5 6 7 8 9
Arabic	٠ ١ ٢ ٣ ٤ ٥ ٦ ٧ ٨ ٩

Table 1.4

Exercise 1g (Oral or Written)

1. Change the following Arabic numerals to Hindu–Arabic numerals:

   a ١٢   b ٦٥١   c ٩٠٧
   d ٥٥٠   e ٨٠٠٤٠

2. The value of the 5 in 6 508 is five hundred. What is the value of each of the following?

   a the 4 in 6 402   b the 4 in 2 984
   c the 2 in 6 402   d the 2 in 2 984
   e the 2 in 10 269   f the 9 in 2 984
   g the 9 in 10 269   g the 6 in 6 402
   i the 6 in 10 269   j the 0 in 6 402
   k the 0 in 10 269   l the 1 in 10 269

3. A student does the sum 352 + 79, and writes:

   ```
     352
   + 79
   ```

   Why is it not correct to write the sum like this? Write the sum correctly.

4. The following additions and subtractions have been set out badly. Set them out correctly. (Do not work out the answers.)

   a   3107   b   6203
         26   − 97
      + 147

   c   1429   d   6700
      + 6580   −   34

17

5 Rearrange the digits in the following numbers to make (i) the highest possible number, (ii) the lowest possible number.
   a 263   b 728   c 506
   d 2815   e 2471   f 450312

a 60·91
 + 3·2

b 26·3
 − 1·7

c 4·50
 + 56·50

d 42·5
 − 9·65

Decimal fractions

An advantage of the place-value system is that we can extend it to include fractions.

Just as there are places for whole numbers such as the hundreds, tens and units, so we can make places for fractions such as the **tenths**, **hundredths**, **thousandths**, and so on. However, we also need to show where the whole numbers end and the fractions begin. We use a **decimal point** to separate the whole numbers from the fractions (Fig. 1.13).

```
hundreds
 tens
  units
   decimal point
    tenths
     hundredths
      thousandths
3 7 6 · 2 9 5
```

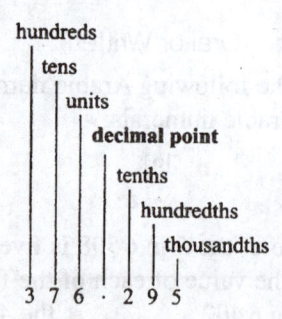

Fig. 1.13

In the number 376·295, the 2 in the first position after the decimal point shows that there are two tenths. The 9 is in the second position after the decimal point; this stands for nine hundredths. The 5 is in the third position after the decimal point and shows five thousandths.

Exercise 1h   (Oral/QR)

1 What is the value of each of the following?
   a the 8 in 1·85   b the 8 in 16·08
   c the 5 in 1·85   d the 5 in 5·691
   e the 6 in 5·691   f the 6 in 16·08
   g the 1 in 1·85   h the 1 in 5·691
   i the 1 in 16·08   j the 0 in 16·08

2 The following additions and subtractions have been set out carelessly. Set them out correctly. (Do not work out the answers.)

SUMMARY

1 All civilisations have developed words and symbols for numbers.
2 Most countries of the world use the Hindu–Arabic *base ten* numerical system, which has ten *digits*: 1, 2, 3, 4, 5, 6, 7, 8, 9, 0.
3 We record numbers using a *place-value system*, where the position of a digit in a number represents its value. (See Fig. 1.13.)
4 We use a *decimal point* to separate whole numbers from fractions.
5 In a place-value system, when doing calculations it is important to be careful to write units under units, tens under tens, and so on.

PUZZLE CORNER

Switching Units and Tens

Look at these multiplications:

$$32 \times 46 = 1\,472$$

$$23 \times 64 = 1\,472$$

Check that they are correct and explain why this works?

Can you make up others like this?

PUZZLE CORNER

P's and Q's

p q q p p q

How many different ways are there of arranging three p's and three q's in a line?

2 Large and small numbers

OBJECTIVES

You should be able to:
1. Count, read and write large numbers (millions, billions, trillions)
2. Write and read small numbers and express them accurately
3. Solve problems expressed in large and small numbers.

Teaching and learning materials

Teacher: Graph paper divided into mm; 1 square metre made out of 1 mm graph paper; poster made from newspaper headlines that contain numerical references

Students: Bring a newspaper article to school that uses large numbers

2-1 Large numbers

There is no such thing as 'the biggest number in the world'. It is always possible to count higher. Science and economics use very large numbers. Thus we need special names for large numbers. Table 2.1 gives the names and values of some large numbers.

name	value	
thousand	1 000	
million	1 000 thousand	= 1 000 000
billion	1 000 million	= 1 000 000 000
trillion	1 000 billion	= 1 000 000 000 000

Table 2.1

How big is a million?

The following examples may give you some idea of the size of a million.

1. A 1 cm by 1 cm square of 1 mm graph paper contains 100 small 1 mm × 1 mm squares.

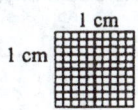

Fig. 2.1 100 small squares

A 1 m by 1 m square of the same graph paper contains 1 million of these small squares.

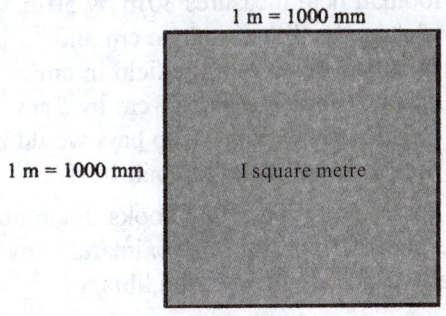

Fig. 2.2 1 000 mm × 1 000 mm = 1 000 000 mm²

2. A cubic metre measures 100 cm by 100 cm by 100 cm.

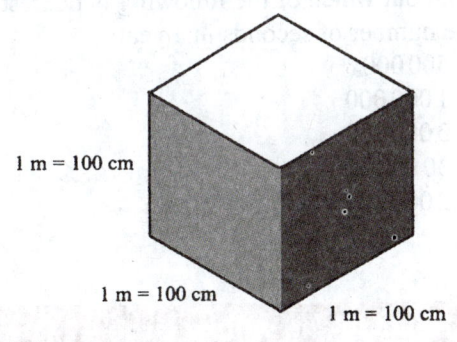

Fig. 2.3 1 cubic metre

Volume of cubic metre
= 100 cm × 100 cm × 100 cm
= 1 000 000 cm³
Thus 1 million cubic centimetres, cm³, will exactly fill a 1 cubic metre box.

19

Fig. 2.4 One million of these make 1 cubic metre

☞ *Optional:* Do Exercise 3 of your Students' Practice Book.

Exercise 2a

1. What is the correct name for **(a)** a thousand thousand, **(b)** a thousand million, **(c)** a million million?

2. A football field measures 80 m by 50 m.
   a Change the dimensions to cm and calculate the area of the field in cm².
   b A bar of soap measures 8 cm by 5 cm. Calculate how many soap bars would be needed to cover the football field.

3. A library has about 4 000 books. Each book has about 250 pages. Approximately how many pages are there in the library?

4. How long would it take to count to 1 million if it takes an average of 1 second to say each number? Give your answer to the nearest $\frac{1}{2}$ day.

5. Find out which of the following is nearest to the number of seconds in a year.
   a 500 000
   b 1 000 000
   c 3 000 000
   d 30 000 000
   e 2 000 000 000

2-2 Reading and writing large numbers

Grouping digits

Read the number 31556926 out aloud. Was it easy to do? It may have been quite difficult. You had to decide, 'Is the number bigger than a million or not?', 'Does it begin with 3 million, 31 million or 315 million?'.

It is necessary to write large numbers in a helpful way. It is usual to group the digits of large numbers in threes from the decimal point. A small gap is left between each group.

31556926 should be written as 31 556 926. Now it is easy to see that the number begins with 31 million. In words we would say or write this number as

thirty one million,
  five hundred and fifty-six thousand,
    nine hundred and twenty-six.

Example 1

Write the number 8702614235 *correctly, then express it in words.*

Grouping the number in sets of three digits from the right-hand side:

8 702 614 235

In words:

eight billion,
  seven hundred and two million,
    six hundred and fourteen thousand,
      two hundred and thirty-five.

Note: We no longer use commas between the groups of digits. Many countries use a comma as a decimal point; thus, to avoid confusion do not use commas for grouping the digits.

Exercise 2b

Write the following numbers, grouping digits in threes from the decimal point. (Use spaces, not commas.) Then, working in pairs and taking turns, say each number aloud to your partner.

1. 1 million
2. 59244
3. 721,568,397
4. 2,312,400
5. 8 trillion
6. 3 billion
7. 9215
8. 14682053
9. 108,412
10. 12345
11. 100000000
12. 987654
13. 923006110317
14. 21 billion
15. 6006006006
16. 727744
17. 6,401,000,000,000
18. 58974308

Digits and words

Editors of newspapers know that large numbers sometimes confuse readers. They often use a mixture of digits and words when writing large numbers.

Example 2

What do the numbers in the following headlines stand for?

a FOOD IMPORTS RISE TO ₦1 BILLION
b OIL PRODUCTION NOW 2·3 MILLION BARRELS DAILY
c FLOODS IN INDIA – 0·6 MILLION HOMELESS
d NEW ROAD TO COST ₦2¼ TRILLION

a ₦1 billion is short for ₦1 000 000 000
b 2·3 million = 2·3 × 1 000 000
             = 2 300 000
c 0·6 million = 0·6 × 1 000 000
             = 600 000
d ₦2¼ trillion = ₦2·25 trillion
              = ₦2 250 000 000 000

Example 3

Express the following in a mixture of digits and words.

a ₦3 000 000   *b* 6 800 000 000
c 240 000 000   *d* 500 000 000 000

a ₦3 000 000 = ₦3 × 1 000 000
            = ₦3 million

b 6 800 000 000 = 6·8 × 1 000 000 000
                = 6·8 billion

c 240 000 000 = 240 × 1 000 000
              = 2409 million
or
240 000 000 = 0·24 × 1 000 000 000
            = 0·24 billion (or 240 million)

d 500 000 000 000 = 0·5 × 1 000 000 000 000
                  = 0·5 trillion or 500 billion

Exercise 2c

1. Express the following numbers in digits only.
   a ₦2 million   b 150 million km
   c 3 billion   d 5½ million
   e ₦2·1 trillion   f 4·2 million litres
   g 0·4 billion   h ₦1¼ million
   i 0·7 million tonnes   j US$¾ billion
   k 0·45 million   l ₦0·58 billion

2. Imagine you are a newspaper editor. Write the following number using a mixture of digits and words.
   a 8 000 000 tonnes   b ₦6 000 000
   c 2 000 000 000   d ₦3 700 000 000
   e US$7 400 000 000   f ₦750 000
   g 200 000 litres   h 500 000 000
   i 300 000 tonnes   j 250 000
   k 980 000 barrels   l 490 000 000 000 000

2-3 Small numbers

Decimal fractions

Decimal fractions also have names.

8 tenths   = 0·8
8 hundredths   = 0·08
8 thousandths   = 0·008
8 ten thousandths   = 0·0008
8 hundred thousandths = 0·00008

Notice that digits are grouped in threes from the decimal point as before.

Example 4

Write the following as decimal fractions.

a 28 *thousandths*   *b* $\frac{865}{100\,000}$
c 350 *millionths*   *d* $\frac{400}{10\,000}$

a 28 thousandths = 1 thousandth × 28
                  = 0·001 × 28
                  = 0·028

b $\frac{865}{100\,000}$ = 0·008 65

There are five zeros in the denominator. The decimal fraction is obtained by moving the digits in the numerator five places to the right.

c 350 millionths = 1 millionth × 350
= 0·000 001 × 350
= 0·000 350 = 0·000 35

In a decimal fraction it is not necessary to write any zeros after the last non-zero digit.

d $\frac{400}{10\,000}$ = 0·040 0
= 0·04

SUMMARY

1 We use the words *million, billion* and *trillion* for large numbers. They are connected as follows:

1 million = 1 thousand × 1 000
1 billion = 1 million × 1 000
1 trillion = 1 billion × 1 000

2 To avoid confusion, when writing large numbers or small decimal fractions, group the digits in threes from the decimal point; e.g. 49 560 216 and 0·003 48.

3 The number 49 560 216 830 is written in words as

forty-nine billion
five hundred and sixty million
two hundred and sixteen thousand
eight hundred and thirty

4 We often write large numbers using a mixture of words and numbers; e.g. $3\frac{1}{2}$ billion = 3 500 million or 3 500 000 000.

Exercise 2d

Write the following as decimal fractions.

1. 6 hundredths
2. 4 thousandths
3. 9 tenths
4. 8 millionths
5. 4 ten thousandths
6. 6 hundred thousandths
7. $\frac{3}{1\,000}$
8. $\frac{9}{100\,000}$
9. $\frac{7}{10\,000}$
10. 16 hundredths
11. 34 thousandths
12. 26 ten thousandths
13. $\frac{28}{100\,000}$
14. $\frac{84}{1\,000}$
15. $\frac{756}{10\,000}$
16. 27 tenths
17. 65 hundredths
18. 402 thousandths
19. 20 hundredths
20. 240 millionths
21. 700 thousandths
22. $\frac{620}{100\,000}$
23. $\frac{330}{100\,000}$
24. $\frac{4\,020}{100\,000}$
25. 90 hundredths
26. 900 thousandths
27. 300 ten thousandths
28. $\frac{720}{1\,000}$
29. $\frac{720}{10\,000}$
30. $\frac{720}{100\,000}$

PUZZLE CORNER

Infinity and Beyond

In this series, each number is $\frac{1}{4}$ of the previous number:

$$\frac{1}{4} + \frac{1}{4^2} + \frac{1}{4^3} + \frac{1}{4^4} + \ldots$$

What do you get if you add these numbers together?

What if you extend the series by more terms ... until you get to ... **infinity**?

Is a calculator any help?
Is there a smarter way?

3 Factors and multiples

OBJECTIVES

You should be able to:
1. Define and identify prime numbers
2. Find the factors of a given whole number
3. Express a number as product of its factors in index form
4. Find the Highest Common Factor (HCF) of two or more whole numbers
5. Write down two or more multiples of a given number
6. Find the Lowest Common Multiple (LCM) of two or more whole numbers.

Teaching and learning materials

Teacher: 1 to 100 number square chart or poster

3-1 Factors

$40 \div 8 = 5$ and $40 \div 5 = 8$.
We say that 8 and 5 are factors of 40.
If we can divide a whole number by another whole number without remainder, the second number is a **factor** of the first.

The numbers 1, 2, 4, 5, 8, 10, 20 and 40 all divide into 40. They are all factors of 40. We can write 40 as a product of two factors in eight ways:

$$40 = 1 \times 40 = 2 \times 20 = 4 \times 10 = 5 \times 8$$
$$= 8 \times 5 = 10 \times 4 = 20 \times 2 = 40 \times 1$$

Exercise 3a (Oral or Written)

1. Find all the factors of the following numbers:
   a 12 b 18 c 20 d 24
   e 28 f 30 g 32 h 48
   i 63 j 72

2. Which of the numbers 2, 3, 4, 5, 6, 7, 8, 9 are factors of the following numbers?
   a 27 b 36 c 54 d 56
   e 60 f 90 g 120 h 144
   i 180 j 210

Prime numbers

A **prime number** has only two factors, itself and 1.
2, 3, 5, 7, 11, 13, … are prime numbers. 1 has only one factor, itself; 1 is *not* a prime number.

Exercise 3b

1. Write down all the prime numbers between 1 and 30.
2. a Copy the 1–100 number square in Fig. 3.1 into your exercise book (or turn to page 2, Exercise 3 in your Students' Practice Book).
   b You are to shade every number that is not a prime number.
   c 1 is not a prime number; shade the square with 1 in it.
   d 2 is a prime number. Leave this square unshaded, then shade every second number following the number 2. This has been done in Fig. 3.1.

1	2	3	4	5	6	7	8	9	10
11	12	13	14	15	16	17	18	19	20
21	22	23	24	25	26	27	28	29	30
31	32	33	34	35	36	37	38	39	40
41	42	43	44	45	46	47	48	49	50
51	52	53	54	55	56	57	58	59	60
61	62	63	64	65	66	67	68	69	70
71	72	73	74	75	76	77	78	79	80
81	82	83	84	85	86	87	88	89	90
91	92	93	94	95	96	97	98	99	100

Fig. 3.1

e 3 is a prime number. Leave this square unshaded, then shade every third number following 3.
f Carry on with the next unshaded number, 5, and shade every fifth number after 5.
g Carry on until you can shade no more numbers. This method of finding prime numbers is called the **sieve of Eratosthenes**. Eratosthenes was a Greek who lived over 2000 years ago.

Prime factors

The **prime factors** of a number are the factors of the number that are prime. It is possible to write every non-prime number as a product of prime factors. For example:

$15 = 3 \times 5$
$24 = 2 \times 2 \times 2 \times 3$
$42 = 2 \times 3 \times 7$

To find the prime factors of a number:
a Start with the lowest prime number, 2. Find out if this will divide into the number. If it will not divide, try the next prime number, 3. And so on, trying 5, 7, 11, 13, … in turn.
b If a prime number will divide, check if it will divide again before moving on to the next prime.

Example 1

Express 15 288 as a product of prime factors.

$15\,288 = 2 \times 7644$
$= 2 \times 2 \times 3822$
$= 2 \times 2 \times 2 \times 1911$
$= 2 \times 2 \times 2 \times 3 \times 637$
$= 2 \times 2 \times 2 \times 3 \times 7 \times 91$
$= 2 \times 2 \times 2 \times 3 \times 7 \times 7 \times 13$

The working can be set out as a continued division as follows:

2	15 288
2	7644
2	3822
3	1911
7	637
7	91
13	13
	1

Thus $15\,288 = 2 \times 2 \times 2 \times 3 \times 7 \times 7 \times 13$

Exercise 3c

Use the above method to express the following as products of prime factors.

1) 12   2) 18   3) 28   4) 30
5) 72   6) 84   7) 108   8) 105
9) 180   10) 216   11) 288   12) 875
13) 900   14) 880   15) 1512   16) 17 325

Index form

In Example 1 we saw that
$15\,288 = 2 \times 2 \times 2 \times 3 \times 7 \times 7 \times 13$.
It is possible to write the product in a shorter way. 2^3 is a short way of writing $2 \times 2 \times 2$. The number 3 in 2^3 is called the **index** or **power**. It shows that three 2's are to be multiplied together.

In the same way, 7^2 is a short way of writing 7×7. The index 2 shows that two 7's are to be multiplied together.

In index form,
$15\,288 = 2^3 \times 3 \times 7^2 \times 13$.
The use of index form saves space and can help to prevent errors in counting and copying. It would be easy to make a mistake when copying the product of factors of 256.
$256 = 2 \times 2 \times 2 \times 2 \times 2 \times 2 \times 2 \times 2$
In index form, $256 = 2^8$. This saves space and clearly shows that eight 2's are to be multiplied together.

We say 2^8 as 'two to the power of eight', or 'two to the eighth power' or 'two raised to the power of eight' or, often, just 'two to the eighth'.

The plural of index is **indices**. The indices 2 and 3 are usually said in a special way: 7^2 as 'seven **squared**', 2^3 as 'two **cubed**'.

Example 2

Express

a $9 \times 9 \times 9 \times 9$ *in index form,*
b 675 *as a product of primes in index form.*

a $9 \times 9 \times 9 \times 9 = 9^4$
  (There are four 9's multiplied together.)

b $675 = 3 \times 3 \times 3 \times 5 \times 5$
  $= 3^3 \times 5^2$

Exercise 3d

1. Write the following in index form.
   a $7 \times 7 \times 7$
   b $3 \times 3 \times 3 \times 3 \times 3$
   c $10 \times 10 \times 10 \times 10$
   d 2×2
   e $6 \times 6 \times 6 \times 6 \times 6 \times 6 \times 6$
   f $8 \times 8 \times 8 \times 8 \times 8 \times 8 \times 8 \times 8 \times 8 \times 8$

2. Re-write your answers to Exercise 3c in index form where possible.

3. Express the following as a product of primes in index form.

a 24	b 48	c 63	d 92
e 136	f 441	g 360	h 625
i 512	j 720	k 729	l 1 000
m 1 232	n 1 404	o 1 225	p 7 290

4. The prime factors of 28 are 2 and 7. We can write this as $28 = 2^2 \times 7$ or $28 \rightarrow 2^2 . 7$. In the second version we use an arrow for 'is equivalent to' and a dot for the multiplication sign. Complete the following, using the arrow and dot notation. The first one has been done.

   a $36 \rightarrow 2^2 . 3^2$ b $44 \rightarrow \square$
   c $50 \rightarrow \square$ d $117 \rightarrow \square$
   e $72 \rightarrow \square$ f $132 \rightarrow \square$
   g $100 \rightarrow \square$ h $800 \rightarrow \square$

Common factors

The numbers 12, 21 and 33 are all divisible by 3. We say that 3 is a **common factor** of 12, 21 and 33.

There may be more than one common factor of a set of numbers. For example, both 2 and 7 are common factors of 28, 42 and 70. Since 2 and 7 are common factors and are both prime numbers, then 14 ($= 2 \times 7$) must also be a common factor of the set of numbers.

1 is a common factor of all numbers.

Exercise 3e (Oral/QR)

Find the common factors, other than 1, of the following.

1. 10 and 14
2. 15 and 24
3. 21 and 28
4. 9 and 15
5. 8 and 18
6. 27 and 30
7. 6 and 12
8. 10 and 20
9. 30 and 36
10. 9 and 18
11. 8 and 100
12. 24 and 40
13. 14, 24 and 38
14. 21, 35 and 56
15. 27, 36 and 39
16. 44, 66 and 88
17. 15, 60 and 75
18. 48, 60 and 72

3-2 Highest common factor (HCF)

2, 7 and 14 are common factors of 28, 42 and 70; 14 is the greatest of the three common factors. We say that 14 is the **highest common factor** of 28, 42 and 70. HCF is short for highest common factor.

To find the HCF of a set of numbers:
a express the numbers as a product of prime factors;
b find the common prime factors;
c multiply the common prime factors together to give the HCF.

Example 3

Find the HCF of 18, 24 *and* 42.

$18 = 2 \times 3 \times 3$
$24 = 2 \times 2 \times 2 \times 3$
$42 = 2 \times 3 \times 7$

The common prime factors are 2 and 3.
The HCF $= 2 \times 3 = 6$.

Example 4

Find the HCF of 216, 288 and 360.

Working:

2	216		2	288		2	360
2	108		2	144		2	180
2	54		2	72		2	90
3	27		2	36		3	45
3	9		2	18		3	15
3	3		3	9		5	5
	1		3	3			1
				1			

In index notation,

$216 = 2^3 \times 3^3$
$288 = 2^5 \times 3^2$
$360 = (2^3 \times 3^2) \times 5$

2^3 is the lowest power of 2 contained in the three numbers. Thus the HCF contains 2^3. 3^2 is the lowest power of 3 contained in the three numbers. The HCF contains 3^2.

$216 = (2^3 \times 3^2) \times 3$
$288 = (2^3 \times 3^2) \times 2^2$
$360 = (2^3 \times 3^2) \times 5$

The HCF $= 2^3 \times 3^2 = 8 \times 9 = 72$.

Exercise 3f

1. Find the HCF of the following. Leave the answers in prime factors.
   a $2 \times 3 \times 3 \times 5$; $2 \times 2 \times 3 \times 3 \times 3$; $3 \times 3 \times 5 \times 7$
   b $2 \times 2 \times 3 \times 5$; $2 \times 2 \times 3 \times 3 \times 7$; $2 \times 3 \times 3 \times 7$
   c $2 \times 3 \times 3 \times 5$; $2 \times 2 \times 2 \times 5$; $2 \times 2 \times 3 \times 5 \times 7$
   d $2 \times 2 \times 2 \times 3 \times 3 \times 7$; $2 \times 2 \times 3 \times 3 \times 3$; $2 \times 3 \times 3 \times 3 \times 7$
   e $2 \times 3 \times 3 \times 5 \times 7$; $3 \times 5 \times 5 \times 7 \times 7$; $2 \times 2 \times 3 \times 5 \times 5 \times 7$

2. Find the HCF of the following.
   a 9, 15 and 24
   b 18, 24 and 32
   c 12, 30 and 42
   d 24, 40 and 64
   e 35, 50 and 65
   f 30, 45 and 75
   g 42, 70 and 56
   h 36, 72 and 63

3. Find the HCF of the following. Leave the answers in prime factors and use index notation.
   a $2^3 \times 3^2 \times 7$; $2^2 \times 3 \times 5^2$; $2^2 \times 3^3 \times 5$
   b $2^2 \times 3^3 \times 5$; $2^3 \times 3^4 \times 5$; $2 \times 3^5 \times 7^2$
   c $2^2 \times 3^3 \times 5^2$; $3^2 \times 5^3 \times 7$; $2 \times 3^2 \times 5^2 \times 7$
   d $2^3 \times 3^3 \times 5^3$; $2^4 \times 3 \times 5^2 \times 7$; $2^5 \times 3^2 \times 5 \times 7^2$
   e $2^3 \times 5^2 \times 7$; $2^2 \times 3^2 \times 5$; $3^3 \times 5^3 \times 7^2$

4. Find the HCF of the following. Use index notation.
   a 63, 42 and 21
   b 144, 216 and 360
   c 280, 105 and 175
   d 126, 234 and 90
   e 160, 96 and 224
   f 189, 270 and 108
   g 288, 180 and 108

3-3 Multiples

Common multiples

6 is a factor of 12, 18, 24, 30, ... We say that 12, 18, 24, 30, ..., etc. are all **multiples** of 6. In the same way, 8, 12, 16, 20, ..., etc. are all multiples of 4.

Exercise 3g   (Oral/QR)
Give five multiples of each of the following.

1. 2
2. 3
3. 5
4. 7
5. 8
6. 9
7. 10
8. 11
9. 12
10. 20

Notice that 12 is a multiple of both 6 and 4. We say that 12 is a **common multiple** of 6 and 4; 24, 36, 48, ..., etc. are also common multiples of 6 and 4.

Example 5

Give three common multiples of

a 3 and 11,
b 4, 5 and 6.

a 33 is a common multiple of 3 and 11.
   Likewise, 66 and 99.
b 120 is a common multiple of 4, 5 and 6.
   Likewise, 240 and 360.

Note: To find a common multiple of a set of numbers, multiply the numbers together.

Exercise 3h
Write down three common multiples of the following sets of numbers.

1) 3 and 4   2) 2 and 5   3) 3 and 7
4) 2, 3 and 5 5) 3, 4 and 5 6) 2, 3 and 7
7) 5 and 6   8) 6 and 8   9) 10 and 15
10) 2, 5 and 6 11) 2, 6 and 8 12) 3, 10 and 15

3-4 Lowest common multiple (LCM)

30, 60, 90 are all common multiples of 6, 10 and 15. 30 is the lowest number that 6, 10 and 15 will divide into. We say that 30 is the **lowest common multiple** of 6, 10 and 15. LCM is short for lowest common multiple. In Example 5(b), the LCM of 4, 5 and 6 is 60 (not 120).
To find the LCM of a set of numbers:
a express the numbers as a product of prime factors;
b find the lowest product of factors which contains all of the prime factors of the numbers.

Example 6
Find the LCM of 8, 9 and 12.

$8 = 2 \times 2 \times 2$
Any multiple of 8 must contain $2 \times 2 \times 2$.

$9 = 3 \times 3$
Any multiple of 9 must contain 3×3.

$12 = 2 \times 2 \times 3$
Any multiple of 12 must contain $2 \times 2 \times 3$.

The lowest product containing all three is
$2 \times 2 \times 2 \times 3 \times 3$

The LCM of 8, 9 and 12 is
$2 \times 2 \times 2 \times 3 \times 3 = 72$

Example 7
Find the LCM of 24, 28, 36 and 50.

In indices $24 = 2^3 \times 3$
             $28 = 2^2 \times 7$
             $36 = 2^2 \times 3^2$
             $50 = 2 \times 5^2$

The LCM $= 2^3 \times 3^2 \times 5^2 \times 7 = 12\,600$.

Note: The prime factors are 2, 3, 5 and 7. The LCM contains the highest powers of 2, 3, 5 and 7 that appear in the factorised numbers.

☞ *Optional*: Do Exercise 4 of your Students' Practice Book.

Exercise 3i

1) Find the LCM of the following. Leave the answers in prime factors.
   a $2 \times 2 \times 3$; $2 \times 3 \times 3 \times 5$; $2 \times 2 \times 5$
   b $2 \times 3 \times 3$; $2 \times 2 \times 2 \times 3$; $2 \times 2 \times 3 \times 5$
   c $2 \times 2 \times 2 \times 3 \times 3$; $2 \times 3 \times 5 \times 5$; $2 \times 2 \times 3 \times 3 \times 5$
   d $3 \times 3 \times 5$; $2 \times 5 \times 5 \times 7$; $2 \times 3 \times 7$; $3 \times 5 \times 7$
   e $2 \times 3 \times 5$; $3 \times 5 \times 7$; $2 \times 3 \times 3 \times 3$; $3 \times 5 \times 5 \times 7$

2) Find the LCM of the following. Leave the answers in prime factors, in index form.
   a $2 \times 3 \times 5$; $2^2 \times 3 \times 5$; $2 \times 3 \times 5^2$
   b $2 \times 3^2 \times 7$; $2^3 \times 3 \times 5$; $2 \times 5^2 \times 7$
   c $3 \times 5 \times 7^2$; $2 \times 3^3 \times 5$; $2^2 \times 3 \times 7$
   d $2^2 \times 3 \times 5^3$; $2^3 \times 3 \times 7^2$; $3^2 \times 5^2 \times 7$
   e $2^3 \times 3^2 \times 5$; $3 \times 5^3 \times 7^2$; $2^4 \times 3 \times 7^2$; $3^2 \times 5^2 \times 7^3$

3 Find the LCM of the following.
  a 4 and 6
  b 6 and 8
  c 6 and 9
  d 7 and 8
  e 8 and 12
  f 9 and 12
  g 2, 3 and 4
  h 3, 4 and 6
  i 4, 6 and 9
  j 6, 8 and 12

4 Find the LCM of the following.
  a 8, 10 and 15
  b 6, 8 and 10
  c 10, 12 and 15
  d 5, 6 and 9
  e 7, 8 and 12
  f 9, 12 and 15
  g 10, 16 and 18
  h 4, 5, 6 and 9
  i 6, 8, 10 and 12
  j 9, 10, 12 and 15

---

1. If a number divides another number exactly, without remainder, the first number is a *factor* of the second. 1 is a factor of all numbers.

2. A *prime number* has only two factors: itself and 1. There are an infinite number of prime numbers; the first ten are 2, 3, 5, 7, 11, 13, 17, 19, 23, 29.

3. The *prime factors* of a number are the factors of a number that are prime.

4. If we write 2 × 2 × 2 × 2 × 2 in the form 2^5, the 5 is called the *index* or *power*. *Indices* is the plural of index. The indices 2 and 3 have special names: *square* and *cube*, respectively.

5. If two or more numbers all have the same factor, we call it a *common factor*; e.g. 5 is a common factor of 15, 20 and 30.

6. The largest number that is a common factor of two or more numbers is called their *highest common factor*, or HCF; e.g. 8 is the HCF of 24, 40 and 56.

7. If two or more numbers all have a common factor, then the numbers are *multiples* of the common factor; e.g. 5, 10, 15, 20, ... are multiples of 5.

8. If a number is a multiple of two or more numbers, we say it is a *common multiple*; e.g. 20 is common multiple of 5 and 2.

9. The smallest number that is a common multiple of two or more numbers is called the *lowest common multiple*, or *LCM*; e.g. 10 is the LCM of 5 and 2.

PUZZLE CORNER

Got the Wrong Buckets?

You have a 10-litre bucket, a 7-litre bucket and a tap.

How can you get exactly 9 litres?

PUZZLE CORNER

Factor this

The factors of 9 are 1, 3 and 9
Three factors altogether = an odd number of factors

The factors of 10 are 1, 2, 5 and 10
Four factors altogether = an even number of the factors

How many numbers from 1 to 100 have an even number of factors?

What do the rest have in common?

4 Fractions 1: Fractions and percentages

OBJECTIVES

You should be able to:
1. Express quantities in terms of common fractions and mixed numbers where appropriate
2. Change mixed numbers to improper fractions and vice versa
3. Obtain equivalents of a given fraction
4. Reduce fractions to their lowest terms
5. Arrange fractions in ascending or descending order of size
6. Add, subtract, multiply and divide fractions
7. Express a quantity as a fraction or percentage of another quantity
8. Convert fractions to percentages and vice versa
9. Solve word problems involving fractions.

Teaching and learning materials

Teacher: Objects that can be divided into fractional parts, e.g. food (oranges, bananas, bread, pie) or other items such as money, chalk, pencils, sheets of paper, string

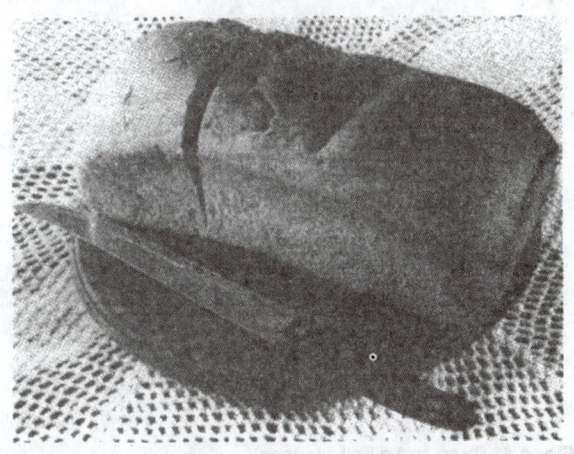

Fig. 4.1 I will eat one-third of the loaf now and the rest later.

Fig. 4.2 Three-fifths of the people are wearing white shirts.

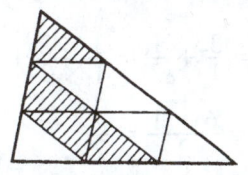

Fig 4.3 Four-ninths of the triangle has been shaded.

4-1 Common fractions

It is not always possible to use whole numbers to describe quantities (Figs 4.1, 4.2, 4.3).

We use **fractions** to describe parts of quantities. We write the fractions like this:

one-third $\frac{1}{3}$
three-fifths $\frac{3}{5}$
four-ninths $\frac{4}{9}$

The number below the line is called the **denominator**. The denominator shows the number of equal parts the whole has been divided into. The number above the line is called the **numerator**. The numerator shows the number of parts in the fraction.

29

Mixed numbers

Some quantities need whole numbers and fractions to describe them (Figs. 4.4, 4.5).

Fig. 4.4 Three and a half oranges.

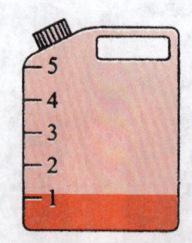

Fig. 4.5 One and one-third litres of kerosene.

The number three and a half, written $3\frac{1}{2}$, is a **mixed number**. A mixed number has a whole number part and a fractional part: $3\frac{1}{2} = 3 + \frac{1}{2}$.

It is possible to express a mixed number as a single fraction:

$$3\frac{1}{2} = 3 + \frac{1}{2} = \frac{3}{1} + \frac{1}{2} = \frac{3 \times 2}{1 \times 2} + \frac{1}{2}$$

$$= \frac{6}{2} + \frac{1}{2} = \frac{6+1}{2} = \frac{7}{2}$$

$$3\frac{1}{2} = \frac{7}{2}$$

The numerator of the fraction $\frac{7}{2}$ is greater than the denominator. This is an example of an **improper fraction**. If the numerator is less than the denominator, the fraction is a **proper fraction**. For example, $\frac{2}{7}$ is a proper fraction.

Example 1
Express $4\frac{5}{6}$ as an improper fraction.

$$4\frac{5}{6} = 4 + \frac{5}{6} = \frac{24}{6} + \frac{5}{6} = \frac{24+5}{6} = \frac{29}{6}$$

or, more quickly,

$$4\frac{5}{6} = \frac{4 \times 6 + 5}{6} = \frac{24+5}{6} = \frac{29}{6}$$

Example 2
Express $\frac{19}{8}$ as a mixed number.

$$\frac{19}{8} = \frac{16+3}{8} = \frac{16}{8} + \frac{3}{8} = 2 + \frac{3}{8} = 2\frac{3}{8}$$

or, more quickly,

$$\frac{19}{8} = 19 \div 8 = 2 \text{ with remainder } 3,$$

but the remainder is also divided by 8:

$$19 \div 8 = 2 + \frac{3}{8} = 2\frac{3}{8}$$

Exercise 4a (Oral)

1. Express as mixed numbers.

a $\frac{4}{3}$	b $\frac{5}{2}$	c $1\frac{1}{4}$	d $\frac{7}{5}$
e $\frac{11}{5}$	f $\frac{25}{7}$	g $\frac{25}{6}$	h $\frac{19}{8}$
i $\frac{26}{9}$	j $\frac{41}{5}$	k $\frac{60}{7}$	l $\frac{55}{6}$
m $\frac{89}{9}$	n $\frac{40}{11}$	o $\frac{113}{3}$	p $\frac{119}{9}$
q $\frac{123}{7}$	r $\frac{57}{10}$	s $\frac{93}{20}$	t $\frac{129}{100}$

2. Express as improper fractions.

a $1\frac{3}{4}$	b $3\frac{1}{3}$	c $6\frac{1}{2}$	d $4\frac{3}{5}$
e $9\frac{1}{4}$	f $3\frac{5}{6}$	g $4\frac{2}{7}$	h $7\frac{3}{5}$
i $5\frac{3}{8}$	j $6\frac{5}{7}$	k $12\frac{2}{3}$	l $13\frac{1}{3}$
m $5\frac{6}{7}$	n $4\frac{1}{12}$	o $3\frac{7}{13}$	p $8\frac{5}{9}$
q $7\frac{1}{2}$	r $9\frac{7}{10}$	s $6\frac{7}{20}$	t $2\frac{13}{100}$

4-2 Equivalent fractions

Look at the diagrams and the fractions in Table 4.1. Imagine that the diagrams show a circular pizza or cake cut into slices.

diagram	number of equal parts	number of parts shaded	fraction shaded
	3	1	$\frac{1}{3}$
	6	2	$\frac{2}{6}$
	9	3	$\frac{3}{9}$
	12	4	$\frac{4}{12}$
	15	5	$\frac{5}{15}$

Table 4.1

In each diagram the whole has stayed the same and the same amount has been shaded.

The fractions $\frac{1}{3}, \frac{2}{6}, \frac{3}{9}, \frac{4}{12}, \frac{5}{15}$ all represent the same amount of the pizza or cake. Thus

$$\frac{1}{3} = \frac{2}{6} = \frac{3}{9} = \frac{4}{12} = \frac{5}{15}.$$

We say that fractions which are equal in this way are **equivalent fractions**. $\frac{2}{6}$ is equivalent to $\frac{5}{15}$ or, simply,

$$\frac{2}{6} = \frac{5}{15}.$$

Optional: Do Exercise 7 of your Students' Practice Book.

Exercise 4b (Oral/QR)
Find the missing numbers.

1. $\frac{1}{3} = \frac{3}{9} = \frac{6}{\square} = \frac{\square}{24} = \frac{50}{\square} = \frac{\square}{900} = \frac{100}{\square}$
2. $\frac{1}{2} = \frac{2}{4} = \frac{3}{\square} = \frac{\square}{8} = \frac{\square}{10} = \frac{\square}{100} = \frac{25}{\square}$
3. $\frac{2}{3} = \frac{8}{12} = \frac{20}{\square} = \frac{\square}{6} = \frac{\square}{900} = \frac{\square}{24} = \frac{10}{\square}$
4. $\frac{1}{4} = \frac{5}{20} = \frac{\square}{8} = \frac{3}{\square} = \frac{\square}{60} = \frac{\square}{100} = \frac{7}{\square}$
5. $\frac{3}{4} = \frac{6}{8} = \frac{15}{\square} = \frac{24}{\square} = \frac{\square}{28} = \frac{\square}{100} = \frac{\square}{24}$
6. $\frac{1}{5} = \frac{10}{50} = \frac{\square}{10} = \frac{4}{\square} = \frac{\square}{100} = \frac{24}{\square} = \frac{5}{\square}$

Sets of equivalent fractions can be made by multiplying the numerator and denominator by the same number. For example:

$$\frac{1}{4} = \frac{1 \times 5}{4 \times 5} = \frac{5}{20}$$

$$\frac{7}{9} = \frac{7 \times 4}{9 \times 4} = \frac{28}{36}$$

In general for any fraction $\frac{a}{b}$ we can make an equivalent fraction by multiplying above and below by the same number. Therefore

$$\frac{a}{b} = \frac{a \times 2}{b \times 2} = \frac{a \times 3}{b \times 3} = \frac{a \times 4}{b \times 4} = \ldots = \frac{a \times n}{b \times n}$$

where n is any whole number.

Example 3

Express each of the fractions $\frac{3}{4}, \frac{5}{8}, \frac{7}{12}, \frac{2}{3}$ with a denominator of 24. Hence arrange the fractions in ascending order (i.e. from lowest to highest).

$$\frac{3}{4} = \frac{3 \times 6}{4 \times 6} = \frac{18}{24}$$

$$\frac{5}{8} = \frac{5 \times 3}{8 \times 3} = \frac{15}{24}$$

$$\frac{7}{12} = \frac{7 \times 2}{12 \times 2} = \frac{14}{24}$$

$$\frac{2}{3} = \frac{2 \times 8}{3 \times 8} = \frac{16}{24}$$

The order is $\frac{14}{24}, \frac{15}{24}, \frac{16}{24}, \frac{18}{24}$, i.e. $\frac{7}{12}, \frac{5}{8}, \frac{2}{3}, \frac{3}{4}$.

Note: In Example 3, 24 is the LCM of 4, 8, 12 and 3. We say that 24 is the **lowest common denominator** of the set of fractions.

Exercise 4c
1. [QR] Find the missing numbers.

a. $\frac{2}{3} = \frac{\square}{18}$ b. $\frac{5}{6} = \frac{20}{\square}$

c. $\frac{3}{5} = \frac{\square}{15}$ d. $\frac{7}{9} = \frac{14}{\square}$

e. $\frac{3}{7} = \frac{9}{\square}$ f. $\frac{9}{11} = \frac{18}{\square}$

g. $\frac{1}{6} = \frac{\square}{18}$ h. $\frac{3}{5} = \frac{\square}{20}$

i. $\frac{5}{8} = \frac{25}{\square}$ j. $\frac{5}{7} = \frac{35}{\square}$

k. $\frac{3}{8} = \frac{\square}{48}$ l. $\frac{5}{9} = \frac{\square}{36}$

2 Use the given common denominators to arrange the fractions in ascending order (i.e. from lowest to highest).

a $\frac{2}{3}, \frac{5}{6}, \frac{7}{12}, \frac{3}{4}$ common denominator 12

b $\frac{3}{4}, \frac{4}{5}, \frac{9}{10}, \frac{17}{20}$ common denominator 20

c $\frac{2}{3}, \frac{5}{9}, \frac{7}{12}, \frac{11}{18}$ common denominator 36

3 Find the lowest common denominator of the following sets of fractions. Use this to arrange the fractions in ascending order of size.

a $\frac{1}{3}, \frac{2}{9}, \frac{5}{18}$ b $\frac{1}{2}, \frac{3}{5}, \frac{8}{15}, \frac{17}{30}$ c $\frac{3}{5}, \frac{5}{8}, \frac{7}{10}, \frac{13}{20}$

Lowest terms

The value of a fraction stays the same if both the numerator and denominator are divided by the same number. For example.

$$\frac{16}{24} = \frac{16 \div 8}{24 \div 8} = \frac{2}{3}$$

$$\frac{15}{60} = \frac{15 \div 15}{60 \div 15} = \frac{1}{4}$$

When the numerator and denominator have no common factor, we say that the fraction is in its **lowest terms**, or in its **simplest form**. Thus $\frac{16}{24}$ in its lowest terms is $\frac{2}{3}$; $\frac{1}{4}$ is the simplest form of $\frac{15}{60}$. To express a fraction in its lowest terms:

a look for common factors of the numerator and denominator;

b divide the numerator and denominator by their common factors;

c repeat until there are no more common factors.

Example 4

Express a $\frac{42}{70}$ and b $\frac{26}{78}$ in their lowest terms.

a By inspection:

$$\frac{42}{70} = \frac{42 \div 7}{70 \div 7} = \frac{6}{10} = \frac{6 \div 2}{10 \div 2} = \frac{3}{5}$$

or by using prime factors:

$$\frac{42}{70} = \frac{2 \times 3 \times 7}{2 \times 5 \times 7} = \frac{2 \div 2 \times 3 \times 7 \div 7}{2 \div 2 \times 5 \times 7 \div 7}$$

$$= \frac{1 \times 3 \times 1}{1 \times 5 \times 1} = \frac{3}{5}$$

b By inspection:

$$\frac{26}{78} = \frac{26 \div 2}{78 \div 2} = \frac{13}{39} = \frac{13 \div 13}{39 \div 13} = \frac{1}{3}$$

After practice, you will be able to leave out many of the steps shown in the above example.

Exercise 4d

1 [QR] Find the missing numbers.

a $\frac{15}{20} = \frac{15 \div \square}{20 \div 5} = \frac{\square}{4}$ b $\frac{12}{21} = \frac{12 \div 3}{21 \div \square} = \frac{4}{\square}$

c $\frac{18}{24} = \frac{18 \div 6}{24 \div \square} = \frac{3}{\square}$ d $\frac{80}{100} = \frac{8}{\square} = \frac{4}{\square}$

e $\frac{25}{100} = \frac{\square}{20} = \frac{\square}{4}$ f $\frac{42}{56} = \frac{21}{\square} = \frac{3}{\square}$

g $\frac{18}{27} = \frac{2}{\square}$ h $\frac{10}{16} = \frac{\square}{8}$

i $\frac{28}{36} = \frac{7}{\square}$ j $\frac{48}{100} = \frac{12}{\square}$

k $\frac{32}{40} = \frac{4}{\square}$ l $\frac{16}{48} = \frac{\square}{3}$

2 Reduce the following fractions to their lowest terms.

a $\frac{7}{35}$ b $\frac{3}{18}$ c $\frac{5}{100}$

d $\frac{38}{80}$ e $\frac{14}{21}$ f $\frac{24}{32}$

g $\frac{30}{36}$ h $\frac{48}{60}$ i $\frac{24}{54}$

j $\frac{45}{105}$ k $\frac{90}{126}$ l $\frac{128}{176}$

4-3 Basic operations on fractions

Addition and subtraction

We can only add or subtract fractions if they have the same denominators.

Example 5

$$\frac{2}{9} + \frac{5}{9} = \frac{2+5}{9} = \frac{7}{9}$$

Example 6

$$\frac{13}{15} - \frac{2}{15} = \frac{13-2}{15} = \frac{11}{15}$$

If fractions have different denominators:

a find a common denominator (preferably the lowest);
b express each fraction as an equivalent fraction using that denominator;
c add or subtract as above.

Example 7
Simplify $\frac{5}{6} + \frac{3}{8}$.

The LCM of 6 and 8 is 24.

$\frac{5}{6} + \frac{3}{8} = \frac{5 \times 4}{6 \times 4} + \frac{3 \times 3}{8 \times 3} = \frac{20}{24} + \frac{9}{24}$

$= \frac{20 + 9}{24} = \frac{29}{24} = 1\frac{5}{24}$

Example 8
Simplify $\frac{7}{10} - \frac{4}{15}$.

The LCM of 10 and 15 is 30.

$\frac{7}{10} - \frac{4}{15} = \frac{7 \times 3}{10 \times 3} - \frac{4 \times 2}{15 \times 2} = \frac{21}{30} - \frac{8}{30}$

$= \frac{21 - 8}{30} = \frac{13}{30}$

If the numbers are mixed, express them as improper fractions.

Example 9
Simplify $6\frac{5}{12} - 3\frac{3}{4}$.

$6\frac{5}{12} - 3\frac{3}{4} = \frac{77}{12} - \frac{15}{4} = \frac{77}{12} - \frac{45}{12} = \frac{32}{12}$

$= \frac{32 \div 4}{12 \div 4} = \frac{8}{3} = 2\frac{2}{3}$

Example 10
Simplify $3\frac{2}{5} + 2\frac{2}{3}$.

$3\frac{2}{5} + 2\frac{2}{3} = \frac{17}{5} + \frac{8}{3} = \frac{51}{15} + \frac{40}{15} = \frac{91}{15} = 6\frac{1}{15}$

Exercise 4e
Simplify the following.

① $\frac{3}{4} + \frac{2}{3}$
② $\frac{3}{4} - \frac{2}{3}$
③ $\frac{5}{6} + \frac{2}{9}$
④ $\frac{5}{6} - \frac{2}{9}$
⑤ $\frac{7}{12} - \frac{3}{8}$
⑥ $\frac{7}{12} + \frac{3}{8}$
⑦ $\frac{11}{15} - \frac{2}{5}$
⑧ $\frac{11}{15} + \frac{1}{5}$
⑨ $1\frac{1}{2} + \frac{3}{4}$
⑩ $1\frac{3}{4} - \frac{1}{2}$
⑪ $1\frac{1}{2} + 2\frac{1}{3}$
⑫ $1\frac{1}{4} - \frac{2}{3}$
⑬ $3\frac{7}{8} + 2\frac{3}{4}$
⑭ $2\frac{5}{6} + 5\frac{7}{9}$
⑮ $5\frac{3}{4} - 2\frac{4}{5}$
⑯ $4\frac{1}{6} - 1\frac{5}{8}$
⑰ $1\frac{1}{2} + 2\frac{1}{3} + 3\frac{1}{4}$
⑱ $5\frac{3}{4} - 2\frac{7}{8} + 1\frac{1}{2}$
⑲ $3\frac{7}{8} + 7\frac{3}{4} - 6\frac{1}{2}$
⑳ $5\frac{1}{6} - 3\frac{2}{3} + 6\frac{7}{12}$

Exercise 4f

① What is the sum of $1\frac{7}{12}$ and $3\frac{5}{8}$?

② What is the difference between $4\frac{3}{8}$ and $3\frac{11}{12}$?

③ Find the sum of $2\frac{3}{4}$ and $2\frac{4}{5}$. Find the difference between this sum and 6.

④ A girl spends $\frac{1}{4}$ of her pocket money on Monday and $\frac{3}{8}$ on Wednesday. What fraction of her money is left?

⑤ A fruit grower uses $\frac{1}{3}$ of his land for bananas, $\frac{3}{8}$ for pineapples, $\frac{1}{6}$ for mangoes and the remainder for oranges. What fraction of his land is used for oranges?

⑥ $\frac{1}{5}$ of the timetable for a class is given to English and $\frac{1}{8}$ to Mathematics. What fraction is left for the other subjects?

⑦ During a week, a student spends $\frac{1}{3}$ of her time in bed, $\frac{5}{24}$ of her time in lessons and $\frac{1}{8}$ of her time doing homework. What fraction of her time is left for doing other things?

⑧ A man goes on a journey. He does $\frac{1}{6}$ of it on a bicycle, $\frac{4}{5}$ on a lorry and walks the rest. What fraction of the journey does he walk?

⑨ A boy plays football for $1\frac{3}{4}$ hours, listens to the radio for $\frac{3}{4}$ hour and then spends $1\frac{1}{4}$ hours doing his homework. How much time does he spend altogether doing these things?

⑩ By how much is the sum of $2\frac{4}{5}$ and $4\frac{1}{2}$ less than $8\frac{1}{10}$?

Multiplication

Whole number × fraction

$4 \times \frac{1}{3}$ means 4 lots of $\frac{1}{3}$ of something. We can show this in pictures (Fig. 4.6) and in numbers.

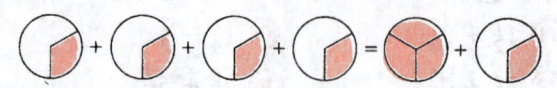

Fig. 4.6

$$4 \times \frac{1}{3} = \frac{1}{3} + \frac{1}{3} + \frac{1}{3} + \frac{1}{3} = \frac{4}{3} = 1\frac{1}{3}$$

or $4 \times \frac{1}{3} = \frac{4 \times 1}{3} = \frac{4}{3}$

Similarly, $3 \times \frac{2}{9}$ (Fig. 4.7).

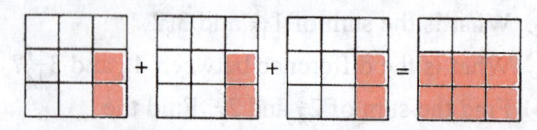

Fig. 4.7

$$3 \times \frac{2}{9} = \frac{2}{9} + \frac{2}{9} + \frac{2}{9} = \frac{6}{9} \left(= \frac{2}{3}\right)$$

or $3 \times \frac{2}{9} = \frac{3 \times 2}{9} = \frac{6}{9} \left(= \frac{2}{3}\right)$

Fraction × whole number

$\frac{2}{5} \times 3$ means $\frac{2}{5}$ of 3 objects. Let the objects be 3 squares (Fig. 4.8).

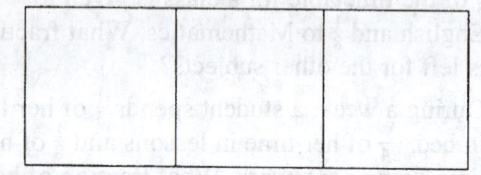

Fig. 4.8

The 3 squares can be divided into fifths. Two of the fifths are shaded in each square (Fig. 4.9).

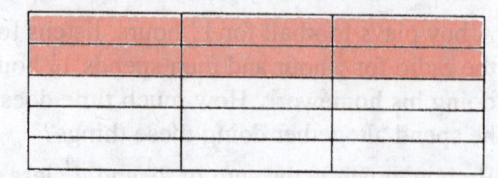

Fig. 4.9

The fifths can be rearranged to make 1 square and $\frac{1}{5}$ of a square altogether (Fig. 4.10).

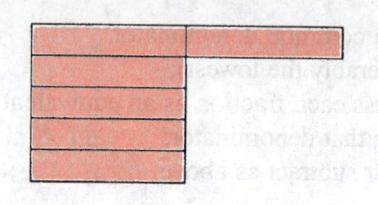

Fig. 4.10

Thus $\frac{2}{5}$ of $3 = \frac{2}{5} \times 3 = 1\frac{1}{5}$. Also notice that

$\frac{2}{5} \times 3 = \frac{2 \times 3}{5} = \frac{6}{5} = 1\frac{1}{5}$ as before.

Exercise 4g

Simplify the following.

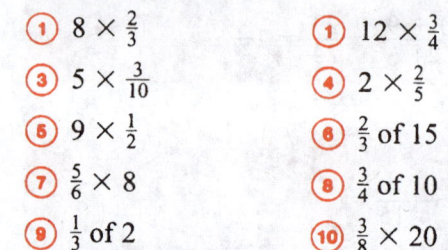

(1) $8 \times \frac{2}{3}$ (2) $12 \times \frac{3}{4}$

(3) $5 \times \frac{3}{10}$ (4) $2 \times \frac{2}{5}$

(5) $9 \times \frac{1}{2}$ (6) $\frac{2}{3}$ of 15

(7) $\frac{5}{6} \times 8$ (8) $\frac{3}{4}$ of 10

(9) $\frac{1}{3}$ of 2   (10) $\frac{3}{8} \times 20$

Fraction × fraction

$\frac{2}{3} \times \frac{5}{7}$ means $\frac{2}{3}$ of $\frac{5}{7}$ of something. The pictures in Fig. 4.11 show how to find $\frac{2}{3}$ of $\frac{5}{7}$ of a rectangle.

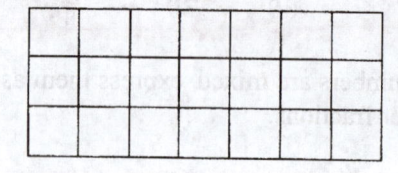

First, shade $\frac{5}{7}$ of the rectangle.

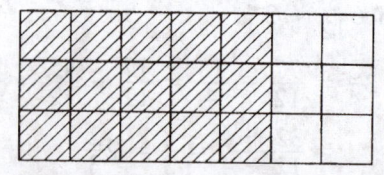

Then cross-shade $\frac{2}{3}$ of the shaded part.

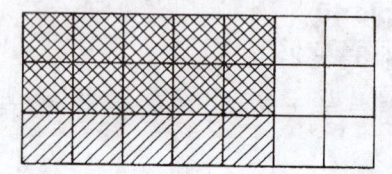

Fig. 4.11

10 small squares represent $\frac{2}{3}$ of $\frac{5}{7}$ of the rectangle.

Since the rectangle contains 21 small squares, then $\frac{2}{3} \times \frac{5}{7} = \frac{10}{21}$. Notice that

$$\frac{2}{3} \times \frac{5}{7} = \frac{2 \times 5}{3 \times 7} = \frac{10}{21}$$

To multiply a fraction by a fraction:
a multiply the numerators to make the numerator of the product;
b multiply the denominators to make the denominator of the product; also,
c always change mixed numbers to improper fractions *before* multiplying.

Example 11
Simplify $\frac{3}{8}$ of $2\frac{2}{9} \times 1\frac{3}{5}$.

$\frac{3}{8}$ of $2\frac{2}{9} \times 1\frac{3}{5} = \frac{3}{8} \times \frac{20}{9} \times \frac{8}{5} = \frac{3 \times 20 \times 8}{8 \times 9 \times 5}* = \frac{4}{3} = 1\frac{1}{3}$

*Divide the numerator and denominator by the common factors 3, 5 and 8 to simplify.

☞ *Optional:* Do Exercise 8 of your Students' Practice Book.

Exercise 4h
Simplify the following.

1. $\frac{1}{2} \times \frac{3}{4}$
2. $\frac{2}{3}$ of $\frac{3}{4}$
3. $\frac{3}{4} \times \frac{1}{3}$
4. $\frac{3}{5} \times \frac{2}{3}$
5. $\frac{5}{6} \times \frac{3}{8}$
6. $\frac{1}{2} \times \frac{8}{9}$
7. $1\frac{1}{4} \times \frac{3}{5}$
8. $\frac{3}{5}$ of $2\frac{1}{2}$
9. $2\frac{1}{2} \times \frac{2}{5}$
10. $1\frac{1}{2} \times 1\frac{2}{3}$
11. $2\frac{3}{4} \times \frac{4}{5}$
12. $\frac{4}{11}$ of $3\frac{2}{3}$
13. $\frac{6}{7}$ of $5\frac{1}{4}$
14. $5\frac{1}{3} \times 2\frac{1}{4}$
15. $2\frac{1}{3} \times \frac{1}{14}$
16. $\frac{5 \times 21}{14 \times 15}$
17. $\frac{12 \times 25}{10 \times 18}$
18. $\frac{16 \times 29 \times 28}{21 \times 24 \times 15}$
19. $\frac{4}{7}$ of $8\frac{3}{4}$
20. $1\frac{7}{8} \times 3\frac{1}{5}$
21. $(2\frac{1}{2})^2$
22. $3\frac{3}{4} \times \frac{4}{9} \times 1\frac{1}{5}$
23. $1\frac{7}{9} \times 3\frac{3}{4} \times \frac{3}{8}$
24. $\frac{12}{25}$ of $(1\frac{1}{4})^2$

Division

Look at the following working very carefully.

$$2 \div \frac{5}{8} = \frac{2}{\frac{5}{8}} = \frac{2 \times \frac{8}{5}}{\frac{5}{8} \times \frac{8}{5}} = \frac{2 \times \frac{8}{5}}{1} = 2 \times \frac{8}{5}$$

Thus, $2 \div \frac{5}{8} = 2 \times \frac{8}{5}$.
$\frac{8}{5}$ is the **reciprocal** of $\frac{5}{8}$; i.e. it is the same fraction turned upside down.

To divide by a fraction, simply multiply by its reciprocal.

Example 12
Find the value of $2\frac{1}{4} \div \frac{3}{7}$.

$2\frac{1}{4} \div \frac{3}{7} = 2\frac{1}{4} \times \frac{7}{3} = \frac{9}{4} \times \frac{7}{3} = \frac{9 \times 7}{4 \times 3} = \frac{21}{4} = 5\frac{1}{4}$

Notice that this example shows that it is possible to get a result which is greater than either of the given numbers.

We saw before that the value of a fraction is unchanged if we multiply the numerator and denominator by the same number. This gives another method of dividing by fractions.

$2\frac{1}{4} \div \frac{3}{7} = \frac{\frac{9}{4}}{\frac{3}{7}} = \frac{\frac{9}{4} \times 28*}{\frac{3}{7} \times 28} = \frac{9 \times 7}{4 \times 3} = \frac{21}{4} = 5\frac{1}{4}$

*28 is the LCM of the denominators of the two fractions.

Example 13
Simplify $\dfrac{2\frac{2}{3} \times 1\frac{1}{2}}{4\frac{4}{5}}$.

Multiplying by the reciprocal:

$\dfrac{2\frac{2}{3} \times 1\frac{1}{2}}{4\frac{4}{5}} = \frac{8}{3} \times \frac{3}{2} \div \frac{24}{5} = \frac{8}{3} \times \frac{3}{2} \times \frac{5}{24} = \frac{24 \times 5}{6 \times 24} = \frac{5}{6}$

or by equal multiplication:

$\dfrac{2\frac{2}{3} \times 1\frac{1}{2}}{4\frac{4}{5}} = \dfrac{\frac{8}{3} \times \frac{3}{2}}{\frac{24}{5}} = \dfrac{\frac{8}{3} \times \frac{3}{2} \times 30*}{\frac{24}{5} \times 30} = \frac{8 \times 3 \times 5}{24 \times 6} = \frac{5}{6}$

*30 is the LCM of the denominators 2, 3 and 5.

Exercise 4i
Simplify the following.

1. $1\frac{2}{3} \div 5$
2. $2\frac{1}{4} \div 3$
3. $4\frac{1}{5} \div 3$
4. $6\frac{3}{7} \div 5$
5. $1\frac{3}{5} \div 6$
6. $3\frac{2}{3} \div 4$
7. $\frac{3}{4} \div \frac{1}{2}$
8. $2\frac{1}{5} \div \frac{1}{5}$
9. $6 \div \frac{3}{5}$
10. $10 \div \frac{2}{7}$
11. $4\frac{1}{5} \div 7$
12. $13\frac{3}{4} \div 11$
13. $\frac{9}{14} \div \frac{3}{7}$
14. $\frac{12}{25} \div \frac{9}{10}$
15. $\frac{16}{33} \div \frac{8}{11}$
16. $1\frac{1}{7} \div \frac{4}{21}$
17. $2\frac{2}{5} \div 1\frac{1}{3}$
18. $4\frac{2}{5} \div 1\frac{1}{10}$
19. $3\frac{1}{5} \div 6\frac{2}{3}$
20. $5\frac{1}{7} \div 2\frac{2}{5}$
21. $\frac{3}{8} \div 5\frac{1}{4}$
22. $\frac{5}{6} \div 2\frac{1}{12}$
23. $1\frac{4}{5} \div 6\frac{3}{10}$
24. $2\frac{5}{8} \div 8\frac{1}{6}$
25. $8\frac{1}{6} \div 3\frac{8}{9}$
26. $7\frac{7}{8} \div 6\frac{5}{12}$
27. $9\frac{2}{7} \div 3\frac{9}{10}$
28. $7\frac{1}{8} \div 4\frac{3}{4}$
29. $\dfrac{\frac{3}{10} \times \frac{35}{36}}{\frac{14}{15}}$
30. $\dfrac{\frac{9}{10} \times 3\frac{1}{5}}{\frac{3}{8}}$
31. $\dfrac{7\frac{3}{7}}{9\frac{3}{4}} \div \dfrac{5}{21}$
32. $\dfrac{8\frac{1}{6} \times 3\frac{3}{7}}{11\frac{2}{3}}$
33. $\dfrac{3\frac{3}{5} \times 1\frac{5}{9}}{2\frac{1}{10}}$
34. $\dfrac{5\frac{1}{4} \div 2\frac{4}{5}}{3\frac{3}{4}}$
35. $\dfrac{9\frac{3}{5}}{5\frac{1}{7}} \times 1\frac{1}{4}$

6. A tank holds 15 litres of water. The capacity of a cup is $\frac{3}{10}$ of a litre. How many cups of water does the tank hold?

7. LP records turn round $33\frac{1}{3}$ times every minute. If one side of an LP plays for 24 minutes, how many times does it turn round?

8. One lecture at an evening course lasts $1\frac{1}{2}$ hours. If the course lasts 30 hours altogether, how many lectures are there?

9. Some shop-soiled goods are sold for $\frac{2}{5}$ of their original price. What will be the selling price of a T-shirt originally costing ₦850?

10. In a school, $\frac{9}{10}$ of the students play sports. $\frac{2}{3}$ of these play football. What fraction of the students play football?

11. It takes $1\frac{3}{4}$ m of cloth to make a skirt. How many skirts can be made from $10\frac{1}{2}$ m of cloth?

12. A ball always bounces to $\frac{3}{5}$ of the height from which it falls. If it falls from a height of 1 m, how high will it rise after the second bounce?

13. A farmer uses $\frac{9}{16}$ of a field for growing cassava. He uses $\frac{2}{7}$ of the remainder for growing corn. What fraction of the field is used for growing corn?

14. Three sisters share some money. The oldest gets $\frac{5}{11}$ of the money. The next girl gets $\frac{7}{12}$ of the remainder. What fraction of the money does the youngest girl get?

Exercise 4j

1. Find the product of $3\frac{1}{4}$ and $2\frac{2}{5}$.
2. Find the value of $6\frac{2}{3}$ divided by $1\frac{7}{9}$.
3. What is three-quarters of $3\frac{3}{7}$?
4. Does $4\frac{1}{2}$ divided into $1\frac{4}{5}$ mean $4\frac{1}{2} \div 1\frac{4}{5}$ or $1\frac{4}{5} \div 4\frac{1}{2}$? Find the values of $4\frac{1}{2} \div 1\frac{4}{5}$ and $1\frac{4}{5} \div 4\frac{1}{2}$ and say which one is $4\frac{1}{2}$ divided into $1\frac{4}{5}$.
5. The mass of each book of an encyclopaedia is $1\frac{3}{4}$ kg. There are 20 books in the encyclopaedia. Find the total mass of the encyclopaedia.

4-4 Percentages

20% means $\frac{20}{100}$. The symbol % is short for *per cent*. **Per cent** means hundredths. A fraction in the form 20% is called a **percentage**.

100% means $\frac{100}{100}$. $\frac{100}{100} = 1$. So, when we say we want 100% of something, we mean we want *all* of it.

To express a percentage as a fraction:
a write the percentage as a fraction of 100;
b reduce the fraction to its lowest terms.

Example 14
Express 15% as a fraction in its lowest terms.

$15\% = \frac{15}{100} = \frac{3 \times 5}{20 \times 5} = \frac{3}{20}$

Exercise 4k
Express the following percentages as fractions in their lowest terms.

1. 5%
2. 50%
3. 25%
4. 40%
5. 70%
6. 4%
7. 35%
8. 12%
9. 80%
10. 75%
11. 24%
12. 65%
13. 64%
14. 60%
15. 45%
16. 84%

☞ *Optional:* Do Exercise 9 of your Students' Practice Book.

To express a fraction as a percentage make an equivalent fraction with a denominator of 100.

Example 15
Express the following fractions as percentages:

a $\frac{2}{5}$, b $\frac{176}{300}$.

a $\frac{2}{5} = \frac{2 \times 20}{5 \times 20} = \frac{40}{100} = 40\%$

b $\frac{176}{300} = \frac{176 \div 3}{300 \div 3} = \frac{58\frac{2}{3}}{100} = 58\frac{2}{3}\%$

Notice in the last example that $\frac{2}{5} \times 100 = 40$ and $\frac{176}{300} \times 100 = 58\frac{2}{3}$. Thus to change a fraction to a percentage it is quicker and easier to multiply the fraction by 100. For example,

$\frac{3}{8} = \frac{3}{8} \times 100\% = \frac{300}{8}\% = 37\frac{1}{2}\%$

Exercise 4l
Express the following fractions as percentages.

1. $\frac{1}{2}$
2. $\frac{1}{4}$
3. $\frac{1}{3}$
4. $\frac{3}{4}$
5. $\frac{1}{5}$
6. $\frac{1}{10}$
7. $\frac{1}{20}$
8. $\frac{1}{25}$
9. $\frac{3}{10}$
10. $\frac{3}{5}$
11. $\frac{2}{15}$
12. $\frac{17}{20}$
13. $\frac{5}{8}$
14. $\frac{1}{6}$
15. $\frac{9}{25}$
16. $\frac{76}{300}$

To express one quantity as a fraction of another

Example 16
Express 7 min 30 s as a fraction of 1 hour.

$\frac{7 \min 30\text{ s}}{1\text{ h}} = \frac{450\text{ s}}{3600\text{ s}}* = \frac{9 \times 50}{72 \times 50} = \frac{9}{72} = \frac{1}{8}\text{h}$

or

$\frac{7 \min 30\text{ s}}{1\text{ h}} = \frac{7\frac{1}{2}\min*}{60\min} = \frac{15}{120} = \frac{1 \times 15}{8 \times 15} = \frac{1}{8}\text{h}$

*Notice that both quantities must be in the same units before fractions can be reduced.

Exercise 4m
1. What fraction of 1 minute is 15 seconds?
2. Express 25 cm as a fraction of 3 m.
3. What fraction is 500 g of 2 kg?
4. What fraction of 6 weeks is 6 days?
5. What fraction of $1 is 40c?
6. Express 40 min as a fraction of 1 hour.
7. Express 650 m as a fraction of 1 km.
8. What fraction is 4 min 30 s of 12 min?
9. Express 13 weeks as a fraction of 1 year.
10. What fraction is 4 mm of 10 cm?
11. Express the first quantity as a fraction of the second. Give your answers in their lowest terms.
    a 2 min 15 s, 7 min 30 s
    b 35 cm, 2 metres
    c 2·25 kg, 3·75 kg
    d 75 mℓ, 1 litre
    e 650 m, 1·95 km
    f 2 weeks, 1 year
    g 360 mℓ, 2 litres
    h 440 m, 1·5 km
    i ₦225, ₦2475
    j 2 h 20 min, 5 h 15 min

To express one quantity as a percentage of another

Make sure that both quantities are in the same units. Express the first quantity as a fraction of the second. Multiply the fraction by 100 to change it to a percentage.

Example 17

A worker hammers a post 2·2 m long into the ground. 66 cm of the post is below the ground. What percentage of the post is above the ground?

Fraction of post below the ground

$$= \frac{66\,cm}{2\cdot 2\,m} = \frac{66\,cm}{220\,cm} = \frac{66}{220}.$$

Percentage of post below the ground

$$= \frac{66}{220} \times 100\% = \frac{6 \times 11 \times 5 \times 20}{11 \times 20}\%$$

$$= 30\%.$$

Percentage of post above the ground

$$= 100\% - 30\% = 70\%.$$

Exercise 4n

1. Express the first quantity as a percentage of the second.
   a ₦10, ₦100   b 25c, €1
   c 400 g, 1 kg d 800 mℓ, 1 ℓ
   e 3 mm, 1 cm f 500 mℓ, 4 ℓ
   g 45 g, 75 g   h 25 m, 1 km
   i 30 cm, 1·5 m j ₦100, ₦250

2. In an exam a student scored 60 marks out of a possible 80. What percentage is this?

3. 3 girls are absent from a class of 25 students. What percentage of the class is absent?

4. 26 cm of wood is cut off a board 130 cm long. What percentage has been cut off?

5. In a box of 200 oranges, 18 are bad. What percentage is bad? What percentage is good?

6. A piece of elastic is 48 cm long. It is stretched to a length of 60 cm. What is the increase in length? What percentage of the original length is the increase?

7. A motorist buys a 5-litre can of oil to maintain her car. She used 800 mℓ. What percentage of oil has she used and what percentage remains?

8. The distance between two villages is 8 km. A student walks from one village to the other. He walks most of the way but runs the last 480 metres. What percentage of the journey did he run?

9. A man bought a second-hand car for ₦700 000. He sold it three years later for ₦560 000. What percentage of his money did he lose?

10. During a physics lesson lasting 1 hour, it took 9 minutes to set up and clear away apparatus. What percentage of the lesson time was used in this way?

11. A cake has a mass of 2·5 kg. It contains 275 g of fruit. What percentage of fruit is there in the cake?

SUMMARY

1. *A fraction* represents part of a whole quantity. A fraction is in two parts, a *numerator* and a *denominator*, as follows:

   $\frac{4}{9}$ ← numerator
   ← denominator

2. *Equivalent fractions* all represent the same amount. For example, $\frac{4}{9}$, $\frac{8}{18}$ and $\frac{40}{90}$ are equivalent fractions.

3. If two or more fractions have the same denominator, we say they have a *common denominator*.

4. The *lowest common denominator* of a set of fractions is the LCM of the denominators.

5. When the numerator and denominator have no common factor, we say a fraction is in its *lowest terms* or in its *simplest form*.

6. A *mixed number* contains a whole and a fractional part, e.g. $2\frac{3}{4}$ is a mixed number.

7. In a fraction, if the numerator is:
   a less than the denominator, it is *proper*;
   b greater than the denominator, it is *improper*.

8. To add or subtract fractions:
   a change mixed numbers to improper fractions;
   b find the lowest common denominator;

c express the fractions as equivalent fractions with the same denominators. (See Examples 5, 6, 7, 8, 9 and 10.)

9 To multiply fractions:
   a change mixed numbers to improper fractions;
   b multiply numerators together to give the numerator of the product;
   c multiply denominators together to give the denominator of the product. (See Example 11.)

10 The *reciprocal* of a fraction is the same fraction turned upside down. (We also say it is the *inverse* of the fraction.) For example, $\frac{9}{4}$ is the reciprocal or inverse of $\frac{4}{9}$.

11 To divide by a fraction, multiply by its reciprocal.

12 *Percentage* or *per cent* means hundredths. The symbol % is short for per cent. Therefore 34% is another way of writing $\frac{34}{100}$.

13 To change a percentage to a fraction, write it as a fraction of 100. Reduce it to its lowest terms where possible.

14 To change a fraction to a percentage, multiply the fraction by 100.

15 To express a quantity as a percentage of another:
   a make sure they are in the same units;
   b express the first as a fraction of the second;
   c multiply the fraction by 100.

PUZZLE CORNER

From A to B

Here is a street map with the streets in a 3 x 3 square.

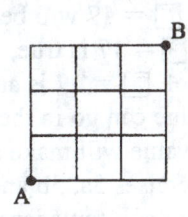

How many ways can you start from A to get to B, if at each junction you either go East or North?

PUZZLE CORNER

Number Pyramid

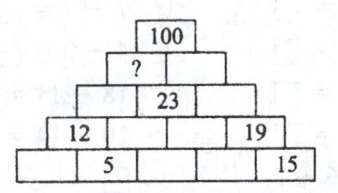

```
        100
      ?
        23
   12      19
     5        15
```

The total of each pair of adjacent squares equals the number above them. What number should replace the question mark?

5 Use of symbols 1: Letters for numbers

OBJECTIVES

You should be able to:

1 Find the missing number in an open sentence
2 Use letters to stand for numbers when writing and solving simple algebraic sentences.

5-1 Open sentences

$14 + \square = 17$. What number in the box will make this true? You may have seen problems like this before. $14 + \square = 17$ will be true if 3 goes in the box: $14 + \boxed{3} = 17$ is true,

We say that $14 + \square = 17$ is an **open sentence**. Any value can go in the box, but usually only one value will make an open sentence true. Exercises 5a, 5b and 5c contain many examples of open sentences. You may have met questions like these earlier in your Basic Education years. However, you should do them before going on to Section 5-2.

Exercise 5a (Oral/QR)

In each sentence, find the number which makes it true.

(1) $3 + 2 = \square$
(2) $8 - 7 = \square$
(3) $7 + 7 = \square$
(4) $7 - 7 = \square$
(5) $0 + 8 = \square$
(6) $4 - 0 = \square$
(7) $9 + 5 = \square$
(8) $18 - 11 = \square$
(9) $6 + 8 = \square$
(10) $20 - 14 = \square$
(11) $\square = 6 + 3$
(12) $\square = 4 - 1$
(13) $\square = 10 + 10$
(14) $\square = 17 - 7$
(15) $\square = 6 + 10$
(16) $\square = 19 - 13$
(17) $\square = 4 + 8$
(18) $\square = 14 - 9$
(19) $\square = 7 + 4$
(20) $\square = 13 - 5$
(21) $3 + \square = 5$
(22) $8 - \square = 2$
(23) $6 + \square = 9$
(24) $10 - \square = 9$
(25) $1 + \square = 8$
(26) $7 - \square = 3$
(27) $0 + \square = 5$
(28) $14 - \square = 14$
(29) $7 + \square = 11$
(30) $12 - \square = 8$
(31) $\square + 2 = 5$
(32) $\square - 1 = 6$
(33) $\square + 8 = 9$
(34) $\square - 3 = 1$
(35) $\square + 4 = 8$
(36) $\square - 2 = 9$
(37) $\square + 7 = 7$
(38) $\square - 6 = 0$
(39) $\square + 5 = 12$
(40) $\square - 5 = 7$
(41) $3 = 2 + \square$
(42) $8 = 10 - \square$
(43) $8 = 3 + \square$
(44) $10 = 13 - \square$
(45) $10 = 7 + \square$
(46) $1 = 5 - \square$
(47) $15 = 10 + \square$
(48) $6 = 16 - \square$
(49) $18 = 6 + \square$
(50) $7 = 19 - \square$
(51) $6 = \square + 2$
(52) $5 = \square - 2$
(53) $8 = \square + 5$
(54) $13 = \square - 3$
(55) $9 = \square + 7$
(56) $0 = \square - 8$
(57) $10 = \square + 4$
(58) $9 = \square - 10$
(59) $16 = \square + 9$
(60) $11 = \square - 6$
(61) $3 \times 4 = \square$
(62) $\square = 9 \times 2$
(63) $25 = 5 \times \square$
(64) $\square \times 6 = 18$
(65) $\square = 6 \times 6$
(66) $9 \times 0 = \square$
(67) $11 = \square \times 1$
(68) $9 \times 0 = \square$
(69) $36 \div 9 = \square$
(70) $\square = 10 \div 2$
(71) $15 \div \square = 5$
(72) $6 \div \square = 3$
(73) $18 \div 3 = \square$
(74) $\square \div 8 = 10$
(75) $3 \div 3 = \square$
(76) $\square \div 9 = 1$

Exercise 5b (Oral/QR)

In each sentence there are two or three boxes. The *same* number should go in every box and make the sentence true.

1. $\Box + \Box = 4$
2. $\Box + \Box = 6$
3. $\Box + \Box = 10$
4. $12 = \Box + \Box$
5. $8 = \Box + \Box$
6. $2 = \Box + \Box$
7. $\Box + \Box + \Box = 6$
8. $\Box + \Box + \Box = 15$
9. $\Box + \Box + \Box = 21$
10. $9 = \Box + \Box + \Box$
11. $18 = \Box + \Box + \Box$
12. $30 = \Box + \Box + \Box$
13. $10 - \Box = \Box$
14. $16 - \Box = \Box$
15. $\Box = 14 - \Box$
16. $\Box = 2 - \Box$
17. $\Box \times \Box = 49$
18. $100 = \Box \times \Box$
19. $\Box \times 1 = \Box$
20. $\Box \div \Box = 1$

What is the value of $5 + \Box$? The value depends on what number goes in the box. If 4 goes in the box, the value is 9. If 11 goes in the box the value is 16.

Exercise 5c (Oral/QR)

1. Find the value of the following if 5 goes in each box.
   a $\Box + 3$ b $\Box + 7$ c $4 + \Box$
   d $7 + \Box$ e $6 - \Box$ f $10 - \Box$
   g $\Box - 1$ h $\Box - 4$ i $5 - \Box$
   j $\Box \times 3 =$ k $8 \times \Box$ l $35 \div \Box$

2. Find the value of the following if 8 goes in each box.
   a $\Box + 9$ b $15 + \Box$ c $16 - \Box$
   d $\Box - 6$ e $\Box + 0$ f $\Box + 6$
   g $11 + \Box$ h $9 - \Box$ i $\Box - 7$
   j $\Box \times 4$ k $\Box \div 4$ l $\Box \div \Box$

3. Find the value of the following if 9 goes in each box.
   a $\Box + \Box$ b $\Box - \Box$
   c $\Box + \Box + 2$
   e $\Box + 7 + \Box$
   g $5 + \Box + \Box$
   i $\Box \times \Box + 4$
   d $\Box + \Box - 6$
   f $\Box - 3 + \Box$
   h $26 - \Box - \Box$
   j $\Box - (\Box \div 3)$

5-2 Letters for numbers

In mathematics we use letters of the alphabet to stand for numbers instead of boxes. We write $14 + x$ instead of $14 + \Box$. Any letter can be used. For example, $14 + a$ would be just as good as $14 + x$. Capital letters are not used; only small letters are used.

When using a letter instead of a number, the letter can stand for any number in general. Thus the value of $14 + x$ depends on the value of x.

For example,

if x stands for 2, $14 + x$ has the value 16;
if x stands for 12, $14 + x$ has the value 26;
if x stands for 5, $14 + x$ has the value 19.

When letters and numbers are used together in this way, the mathematics is called **generalised arithmetic** or **algebra**. The word algebra comes to us from an important book written around AD 830 by Mohammed Musa al Khowarizmi, a noted mathematician from Baghdad. The title of the book was *Al-jabr wa'l Muqābalah*.

The statement $14 + x = 17$ is called an **algebraic sentence**. It means 14 plus a number x makes 17, or, 14 plus x equals 17.

In the next exercise, each letter stands for a number. The number that the letter stands for should make the sentence true. For example, $14 + x = 17$ will be true if x stands for 3. We write this:
   If $14 + x = 17$
   Then $x = 3$

Exercise 5d (Oral/QR)

Each sentence is true. Find the number that each letter stands for.

1. $x = 2 + 7$
2. $y = 9 + 5$
3. $x = 3 - 0$
4. $y = 14 - 4$

41

(5) $z = 18 + 11$

(6) $z = 15 - 8$

(7) $a = 5 + 16$

(8) $a = 23 - 6$

(9) $b = 8 + 18$

(10) $b = 24 - 19$

(11) $6 + 3 = c$

(12) $6 - 4 = c$

(13) $12 + 8 = p$

(14) $18 - 7 = p$

(15) $9 + 7 = q$

(16) $17 - 8 = q$

(17) $13 + 9 = r$

(18) $25 - 18 = r$

(19) $5 + 18 = s$

(20) $21 - 12 = s$

(21) $2 + m = 5$

(22) $7 - m = 6$

(23) $11 + n = 14$

(24) $15 - n = 10$

(25) $22 + d = 30$

(26) $17 - d = 9$

(27) $19 + e = 30$

(28) $25 - e = 15$

(29) $8 + f = 23$

(30) $17 - f = 11$

(31) $z + 4 = 8$

(32) $z - 6 = 2$

(33) $y + 12 = 22$

(34) $y - 1 = 27$

(35) $x + 6 = 29$

(36) $x - 14 = 0$

(37) $c + 11 = 30$

(38) $c - 15 = 15$

(39) $b + 7 = 21$

(40) $b - 17 = 12$

(41) $5 = 4 + a$

(42) $6 = 7 - a$

(43) $10 = 5 + r$

(44) $8 = 13 - r$

(45) $17 = 9 + q$

(46) $16 = 20 - q$

(47) $26 = 12 + p$

(48) $4 = 21 - p$

(49) $24 = 17 + s$

(50) $11 = 29 - s$

(51) $4 = n + -$

(52) $9 = n - 5$

(53) $12 = m + 5$

(54) $16 = m - 9$

(55) $30 = f + 7$

(56) $10 = f - 17$

(57) $28 = e + 13$

(58) $6 = e - 18$

(59) $22 = d + 15$

(60) $21 = d - 6$

(61) $2 \times 14 = y$

(62) $z = 3 \times 7$

(63) $28 = 7 \times g$

(64) $h \times 4 = 20$

(65) $j = 4 \times 6$

(66) $7 \times 0 = k$

(67) $14 = m \times 1$

(68) $6 \times 0 = n$

(69) $32 \div 4 = p$

(70) $q = 12 \div 2$

(71) $14 \div r = 2$

(72) $22 \div s = 2$

(73) $33 \div 11 = t$

(74) $v \div 4 = 20$

(75) $12 \div 12 = w$

(76) $a \div 5 = 1$

Exercise 5e (Oral/QR)

Each sentence is true. Find the numbers that the letters stand for.

(1) $x + x = 8$

(2) $y + y = 12$

(3) $z + z = 14$

(4) $4 = a + a$

(5) $18 = b + b$

(6) $16 = c + c$

(7) $e + e + e = 3$

(8) $f + f + f = 12$

(9) $g + g + g = 30$

(10) $6 = h + h + h$

(11) $24 = j + j + j$

(12) $27 = k + k + k$

(13) $12 - m = m$

(14) $20 - n = n$

(15) $p = 28 - p$

(16) $64 = b \times b$

(17) $q \times q = 4$

(18) $25 = r \times r$

(19) $s \div 1 = s$

(20) $t \div t = 1$

What is the value of $x + 6$? The value of $x + 6$ depends on what x stands for.

If $x = 3$, then $x + 6 = 3 + 6 = 9$

If $x = 8$, then $x + 3 = 8 + 6 = 14$

Exercise 5f (Oral/QR)

(1) Find the value of the following when $x = 4$.

a $x + 5$ b $x + 8$ c $x - 1$
d $x - 4$ e $9 + x$ f $0 + x$
g $10 - x$ h $19 - x$ i $x \times 3$
j $x \div 2$ k $6 \times x$ l $28 \div x$

(2) Find the value of the following when $m = 15$.

a $m + 1$ b $m + 9$ c $m - 3$
d $m - 14$ e $5 + m$ f $13 + m$
g $22 - m$ h $15 - m$ i $m \times 2$
j $m \div 5$ k $3 \times m$ l $60 \div m$

(3) Find the value of the following when $a = 7$.

a $a + a$ b $a - a$
c $a + a + 6$ d $a + a + 3$
e $a + 5 + a$ f $a - 2 + a$
g $9 + a + a$ h $16 + a - a$
i $11 - a + a$ j $a - 8 + a$
k $a - 13 + a$ l $2 - a + a$
m $a \times a - 7$ n $a \div a + 9$

Exercise 5g (Oral/QR)

(1) A bicycle costs ₦10 000 and a radio costs ₦x. They cost ₦16 000 altogether. What is the value of x?

② Amina is *a* years old. Next year she will be 14 years old. What is the value of *a*?

③ A bag of sugar has a mass of *m* kg. The mass of three bags of sugar is 6 kg. What is the value of *m*? What would be the total mass of one bag of sugar and a 5 kg bag of flour?

④ There are two pencils. One is 14 cm long. The other is *x* cm long. Someone puts the pencils together as shown in Fig. 5.1. If $x = 10$, what is the total length of the two pencils?

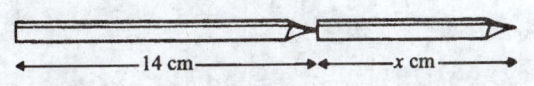

Fig. 5.1

⑤ There are *n* students in a classroom. 12 more students come into the classroom. If $n = 22$, how many students are there in the classroom altogether?

⑥ A man has 28 goats. He gives *n* of them to his sons and keeps the rest. If he keeps 10 goats, what is the value of *n*?

⑦ A student has *n* naira. She spends ₦150. If she now has ₦320, what is the value of *n*?

⑧ A father is 42 years old and his son is *y* years old. If the difference of their ages is 28 years, what is the value of *y*?

⑨ A girl has 14 sweets. She eats *n* of them. Find how many sweets she has left when $n = 5$. What is the value of *n* when she has no sweets left?

⑩ There are 21 matches left in a matchbox. Originally there were *m* matches in the box and 27 have been used. What is the value of *m*?

⑪ Initially a school HIV&AIDS club has 30 members. After a publicity campaign it increases its membership *k* times. If the new membership is 120, what is the value of *k*?

⑫ The cost of a new water pump for a school community is ₦250 000. There are *n* people in the community. When the cost is shared equally among the community members, they each have to pay ₦250. What is the value of *n*?

☞ *Optional:* Do Exercise 10 of your Students' Practice Book.

SUMMARY

1 In mathematics we often use letters of the alphabet, for example *a*, *b*, *x*, *y*, to stand for unknown numbers.

2 *Algebra* is a branch of mathematics in which letters and numbers are used together.

3 An *algebraic sentence* is usually a statement about numbers and unknown values and is usually written in symbols, e.g. $9 - x = 5$ is an algebraic sentence and is short for 'Nine subtract an unknown value (*x*) is equal to five'.

4 An algebraic sentence may be *true* or *false*: it depends on the value(s) of the unknown(s). For example, $9 - x = 5$ is true if $x = 4$; it is false for any other value of *x*.

PUZZLE CORNER

Add the rows and columns

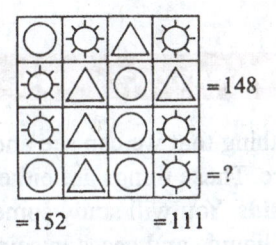

= 148
= ?
= 152   = 111

What should be the total of the bottom row?

PUZZLE CORNER

Funny Fractions

$$\frac{\heartsuit}{\heartsuit} - \frac{\heartsuit}{6} = \frac{\heartsuit}{12}$$

What does the ♥ stand for?

6 Solids 1: Properties

OBJECTIVES

You should be able to:
1. Identify and name common three-dimensional shapes (cuboids, cubes, cylinders, prisms, cones, pyramids, spheres)
2. Identify, count and name the faces, edges and vertices of a solid shape
3. Draw skeleton views of solids
4. Make nets of solids.

Teaching and learning materials
Teacher: Empty containers (matchboxes, chalk boxes, soap packets, tin cans), wooden off-cuts, building blocks, balls; cardboard, wire, drinking straws, glue, sticky tape, scissors or a sharp knife for making models
Students: Empty matchbox (one each) and other packets and solid shapes (as above)

6-1 Three-dimensional shapes

Nearly everything that we can see and touch takes up space. These things are either **gases**, **liquids** or **solids**. You will study some of the properties of liquids and gases in science.

Most solids, or **three-dimensional shapes**, such as stones and trees, have rough and **irregular** shapes. These usually occur in nature. However, some three-dimensional shapes, such as tin cans and houses, have **regular** shapes. These are usually made by people. We often call them **geometrical solids**.

This photograph of a groundnut pyramid (Fig. 6.1) shows how it is made up of two basic shapes.

Exercise 6a
Look at the photographs in Figs 6.1 and 6.2.

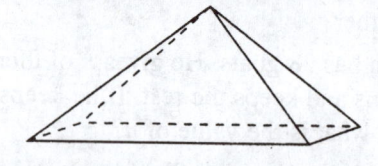

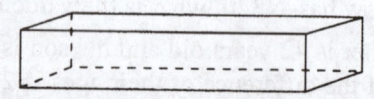

Fig. 6.1 The photograph shows groundnut pyramids. The diagram shows that each pyramid is made up from a square-based pyramid and a cuboid.

a

b

c

d

e

Fig. 6.2 **a** Cuboids   **b** Cubes
       c Cones   **d** Cylinders
       e Spheres

Make a table like the one in Fig. 6.3. Name at least 10 objects you can see in the photographs. Make a freehand sketch of each object and name its basic shape. An example is shown in Fig. 6.3.

No.	Name of object	Freehand drawing	Name of basic shape
1	tin of margarine		cylinder
2			
3			

Fig. 6.3

45

6-2 Cuboids and cubes

Cuboid

Look at a matchbox. The name of its shape is a **cuboid** (Fig. 6.4).

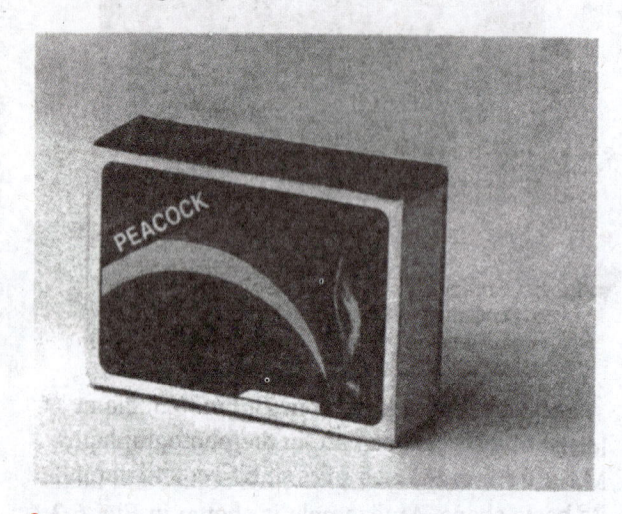

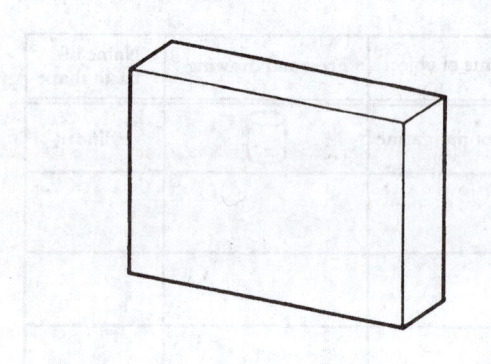

Fig. 6.4 a Matchbox
b Outline of matchbox: a cuboid.

The cuboid is one of the most common manufactured solids (Fig. 6.5). All solids have surfaces, or **faces**. Most solids also have **edges**.

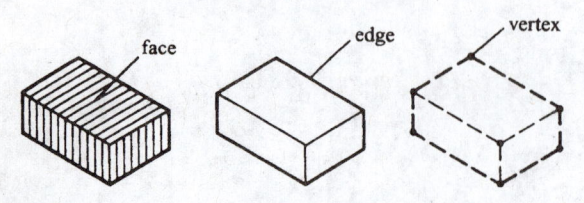

Fig. 6.5

A **face** may be flat (**plane**) or curved. A cuboid has 6 plane faces. Each face is in the shape of a rectangle (Fig. 6.6).

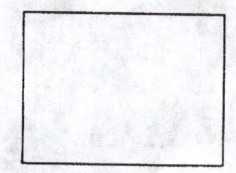

Fig. 6.6 A rectangle

An **edge** is a line where two faces meet. It may be straight or curved. A cuboid has 12 straight edges.

A **vertex** is a point or corner where three or more edges meet. The plural of vertex is **vertices**. A cuboid has 8 vertices.

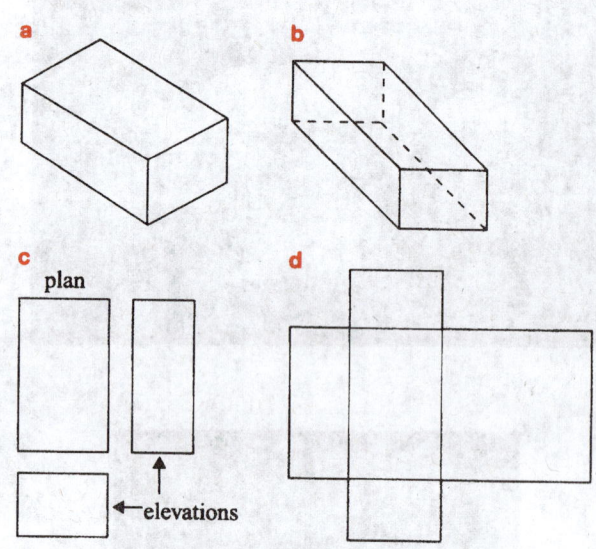

Fig. 6.7 Ways of drawing a cuboid.
a Isometric projection.   **b** Skeleton view.
c Engineer's drawing.   **d** Net.

Drawing cuboids

There are many ways of drawing cuboids (Fig. 6.7). In each case it is impossible to show the solid as it really is. A **skeleton view** is very useful since it shows all the edges. The drawings in Fig. 6.8 show how to draw a skeleton view very quickly. Notice that some edges are hidden from view. We usually show these as broken lines.

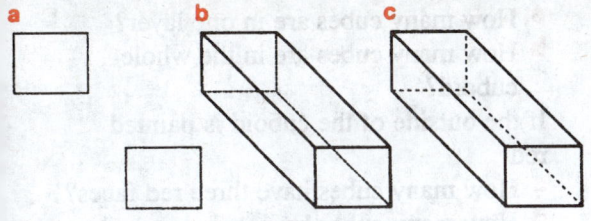

Fig. 6.8 How to draw a skeleton view of a cuboid.
  a Draw two rectangles.
  b Join corner to corner.
  c Go over the drawing. Make the hidden edges broken.

Net of a cuboid

Get a tray from a matchbox. Cut the edges shown in Fig. 6.9. Flatten the shape. The flat shape is called the **net** of the matchbox.

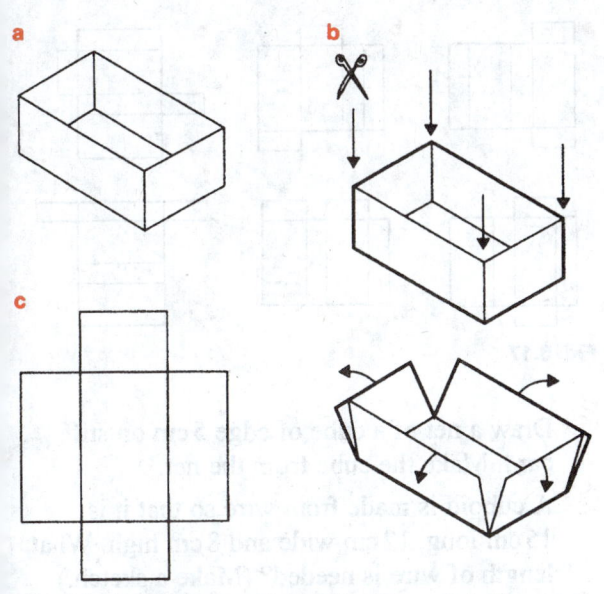

Fig. 6.9 How to use a matchbox to demonstrate the net of a cuboid.
  a This is an open cuboid.
  b Cut along the edges shown.
  c The flat shape is the net of the cuboid.

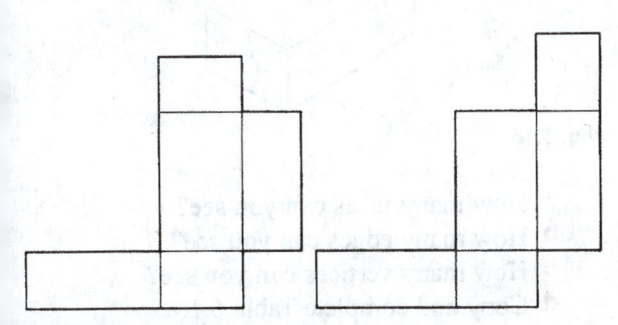

Fig. 6.10

The shape of the net depends on where you make the cuts. You should be able to make the nets shown in Fig. 6.10 from a matchbox tray. Notice that in each case the net is made up of five rectangles.

Normally a cuboid has six rectangular faces and its net contains six rectangles. Fig. 6.11 shows a cuboid and its net.

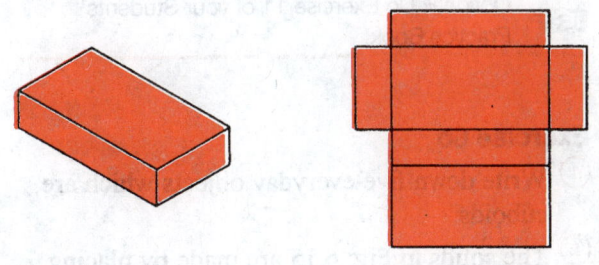

Fig. 6.11

Cubes

A **cube** is a cuboid in which all six faces are squares (Figs 6.12, 6.13, 6.14).

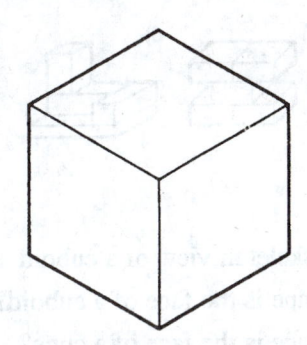

Fig. 6.12

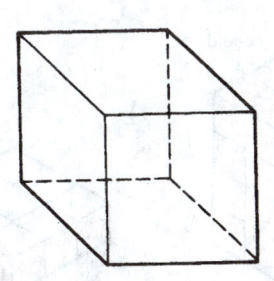

Fig. 6.13 Skeleton view of a cube.

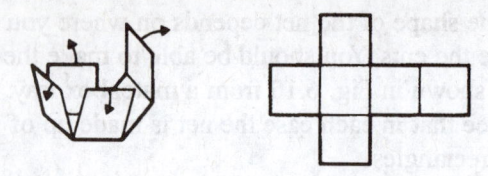

Fig. 6.14 Net of a cube.

☞ *Optional:* Do Exercise 11 of your Students' Practice Book.

Exercise 6b

1. Write down five everyday objects which are cuboids.
2. The solids in Fig. 6.15 are made by placing cuboids together. How many cuboids are in each solid?

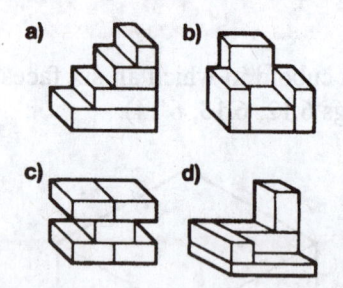

Fig. 6.15

3. Draw a skeleton view of a cuboid and a cube.
4. What shape is the face of a cuboid?
5. What shape is the face of a cube?
6. The cuboid in Fig. 6.16 is made by building up four layers of cubes.

cuboid

one layer

Fig. 6.16

a How many cubes are in one layer?
b How many cubes are in the whole cuboid?

If the outside of the cuboid is painted red:

c How many cubes have three red faces?
d How many cubes have only two red faces?
e How many cubes have only one red face?
f How many cubes have no red faces?

7. Which of the diagrams in Fig. 6.17 can be folded to make a cuboid? (It may help if you copy the shapes onto paper and try to fold them.)

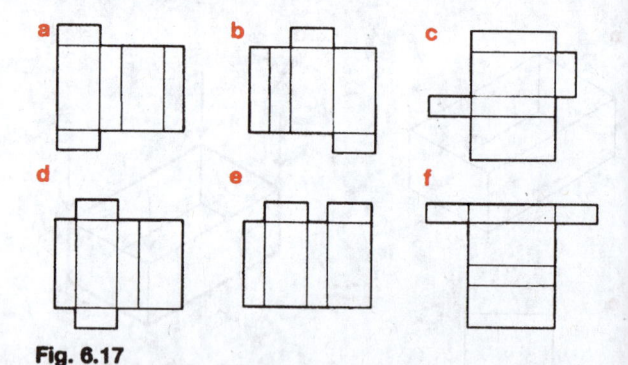

Fig. 6.17

8. Draw a net of a cube of edge 5 cm on stiff card. Make the cube from the net.
9. A cuboid is made from wire so that it is 15 cm long, 12 cm wide and 8 cm high. What length of wire is needed? (Make a sketch.)
10. In Fig. 6.18

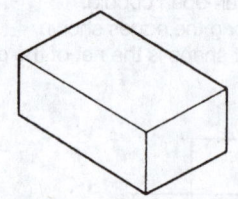

Fig. 6.18

a How many faces can you see?
b How many edges can you see?
c How many vertices can you see?
d Copy and complete Table 6.1.

	total number of vertices	total number of faces	total number of edges
cuboid			
cube			

Table 6.1

☞ *Optional:* Do Exercise 12 of your Students' Practice Book.

6-3 Cylinders and prisms

Cylinder

Look at the tin of coffee (Fig. 6.19). The name of its shape is a **cylinder**.

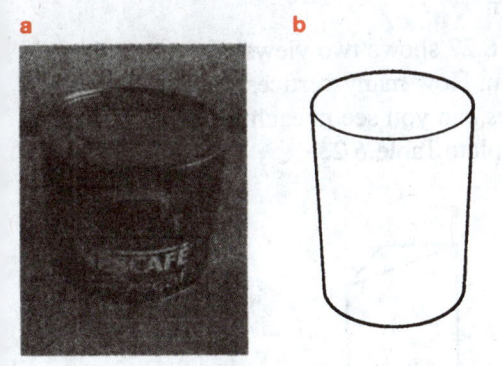

Fig. 6.19 a Tin of coffee **b** Outline of tin: cylinder.

The cylinder has two plane faces and one curved face. It has no vertices and two curved edges. The two plane faces are both circles (Fig. 6.20).

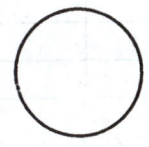

Fig. 6.20 A circle

Drawing cylinders

Some ways of drawing a cylinder are shown in Fig. 6.21.

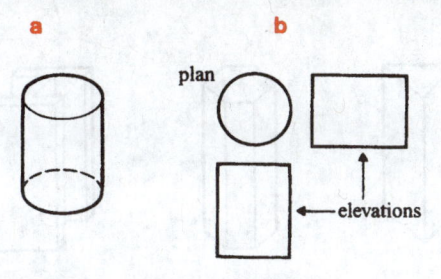

Fig. 6.21 Ways of drawing a cylinder.
 a Skeleton view. **b** Engineer's drawing.

A skeleton view of a cylinder (Fig. 6.22) is drawn in much the same way as that of a cuboid.

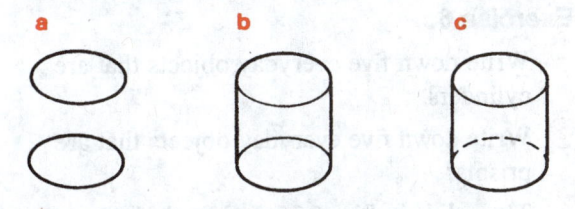

Fig. 6.22 How to draw a skeleton view of a cylinder.
a Draw two flattened circles (ellipses).
b Join the ellipses by two straight lines.
c Make the hidden edge a broken line.

Fig. 6.23 shows how to cut a cylinder to give its net. The net is made up of two circles and one rectangle.

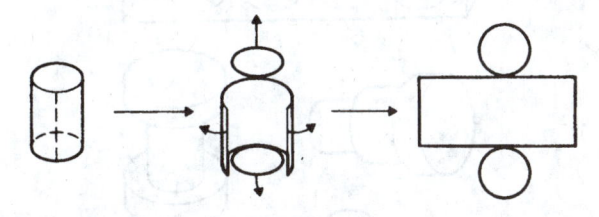

Fig. 6.23 How to cut a cylinder to give its net.

Prism

The base and top faces of a prism are always the same shape. The names of prisms come from the shape of their base and top faces. The side faces of right prisms are always rectangles (Fig. 6.24).

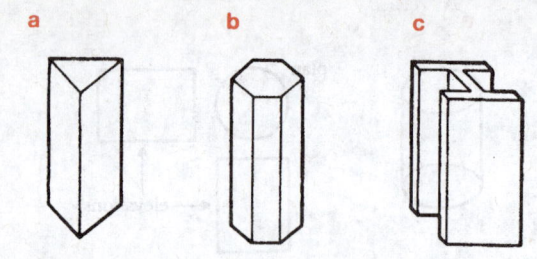

Fig. 6.24 a Triangular prism.
  b Hexagonal prism.
  c I-shaped prism.

The cuboid is a rectangular prism and the cylinder can be thought of as a special prism.

Exercise 6c

1. Write down five everyday objects that are cylinders.
2. Write down five everyday objects that are prisms.
3. The solids in Fig. 6.25 each include cylinders. How many cylinders are in each solid?

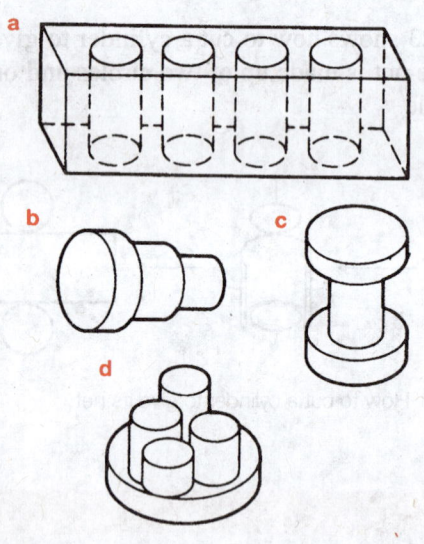

Fig. 6.25

4. Draw a skeleton view of a cylinder and a triangular prism.
5. What is the shape of the plane faces of a cylinder?
6. What is the shape of the end faces of a triangular prism? What is the shape of the other faces of a triangular prism?
7. Name the solids which have the nets shown in Fig. 6.26.

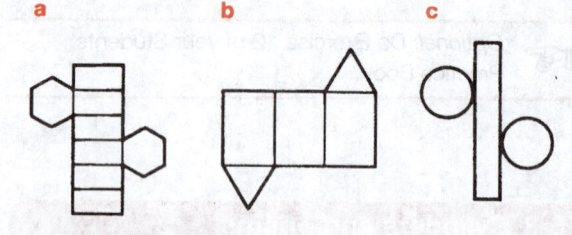

Fig. 6.26

8. How many faces, edges and vertices does a triangular prism have?
9. Sketch three different nets of a triangular prism.
10. Fig. 6.27 shows two views of a triangular prism. How many vertices, faces and edges can you see in each view? Copy and complete Table 6.2.

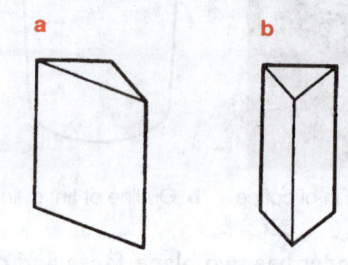

Fig. 6.27

view	number of vertices seen	number of faces seen	number of edges seen
a			
b			

Table 6.2

50

6-4 Cones and pyramids

Cones

a **b**

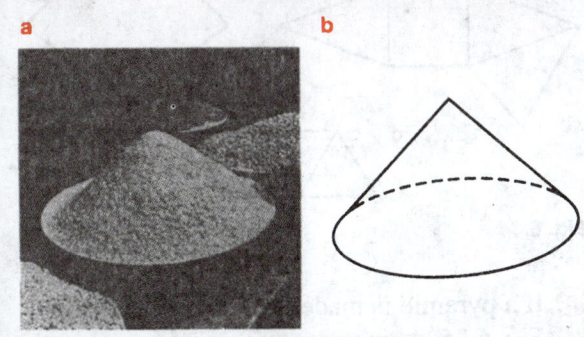

Fig. 6.28 a A cone-shaped mound of rice.
b Outline of mound: cone.

A mound of rice is often cone-shaped (Fig. 6.28). The base of a cone is a plane circle. The cone is quite a common shape but it is usually part of a bigger object (Fig. 6.29).

a **b**

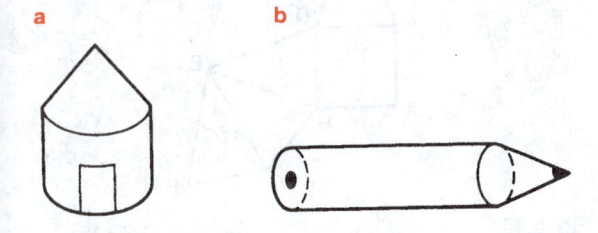

Fig. 6.29 a The roof of the house.
b The sharp end of the pencil.

Fig. 6.30 shows how to cut a cone to give its net.

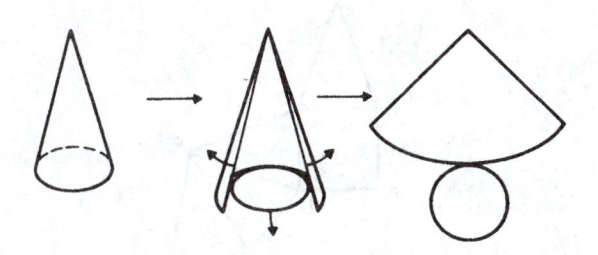

Fig. 6.30

Optional: Do Exercise 48 of your Students' Practice Book.

Pyramids

The names of pyramids come from the shape of their base faces (Fig. 6.31).

a **b** **c**

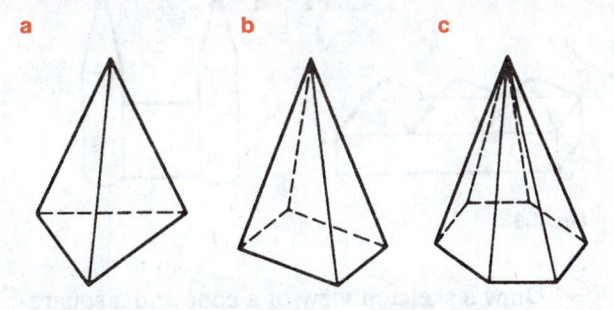

Fig. 6.31 a Triangular-based pyramid (tetrahedron).
b Square-based pyramid.
c Hexagonal-based pyramid.

Note: *Tetrahedron* means *four faces*.

The nets of a square-based pyramid (Fig. 6.32) show that, apart from its base, all its faces are triangular in shape.

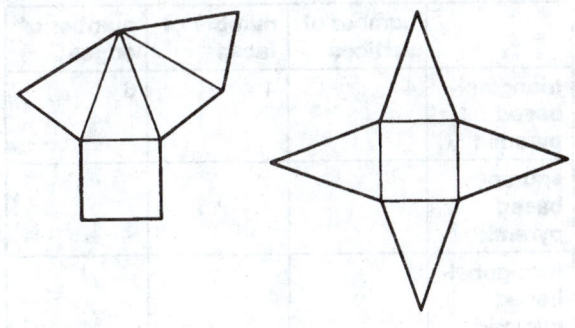

Fig. 6.32

Exercise 6d

1. Write down five everyday objects which are wholly or partly cone-shaped.
2. Write down five everyday objects which are wholly or partly pyramid-shaped.
3. The solids in Fig. 6.33 include either cones or pyramids. How many cones or pyramids can you see in each solid?

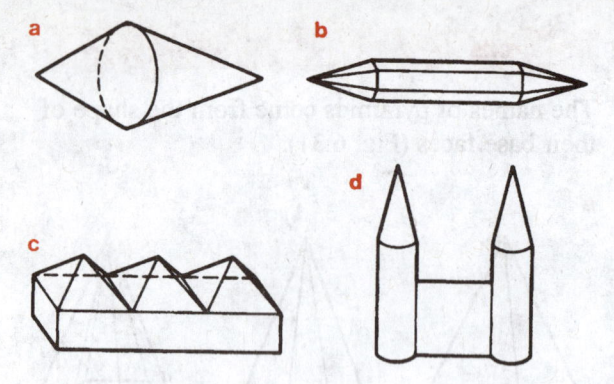

Fig. 6.33

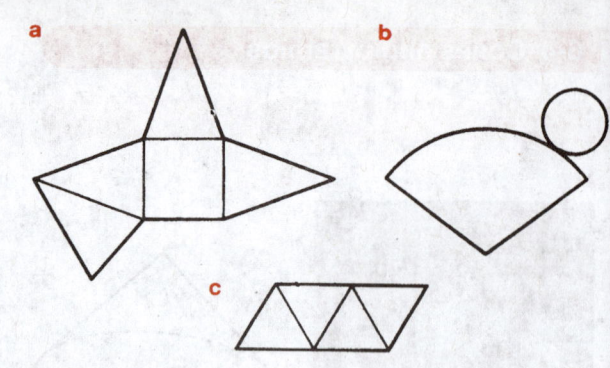

Fig. 6.34

④ Draw a skeleton view of a cone and a square-based pyramid.

⑤ The faces of a pyramid are all triangular. What kind of pyramid is it?

⑥ A pyramid has a total of six triangular faces. How many faces does it have altogether? What is the shape of its other face(s)?

⑦ Copy and complete Table 6.3.

	number of vertices	number of faces	number of edges
triangular-based pyramid	4	4	6
square-based pyramid			
hexagonal-based pyramid			
triangular prism			
cube			
cuboid			

Table 6.3

⑧ Name the solids which have the nets shown in Fig. 6.34.

⑨ If a pyramid is made from the net shown in Fig. 6.35, which edge will join to
   a DE   b EF   c AB   d HG?
   e Which letters will be at the vertex of the pyramid?

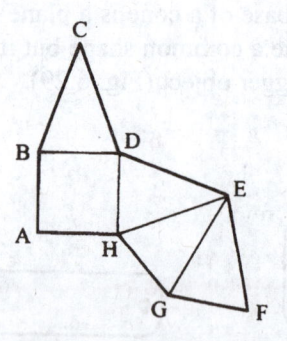

Fig. 6.35

⑩ Fig. 6.36 shows a view of a square-based pyramid. How many vertices, faces and edges can you see in this view of the pyramid?

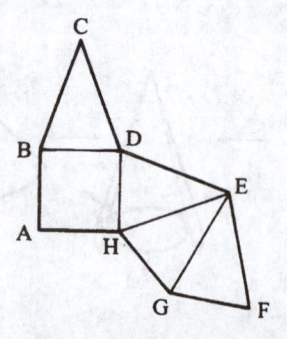

Fig. 6.36

☞ *Optional:* Do Exercise 13 of your Students' Practice Book.

6-5 Spheres

Nearly every ball is sphere-shaped (Fig. 6.37).

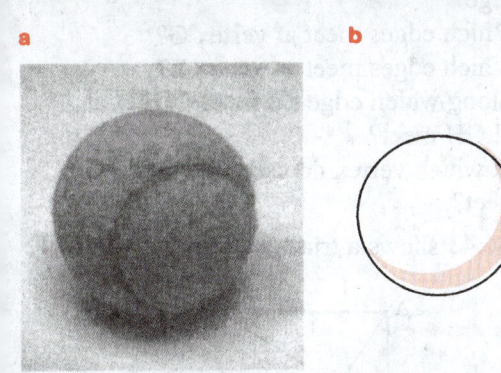

Fig. 6.37 **a** A tennis ball. **b** Outline of ball: sphere.

Half a sphere is called a **hemisphere** (Fig. 6.38).

Fig. 6.38 Hemisphere.

Optional: Do Exercise 14 of your Students' Practice Book.

Exercise 6e

1. Write down five everyday objects each of which is either sphere-shaped or contains part of a sphere in its shape.

2. State which shapes make up the solids in Fig. 6.39.

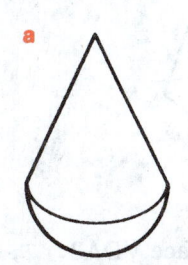

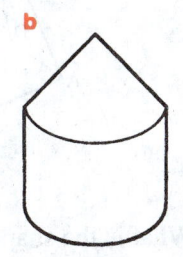

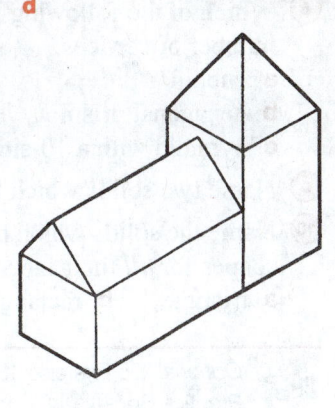

Fig. 6.39

3. Which of the following solids will roll smoothly:
   a cube   **b** cone
   c sphere   **d** square-based pyramid
   e tetrahedron **f** cylinder
   g cuboid?

4. A skeleton square-based pyramid is made from wire. All its edges are the same length. If 40 cm of wire is used, find the length of each edge of the pyramid. (Make a sketch.)

5. Name two solids which have five faces.

6. Sketch four different nets of a square-based pyramid.

7. If the net shown in Fig. 6.40 is folded to make a cuboid, which edge will join to
   a AB   **b** CD   **c** FG   **d** KL?

   Which points will join to
   e point A   **f** point D?

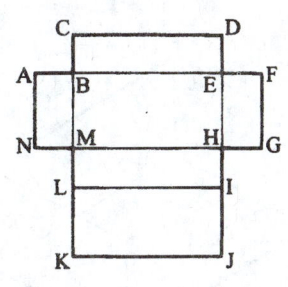

Fig. 6.40

8 Which of the following has the greatest number of vertices:
  a cuboid
  b hexagonal prism
  c pyramid with a 10-sided base?

9 Name two solids which have no vertices.

10 Name the solids which have the following shapes for *all* their faces.
  a triangle   **b** rectangle   **c** square.

Optional: Do Exercise 15 of your Students' Practice Book.

6-6 Naming vertices, edges, faces

We use capital letters of the alphabet to name the vertices of a solid. The left-hand edge in Fig. 6.41 is edge AD. The top face is face ABFE.

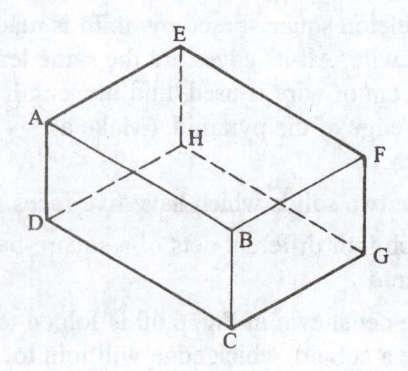

Fig. 6.41

Exercise 6f

1 Fig. 6.42 shows the cuboid ABCDEFGH.

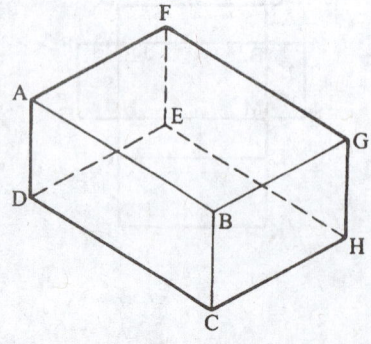

Fig. 6.42

a Faces ABCD and ABGF meet along which edge?
b Faces BCHG and ABGF meet along which edge?
c Which edges meet at vertex G?
d Which edges meet at vertex E?
e Along which edge do faces CDEH and EFGH meet?
f At which vertex do edges AF and FG meet?

2 Fig. 6.43 shows a triangular prism ABCDEF.

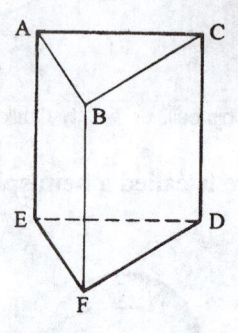

Fig. 6.43

Name the vertices or edges where the following intersect.
a edge AE and edge EF
b edge CD, edge DE and edge DF
c edge BF and face ABC
d face ACDE and edge DF
e face ACDE and face ABC
f face BCDF and face ABFE

3 The skeleton view of square-based pyramid VABCD is shown in Fig. 6.44.

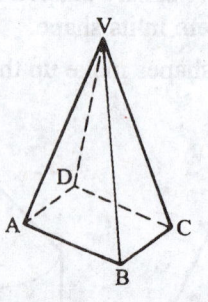

Fig. 6.44

a What is the shape of face VDA?
b What is the true shape of face ABCD?
c How many edges meet at the vertex V?

Name the vertices or edges where the following meet.

d edge AB and edge VB
e edge VB and face AVD
f face AVB and face DVC
g face ABCD and face DVC

SUMMARY

1 *Cuboids, cubes, cones, pyramids, cylinders and spheres* are special *three-dimensional shapes* called *geometrical solids*. See the photographs on pages 44 and 45.
2 All geometrical solids have one or more *faces*. The faces may be plane (flat) or curved.
3 Many geometrical solids also have *edges* and *vertices* (singular: *vertex*). The edges may be straight or curved. See Fig. 6.5.
4 A *skeleton view* of a solid shows its faces, edges and vertices. See Fig. 6.8.
5 The *net* of solid is the flat shape that can be folded to make the solid. See Fig. 6.9.

PUZZLE CORNER

Complete the square

Use the numbers 1, 2, 3, 4, 5 so that no row, column or diagonal line of any length contains the same number more than once.

				4
	5			?
2				5
	4			

What number replaces the ?

PUZZLE CORNER

Look before you leap!

See how long it takes you to work out the following:

(1 × 2) × (3 × 4) × (5 × 6) × (7 × 8) × (9 × 0)

7 Algebraic simplification 1: Grouping

OBJECTIVES

You should be able to:
1. State the coefficient of an algebraic term
2. Group positive and negative terms to simplify an algebraic expression
3. Group like and unlike terms to simplify an algebraic expression
4. Solve work problems by forming and simplifying algebraic expressions.

7-1 Coefficients

In arithmetic 3×4 is a short way of writing $4 + 4 + 4$. Similarly, in algebra, $3 \times a$ is short for $a + a + a$. $3 \times a$ is usually shortened to $3a$. Say this as 'three a'.

$$3a = 3 \times a = a + a + a$$

Notice the difference between 34 in arithmetic and $3a$ in algebra. 34 means 3 tens and 4 or $30 + 4$. 34 does *not* mean 3×4. In algebra, $3a$ always means $3 \times a$.

Exercise 7a
Write the following in the shortest possible way.
1. $a + a + a$
2. $x + x + x$
3. $p + p$
4. $r + r + r + r + r$
5. $t + t + t + t + t + t + t + t$
6. $m + m + m + m$
7. $z + z + z + z + z + z + z + z + z$
8. $y + y$
9. $c + c + c + c + c + c$
10. $k + k + k + k + k$

Exercise 7b (Oral)
1. What do the following mean in arithmetic?
   a 3×4 b 34 c 3×6 d 36
   e 2×9 f 29 g 5×1 h 51
   i 77 j 98
2. What do the following mean in algebra?
   a $3a$ b $5x$ c $2y$ d $4n$
   e $3m$ f $6d$ g $2f$ h $10e$
   i $7r$ j $5s$

$3a$, $x + 1$, $7 - r$, $7y$ are all examples of **algebraic expressions**. In the expression $3a$, the 3 is called the **coefficient** of a. The 3 shows that three a's have been added together. For example,
a in $7y$, 7 is the coefficient of y; seven y's have been added together;
b in x, there is only *one* x; x is the same as $1x$; the coefficient of x is 1.
Note: It is usual to write x, not $1x$.

Coefficients are not always whole numbers. Coefficients can also be fractions. In arithmetic $\frac{1}{3} \times 12$ or $\frac{12}{3}$ are short ways of writing $\frac{1}{3}$ of 12 or $12 \div 3$. In algebra $\frac{1}{3}a$ or $\frac{a}{3}$ are short ways of writing $\frac{1}{3}$ of a or $a \div 3$.
In the expression $\frac{1}{3}a$, the coefficient of a is $\frac{1}{3}$.
$\frac{1}{3}a = \frac{a}{3}$, so the coefficient of a in $\frac{a}{3}$ is also $\frac{1}{3}$.

For example,
c in $\frac{3}{4}x$, $\frac{3}{4}$ is the coefficient of x;
d in $\frac{2a}{3}$, $\frac{2}{3}$ is the coefficient of a (since $\frac{2a}{3} = \frac{2}{3}a$)
e in $\frac{z}{5}$, $\frac{1}{5}$ is the coefficient of z.

Exercise 7c (Oral)
What is the coefficient of x in each of the following?
1. $3x$
2. $7x$
3. $4x$
4. $8x$
5. $15x$
6. $9x$
7. $18x$
8. $2x$
9. x
10. $10x$
11. $\frac{1}{3}x$
12. $\frac{1}{2}x$

⑬ $\frac{1}{4}x$ ⑭ $\frac{2}{3}x$ ⑮ $\frac{3}{4}x$ ⑯ $\frac{x}{5}$
⑰ $\frac{x}{10}$ ⑱ $\frac{2x}{3}$ ⑲ $\frac{3x}{4}$ ⑳ $\frac{3x}{5}$

7-2 Grouping positive and negative terms

Expressions such as $3x$, x, $8x$, $12x$, $\frac{1}{2}x$ are called **terms in x**. We can add terms in x together.
  $3x + 2x$ means 3 x's add 2 x's.
This gives 5 x's altogether. Thus
  $3x + 2x = 5x$
$5x$ uses less space, or is simpler, than
  $3x + 2x$.
Thus two terms in x have been **simplified** to one term in x.
  We can also subtract terms.
  $7y - 4y$ means 7 y's take away 4 y's.
This leaves 3 y's. Thus
  $7y - 4y = 3y$
Again, two terms have been simplified to one term.

Exercise 7d (Oral)
Simplify the following.

① $2a + 3a$ ② $5x - 3x$ ③ $4b + 4b$
④ $6y - 2y$ ⑤ $4c + c$ ⑥ $7z - z$
⑦ $p + 2p$ ⑧ $8k - 7k$ ⑨ $4q + 6q$
⑩ $5m - 2m$ ⑪ $r + r$ ⑫ $3n - 3n$
⑬ $5d - 4d$ ⑭ $x + 9x$ ⑮ $20x - 2x$

We can simplify expressions which contain many terms. For example, the expression
  $3a - 8a + 5a + 9a - 2a$
means: add $3a$, $5a$ and $9a$ together, take away $8a$ and $2a$. This gives $17a$ take away $10a$. The result is $7a$. We can write this as follows.

$3a - 8a + 5a + 9a - 2a$
$= 3a + 5a + 9a - 8a - 2a$
$= 17a - 10a$
$= 7a$

The first line in this example is important. We have grouped all the terms with a + sign before them together, and all the terms with a − sign before them together. This method is called **grouping positive and negative terms**. It is usually the best way of simplifying big expressions.

Example 1
Simplify $3m - 8m - 2m + 16m - 4m$.

  $3m - 8m - 2m + 16m - 4m$
  $= 3m + 16m - 8m - 2m - 4m$
  $= 19m - 14m$
  $= 5m$

Exercise 7e

① Simplify the following.

a $4a + 3a$ b $5b - 2b$
c $9c + c$ d $12d - 7d$
e $11e + 8e$ f $20f - 16f$
g $5g + 9g$ h $13h - h$
i $18j + 7j$ j $21k - 20k$
k $6m + 17m$ l $22n - 8n$
m $p + 5p$ n $7q - 7q$
o $2r - r$ p $12s - 2s$
q $22t + 8t$ r $21u - 12u$
s $3v + 4v + 5v$ t $w + 4w + 4w$
u $8x + x + 3x$ v $5y + 13y + 2y$
w $z + 9z + z$ x $4a + 5a + a$

② Simplify the following. Set out your work as in Example 1 above.

a $10b + b - 3b$ b $3c + 5c - 8c$
c $7d + 4d - 8d$ d $16e + 12e - 13e$
e $6f - 2f + 3f$ f $4g - 7g + 10g$
g $20h - 15h + 6h$ h $2j - 9j + 9j$
i $11k - 16k + 9k$ j $8m - 3m - 2m$
k $9n - 5n - 3n$
l $17p - 8p - 2p$
m $13q - 4q - 4q$
n $22r - 14r - 8r$
o $5s + s + 2s + 4s$
p $3t + 6t + t + t$
q $4u + u + 6u - 5u$
r $9v + 2v + 3v - 8v$
s $6w + 4w - 3w - 2w$
t $12x + 3x - 5x - 2x$
u $3y - 5y + 10y - 4y$

57

v $7z - 2z + 7z - 2z$
w $11a + 5a - 2a + a$
x $4b + 2b - 9b + 8b$
y $20c - 9c - c + 2c$
z $12d - 5d - 3d + 4d$

3 Simplify the following. Set out your work as in Example 1 above.
a $22e - 5e - 8e - 4e$
b $12f - 5f - 3f - 4f$
c $6g + 5g - 2g - 4g - 2g$
d $7h + h + 3h - 2h - 4h$
e $8j - 10j + 6j - 7j + 4j$
f $13k - 5k - 9k + 6k - k$
g $4m - 22m + 13m + 10m - 3m$
h $14n + 2n - 6n - 12n + 7n$
i $p - 15p - 5p - 2p + 25p$
j $2q - 20q + 11q + 8q + 5q$

7-3 Grouping like and unlike terms

What is the sum of 5 plantains and 8 plantains? 13 plantains. Similarly, in algebra,
   $5p + 8p = 13p$
What is the sum of 3 plantains and 7 torches? All that can be said is that there is a mixture of plantains and torches. Similarly, in algebra, it is impossible to simplify
   $3p + 7t$
$5p$ and $8p$ are **like terms**. Their sum is $13p$.
$3p$ and $7t$ are **unlike terms**. Their sum is $3p + 7t$.
   Notice that:

3 plantains + 8 torches + 6 plantains + 5 torches
   = 9 plantains + 13 torches

In real life, the same things can be grouped together. Similarly in algebra, like terms can be grouped:

$3p + 8t + 6p + 5t = 3p + 6p + 8t + 5t$
$= 9p + 13t$

Example 2
Simplify $7h - 4 - 3h + 11$.

Notice that terms in h and number terms are unlike.

$7h - 4 - 3h + 11 = 7h - 3h + 11 - 4$
$= 4h + 7$

Example 3
Simplify $8x - 6y - 9y - 2x$.

$8x - 6y - 9y - 2x = 8x - 2x - 6y - 9y$
$= 6x - 15y$

Example 4
Simplify $10r - 3r - 8 - 4r$.

Notice that there are three terms in r.

$10r - 3r - 8 - 4r = 10r - 3r - 4r - 8$
$= 10r - 7r - 8$
$= 3r - 8$

Exercise 7f
Simplify the following. Set your work out as in the examples above.

1. $2x + 3x + 7$
2. $6x - 3x + 2$
3. $5x + 6x + 8y$
4. $10x - 4x + 1$
5. $4x + x - 2$
6. $7x - 2x - 2y$
7. $5y + 7x + 2x$
8. $3y + 9x - 4x$
9. $9y + 4x + 8x$
10. $15 - 2x + 10x$
11. $1 + x + x$
12. $4y - 8x + 12x$
13. $3x + 8y + 3x$
14. $10x + 5 - 4x$
15. $10x - 5 + 4x$
16. $2x + 11y - 2x$
17. $x + 2 + 9x$
18. $5x - 8 - 4x$
19. $6y + 7y + 12x$
20. $8y - 7y - x$
21. $14x + 14 + 3$
22. $3x + 11 - 2$
23. $7y - 3x + 4y$
24. $14y - 9x - 6y$
25. $6a + 2a + 3 + 10$
26. $8a - 5a + 14 - 6$
27. $3x + 8x + 9y - 4y$
28. $11x - 2x + 3y + 5y$
29. $4a - a + 5b - 4b$

58

30. $7m + 3 + 2m + 1$
31. $19n + 19 + n - 10$
32. $12p + 3 - 2p - 2$
33. $2p + 7t + 5p + 3t$
34. $18a - 3b - 6a + 10b$
35. $2x - 8 - 3 + 5x$
36. $20x - 4y - y - 3x$
37. $20 + 2x + x + 3x$
38. $12n - 3p - 3p - 5p$
39. $6c - 10c + 13c - 7$
40. $4y - 2x + 5x - 3y$

Exercise 7g (Further practice)
Simplify the following *where possible*.

1. $2x + 7x$
2. $6d + d$
3. $a + 8a$
4. $9b + 3b$
5. $3m + 5n$
6. $3y + 2y + 5y$
7. $4h + 9h + 12h$
8. $2x + 6y$
9. $8n - 5n$
10. $14k - 6k$
11. $8e + 5e - 7e$
12. $4g - g + 3g$
13. $15a - 2$
14. $19b - 12b$
15. $5x - 14x + 9x$
16. $17d - 8d - 3d$
17. $6m - 9m + 4m$
18. $8a + 14a - 21a$
19. $35b - 27b$
20. $31p - 9q$
21. $28f - 11$
22. $4c - 9c + 15c - 7c$
23. $7d + 15d - 9d - 11d$
24. $8m - 9m - 5m + 10m$
25. $11n - 3n - 6n + 9n - 5n$
26. $4x + 9x - 7x - 6x + 8x - 3x$
27. $3m + 5n + 4m + 6n$
28. $9a + 10b - 5a - 4b$
29. $8h - 3 - 5h + 9$
30. $7x + 5y - 4$
31. $11x + 9y - 7x$
32. $13a + -b - 9a + 7b$
33. $5f - 3g - 7f + 9g + 3f - 4g$
34. $7m - 2n + 6 - 5m + 7n + 3$
35. $3x + 2 - 7x - 4 + 5x + 6$
36. $a - 7b + 3c + 8b + 2a$
37. $5h + 8k + 2 - 3k - 2h$
38. $6m + 3n - 1 - 6m + 4$
39. $a - 2b - 4a + 3c + 4a + 5b$
40. $6p - 2q + 4r - 2p + 3s + 5q$

Exercise 7h

1. A carpenter has two planks of wood. One plank is x cm long, the other plank is $3x$ cm long. What is the total length of the two planks?

2. A shop sells x books at ₦500 each, y books at ₦600 each, and z books at ₦900 each. How many books are sold? How much money is paid for the books?

3. 180 people attend a meeting. There are n men and n women and the rest are children. How many children are at the meeting?

4. A salesperson earns ₦19 000 per month. Each month she spends ₦$3x$ on food and ₦$2x$ on rent. How much money does she have left each month?

5. A man weighs k kg. He goes on a diet and loses one-tenth of his weight. What is his weight after going on the diet?

6. A villager has $6x$ sheep and $5y$ goats. She sells $3x$ sheep and $2y$ goats. How many animals is she left with?

7. A man has x matches in a matchbox. On Monday he uses one-quarter of them. On Tuesday he uses five more. How many matches has he used? How many has he left?

8. A girl gets n naira pocket money each week. She saves her money for five weeks and buys a present for her mother which costs ₦1 200. How much money does she have left?

9. A woman has x eggs in a basket. She sells one-third of them to another woman. Two of the eggs get broken. How many eggs are left in the basket?

10. Table 7.1 shows the number of goals for and against a team during four weeks of a month.

	goals for	goals against
week 1	x	2y
week 2	2x	y
week 3	3y	y
week 4	y	x

Table 7.1

a How many 'goals for' in the month?
b How many 'goals against' in the month?

SUMMARY

1. Expressions such as $3x$, $12x$, ... are called *terms in x*. In the term $12x$, 12 is called the *coefficient of x*.
2. *Like terms* are terms which have the same letter. $3x$ and $8x$ are like terms. $4a$ and $11b$ are *unlike terms*. y and 2 are also unlike terms.
3. An *algebraic expression* is a collection of algebraic terms.
4. To *simplify* an expression means to reduce it to its lowest or neatest form.
5. To simplify an expression:
   a group like terms together;
   b within like terms, group positive terms and negative terms together;
   c add or subtract in the usual way.

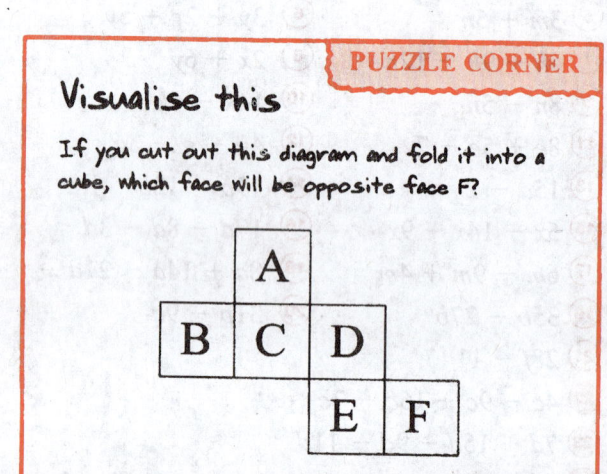

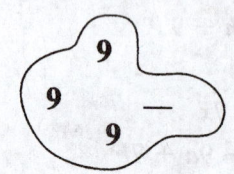

PUZZLE CORNER

Visualise this

If you cut out this diagram and fold it into a cube, which face will be opposite face F?

```
    A
B C D
    E F
```

PUZZLE CORNER

Three 9's and a Minus

9
9   —
  9

Use three 9's and a minus sign, to represent the number 1.

8 Angles 1: Measurement

OBJECTIVES

You should be able to:
1 Identify angles between two lines
2 Interpret angle as a measure of rotation and its measurement in terms of revolution (or parts of a revolution)
3 Name angles using capital letters
4 Measure a given angle to the nearest degree using a protractor
5 Construct a given angle using a protractor.

Teaching and learning materials
Teacher: Chalk board instruments (ruler and protractor); cardboard, paper, scissors
Students: Mathematical set: protractor and ruler are essential for this topic

8-1 Angle as rotation

We use the word **angle** for amount of turn. For example, Fig. 8.1 shows how the hands of a clock move between 9 o'clock and 10 o'clock.

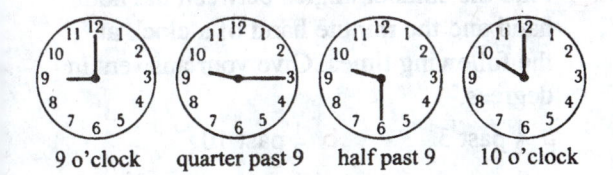

9 o'clock   quarter past 9   half past 9   10 o'clock

Fig. 8.1

Both hands turn. In one hour the amount that each hand turns is different.

The minute hand makes one complete **turn**, or one **revolution** (Fig. 8.2).
The angle turned = 1 revolution.

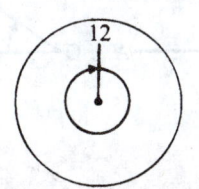

Fig. 8.2

The hour hand turns through $\frac{1}{12}$ of a revolution (Fig. 8.3).
The angle turned = $\frac{1}{12}$ revolution.

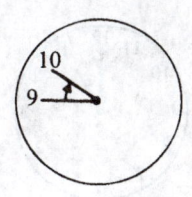

Fig. 8.3

This shows that just as we can measure length, so we can measure angle. To avoid fractions, one revolution is divided into 360 equal parts. Each part is called a **degree**. We use the symbol ° for degree.

1 revolution = 360 degrees or 360°
1° = $\frac{1}{360}$ revolution

☞ *Optional:* Do Exercise 16 of your Students' Practice Book.

8-2 Angles between lines

Fig. 8.4 shows two lines OA and OB. The lines meet at the point O.

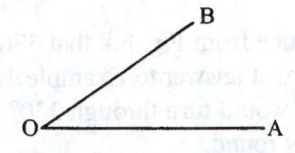

Fig. 8.4

61

The angle between the two lines is the amount that one line must turn so that it points the same way as the other line (Fig. 8.5).

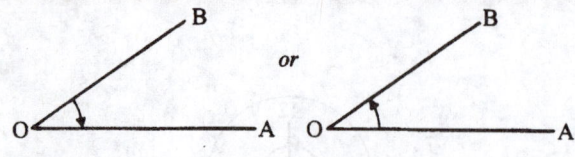

Fig. 8.5

Fig. 8.8

Example 1

What is the angle between the hour hand and the minute hand of a clock at 1 o'clock?

The angle between the hands is the amount that one hand must turn to reach the position of the other (Fig. 8.6). That is $\frac{1}{12}$ of a revolution.

Fig. 8.6

angle between hands = $\frac{1}{12}$ of a revolution
= $\frac{1}{12}$ of 360° = 30°

Notice, in the above example, that the size of the angle does not depend on the size of the hands. At 1 o'clock the angle between the hour hand and the minute hand is 30° whether on a watch or on a clock (Fig. 8.7).

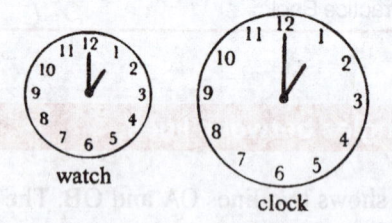

watch   clock

Fig. 8.7

Again, notice from Fig. 8.8 that 330° would also be a correct answer to Example 1. The minute hand would turn through 330° if it went the other way round.
330° + 30° = 360°

Exercise 8a

1. Copy and complete Table 8.1.

revs	degrees
1	360°
2	
3	1 080°
10	
$\frac{1}{12}$	180°

revs	degrees
$\frac{1}{3}$	
	90°
$\frac{1}{10}$	
$\frac{1}{8}$	
$1\frac{1}{2}$	

Table 8.1

2. Find the smaller angles between the hour hand and the minute hand of a clock at the following times. Give your answers both in revolutions and in degrees.
   a 2 o'clock b 3 o'clock c 4 o'clock
   d 5 o'clock e 6 o'clock f 7 o'clock
   g 9 o'clock h 10 o'clock i 11 o'clock

3. a Where does the hour hand of a clock point at $\frac{1}{2}$ past 2?
   b What is $\frac{1}{2}$ of 30°?
   c What is the smaller angle between the hour hand and the minute hand of a clock at $\frac{1}{2}$ past 2?

4. Find the smaller angles between the hour hand and the minute hand of a clock at the following times. Give your answers in degrees.
   a $\frac{1}{2}$ past 3 b $\frac{1}{2}$ past 10
   c $\frac{1}{2}$ past 8 d $\frac{1}{2}$ past 12
   e $\frac{1}{2}$ past 5 f $\frac{1}{2}$ past 6

5. a Where does the hour hand of a clock point at $\frac{1}{4}$ past 2?
   b What is $\frac{1}{4}$ of 30°?
   c What is $\frac{3}{4}$ of 30°?

d What is the angle between the hour hand and the minute hand of a clock at $\frac{1}{4}$ past 2?

6 Find the smaller angles between the hour hand and the minute hand of a clock at the following times. Give your answers in degrees.

a $\frac{1}{4}$ past 11   b $\frac{1}{4}$ past 9
c $\frac{1}{4}$ to 9   d $\frac{1}{4}$ past 12
e $\frac{1}{4}$ to 5   f $\frac{1}{4}$ past 3

Naming angles

When lines OA and OB meet at the point O (Fig. 8.9), we say that angle AOB or angle BOA is the angle between them. AÔB is short for angle AOB. Notice that O, the middle letter, is the vertex of the angle. The lines OA and OB are the arms of the angle.

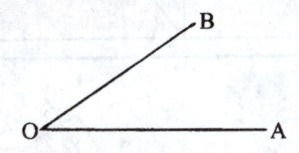

Fig. 8.9

If OA is fixed and OB can turn, we get angles of different sizes. Some of these have special names.

In Fig. 8.10, AÔB is less than 90°; AÔB is an **acute angle**.

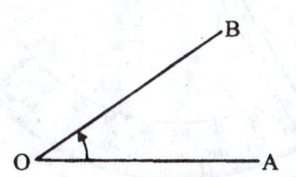

Fig. 8.10

In Fig. 8.11, AÔB = 90°; AÔB is a **right angle** or **quarter turn**.

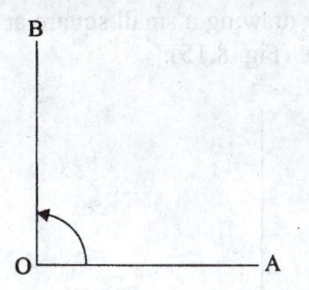

Fig. 8.11

In Fig. 8.12, AÔB is greater than 90° but less than 180°; AÔB is an **obtuse angle**.

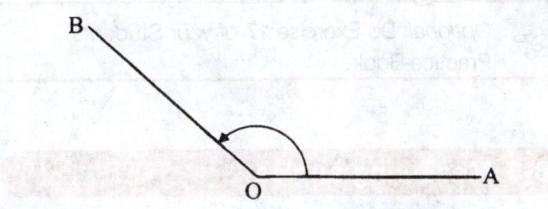

Fig. 8.12

In Fig. 8.13, AÔB = 180° = 2 right angles; AÔB is a **straight angle** or **half turn**.

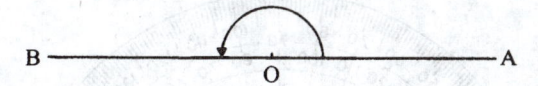

Fig. 8.13

In both diagrams in Fig. 8.14, AÔB is less than 360° but greater than 180°; AÔB is a **reflex angle**.

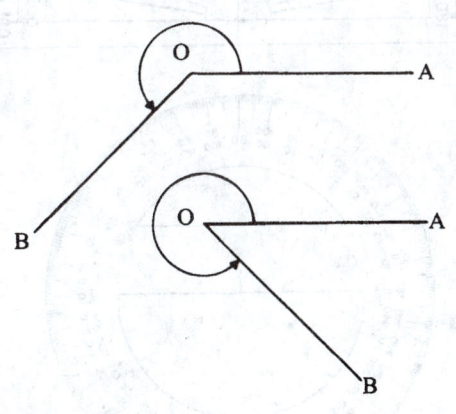

Fig. 8.14

The right angle is especially important. There are many examples where lines meet at right angles. A right angle is often shown on a

63

diagram by drawing a small square at the vertex of the angle (Fig. 8.15).

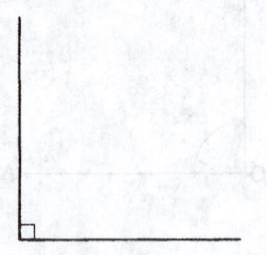

Fig. 8.15

☞ *Optional:* Do Exercise 17 of your Students' Practice Book.

8-3 Measuring angles

We use a **protractor** to measure the number of degrees in an angle. There are many kinds of protractor; two are shown in Fig. 8.16.

a

b

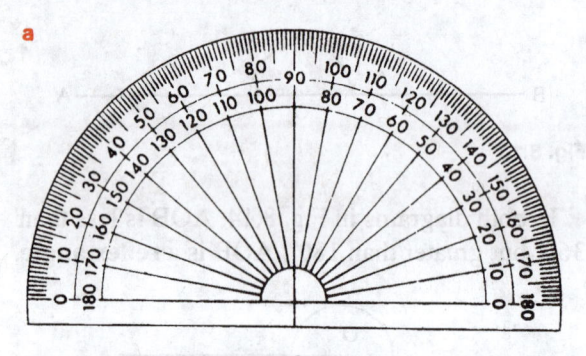

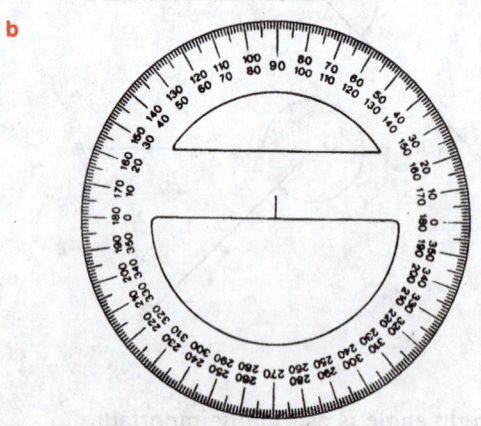

Fig. 8.16 a Semi-circular protractor.
  b Circular protractor.

To measure an angle:
a Place the protractor over the angle so that its centre, O, is exactly over the vertex of the angle and the base line is exactly along one arm of the angle.
b Count the degrees *from* the base line *to* the other arm of the angle. Most protractors have two rows of numbers. This is because you can measure the angle either **anticlockwise** (as in ig. 8.17(a)) or **clockwise** (as in Fig. 8.17(b)). This can be confusing because the reading seems to be either 52° or 128°. However, since the angle is acute, it must be 52°.

a

b

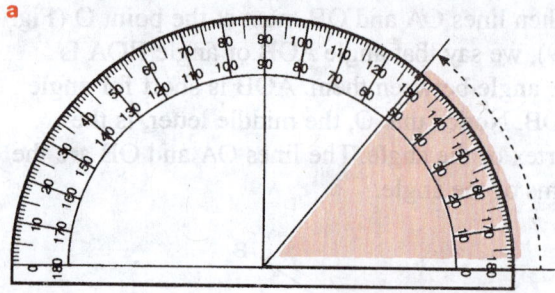

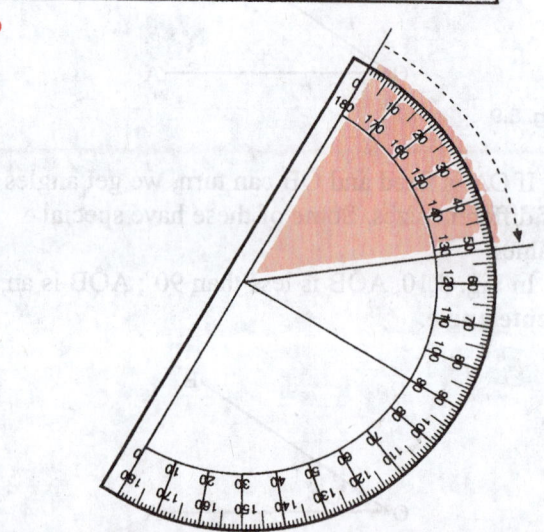

Fig. 8.17

Example 2

Measure the size of the obtuse angle PÔQ *in Fig. 8.18.*
Calculate the size of reflex angle PÔQ.

Place the protractor on the angle with its centre on O and its base line on OP or OQ as shown in Fig. 8.19.

64

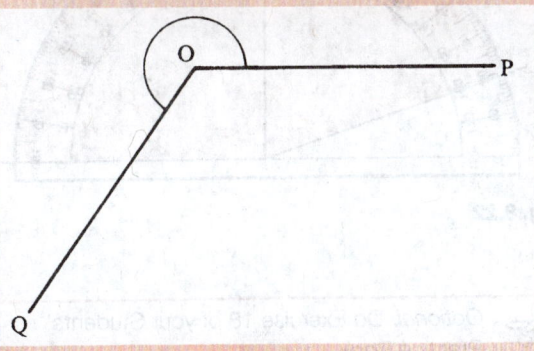

obtuse PÔQ = 125° (by measurement)
reflex PÔQ = 360° − 125° = 235°

Fig. 8.18

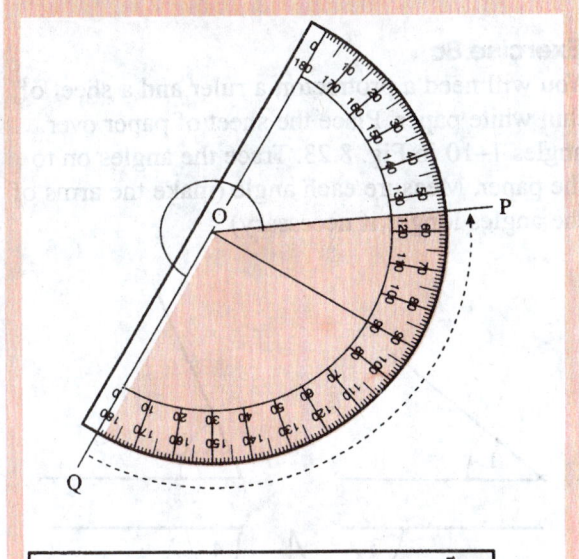

Fig. 8.19

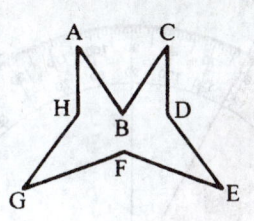

Fig. 8.20

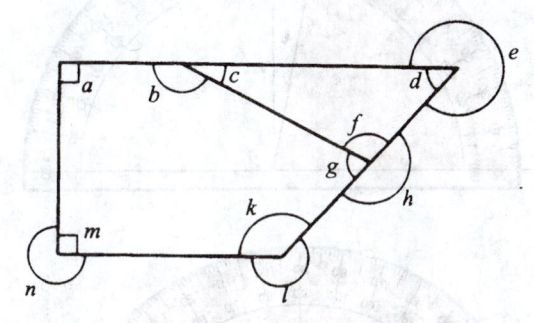

Fig. 8.21

② In Fig. 8.21, 12 angles have been marked using small letters of the alphabet. State whether each is an acute, right, obtuse or reflex angle.

③ Read the sizes of the angles in Fig. 8.22.

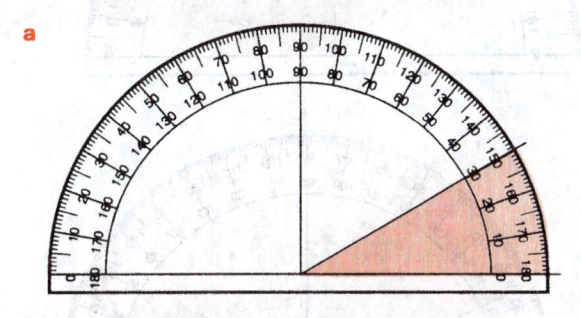

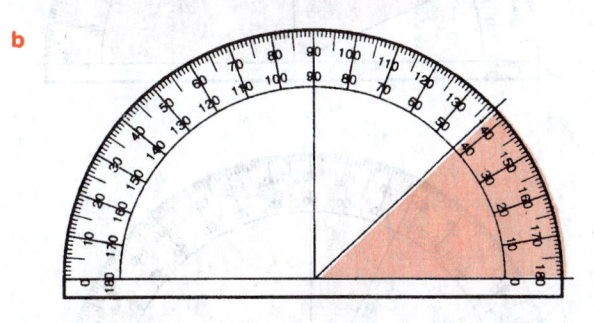

a

b

Exercise 8b (Oral)

① In Fig. 8.20,
   a name all the acute angles (five of them).
   b name all the obtuse angles (three of them).
   c name all the reflex angles (eight of them).

65

c

d

e

f

g

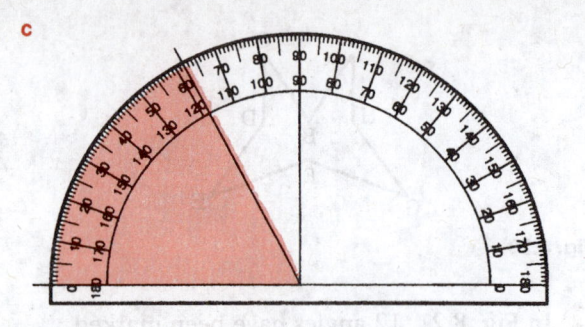

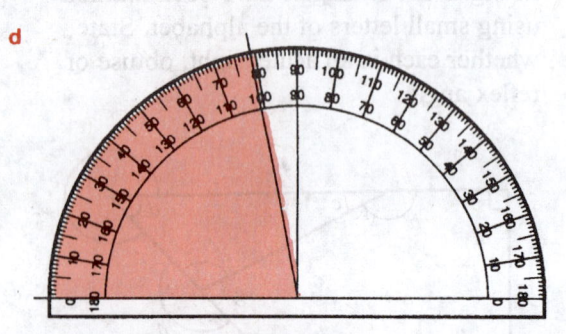

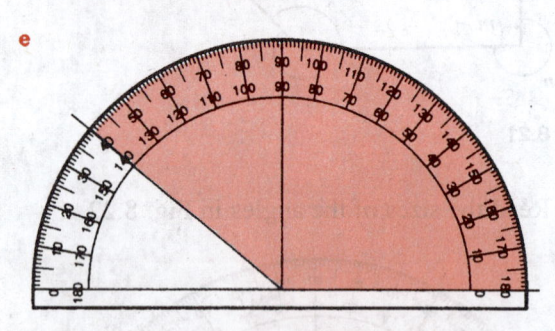

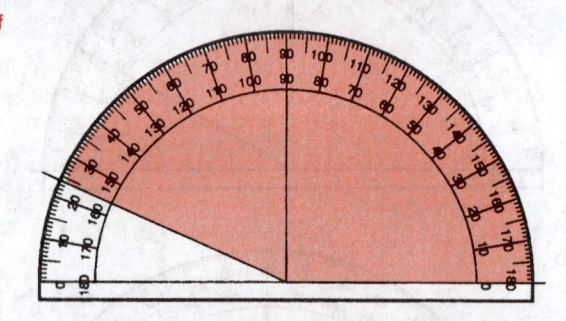

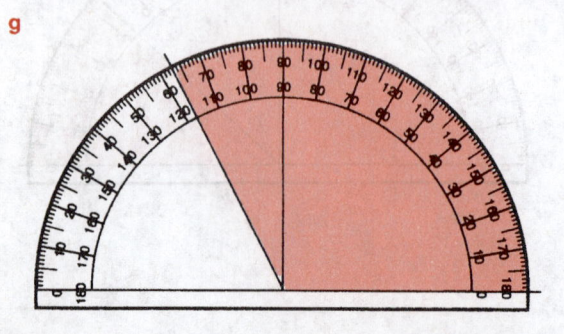

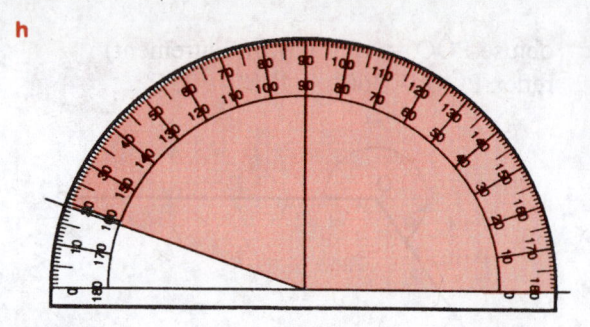

h

Fig. 8.22

☞ *Optional:* Do Exercise 18 of your Students' Practice Book.

Exercise 8c

You will need a protractor, a ruler and a sheet of thin white paper. Place the sheet of paper over angles 1–10 in Fig. 8.23. Trace the angles on to the paper. Measure each angle (make the arms of the angles longer if necessary).

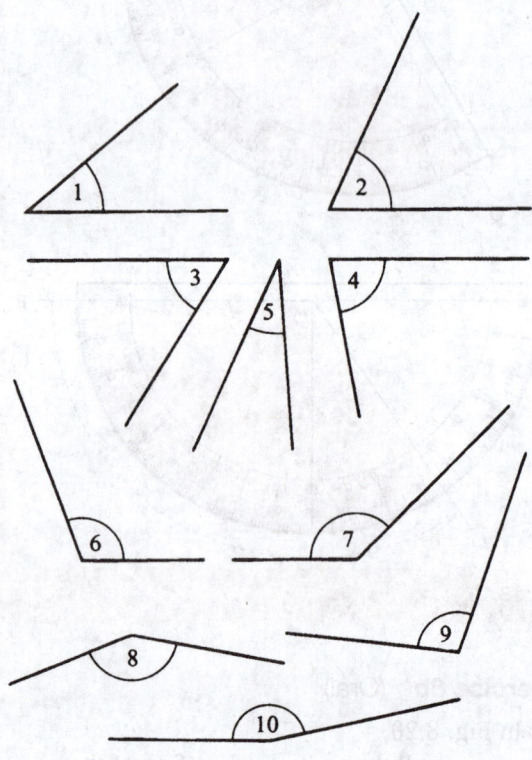

Fig. 8.23

Optional: Do Exercise 19 of your Students' Practice Book.

8-4 Constructing angles

Example 3

Construct an angle of 47°.

Draw a line and mark a point O on it (Fig. 8.24).

Fig. 8.24

Place a protractor so that its centre is over O and its base line is exactly over the line already drawn. Count round until 47° is reached. Make a mark on the paper opposite 47° (Fig. 8.25).

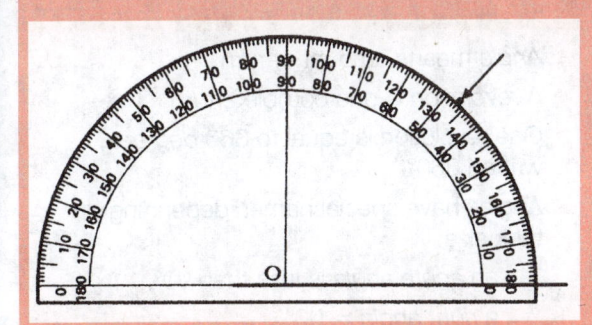

Fig. 8.25

Remove the protractor. Join the mark to O with a ruler (Fig. 8.26).

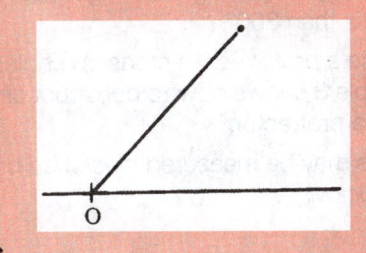

Fig. 8.26

Exercise 8d

1. Use a protractor to construct the following angles.
   a 40°   **b** 65°   **c** 74°
   d 130° **e** 105   **f** 143°

2. Use a protractor to construct the following reflex angles.
   a 300° **b** 285° **c** 215° **d** 238°
   (*Hint*: Subtract the given angles from 360° to get acute or obtuse angles.)

3. Construct a copy of Fig. 8.27 such that AĈD = 68°. Measure BĈD. What do you notice?

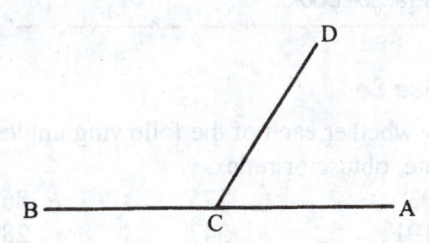

Fig. 8.27

4. Make a copy of Fig. 8.28 such that EF̂G = 90° and EF̂H = 25°. Measure HF̂G. What do you notice?

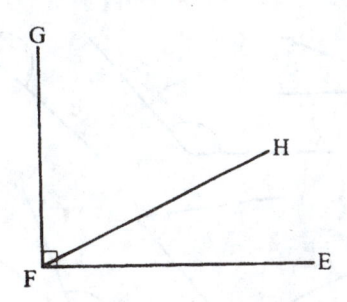

Fig. 8.28

5. In Fig. 8.29 WOX and YOZ are straight lines. Make a copy of the diagram such that ZÔX = 53°. Measure ZÔW, WÔY and YÔX. What do you notice?

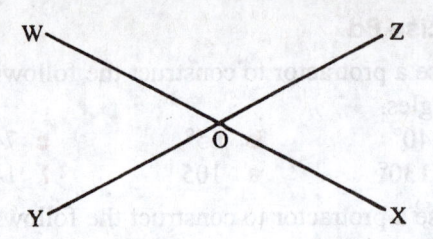

Fig. 8.29

6 Draw any large triangle. Measure its three angles. Find the sum of the three angles of the triangle. What do you notice?

☞ *Optional:* Do Exercise 20 of your Students' Practice Book.

Exercise 8e

1 Say whether each of the following angles is acute, obtuse or reflex.
- a 93°
- b 175°
- c 86°
- d 191°
- e 347°
- f 28°
- g 79°
- h 112°
- i 63°
- j 156°
- k 211°
- l 167°
- m 183°
- n 72°
- o 98°

2 Estimate the sizes of the angles in Fig. 8.30 to the nearest 10°.

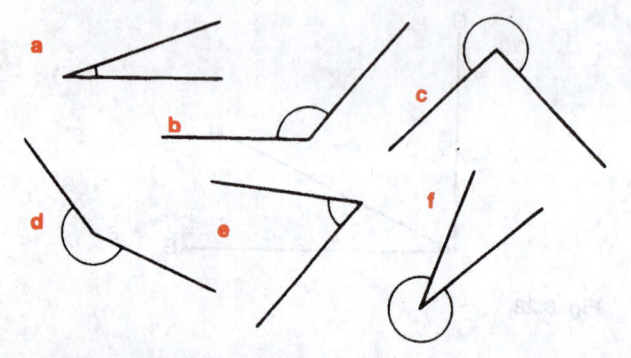

Fig. 8.30

3 Use the method of Exercise 8c to trace the angles in question 2 on to a piece of paper. Measure each angle. How good were your estimates?

4 *Without using a protractor*, try to draw angles of the following sizes.
- a 90°
- b 45°
- c 80°
- d 100°
- e 120°

5 Measure the angles you drew in question 4. How accurate were your drawings?

6 Draw any four-sided shape. A shape with four sides is called a **quadrilateral**. Measure the four angles of the quadrilateral you have drawn. Find the sum of the four angles. What do you notice?

7 Draw a triangle such that two of its sides are 10 cm long. The third side can be any length. Measure the three angles of the triangle. What do you notice? Find the sum of the three angles. What do you notice?

8 Draw a triangle such that one of its angles is obtuse. Measure the three angles of the triangle. Find their sum. What do you notice?

☞ *Optional:* Do Exercise 21 of your Students' Practice Book.

SUMMARY

1 *Angle* means amount of turn.

2 A *revolution* is one complete turn.

3 One revolution is equal to 360 *degrees*, written 360°.

4 Angles have special names depending on their size:

an *acute angle* is less than 90°,

a *right angle* = 90°,

an *obtuse angle* is greater than 90° and less than 180°,

a *straight angle* = 180°,

a *reflex angle* is greater than 180° and less than 360°.

We use a *protractor* to measure angles. Example 3 shows how to construct an angle using a protractor.

Angles may be measured *clockwise* or *anticlockwise*.

Chapters 1–8 Revision exercises and tests

Revision exercise 1 (Chapters 1, 2, 3)

1. What is the value of the following?
   a the 5 in 253   b the 7 in 367
   c the 2 in 2403
2. What is the value of the following?
   a the 6 in 4·62   b the 8 in 0·238
   c the 1 in 3·815
3. Express the number 243 as a Roman numeral.
4. Express the following numbers as a product of prime factors.
   a 18   b 26   c 45
5. Calculate the value of
   a 7^2 b 5^3 c $2^3 \times 3^2$
6. Find the HCF of 63 and 90.
7. Find the LCM of 12 and 15.
8. Express 458 m in kilometres.
9. Add 7·5 m, 2·25 m and 50 cm and give the result in metres.
10. Find the number of seconds in $10\frac{1}{2}$ min.

Revision test 1 (Chapters 1, 2, 3)

1. The value of the 8 in 18 214 is
   A 8 units   B 8 tens   C 8 hundreds
   D 8 thousands   E 8 ten thousands
2. The Roman numeral CXCIV represents the number
   A 194   B 196   C 214   D 215   E 216
3. The value of 6^2 is
   A 12   B 24   C 26   D 36   E 62
4. 5300 mℓ expressed in litres is
   A 0·053   B 0·53   C 5·3   D 53   E 530
5. The number of minutes in $1\frac{1}{2}$ hours is
   A 30   B 45   C 65   D 75   E 90
6. Express 60 as a product of prime factors.
7. Find the LCM of 6 and 14.
8. Find the HCF of 32, 40 and 56.
9. Find the sum of 2·82 t and 893 kg. Express the answer in tonnes.
10. Find the difference between 1·42 m and 29 cm. Express the answer in cm.

Revision exercise 2 (Chapter 4)

1. Find the missing numbers.
   a $\frac{3}{4} = \frac{\square}{12}$ b $\frac{9}{10} = \frac{\square}{90}$ c $\frac{15}{27} = \frac{5}{\square}$
2. Reduce the following to their lowest terms.
   a $\frac{12}{20}$ b $\frac{30}{45}$ c $\frac{48}{60}$
3. Express $4\frac{2}{3}$ as an improper fraction.
4. Simplify the following.
   a $\frac{1}{4} + \frac{1}{3}$ b $\frac{3}{5} - \frac{1}{4}$
   c $\frac{5}{9} \times \frac{3}{10}$ d $\frac{5}{6} \div \frac{2}{3}$
5. Simplify the following.
   a $2\frac{3}{4} + 5\frac{1}{8} - 3\frac{1}{2}$ b $4\frac{3}{8} \times \frac{4}{25}$ c $3\frac{1}{9} \div 11\frac{2}{3}$
6. A boy eats $\frac{1}{4}$ of a loaf at breakfast and $\frac{5}{8}$ of it for lunch. What fraction of the loaf is left?
7. In a class $\frac{4}{5}$ of the students have mathematical instruments. $\frac{1}{4}$ of these students have lost their protractors. What fraction of students in the class have protractors?
8. Express the following percentages as fractions in their lowest terms.
   a 25%   b 28%   c 55%
9. What fraction of 2 weeks is 4 days?
10. What percentage of the letters in the word 'protractor' are vowels?

Revision test 2 (Chapter 4)

1. Which one of the following is *not* equivalent to $\frac{1}{2}$?
   A $\frac{9}{18}$ B $\frac{11}{22}$ C $\frac{15}{30}$ D $\frac{16}{32}$ E $\frac{24}{42}$
2. If $5\frac{1}{7}$ is expressed as an improper fraction, its numerator will be
   A 8   B 12   C 13   D 35   E 36

3. To express the fraction $\frac{30}{48}$ in its lowest terms, divide the numerator and denominator by
   A 2   B 3   C 5   D 6   E 8

4. 45 minutes, expressed as a fraction of one hour, is
   A $\frac{1}{60}$ B $\frac{1}{45}$ C $\frac{3}{4}$ D $\frac{4}{5}$ E $\frac{4}{3}$

5. $\frac{4}{25}$, expressed as a percentage, is
   A 4%   B $6\frac{1}{4}$%   C 8%   D 12%   E 16%

6. Simplify $5\frac{1}{4} + 1\frac{1}{6} - 3\frac{2}{3}$.

7. Simplify $6\frac{1}{4} \times 1\frac{3}{5}$.

8. Simplify $6\frac{3}{4} \div 5\frac{5}{8}$.

9. During a radio programme lasting 1 hour there were 18 minutes of talking; the rest was music. What percentage of the radio programme was music?

10. One-sixth of a stick is cut off and then three-tenths of the remaining piece is thrown away. What fraction of the original stick remains?

Revision exercise 3 (Chapters 5, 7)

1. Find the values of the following when $x = 6$.
   a $x - 1$ b $11 + x$
   c $x + 5 - x$ d $6x$

2. Find the value of a in each of the following true sentences.
   a $6 = 5 + a$ b $9 - a = 4$
   c $4 + a = 11$

3. Write down the number which is
   a 5 more than m b 5 less than m
   c 5 times as big as m

4. An exercise book has x pages. Two exercise books have 64 pages. What is the value of x?

5. If $x = 2$, find the value of
   a $3x$ b $3x - 1$ c $17 - 5x$

6. A girl has ₦320. She gives ₦n to a friend and keeps the rest. If she keeps ₦180, what is the value of n?

7. Simplify the following.
   a $6a + 3a$ b $10x + 4x - 8x$
   c $3n - 8n + 7n$

8. Simplify the following.
   a $8n - 5 + 2n$ b $5 - x - 5x$
   c $3a + 4b - a + 2b$

9. A student buys 2 packets each containing x biscuits. He eats 6 biscuits. How many biscuits does he have left?

10. A trader sells x pencils at ₦90 each, y pens at ₦120 each, and 5 rubbers at ₦x each. How much money does the trader get altogether?

Revision test 3 (Chapters 5, 7)

1. When $x = 8$, the value of $18 - x$ is
   A 1   B 8   C 10   D 18   E 26

2. If $13 = a - 9$ is a true sentence, then $a =$
   A 0   B 4   C 9   D 13   E 22

3. Maria is x years old. In two years time she will be 16 years old. $x =$
   A 2   B 7   C 8   D 14   E 18

4. The number which is 6 less than m is
   A $m - 6$ B $6 - m$ C $6m$
   D $\frac{m}{6}$ E $m + 6$

5. When $x = 4$, the value of $8x$ is
   A 2   B 4   C 12   D 32   E 84

6. Simplify $a - 5a + 8a - 2a$.

7. Simplify $6x - 2y - 5y - 3x$.

8. A girl has ₦n. She gives ₦180 to her brother and spends the other ₦220. What is the value of n?

9. A cup holds d mℓ of tea. A student drinks one-fifth of the tea. How much tea is left?

10. A trader buys 30 shirts for ₦x each. He sells them all for ₦y each. What is his profit?

Revision exercise 4 (Chapters 6, 8)

1. How many edges has a cube?

2. How many faces has a triangular prism? How many of these faces are rectangular?

3. How many vertices has a square-based pyramid?

4. All the edges of a triangular-based pyramid are 10 cm long. A skeleton model of the pyramid is made of wire. What length of wire is needed?

5. How many degrees in
   a a right angle   b $\frac{1}{6}$ of a revolution
   c $2\frac{1}{2}$ revolutions?

6. State whether the following angles are acute, obtuse or reflex.
   a 212°   b 81°   c 95°
   d 198°   e 5°

7. Use a protractor to measure AÔB and BÔC in Fig. R1.

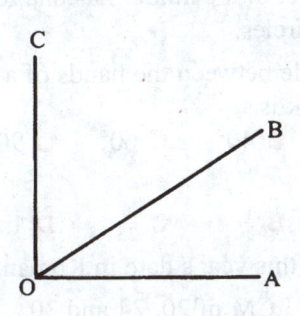

Fig. R1

8. Use a protractor to construct angles of
   a 40°   b 90°   c 150°

9. Construct a copy of Fig. R2 such that AÔB = 66°. Measure BÔC.

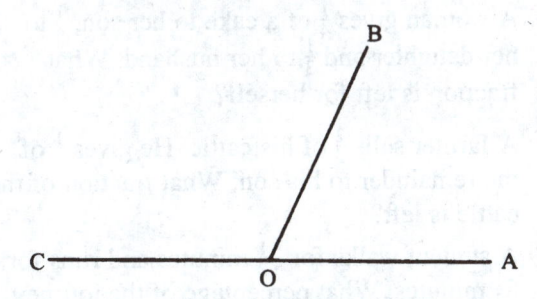

Fig. R2

10. Find, in degrees, the smaller angle between the hour hand and the minute hand of a clock at $\frac{1}{2}$ past 10.

Revision test 4   (Chapters 6, 8)

1. Each face of a cuboid is in the shape of a
   A triangle   B rectangle   C square
   D hexagon   E circle.

2. Which net in Fig. R3 is the net of a triangular prism?

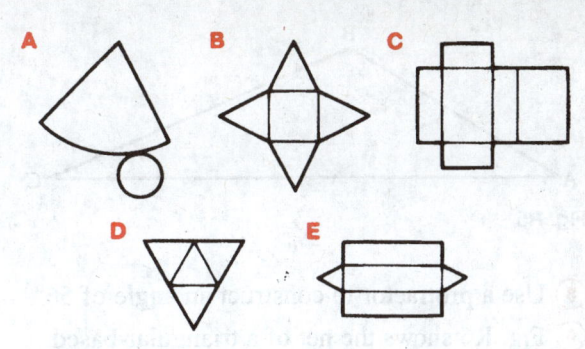

Fig. R3

3. The angle between the hands of a clock at 2 o'clock is
   A 2°   B 24°   C 30°   D 60°   E 72°

4. The number of degrees in 1–8 of a revolution is
   A 8   B $12\frac{1}{2}$ C $22\frac{1}{2}$ D 45   E 90

5. It takes 72 cm of wire to make a skeleton model of a cube. The length of one edge of the cube is
   A 6 cm   B 8 cm   C 9 cm
   D 12 cm   E 18 cm

6. Fig. R4 shows the cuboid ABCDEFGH.

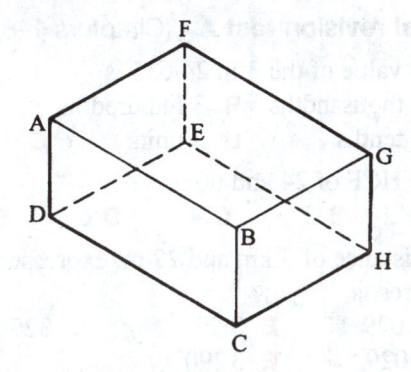

Fig. R4

   a Faces ABGF and BCHG meet along which edge?
   b Which edges meet at vertex H?
   c Edges BG and AB meet at which vertex?

7. Use a protractor to measure AB̂C in the triangle in Fig. R5.

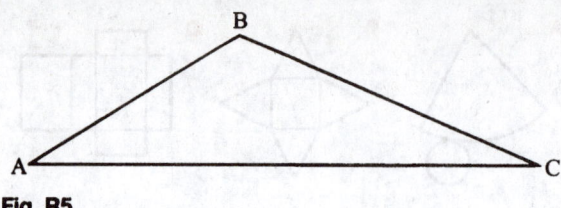

Fig. R5

⑧ Use a protractor to construct an angle of 56°.
⑨ Fig. R6 shows the net of a triangular-based pyramid.

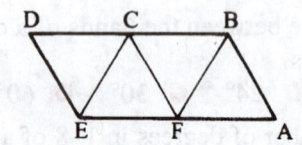

Fig. R6

If the net is folded to make the pyramid,
a which edge will join to edge BC?
b which point will join to point A?

⑩ Find, in degrees, the angle between the hour hand and the minute hand of a clock at $\frac{1}{2}$ past 6.

General revision test A (Chapters 1–8)

① The value of the 3 in 24·635 is
A 3 thousandths   B 3 hundredths
C 3 tenths   D 3 units   E 3 tens

② The HCF of 24 and 60 is
A 2   B 3   C 4   D 6   E 12

③ A distance of 3 km and 29 m, expressed in metres is
A 3·029   B 3·29   C 329
D 3 029   E 3 290

④ The lowest common denominator of $\frac{2}{3}, \frac{4}{5}, \frac{5}{6}$ and $\frac{3}{10}$ is
A 15   B 30   C 50   D 60   E 900

⑤ Four pages of a 16-page newspaper are missing. The percentage missing is
A $\frac{1}{4}$ B 4   C 16   D 25   E 75

⑥ If $26 - x = x$ is a true sentence, the value of x is
A 0   B 2   C 13   D 24   E 26

⑦ If $x = 3$, the value of $7x - 2x$ is
A 6   B 8   C 15   D 21   E 53

⑧ Which one of the following statements about a cylinder is false?
A A cylinder has two vertices.
B A cylinder has two plane faces.
C A cylinder has two curved edges.
D A cylinder has one curved face.
E The net of a cylinder has one rectangle and two circles.

⑨ The angle between the hands of a clock at 8 o'clock is
A 20°   B 40°   C 60°   D 90°   E 120°

⑩ $\frac{3}{5}$ of $\frac{5}{3}$ is
A $\frac{1}{5}$ B $\frac{1}{3}$ C $\frac{9}{25}$ D 1   E $2\frac{7}{9}$

⑪ Express this year's date in Roman numerals.

⑫ Find the LCM of 20, 24 and 30.

⑬ Find the sum of 600 mℓ, 900 mℓ and 60 mℓ. Give your answer in litres.

⑭ Simplify the following.
a $1\frac{1}{20} + \frac{3}{5}$ b $5\frac{3}{8} - 4\frac{3}{4}$
c $3\frac{3}{4} \times 1\frac{1}{2}$ d $3\frac{1}{3} \div 2\frac{2}{9}$

⑮ A woman gives $\frac{1}{4}$ of a cake to her son, $\frac{1}{4}$ to her daughter and $\frac{1}{3}$ to her husband. What fraction is left for herself?

⑯ A farmer sells $\frac{2}{5}$ of his cattle. He gives $\frac{1}{3}$ of the remainder to his son. What fraction of the cattle is left?

⑰ A student walks for $3\frac{1}{2}$ minutes and runs for $8\frac{1}{2}$ minutes. What percentage of the journey time is spent running?

⑱ If $x = 2$, find the value of the following.
a $7 - x$ b $5x - 3$ c $\frac{3}{4}x$ d $4 - 2x$

⑲ I buy 5 metres of cloth at ₦x per metre. How much change will I get from ₦7 000?

⑳ Make a drawing like that in Fig. R7, such that $A\hat{C}D = 114°$. $\hat{A}$ and $\hat{B}$ can be any size. Measure $\hat{A}$ and $\hat{B}$. Find the sum of $\hat{A}$ and $\hat{B}$.

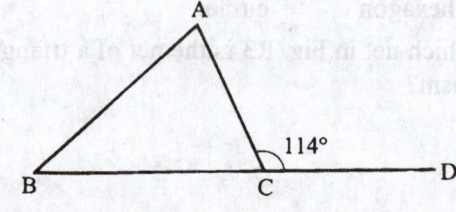

Fig. R7

9 Fractions 2: Decimals and percentages

OBJECTIVES

You should be able to:

1. Add and subtract numbers containing decimal fractions
2. Multiply and divide decimal numbers by powers of 10
3. Multiply and divide numbers containing decimal fractions
4. Convert fractions to decimal fractions and vice versa
5. Convert percentages to decimal fractions and vice versa
6. Solve word problems involving decimal fractions.

Teaching and learning materials

Teacher: Abacus (or paper abacus as in Chapter 1) with a decimal place holder

9-1 Decimals

Decimal fractions

We have seen in Chapter 1 how to extend the place value system to include decimal fractions. The number 3·549 is a way of writing 3 units + $\frac{5}{10} + \frac{4}{100} + \frac{9}{1000}$, or simply 3 units + $\frac{549}{1000}$:

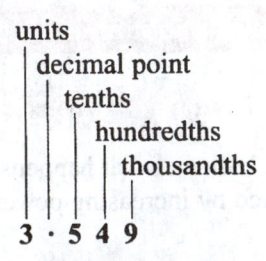

```
        units
         | decimal point
         |  | tenths
         |  |  | hundredths
         |  |  |  | thousandths
         3 · 5  4  9
```

The decimal point acts as a place-holder between the whole-number part and the fractional part of the number. Exercise 9a shows that we often need decimal fractions to be able to read everyday dials and instruments.

Exercise 9a (Oral/QR)

Each part of Figure 9.1 shows a scale and an arrow. The reading opposite each arrow is a decimal number. Find the reading in each case, estimating where necessary.

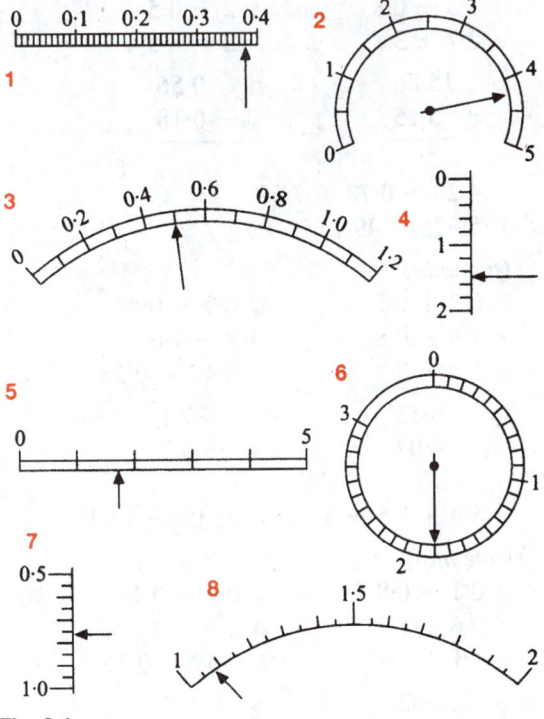

Fig. 9.1

9-2 Addition and subtraction

Be very careful to set out your work correctly. Units must be under units, decimal points under decimal points, ... and so on. For example, 24·8 + 6·5 is set out as

73

```
  24·8              24·8
+  6·5      not      6·5
──────              ─────
```

After you have set out your work correctly, add and subtract in the same way as you do for whole numbers, but remember to write down the decimal point when you come to it.

Exercise 9b

Questions 1–5 each contain ten short QR items. Give yourself ten minutes to do questions 1 and 2. Correct your work. If you make fewer than five mistakes, go on to question 6. If you make more than four mistakes, do questions 3, 4, 5.

1 (*five min*)
  a 0·2 + 0·6   b 0·6 − 0·5
  c 1·3 + 0·8   d 2 − 0·5
  e 2·7 + 3·8   f 8·8 − 5·4
  g   15·86   h   0·56
     + 5·15   − 0·18
  i 4·23 + 0·78 + 7·52
  j 59·25 − 49·17

2 (*five min*)
  a 0·3 + 0·5   b 0·9 − 0·4
  c 1·9 + 0·8   d 3 − 1·6
  e 5·4 + 2·7   f 0·47 − 0·25
  g   6·33   h   7·1
     + 4·07   − 3·7
  i 8·4 + 7·5 + 31·9   j 25·08 − 14·13

3 (*five min*)
  a 0·1 + 0·8   b 0·4 − 0·1
  c 0·6 + 1·7   d 2 − 1·7
  e 6·1 + 1·9   f 0·59 − 0·55
  g   12·62   h   8·2
     + 13·59   − 5·7
  i 3·67 + 2·74 + 5·4 + 0·23
  j 18·33 − 16·55

4 (*five min*)
  a 0·3 + 0·2   b 0·8 − 0·6
  c 0·5 + 0·9   d 3 − 0·3
  e 3·5 + 4·6   f 7·5 − 2·5

  g   13·45   h   0·85
     + 7·55   − 0·26
  i 4·5 + 0·76 + 6·4 + 1·06
  j 24·11 − 14·07

5 (*five min*)
  a 0·4 + 0·4   b 0·3 − 0·2
  c 1·6 + 0·4   d 2 − 1·8
  e 7·5 + 1·7   f 9·3 − 6·2
  g   8·92   h   0·53
     + 4·09   − 0·26
  i 69·3 + 6·93 + 0·693
  j 40·5 − 4·05

6 Find the sum of the following.
  a $1.62, $2.52 and $3.42
  b 1·12 m, 64 cm and 96 cm

7 Find the difference between the following.
  a 28·95 m and 17·58 m
  b 3·062 kg and 855 g

8 A ball of string is 13·5 m long when new. Lengths of 2·3 m, 2·37 m and 95 cm are cut off.
  a What length of string is cut off altogether?
  b How much string is left?
     (Give both answers in metres.)

9 A recipe for bread says: 'Mix 30 g of yeast, 15 g of sugar and 15 g of salt. Add the mixture to 1 kg of flour. Add water and stir.' A cook followed the recipe and the total mass of the mixture was 1·65 kg. What mass of water was added?

10 Find the difference between 9·28 and the sum of 2·31 and 3·92.

9-3 Multiplication and division

Multiplication and division by powers of 10

Table 9.1 shows what happens when 3·07 is multiplied by increasing powers of 10.

3·07 ×	1	=		3·07
3·07 ×	10	= 3·07 × 10^1 =		30·7
3·07 ×	100	= 3·07 × 10^2 =		307·
3·07 ×	1000	= 3·07 × 10^3 =		3070·
3·07 ×	10000	= 3·07 × 10^4 =		30700·

Table 9.1

Notice that when **multiplying** by powers of 10:
a as the power of 10 increases it is as if the decimal point stays where it is and the digits in the number move to the left;
b the digits move as many places to the left as the power of 10 (or as the number of zeros in the multiplier);
c as each place to the right of the digits becomes empty we fill it with a zero to act as a place holder;
d if the fraction to the right of the decimal point becomes zero there is no need to write anything after the point.

Similarly, Table 9.2 shows what happens when 3·07 is divided by increasing powers of 10.

3·07 ÷	1	=		3·07
3·07 ÷	10	= 3·07 ÷ 10^1 =		0·307
3·07 ÷	100	= 3·07 ÷ 10^2 =		0·0307
3·07 ÷	1000	= 3·07 ÷ 10^3 =		0·00307
3·07 ÷	10000	= 3·07 ÷ 10^4 =		0·000307

Table 9.2

Notice that when **dividing** by powers of 10:
a as the power of 10 increases it is as if the decimal point stays where it is and the digits in the number move to the right;
b the digits move as many places to the right as the power of 10 (or as the number of zeros in the divisor);
c as each place to the left of the digits becomes empty we fill it with a zero to act as a place holder;
d if the number to the left of the decimal point becomes zero it is usual to write a zero there.

Example 1

Write the following as decimal numbers.

a $0·036 \times 10000$ b $\frac{23}{1000}$

c $120 \div 100000$ d $0·00045 \times 100$

a $0·036 \times 10000 = 0·036 \times 10^4 = 360$

b $\frac{23}{1000} = 23 \div 1000 = 23 \div 10^3 = 0·023$

c $120 \div 100000 = 120 \div 10^5 = 0·00120$
$ = 0·0012$

It is not necessary to write zeros to the right of a decimal fraction. For example, 0·200000 is just the same as 0·2.

d $0·00045 \times 100 = 0·00045 \times 10^2 = 0·045$

Exercise 9c (Oral)

Give the following as decimal numbers.

1. $2·67 \times 100$
2. $4·55 \times 10000$
3. $8·03 \times 1000$
4. $5·6 \div 1000$
5. $8·11 \div 10$
6. $7·04 \div 100$
7. $0·027 \times 10000$
8. $0·36 \times 100$
9. $0·0085 \times 1000$
10. $\frac{52}{1000}$
11. $\frac{63}{1000}$
12. $\frac{423}{100}$
13. $0·05 \times 1000$
14. 650×100
15. 90×100000
16. $4·37 \times 10^3$
17. $24·5 \times 10^4$
18. $0·207 \times 10^2$
19. $4502 \div 10^2$
20. $20·05 \div 10^3$
21. $0·0036 \div 10^4$
22. $5140 \div 100000$
23. $60 \div 100$
24. $300 \div 10000$
25. $0·00026 \times 100$
26. $0·07 \times 10$
27. $0·00008 \times 1000$
28. $\frac{2·42}{10000}$
29. $\frac{400·7}{100}$
30. $\frac{70·63}{1000}$
31. Express $6.20 in cents
32. Express 344c in dollars.
33. Express 2·41 m in cm.
34. Express 592 cm in metres.
35. Express 6·24 tonnes in a kg, b g.
36. Express 920 kg in a tonnes, b g.

75

37. Express 420 g in **a** kg, **b** tonnes.
38. Express 504 mℓ in **a** ℓ, **b** kℓ.
39. Express 20·9 m in **a** mm, **b** km.
40. Express 7050 ℓ in **a** kℓ, **b** mℓ.

Multiplication of decimals

Example 2
Find the product of 38·6 and 1·64.

$$38·6 \times 1·64 = \frac{386}{10} \times \frac{164}{100} = \frac{386 \times 164}{1000}$$

Use long multiplication to find the numerator:

```
      386
    ×  164
    -----
     1 544
    23 160
    38 600
    ------
    63 304
```

$$38·6 \times 1·64 = \frac{63\,304}{1000} = 63·304$$

The method in Example 2 can be made shorter as follows.

a Multiply the given numbers without decimal points.

b Count the digits after the decimal points in the numbers being multiplied.

c Place the decimal point so that the product has the same number of digits after the point.

Example 3
Calculate 0·25 × 0·009.

25 × 9 = 225

There are five digits after the decimal points in the given numbers. So,

0·25 × 0·009 = 0·00225

Exercise 9d (Oral/QR)
Find the following products.

1. 0·7 × 8
2. 0·2 × 4
3. 0·2 × 6
4. 0·3 × 9
5. 0·8 × 5
6. 9 × 0·4
7. 7 × 0·7
8. 7 × 0·6
9. 5 × 0·6
10. 8 × 0·5
11. 0·6 × 0·3
12. 0·4 × 0·7
13. 0·1 × 0·6
14. 0·3 × 0·4
15. 0·3 × 0·3
16. 0·09 × 0·2
17. 0·7 × 0·06
18. 0·04 × 0·08
19. 0·5 × 0·006
20. 0·003 × 0·05

Exercise 9e
Questions 1–5 each contain five QR items. Give yourself ten minutes to do questions 1 and 2. Correct your work. If you make fewer than four mistakes, go on to question 6. If you make more than three mistakes, do questions 3, 4, 5.

1. *(five min)*
   a 0·6 × 1·8
   b 1·93 × 0·3
   c (0·05)²
   d 0·64 × 2·5
   e 6·83 × 0·62

2. *(five min)*
   a 8 × 0·15
   b 27·9 × 0·5
   c (0·2)²
   d 6·8 × 3·1
   e 7·3 × 0·144

3. *(five min)*
   a 0·4 × 1·4
   b 510 × 0·002
   c (0·8)²
   d 5·4 × 0·052
   e 2·71 × 0·25

4. *(five min)*
   a 5 × 0·6
   b 0·17 × 3
   c (0·004)²
   d 410 × 0·0023
   e 0·87 × 0·306

5. *(five min)*
   a 3 × 0·9
   b 1·3 × 0·7
   c (0·3)²
   d 0·77 × 0·15
   e 3·42 × 9·9

6. What is 0·25 of 6·36?
7. Find the product of 2·03 and 0·055.
8. A ream of paper contains 480 sheets. Each sheet is 0·014 cm thick. Find the thickness of the ream of paper.

9. A dress needs 3·5 m of cloth. If cloth costs ₦480 per metre, how much will it cost to buy enough cloth for a dress?

10. 1 metre of string has a mass of 2·3 g. What is the mass of 112·8 metres of this string? Give your answer **a** in g, **b** in kg.

Division of decimals

If the divisor is a whole number, divide in the usual way. Be careful to include the decimal point in the correct place.

Example 4

Calculate $10·71 \div 63$.

$$\begin{array}{r} 0·17 \\ 63\overline{)10·71} \\ \underline{6·3} \\ 4·41 \\ \underline{4·41} \end{array}$$

$10·71 \div 63 = 0·17$

If the divisor contains a decimal fraction, make an equivalent division such that the divisor is a whole number. See Example 5.

Example 5

Calculate $13·05 \div 2·9$.

$13·05 \div 2·9 = \frac{13·05}{2·9} = \frac{13·05 \times 10}{2·9 \times 10} = \frac{130·5}{29}$

$13·05 \div 2·9 = 130·5 \div 29$

$$\begin{array}{r} 4·5 \\ 29\overline{)130·5} \\ \underline{116} \\ 14·5 \\ \underline{14·5} \end{array}$$

$13·05 \div 2·9 = 130·5 \div 29 = 4·5$

The method in Example 5 can be made shorter as follows.

a Count how many places to the right the digits in the divisor must move to make the divisor a whole number.

b Move the digits of *both* numbers to the right by this number of places.

c Divide as before.

Example 6

Calculate $4·2 \div 0·006$.

$4·2 \div 0·006 = 4200 \div 6 = 700$

Example 7

Calculate $1·938 \div 0·34$.

$1·938 \div 0·34 = 193·8 \div 34$

$$\begin{array}{r} 5·7 \\ 34\overline{)193·8} \\ \underline{170} \\ 23·8 \\ \underline{23·8} \end{array}$$

$1·938 \div 0·34 = 193·8 \div 34 = 5·7$

Exercise 9f (Oral/QR)

Find the value of the following divisions.

1. $18 \div 6$
2. $1·8 \div 6$
3. $0·18 \div 6$
4. $18 \div 0·6$
5. $18 \div 0·06$
6. $1·8 \div 0·6$
7. $180 \div 0·6$
8. $0·18 \div 0·06$
9. $1800 \div 0·06$
10. $0·018 \div 0·6$
11. $\frac{30}{5}$
12. $\frac{3}{5}$
13. $\frac{30}{0·5}$
14. $\frac{0·3}{5}$
15. $\frac{3}{0·005}$
16. $\frac{30}{0·05}$
17. $\frac{300}{0·5}$
18. $\frac{3}{0·05}$
19. $\frac{0·003}{0·5}$
20. $\frac{0·3}{0·05}$

Exercise 9g

Questions 1–5 each contain five items. Give yourself ten minutes to do questions 1 and 2. Correct your work. If you make fewer than four mistakes, go on to question 6. If you make more than three mistakes, do questions 3, 4, 5.

(1) *(five min)*
a $\frac{0.09}{3}$ b $\frac{3.6}{0.4}$
c $0.042 \div 0.06$ d $\frac{7.3}{0.002}$
e $12.24 \div 3.6$

(2) *(five min)*
a $\frac{1.47}{7}$ b $\frac{0.27}{0.09}$
c $0.012 \div 0.4$ d $\frac{3.68}{0.08}$
e $3.172 \div 0.52$

(3) *(five min)*
a $\frac{0.32}{8}$ b $\frac{4}{0.5}$
c $0.28 \div 0.007$ d $\frac{0.6.15}{0.3}$
e $80.5 \div 2.3$

(4) *(five min)*
a $\frac{0.6}{3}$ b $\frac{1.8}{0.2}$
c $4.8 \div 0.08$ d $\frac{4.77}{0.09}$
e $6.44 \div 0.028$

(5) *(five min)*
a $\frac{0.7}{7}$ b $\frac{0.4}{0.8}$
c $36 \div 0.09$ d $\frac{0.432}{0.4}$
e $351 \div 0.45$

(6) If $35 \times 67 = 2345$, what is the value of $2.345 \div 6.7$?

(7) The mass of six equal books is 2·82 kg. Calculate the mass of one book
a in kg b in g.

(8) A pile of boards is 36 cm high. Each board is 0·8 cm thick. How many boards are in the pile?

(9) An electrician pays ₦1 170 for 6·5 metres of armoured wire. What is the cost of 1 metre of wire?

(10) A test car travels 98·6 km on 7·25 litres of petrol. How many km does it travel on 1 litre of petrol?

9-4 Conversion

Changing fractions to decimals

To express a fraction as a decimal, make an equivalent fraction with a denominator which is a power of ten.

Example 8

Express $\frac{4}{5}$ as a decimal.

$\frac{4}{5} = \frac{4}{5} \times \frac{10}{10} = \frac{40}{50} = \frac{40 \div 5}{50 \div 5} = \frac{8}{10} = 0.8$

Example 9

Express $\frac{3}{8}$ as a decimal.

$\frac{3}{8} = \frac{3 \times 1000}{8 \times 1000} = \frac{3000}{8000} = \frac{3000 \div 8}{8000 \div 8} = \frac{375}{1000}$
$= 0.375$

It is usually quicker to divide the numerator of the fraction by its denominator, taking care to write down the decimal point as it arises:

$\frac{3}{8} = 3.000 \div 8 = 0.375 \qquad 8\overline{)3.000}^{\,0.375}$

$\frac{3}{8}$ gives an exact decimal fraction, 0·375. We say it is a **terminating decimal**.

Exercise 9h

Express the following as terminating decimals.

(1) $\frac{1}{2}$ (2) $\frac{1}{5}$ (3) $\frac{1}{4}$ (4) $\frac{3}{5}$
(5) $\frac{3}{4}$ (6) $\frac{11}{20}$ (7) $\frac{2}{5}$ (8) $\frac{6}{25}$
(9) $\frac{1}{20}$ (10) $\frac{3}{20}$ (11) $\frac{7}{20}$ (12) $\frac{4}{5}$
(13) $\frac{1}{25}$ (14) $\frac{18}{25}$ (15) $\frac{3}{25}$ (16) $\frac{17}{25}$
(17) $\frac{5}{8}$ (18) $\frac{3}{8}$ (19) $\frac{13}{50}$ (20) $\frac{33}{50}$
(21) $\frac{23}{25}$ (22) $\frac{3}{40}$ (23) $\frac{17}{20}$ (24) $\frac{39}{40}$
(25) $\frac{9}{25}$ (26) $\frac{12}{25}$ (27) $\frac{43}{50}$ (28) $\frac{6}{125}$
(29) $\frac{7}{8}$ (30) $\frac{11}{40}$ (31) $1\frac{3}{4}$ (32) $\frac{31}{50}$
(33) $3\frac{1}{8}$ (34) $\frac{19}{20}$ (35) $9\frac{3}{5}$ (36) $2\frac{17}{40}$
(37) $4\frac{13}{20}$ (38) $7\frac{19}{25}$ (39) $\frac{9}{16}$ (40) $\frac{7}{16}$

Example 10

Express $\frac{7}{9}$ as a decimal.

$\frac{7}{9} = 7.000 \div 9 \qquad 9\overline{)7.000\ldots}^{\,0.777\ldots}$

$= 0.777\ldots$

In Example 10, $\frac{7}{9}$ results in a never-ending decimal fraction, 0·777 ... The digit 7 is repeated as often as we like. We say it is a **recurring decimal**. We say this as 'zero point seven recurring' and write it as 0·$\dot{7}$.

Many fractions give rise to recurring decimals. For example:

$\frac{4}{11}$ = 0·363636 .. = 0·$\dot{3}\dot{6}$

$\frac{5}{7}$ = 0·714285714285 .. = 0·$\dot{7}1428\dot{5}$ or 0·$\overline{714285}$

$\frac{1}{6}$ = 0·166666 .. = 0·1$\dot{6}$

Exercise 9i
Express the following as recurring decimals.

(1) $\frac{1}{3}$ (2) $\frac{2}{3}$ (3) $\frac{2}{9}$ (4) $\frac{5}{9}$
(5) $\frac{8}{9}$ (6) $\frac{3}{11}$ (7) $\frac{5}{11}$ (8) $\frac{5}{6}$
(9) $\frac{7}{12}$ (10) $\frac{1}{7}$

Changing decimals to fractions

Any decimal fraction can be expressed as a fraction with a denominator which is a power of ten. For example, 0·3 = $\frac{3}{10}$, 0·54 = $\frac{54}{100}$, 0·207 = $\frac{207}{1000}$, and so on.

Example 11
Express 0·62 as a fraction in its lowest terms.

0·62 = $\frac{62}{100}$ = $\frac{62 \div 2}{100 \div 2}$ = $\frac{31}{50}$

Example 12
Express 0·376 as a fraction in its lowest terms.

0·376 = $\frac{376}{1000}$ = $\frac{376 \div 8}{1000 \div 8}$ = $\frac{47}{125}$

Exercise 9j
Express the following as fractions in their lowest terms.

(1) 0·8 (2) 0·7 (3) 0·75
(4) 0·6 (5) 0·2 (6) 0·28
(7) 0·45 (8) 0·32 (9) 0·44
(10) 0·42 (11) 0·54 (12) 0·48
(13) 0·56 (14) 0·52 (15) 0·66
(16) 0·98 (17) 0·84 (18) 0·135
(19) 0·102 (20) 0·525 (21) 0·105
(22) 0·825 (23) 0·375 (24) 0·488
(25) 0·725 (26) 7·4 (27) 0·625
(28) 1·25 (29) 0·624 (30) 4·72

9-5 Decimals and percentages

Remember that 17% means $\frac{17}{100}$. Thus 17% is the same as 0·17.

17% = $\frac{17}{100}$ = 0·17

This shows that to change a percentage to a decimal fraction, divide the percentage by 100. For example,

16% = 16 ÷ 100 = 0·16

To change a decimal fraction to a percentage, multiply by 100. For example,
0·732 = (0·732 × 100)% = 73·2%

Notice also,

$\frac{1}{3}$ = 0·333 ... = 0·$\dot{3}$

$\frac{1}{3}$ = 33·333 ... % = 33·$\dot{3}$% = 33$\frac{1}{3}$%

Exercise 9k (Oral)

(1) Express the following percentages as decimals.
   a 5%   b 50%   c 25%
   d 40% e 70%   f 4%
   g 15% h 12%   i 80%
   j 75% k 24%   l 35%
   m 64% n 60%   o 45%

(2) Express the following decimals as percentages.
   a 0·25 b 0·85 c 0·36
   d 0·81 e 0·08 f 0·125
   g 0·308 h 0·7   i 0·07
   j 0·$\dot{6}$ k 0·5 l 0·022
   m 0·005 n 0·8   o 0·1$\dot{3}$

Exercise 9I

1. Find the value of the following.
   a 24·2 + 6·78
   b 3·55 kg + 7·84 kg
   c 5·25 kg + 6·75 kg
   d 61·7 + 4·05 + 18·86
   e 34 m + 3·75 m + 75 cm
   f 2·2 kg − 0·35 kg
   g 67 cm − 28 mm
   h 852·25 km − 78·50 km
   i 50·4 − 5·04
   j $24 − $10·14
   k 0·5 × 7
   l (0·4)^2
   m 0·08 × 0·7
   n 12·4 × 0·8
   o 21·8 × 0·73
   p 0·1 ÷ 8
   q 0·03 ÷ 0·4
   r 43·4 ÷ 0·7
   s 0·0927 ÷ 0·03
   t 89·6 ÷ 0·35

2. Find the value of the following. Give your answers both in decimals and in fractions where possible.
   a $\frac{1}{4} + 0·34$
   b $0·6 - \frac{1}{3}$
   c $5·8 + 2\frac{3}{4}$
   d $4\frac{1}{2} - 1·06$
   e $\frac{1}{2}$ of 0·48
   f $\frac{3}{4}$ of 2·8
   g $5·4 \times 2\frac{1}{2}$
   h $3·14 \times (\frac{1}{2})^2$
   i $1\frac{4}{5} \div 0·45$
   j $2·88 \div 3\frac{3}{4}$
   k 14 ÷ 5·6
   l $0·7 \div 5\frac{1}{4}$

3. A student spends 37·5% of her money on food, 28·75% on rent, and 15% on books. What percentage of her money is left to spend on other things?

4. What percentage of 10 km is 2·5 km?

5. What is 30% of $180·90? A dealer bought some items for $180·90 each and sold them at a profit of 30%. What was the selling price of each item?

6. If 1·504 ÷ 4·7 = 0·32, what is the value of 320 × 0·47?

7. A person bought a second-hand car for ₦184 000 and later sold it at a loss of 17·5%. What was the selling price of the car?

8. Express 8·705 m in a mm, b km.

9. 12·5 g of medicine costs ₦1 075. What is the cost of 1 g of medicine?

10. A man works 46·5 hours and is paid ₦520 per hour. What is his total pay?

SUMMARY

1. To add or subtract decimals:
   a set out work carefully, placing units under units, decimal points under each other, tenths under tenths and so on;
   b then proceed as you would with ordinary numbers, writing down the decimal point when you come to it.

2. Tables 9.1 and 9.2 show how to multiply and divide decimal numbers by powers of 10.

3. *To express a fraction as a decimal*, make an equivalent fraction with a denominator that is a power of 10.

4. A *terminating* decimal fraction has a fixed number of digits after the decimal point.

5. A recurring decimal has a never-ending number of digits after the decimal point, e.g. 0·333 33 ..., written as 0·$\dot{3}$.

6. To multiply decimals (simple method):
   a multiply the numbers without the decimal points;
   b count the digits after the decimal points in the numbers being multiplied, then place the decimal point in the product so that it has the same total number of digits after the point.
   (See Example 3.)

7. *To divide decimals*, follow the method of Example 5, 6 or 7.

8. *To change a decimal fraction to a percentage*, multiply by 100 (as for fractions).

9. *To change a percentage to a decimal fraction*, divide by 100.

10 Use of symbols 2: Word problems

OBJECTIVES

You should be able to:
1 Use letters to express mathematical statements
2 Solve simple word problems using algebra

10-1 Algebra from words

Here is a story in pictures (Fig. 10.1).

a

b

c

Fig. 10.1

Here is the story in words.
a Ugwu has a bag with some mangoes in it.
b He buys 2 more mangoes.
c Ugwu now has a bag with some mangoes and 2 more mangoes.

Here is the same story with algebraic symbols.
a Ugwu has m mangoes.
b Ugwu buys 2 mangoes.
c Ugwu now has $m + 2$ mangoes.

In this story, m represents the number of mangoes in the bag. $m + 2$ represents the number of mangoes that Ugwu has altogether.

Example 1

A boy has m mangoes. He sells two of them. How many mangoes does he now have?

He sells 2 mangoes. He must have 2 less than he had before. He now has $m - 2$ mangoes.

Sometimes a problem may be difficult because letters are used for numbers. If this happens, first change the letter to an easy number. Use that number instead of the letter. This will show what has to be done with the letter.

Example 2

A girl is 14 years old. How old will she be in x years time?

Use 2 and 10 instead of x:
In 2 years time the girl will be
$14 + 2$ years old (16 years old).
In 10 years time the girl will be
$14 + 10$ years old (24 years old).
So, in x years time the girl will be
$14 + x$ years old.
$14 + x$ will not simplify.
The girl will be $14 + x$ years old.

Remember that, in algebra, letters represent numbers only. If a problem contains units, then units must show in the working. For example, the length of a rope cannot be 7 or x. The units

81

are missing. The rope might be 7 metres long or x centimetres long. Always use units when necessary.

> **Example 3**
>
> How many cm *are there in* n *metres?*
>
> Use 2 m and 5 m instead of n metres.
> Multiply by 100 to change metres to cm.
> $\quad 2\,m = 2 \times 100\,cm = 200\,cm$
> $\quad 5\,m = 5 \times 100\,cm = 500\,cm$
> So, n metres $= n \times 100\,cm = 100n\,cm$.

The following exercises provide practice at making algebraic expressions from English sentences.

Exercise 10a (Oral)
Use addition in this exercise.

1. Baba is 13 years old.
   How old will he be in 8 years from now?
   How old will he be in y years from now?

2. What number is 4 more than 3?
   What number is 4 more than n?
   What number is 7 more than x?

3. A farmer has 6 goats and z cows.
   How many animals does he have altogether?

4. Last year the body-mass of a student was 48 kg. The increase in the student's body-mass this year is m kg.
   What is the student's body-mass this year?

5. A man has k kola nuts. A friend gives him 1 more kola nut.
   How many kola nuts does the man have now?

6. If today is the 6th of September, what will be the date in n days time? (Assume that the month will still be September.)

7. Each side of a square board is d centimetres long. What is the total length of the sides of the board?

8. In a test, Muhammad got 7 marks more than Emmanuel. Emmanuel got x marks.
   a How many marks did Muhammad get?
   b Fatima got y marks more than Muhammad. How many marks did Fatima get?

Exercise 10b (Oral)
Use subtraction in this exercise.

1. What number is 2 less than 9?
   What number is 2 less than n?
   What number is 5 less than r?

2. A woman is 30 years old.
   What was her age 10 years ago?
   What was her age y years ago?

3. A book has x pages. A boy reads 30 pages of the book.
   How many pages has the boy not read?

4. A boy has m mangoes. If he eats 5 of them, how many does he have left?

5. A girl guesses that a line is 15 cm long. She measures the line. She finds that her guess is x cm too long. What is the length of the line?

6. A dealer bought a diamond for ₦x and sold it for ₦165 500. What was the profit?

7. A man cycles x km towards a village which is 20 km away.
   How far does he still have to cycle?

8. Audu has s naira in his savings account. He uses some of this to buy a suit which costs t naira. How much does he have left in his savings?

Exercise 10c (Oral)
Use multiplication in this exercise.

1. a How many metres in 1 kilometre?
   b How many metres in 4 kilometres?
   c How many metres in x kilometres?

2. a How many days in 1 week?
   b How many days in 5 weeks?
   c How many days in w weeks?

3. How many calendar months are there in x years?

4. What is the number which is 9 times greater than d?

5. a What is the cost of 8 books at ₦400 each?
   b What is the cost of x books at ₦400 each?
   c What is the cost of 5 books at ₦t each?

6. A loaf of bread has a mass of x kg.
   What is its mass in grammes?

7 A rubber band is x mm long when unstretched. It is stretched to 3 times its unstretched length.
What is the stretched length?

8 What is the cost of 10 km of road drains at m naira per km?

Exercise 10d (Oral)

Use division in this exercise.

1 a How many weeks are there in 14 days?
b How many weeks are there in d days?

2 a How many metres are there in 3000 millimetres?
b How many metres are there in k mm?

3 6 equal blocks have a mass of b kg.
What is the mass of each block?

4 5 pencils cost ₦400.
a How much does one pencil cost?
b In another shop, 5 pencils cost ₦p. How much does one pencil cost in this shop?

5 A chicken lays h eggs in 9 days. What is the average number of eggs it lays in one day?

6 A stick is 140 cm long. The stick is cut into x pieces, each the same length.
What is the length of each piece?

7 What is the number which is one-third as big as n?

8 Fig. 10.2 shows 5 equal blocks built in a column. The height of the column is x cm.
How thick is each block?

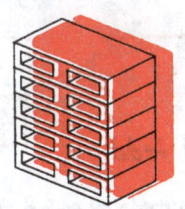

Fig. 10.2

Exercise 10e

1 A radio programme has x minutes of talking and 20 minutes of music.
How long is the programme?

2 A teacher has 6 pens, n of them are red, the rest are blue.
How many blue pens does the teacher have?

3 Find the number of square carpets of length 1 metre each that are needed to cover a rectangular hall of length a metres and width 20 metres.

4 How many kilogrammes are there in x grammes?

5 A packet of sugar costs ₦200.
How much would x packets of sugar cost?

6 A school paid ₦380 000 to buy desks. It bought d desks altogether.
What was the cost of one desk?

7 Mary has 20 oranges. Naomi has x oranges less than Mary.
How many oranges has Naomi?

8 A man walks $3x$ km on the first day, 12 km on the second day and $2x$ km on the third day.
How far does he walk in the three days?

9 Team A scored three times as many points as Team B.
a Which team scored more points?
b If Team A scored n points, how many points did Team B score?

10 A square mat has a side of length 3 metres.
What is the total area of x of these mats?

Exercise 10f

1 Find the difference between x metres and $7x$ cm. Give your answer in cm.

2 A rectangle is such that its length is twice its breadth. If the breadth is d cm, find the total length of the sides of the rectangle.

3 A full matchbox contains x matches. A man has three full matchboxes and a matchbox containing y matches. How many matches does he have altogether?

4 A girl is x years old. Her father is four times as old.
a How old is the father?
What will be the age in y years time of
b the girl   **c** the father?

5 Find the sum of $2x$ kg and $5x$ g. Give your answer in grammes.

6 A car cost ₦c when new. It was sold for four-fifths of its cost price.
How much money was lost on the car?

7. A man has n cattle. He sells half of them. He then gives 8 cattle to his daughter's husband. How many cattle does he have left?

8. How many packets of pins at ₦150 per packet can I buy for x naira?

9. During a period of x weeks there were 13 days when it didn't rain. On how many days did it rain?

10. A sum of ₦5 000 is shared equally between x girls. One of the girls spends ₦360. How many naira does she have left?

☞ *Optional:* Do Exercise 23 of your Students' Practice Book.

SUMMARY

1. In algebra, we use letters to represent numbers.
2. If a problem appears difficult because a letter is used for a number, change the letter to a simple number. This will usually show you the method.
3. Remember that an algebraic expression or sentence gives a very short way of representing words.

PUZZLE CORNER

Freight Train

A freight train 1 km long crosses a bridge 1 km long. If the train travels at 20 km/h, how long does it take to cross the bridge?

PUZZLE CORNER

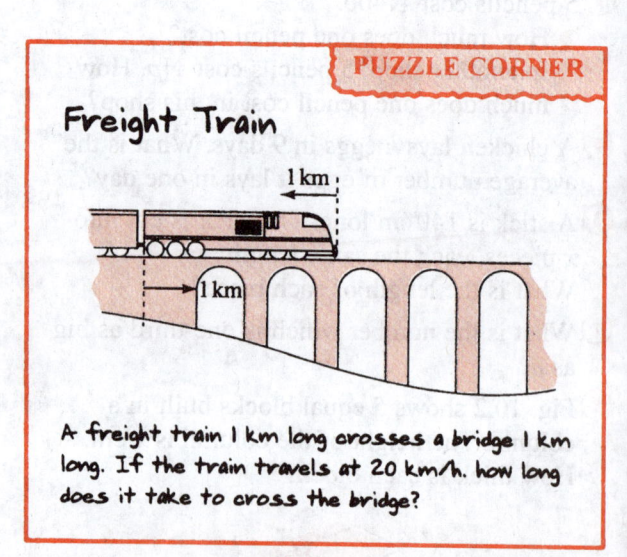

Square and Add

This sequence is made by adding the squares of the digits in each number to make the next:

$$25 \to 29 \to 85 \to 89 \to$$

Carry on for at least 10 more terms. What happens?
Start with a different number. What happens?
Can you discover any rules?

11 Plane shapes 1: Properties

OBJECTIVES

You should be able to:

1. Identify, name and state the properties of common plane shapes (rectangles, squares, triangles, regular polygons, circles)
2. Distinguish between different types of triangle (scalene, isosceles, equilateral)
3. Construct plane shapes by (a) paper folding, (b) using compasses
4. Identify by name the various parts of a circle (circumference, arc, radius, diameter, sector, semi-circle, segment).

Teaching and learning materials

Teacher: Chalk board instruments, cardboard, paper, scissors

Students: Old newspapers; mathematical sets (ruler and compasses)

11-1 Rectangles and squares

Rectangles

Place a matchbox (or other small box) on a sheet of paper. Draw round the shape of the face touching the paper. Repeat for two other different faces. Your drawings should look like Fig. 11.1.

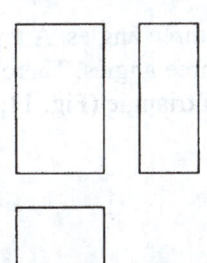

Fig. 11.1

Each shape is a **rectangle**.

A **diagonal** of a rectangle is a straight line from one corner to the opposite corner. Every rectangle has two diagonals as shown in Fig. 11.2.

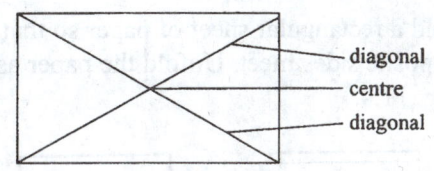

Fig. 11.2

The point where the diagonals cross is the **centre** of the rectangle.

Exercise 11a

1. Name at least ten things in your classroom which have a rectangular shape.
2. How many sides has a rectangle?
3. How many angles are in a rectangle?
4. In each of these rectangles:
   i a page out of your exercise book,
   ii the shape of the top of your desk,
   iii the face of a cuboid (e.g. a chalkbox),
   a measure the lengths of all the sides; what do you notice?
   b measure the sizes of all the angles; what do you notice?
5. What is the total of the four angles of a rectangle?
6. In each rectangle in question 4,
   a measure the lengths of both diagonals; what do you notice?
   b measure the distance from the centre to each corner; what do you notice?
7. At the centre of each rectangle, where the diagonals cross, there are four angles.
   a How many are acute?
   b What kind of angles are the others?

⑧ One pair of sides of a rectangle point in the same direction (Fig. 11.3). We say they are **parallel** to each other. Are the other two sides parallel to each other?

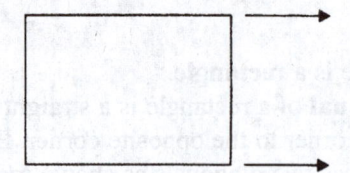

Fig. 11.3

⑨ Fold a rectangular sheet of paper so that opposite sides meet. Unfold the paper as in Fig. 11.4.

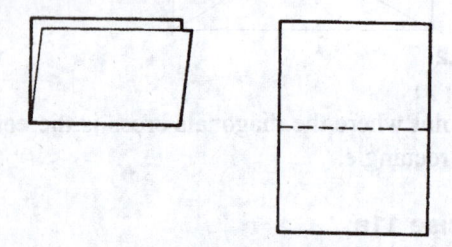

Fig. 11.4

The line of the fold divides the rectangle into two matching halves. This fold is a **line of symmetry** of the rectangle.
 a Does the rectangle have another line of symmetry? If so, fold the paper another way so that both halves match.
 b How many lines of symmetry has a rectangle?

☞ *Optional:* Do Exercise 24 of your Students' Practice Book.

Squares

A **square** is a rectangle in which all the sides are the same length.

Exercise 11b

① Make a square by folding and cutting a rectangular sheet of paper as shown in Fig. 11.5.

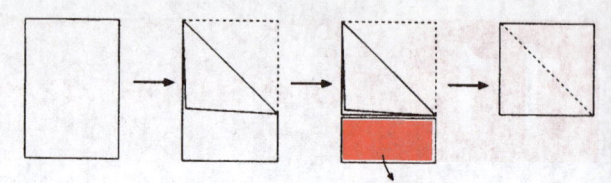

Fig. 11.5

② Name as many things as you can which have square shapes.
③ Measure the lengths of the diagonals of a square. What do you notice?
④ At the centre, where the diagonals meet, there are four angles. What kind of angles are they?
⑤ Each diagonal meets the corner of a square and makes two angles (Fig. 11.6). Measure these angles. What do you notice?

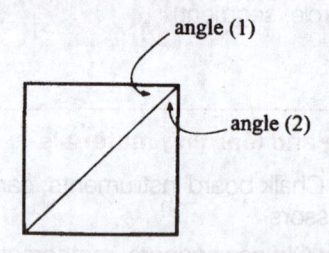

angle (1)
angle (2)

Fig. 11.6

⑥ How many lines of symmetry has a square? Check by folding.
⑦ Write down three properties of both a square and a rectangle.
⑧ Write down three differences between a square and a rectangle.

11-2 Triangles

Tri-angle means three angles. A **triangle** has three sides and three angles. There are many different kinds of triangle (Fig. 11.7).

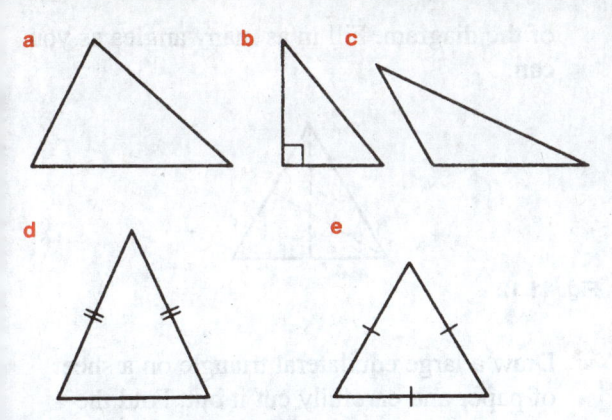

Fig. 11.7 a Scalene triangle
b Right-angled triangle
c Obtuse-angled triangle
d Isosceles triangle
e Equilateral triangle

A **scalene** triangle is a triangle in which all three sides are of different lengths. A **right-angled** triangle contains one right angle. Similarly, an **obtuse-angled** triangle contains one obtuse angle. *Iso-sceles* means same legs; an **isosceles** triangle has two sides equal in length. *Equilateral* means equal sides; an **equilateral** triangle has sides all of the same length.

☞ *Optional:* Do Exercise 25 of your Students' Practice Book.

Isosceles triangle

Exercise 11c

1. Make an isosceles triangle by folding and cutting a sheet of paper as shown in Fig. 11.8.

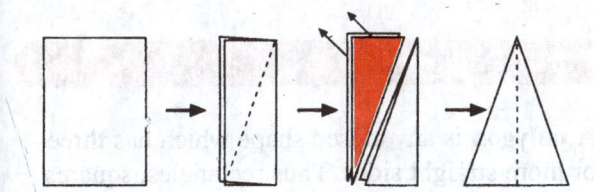

Fig. 11.8

2. Place a model pyramid on your paper so that a triangular face is touching the paper. Draw round this face. Measure the sides of the triangle you have drawn. Have you drawn an isosceles triangle?

3. Measure all three angles of any isosceles triangle you have drawn or made. What do you notice?

4. The folding and cutting method (question 1 above) shows that an isosceles triangle has at least one line of symmetry. In Fig. 11.9, the line of symmetry is the line CM.

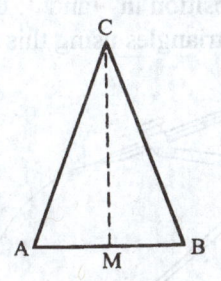

Fig. 11.9

a On *your* triangle, measure the following: $A\hat{C}M$, $B\hat{C}M$, $A\hat{M}C$, $B\hat{M}C$, $C\hat{A}B$, $C\hat{B}A$. What do you notice?
b Also measure the following: AM, BM. What do you notice?
c Does an isosceles triangle normally have any more lines of symmetry?

5. In Fig. 11.10, △ACB is isosceles, CM is the line of symmetry. $A\hat{C}M = 20°$ and BM = 4 cm. Make a sketch of the diagram. Fill in as many other angles and lengths as you can.

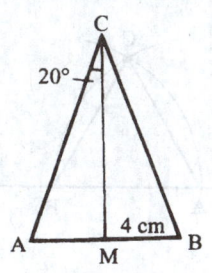

Fig. 11.10

6. Why do you think that the triangle in question 5 is named △ACB and not △ABC?

87

Equilateral triangle

Exercise 11d

1. Fig. 11.11 shows a quick way of drawing an equilateral triangle using ruler and compasses.

   Note that the compasses are kept open at the same position in **a** and **b**. Draw some equilateral triangles using this method.

   a

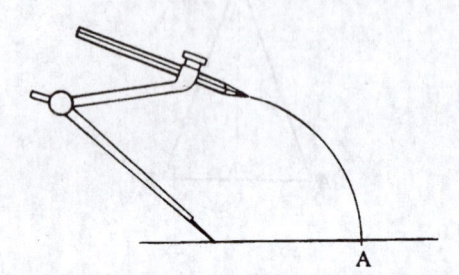

   b

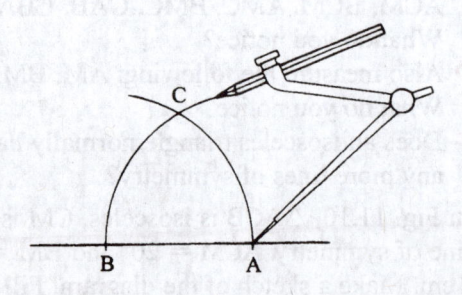

   c

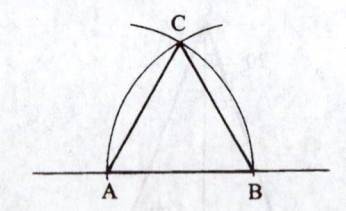

   Fig. 11.11

2. Measure all three angles of an equilateral triangle you have drawn. What do you notice?

3. Write down three differences between an equilateral triangle and an isosceles triangle.

4. Fig. 11.12 shows an equilateral triangle and two of its lines of symmetry. Make a sketch of the diagram. Fill in as many angles as you can.

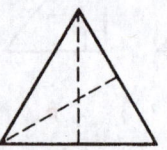

   Fig. 11.12

5. Draw a large equilateral triangle on a sheet of paper and carefully cut it out. Fold the triangle to find its lines of symmetry.
   a How many lines of symmetry has an equilateral triangle?
   b What do you notice about the lines of symmetry?

6. How many equilateral triangles can you see in each of the diagrams in Fig. 11.13?

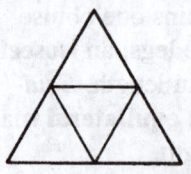

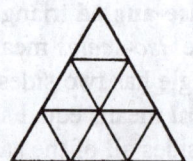

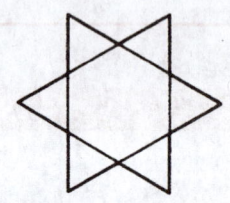

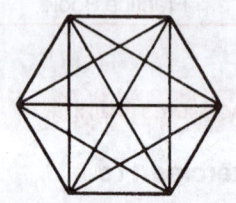

   Fig. 11.13

11-3 Polygons

A **polygon** is any closed shape which has three or more straight sides. Thus rectangles, squares and triangles are all polygons.

Regular polygons

A **regular polygon** is a polygon in which the sides are all equal in length and the angles are all equal to each other. Thus the equilateral triangle and square are regular polygons. Fig. 11.14 shows five regular polygons which you will find in your mathematics course.

☞ *Optional:* Do Exercise 26 of your Students' Practice Book.

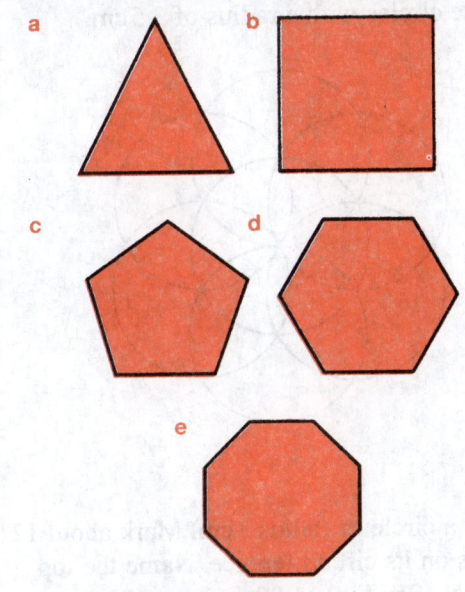

Fig. 11.14 a Equilateral triangle
b Square
c Regular pentagon
d Regular hexagon
e Regular octagon

Quadrilaterals

Quadri-lateral means four-sided. A **quadrilateral** is a polygon with four sides. The rectangle and square are both quadrilaterals. There are many other quadrilaterals which have special names. You will find two of these in Chapters 13 and 14, the **parallelogram** and the **trapezium**.

A parallelogram has two pairs of parallel sides. A trapezium has one pair of parallel sides. In Fig. 11.15, the arrowheads show which sides are parallel.

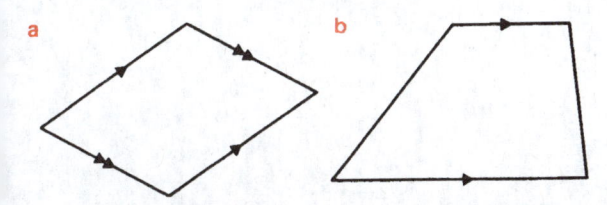

Fig. 11.15 a Parallelogram
b Trapezium

11-4 Circles

The **circle** is a very common and important shape. It is the shape of the floor of a round house. Most wheels are circular.

It is nearly impossible to draw a good circle without help. Fig. 11.16 shows some ways of drawing a circle.

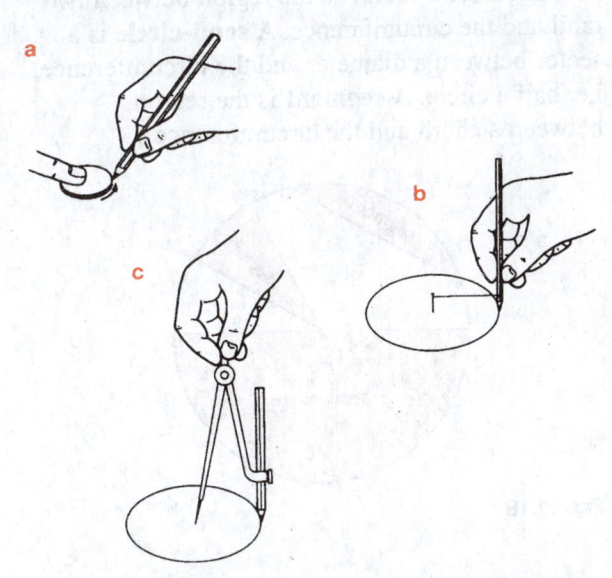

Fig. 11.16 a Drawing round a circular object such as a coin
b Using string
c Using compasses

The parts of a circle

The **centre** is the point at the middle of a circle.

Lines
In Fig. 11.17, the **circumference** is the curved outer boundary of the circle. An **arc** is a curved part of the circumference. A **radius** is any straight line joining the centre to the circumference. The plural of radius is **radii**. A **chord** is any straight line joining two points on the circumference. A **diameter** is any chord which goes through the centre of the circle.

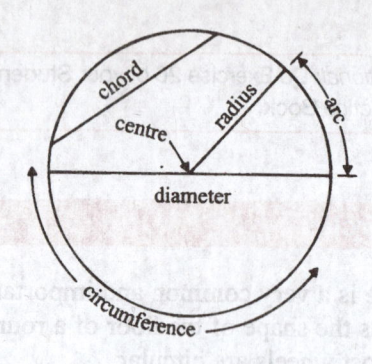

Fig. 11.17

Regions

In Fig. 11.18, a **sector** is the region between two radii and the circumference. A **semi-circle** is a sector between a diameter and the circumference, i.e. half a circle. A **segment** is the region between a chord and the circumference.

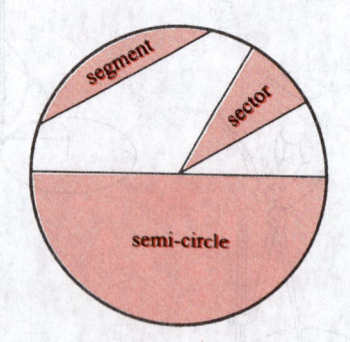

Fig. 11.18

☞ *Optional:* Do Exercise 27 of your Students' Practice Book.

Exercise 11e

Questions 3, 4 and 5 give practice in using compasses.

① Draw a circle and include the following parts on it: two radii, a sector, a chord, a segment, a diameter, an arc. Label each part and shade any regions.

② Draw a circle on a piece of paper. Cut out the circle carefully. Check, by folding, to see whether a circle has any lines of symmetry. How many lines of symmetry does a circle have? (Be careful with your answer.)

③ Draw three circles, with radii 3 cm, 4 cm and 5 cm, so that each circle has the same centre.

④ Draw the pattern shown in Fig. 11.19. Draw all the circles with a radius of 3·5 cm.

Fig. 11.19

⑤ Draw a circle of radius 3 cm. Mark about 12 points on its circumference. Name the top point P. (See Fig. 11.20 and page 31 in your Students' Practice Book.)

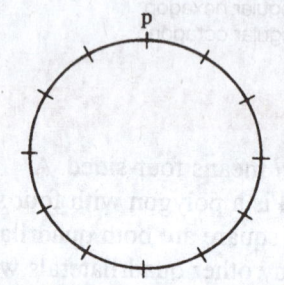

Fig. 11.20

Draw a circle with one of the other points as centre so that the circumference goes through P. Repeat this for every point you draw on the original circle. What shape does your finished pattern look like?

90

SUMMARY

1. A *polygon* is a closed shape with three or more straight sides. A *regular polygon* has sides of equal length and angles of equal size.

2. A *triangle* is a polygon with three sides and three angles. Triangles have special names according to their properties:

   a *scalene triangle* has three sides of different lengths,

   a *right-angled triangle* has an angle of 90°,

   an *isosceles triangle* has two sides of equal length (and therefore two equal angles),

   an *equilateral triangle* has all sides the same length and three angles of 60°.

3. A *quadrilateral* is a four-sided polygon. There are many kinds of quadrilaterals, including *parallelograms*, *trapeziums*, *rectangles* and *squares*.

4. A *rectangle* is a quadrilateral with four right angles.

5. A *square* is a special rectangle, with all four sides equal.

6. A *diagonal* of a rectangle joins a corner to the opposite corner. The diagonals of a rectangle cross at its centre.

7. A *line of symmetry* divides a shape into two matching halves.

8. Figs. 11.17 and 11.18 give the names of the lines and regions of a *circle*.

PUZZLE CORNER

Dots and Squares

Make a sheet of dotty paper

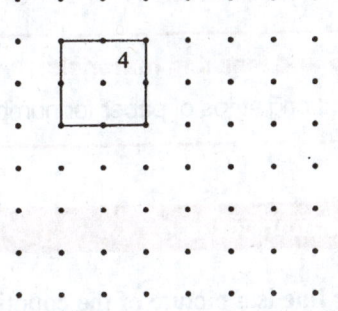

Draw squares of exactly 1, 2, 5, 8, 9, 10, 13, 16, 17 and 18 square units on your dotty paper. Label each square as shown.

PUZZLE CORNER

Who's Who?

There are three friends. Amina is older than the one with the red dress, but younger than the doctor.

Olanna is younger than the one with the yellow dress, while Chiamaka is older than the one with the green dress. The teacher is younger then the lawyer.

Give the colour of dress and profession of each friend from youngest to oldest.

12 Directed numbers: Addition and subtraction

OBJECTIVES

You should be able to:

1. Draw and use a number line to represent directed numbers (positive and negative numbers)
2. Interpret and relate positive and negative numbers to everyday activities
3. Arrange directed numbers in order of size
4. Add and subtract positive and negative numbers, using the number line.

Teaching and learning materials

Teacher: Long strips of paper for number lines

12-1 The number line

A **number line** is a picture of the counting numbers. Fig. 12.1 shows a number line. It starts at 0 (zero) and increases in equal steps to the right.

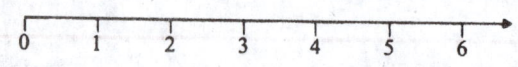

Fig. 12.1

The number line can be used to show addition and subtraction.

Example 1

Use the number line to complete $1 + 4 = \square$.

Fig. 12.2 shows the addition.

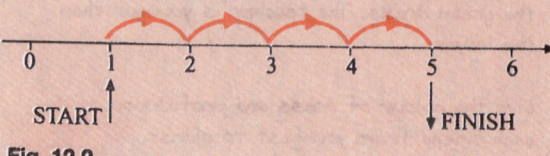

Fig. 12.2

Follow the arrows. Start at 1. Move four places to the *right*. Finish at 5.
$$1 + 4 = 5$$

Example 2

Use the number line to complete $6 - 2 = \square$.

Fig. 12.3 shows the subtraction.

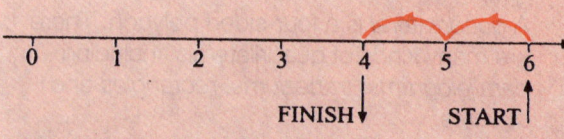

Fig. 12.3

Follow the arrows. Start at 6. Move two places to the *left*. Finish at 4.
$$6 - 2 = 4$$

Exercise 12a

1. Sketch a number line as given in Fig. 12.4.

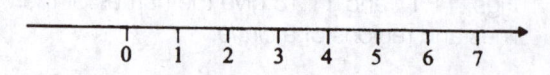

Fig. 12.4

2. Use your number line to complete the following additions.
   a $1 + 5 = \square$ b $2 + 4 = \square$
   c $4 + 2 = \square$ d $3 + 1 = \square$
   e $4 + 3 = \square$ f $2 + 5 = \square$

3. Use your number line to complete the following pattern.
   $5 - 2 = \square$
   $5 - 3 = \square$
   $5 - 4 = \square$
   $5 - 5 = \square$
   $5 - 6 = \square$

5 − 7 = ☐
5 − 8 = ☐

4 Were you able to complete the last three rows of the pattern in question 3? (If not, read the next section carefully.)

Positive and negative numbers

Fig. 12.5 shows the subtraction 5 − 6 on the number line.

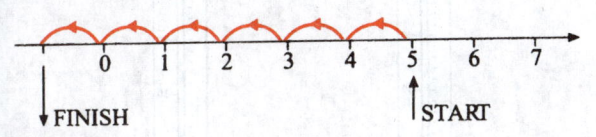

↓ FINISH   ↑ START

Fig. 12.5

In Fig. 12.5, the finishing point is 1 unit to the *left* of 0. We could say,

$$5 - 6 = 1L$$
i.e. 5 − 6 = 1 unit to the left of 0.
Similarly, 5 − 7 = 2L
5 − 8 = 3L

In practice, we say that numbers to the left of 0 are **negative numbers** and numbers to the right of 0 are **positive numbers**. There are many different symbols for positive and negative numbers. For example, **positive five** can be written $+5$, $(+5)$, $^{+}5$ or $\overset{+}{5}$ and **negative three** can be written -3, (-3), $^{-}3$, $\overline{3}$. Fig. 12.6 shows how to write positive and negative numbers on the number line.

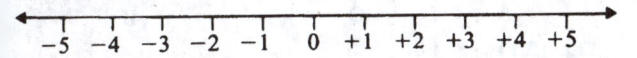

Fig. 12.6

The number line extends in two directions from 0: to the right for positive numbers, to the left for negative numbers.

Exercise 12b (Oral/QR)

1 Fig. 12.7 is a picture of a football team.

Fig. 12.7

The captain, Olu, sits in the middle.

Isa is two places to the *right* of Olu. We can say his position is (+2).

Joe is five places to the *left* of Olu. We can say his position is (−5).

a Use this method to give the position of the following.
  i Mbu   **ii** Ali
  iii Ojo   **iv** Iya
b Name the players in the following positions.
  i (+4)   **ii** (−4)
  iii (−3)   **iv** (+1)
  v 0

2 A line is marked off in metres as shown in Fig. 12.8.

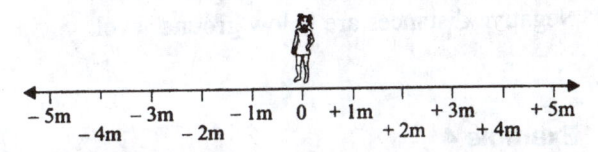

Fig. 12.8

A girl moves to the right and left along the line. Find her final position if she starts at 0 and moves as follows.

a 2 m to the right
b 5 m to the left
c 3 m to the right, then 1 m to the right
d 5 m to the right, then 2 m to the left
e 4 m to the right, then 7 m to the left
f 2 m to the left, then 2 m to the left
g 5 m to the left, then 4 m to the right
h 3 m to the left, then 8 m to the right
i 3 m to the right, then 3 m to the left
j 2 m to the left, then 3 m to the right.

Positive and negative numbers in daily life

Consider the following examples.

Example 3

Fig. 12.9 shows a man tapping a palm tree and a man digging a well.

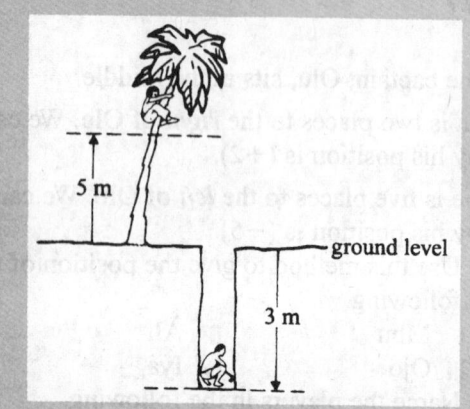

Fig. 12.9

The tapper is 5 m *above* ground level.
The digger is 3 m *below* ground level.
We can say that their distances from ground level are +5 m and −3 m.
Positive distances are above ground level.
Negative distances are below ground level.

Example 4

Fig. 12.10 shows the readings on two thermometers a) and b).
Thermometer **a)** shows the shade temperature on a March day.
It reads 26°C.
Thermometer **b)** shows the temperature inside a refrigerator.
It reads 3°C *below* 0, i.e. −3°C.

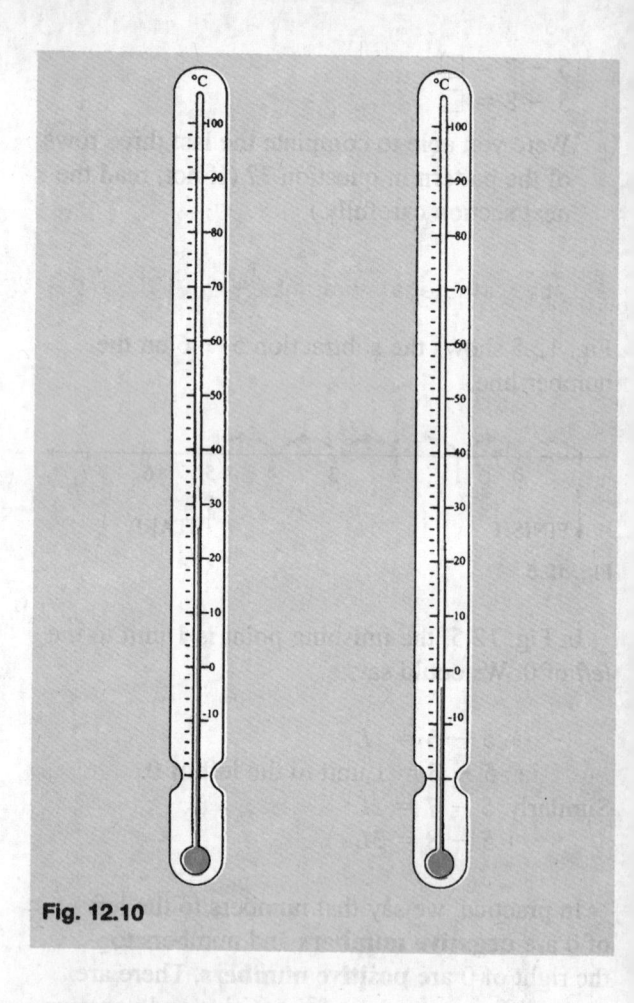

Fig. 12.10

Example 5

A path runs east-west. O is a point on the path as shown in Fig. 12.11.

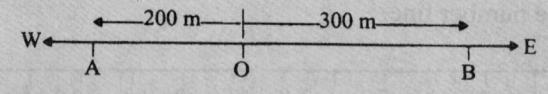

Fig. 12.11

Point A is 200 m west of O. Point B is 300 m east of O. If we take distances east of O to be positive, then the position of A is −200 m and the position of B is +300 m.

94

Example 6

When an important event is due to take place, the time it is due to start is often called 'zero hour'. Times before zero hour are negative. Times after zero hour are positive.

For example, a President may decide to broadcast to the nation at 3 pm one day. 3 pm is zero hour. On that day, the President may have lunch with his Ministers at 1 pm. We say that he has lunch at −2 hours. He may finish his speech at 4 pm. He finishes his speech at +1 hour.

Examples 3, 4, 5 and 6 show that we sometimes have to use terms like *above, below, after, before* to describe quantities such as distances, temperature and time. In these cases we can also describe the quantities by using positive and negative numbers.

Exercise 12c

1. A bird is at the top of a tree 7 m above the surface of a river. A fish swims 2 m below the surface of the river.
   a Give the positions of the bird and the fish as distances from the surface of the river.
   b How far is the fish below the bird?

2. A map shows that the top of a hill is 200 m above sea-level and the bottom of a lagoon is 15 m below sea-level.
   a Express these distances as distances from sea-level.
   b What is the difference between the two heights?

3. The temperature inside a freezer is −3 °C. The temperature falls by a further 12 °C. What is the new temperature?

4. What is the difference between temperatures of 12 °C and −10 °C?

5. A straight road runs east-west through a point O. Distances east of O are positive. Distances west of O are negative.
   a Express the positions of the following points in terms of positive or negative distances.
      i   P is 8 km west of O
      ii Q is 9 km east of O
      iii R is 15 km east of O
      iv T is 11 km west of O
   b From the above data, find the distance between the following pairs of points.
      i   P and Q   ii Q and R
      iii R and T   iv P and T

6. A straight road runs north-south through a point X. Distances north of X are positive. Distances south of X are negative.
   a Express the positions of the following points as positive or negative distances.
      i   A is 330 m north of X
      ii B is 60 m south of X
      iii C is 52 m north of X
      iv D is 128 m south of X
   b From the above data find the distance between these points.
      i   A and B   ii B and C
      iii C and D   iv A and D

7. Zero hour for a meeting is midday (12 noon). Express the following as positive or negative times.
   a 5 h before zero hour
   b 7 h after zero hour
   c $1\frac{1}{2}$ h after zero hour
   d 45 min before zero hour
   e 3 pm   f 10 am
   g 9 pm   h 8.30 am
   i 4.45 pm

8. A girl arrives at school 10 minutes early. Another girl is 3 minutes late. How long has the first girl been at school before the second girl arrives?

9. A man was born 5 years before Independence. His first son was born 19 years after Independence. How old was the man when his son was born?

10. A watch is 9 minutes fast. A clock is 6 minutes slow. A radio announcer says, 'The time is now 11.30 am.' What times do the watch and clock show?

11. The top of an oil drill is 10 m above ground level. The drill is 220 m long. What is the

distance of the bottom of the drill from ground level?

12. Two pieces of wood should be the same length. One is 5 mm too long. The other is 3 mm too short. What is the difference in the lengths of the two pieces of wood?

13. Meat at a temperature of 22 °C is put in a freezer. The freezer cools the meat down by 34 °C. What is the temperature of the frozen meat?

14. A traveller arrives at an airport $1\frac{1}{2}$ hours before her plane is due to take off. The plane takes off $\frac{3}{4}$ hour late. How long does she wait altogether?

15. On Thursday evening, Sola has ₦1 900. Fani has no money and owes ₦600 to Sola. We can say that Fani has ₦(−600). On Friday they each get paid ₦6 400. If Fani repays his debt to Sola, how much money does each have?

16. Maria owes Fatima ₦180, but she has only ₦40. What is the most she can pay back? If Maria pays this back, express her remaining debt as a negative sum of money.

17. A man has ₦1 700. His sister has ₦(−800).
    a How much does the sister owe?
    b By how much is the man better off?

18. A man borrows ₦950 000 to buy a car. We can say that he has ₦(−950 000). In the first year he pays back ₦97 500. Express his remaining debt as a negative number of naira.

12-2 Directed numbers

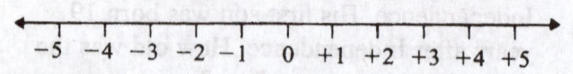

Fig. 12.12

Positive numbers and negative numbers are called **directed numbers**. The sign tells which *direction* to go from zero to reach the position of the number. Zero is neither positive nor negative. As we move to the right along the number line, the numbers increase. As we move to the left, the numbers decrease (Fig. 12.13).

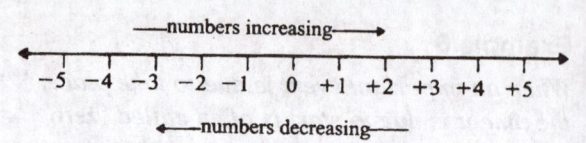

Fig. 12.13

Thus $+2 > -4$, i.e. 12 **is greater than** -4 and $-5, +1$, i.e. 25 **is less than** $+1$.

Exercise 12d (Oral/QR)
Make a number line from -20 to $+20$ by marking a long strip of paper. Use the number line in this exercise.

1. Which is the greatest number in each of the following?
   a $+5, -7, +12, -2, -19, +6$
   b $-3, -2, +2, +5, -8, -10$
   c $-3, -12, -13, -8, -5, -7$
   d $+3, -3, +8, -8, +15, -15$
   e $+4, 0, -4, -8, -12, -16$
   f $-3, -5, 0, -18, -14, -1$

2. [QR] For each of the following write out the complete line. The first line is complete.

	start	move	finish
a	+2	5 units to the left	−3
b	+5	7 units to the left	
c	−1	7 units to the left	
d	+2	4 units to the right	
e	−3	5 units to the right	
f	−10	10 units to the right	
g	+12	9 units to the left	
h	+14	30 units to the left	
i	−20	28 units to the right	
j	+1	2 units to the left	
k	+2		−4
l	+5		+3
m	+6		−6
n	−2		0
o	−15		+15
p	+15		−15
q	−11		+13
r	+12		−2
s	+10		+6
t	+10		−17
u		2 units to the right	+5
v		8 units to the left	+2
w		10 units to the left	−4

x	☐	35 units to the right	+20
y	☐	11 units to the right	+7
z	☐	13 units to the left	−5

3 Arrange the following in order from least to greatest.
a   −3, 0, −2, +1, −8, +5
b   +5, −2, +9, +7, −5, −4
c   +6, −8, −20, +5, −14, 0
d   −6, +6, −18, +18, −11, +11
e   −1, 0, −5, −3, −14, −10
f   −9, −11, +1, −10, +17, +16

4 Place either > (is greater than) or, (is less than) between each of the two numbers to make each a true statement. The first one has been done.
a   −9 < +3   b   −15 ☐ +8
c   +4 ☐ +3   d   +18 ☐ +1
e   −18 ☐ −1   f   0 ☐ −2
g   −1 ☐ +1   h   −7 ☐ −17
i   −13 ☐ +13   j   0 ☐ −4
k   +5 ☐ −5   l   −9 ☐ 0

12-3 Adding and subtracting positive numbers

Addition

The addition 2 + 3 = 5 can be written in directed numbers as: (+2) + (+3) = +5. We can show this addition on the number line in Fig. 12.14. Follow the arrows from start to finish.

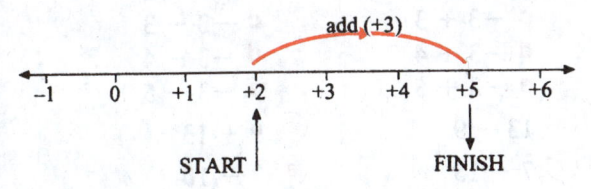

Fig. 12.14

Similarly, we can find the value of −2 + 6. In directed numbers this is: (−2) 1 (+6). Follow the arrows on the number line in Fig. 12.15 from start to finish.

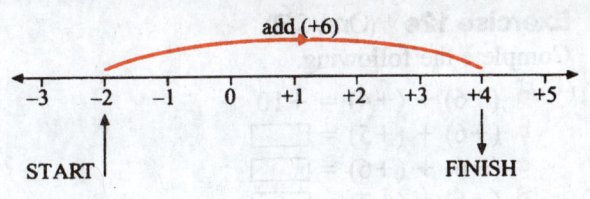

Fig. 12.15

Thus: −2 + 6 = +4.

To add a positive number: move that number of places to the right on the number line.

Subtraction

The subtraction 4 − 3 = 1 can be written in directed numbers as: (+4) − (+3) = +1. We can show this subtraction on the number line in Fig. 12.16. Follow the arrows from start to finish.

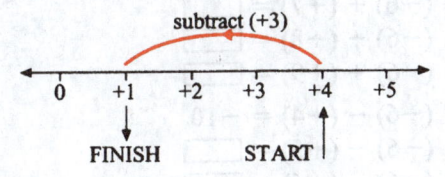

Fig. 12.16

Similarly, we can find the value of 3 − 7. In directed numbers this is: (+3) − (+7). Follow the arrows on the number line in Fig. 12.17 from start to finish.

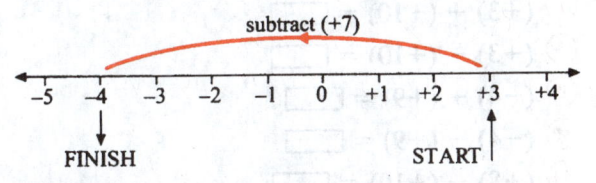

Fig. 12.17

Thus: 3 − 7 = −4.

To subtract a positive number: move that number of places to the left on the number line.

☞ *Optional*: Do Exercise 28 of your Students' Practice Book.

Exercise 12e (Oral/QR)
Complete the following.

1. a $(+6) + (+4) = +10$
   b $(+6) + (+5) =$ ☐
   c $(+6) + (+6) =$ ☐
   d $(+6) + (+7) =$ ☐
   e $(+6) + (+8) =$ ☐
   f $(+6) + (+9) =$ ☐

2. a $(+6) - (+4) = +2$
   b $(+6) - (+5) =$ ☐
   c $(+6) - (+6) =$ ☐
   d $(+6) - (+7) =$ ☐
   e $(+6) - (+8) =$ ☐
   f $(+6) - (+9) =$ ☐

3. a $(-6) + (+4) = -2$
   b $(-6) + (+5) =$ ☐
   c $(-6) + (+6) =$ ☐
   d $(-6) + (+7) =$ ☐
   e $(-6) + (+8) =$ ☐
   f $(-6) + (+9) =$ ☐

4. a $(-6) - (+4) = -10$
   b $(-6) - (+5) =$ ☐
   c $(-6) - (+6) =$ ☐
   d $(-6) - (+7) =$ ☐
   e $(-6) - (+8) =$ ☐
   f $(-6) - (+9) =$ ☐

5. $(+14) + (+5) =$ ☐
6. $(+14) - (+5) =$ ☐
7. $(+3) + (+10) =$ ☐
8. $(+3) - (+10) =$ ☐
9. $(-4) + (+9) =$ ☐
10. $(-4) - (+9) =$ ☐
11. $(+8) - (+10) =$ ☐
12. $(-8) + (+10) =$ ☐
13. $(+8) + (+10) =$ ☐
14. $(-8) - (+10) =$ ☐
15. $(-5) + (+5) =$ ☐
16. $(+11) - (+11) =$ ☐
17. $(-3) + (+5) - (+8) =$ ☐
19. $(+6) - (+9) + (+12) =$ ☐
18. $(+12) - (+5) - (+10) =$ ☐
20. $(-6) - (+7) + (+14) =$ ☐

In many cases, brackets are not given. If a number is not directed, take it to be positive.

Example 7
Simplify $-3 - 9 + 14$.
$$-3 - 9 + 14 = 0 - 3 - 9 + 14$$
$$= 0 - (+3) - (+9) + (+14)$$

This is shown on the number line in Fig. 12.18.

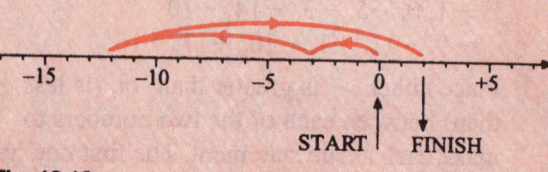

Fig. 12.18

$$0 - (+3) - (+9) + (+14) = 2$$
or $\quad -3 - 9 + 14 \quad = 2$

In practice there is no need to start at zero. The sign in front of the first number shows you where to start.

Exercise 12f (Oral/QR)
Simplify the following.

1. a $3 + 1$
   b $3 + 2$
   c $3 + 3$
   d $3 + 4$
   e $3 + 5$

2. a $3 - 1$
   b $3 - 2$
   c $3 - 3$
   d $3 - 4$
   e $3 - 5$

3. a $-3 + 1$
   b $-3 + 2$
   c $-3 + 3$
   d $-3 + 4$
   e $-3 + 5$

4. a $-3 - 1$
   b $-3 - 2$
   c $-3 - 3$
   d $-3 - 4$
   e $-3 - 5$

5. $13 - 9$
6. $9 - 13$
7. $7 - 15$
8. $3 - 10$
9. $-3 - 7$
10. $11 - 4$
11. $-1 - 8$
12. $12 - 17$
13. $19 - 12$
14. $-4 - 7$
15. $-8 + 7$
16. $-4 + 12$
17. $12 - 6 - 4$
18. $3 - 11 + 2$
19. $-3 - 4 + 10$
20. $-4 + 9 - 7$

Notice that:
a +7 − 4 = +3   a +4 − 7 = −3
c +7 + 4 = +11   d −7 − 4 = −11

In **a** and **b**, the two signs are different. Disregard signs and take the smaller number from the larger. Then:
a if the larger number has a + sign before it, the result is positive;
b if the larger number has a − sign before it, the result is negative.

In **c** and **d**, the two signs are the same. Disregard the signs and add the two numbers. Then:
c if both signs are +, the result is positive;
d if both signs are −, the result is negative.

This helps to simplify directed numbers without using the number line.

Exercise 12g
Simplify the following. Try not to use the number line.

1. 19 − 11
2. 12 − 17
3. −5 − 8
4. 18 − 27
5. 31 − 32
6. −11 − 19
7. −13 − 21
8. 33 − 18
9. 43 − 51
10. 29 − 53
11. −17 − 26
12. 27 − 64
13. −33 − 12
14. −47 − 75
15. 81 − 107
16. 121 − 87
17. 92 − 155
18. 137 − 173
19. 145 − 219
20. 78 − 252

12-4 Adding and subtracting negative numbers

Addition

When adding numbers, it does not matter in which order the numbers are added. For example,
  3 + 5 = 5 + 3 = 8
Consider the addition (+6) + (−2).
  (+6) + (−2)   = (−2) + (+6)
But (−2) + (+6) = +4 (see page 97)
Thus: (+6) + (−2) = +4

On the number line in Fig. 12.19 we know that we start at +6 and finish at +4. The only way this can happen is if we move 2 places to the *left*.

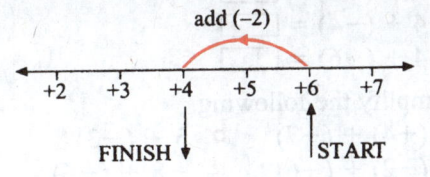

Fig. 12.19

To add a negative number: move that number of places to the left on the number line.

Notice that to add a negative number is equivalent to subtracting a positive number of the same value, for example, see Fig. 12.20.

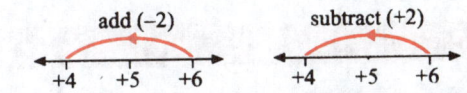

Fig. 12.20

Example 8
Simplify the following.
a 2 + (−5)   b −3 + (−3)

a 2 + (−5) = (+2) + (−5) = (+2) − (+5)
            = −3

b −3 + (−3) = (−3) + (−3) = (−3) − (+3)
             = −6

Exercise 12h (Oral/QR)

1. Complete the following number patterns.
   a (+3) + (+2) = +5
      (+3) + (+1) = ☐
      (+3) + 0   = ☐
      (+3) + (−1) = ☐
      (+3) + (−2) = ☐
      (+3) + (−3) = ☐
   b (−1) + (+1) = 0
      (−1) + 0   = ☐
      (−1) + (−1) = ☐
      (−1) + (−2) = ☐
      (−1) + (−3) = ☐
      (−1) + (−4) = ☐

c 4 + (+4) = +8
   4 + (+2) = ☐
   4 + 0   = ☐
   4 + (−2) = ☐
   4 + (−4) = ☐
   4 + (−6) = ☐

② Simplify the following.
a (+4) + (−7)   b 5 + (−3)
c (−2) + (−6)   d −8 + (−6)
e 20 + (−20)   f (+13) + (−10)
g (−9) + (−9)   h −18 + (−3)
i 0 + (−5)   j 60 + (−40)
k (−12) + (−8)   l 43 + (−23)
m −25 + (−14)   n 100 + (−144)
o −51 + (238)   p 16 + (−9) − (+10)
q −3 + 14 + (−5)

Subtraction

Consider the subtraction 5 − 3. One way of doing this is to say, 'What do we add to 3 to get 5?' Since 3 + 2 = 5, then 5 − 3 = 2.
Now consider the subtraction 5 − (−3). 'What do we add to −3 to get 5?' From earlier work on the number line we know that −3 + 8 = 5. Thus: 5 − (−3) = 8

This can be shown on the number line as in Fig. 12.21. START at +5 and FINISH at +8. The only way this can happen is if we move 3 places to the *right*.

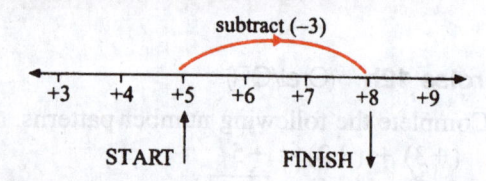

Fig. 12.21

To subtract a negative number: move that number of places to the right on the number line.
Notice that to subtract a negative number is equivalent to adding a positive number of the same value; for example, see Fig. 12.22. This result is so unusual that it is quite easy to remember.

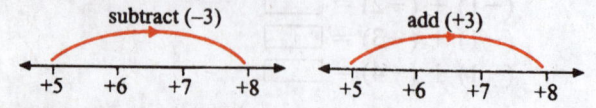

Fig. 12.22

☞ *Optional*: Do Exercise 29 of your Students' Practice Book.

Exercise 12i (Oral/QR)

① Complete the following number patterns.
a 5 − (+2) = +3
   5 − (+1) = ☐
   5 − 0   = ☐
   5 − (−1) = ☐
   5 − (−2) = ☐
b (−3) − (+3) = −6
  (−3) − (+2) = ☐
  (−3) − (+1) = ☐
  (−3) − 0   = ☐
  (−3) − (−1) = ☐
c −2 − (+1) = −3
  −2 − 0   = ☐
  −2 − (−1) = ☐
  −2 − (−2) = ☐
  −2 − (−3) = ☐

② Simplify the following.
a 8 − (−3)   b (−8) − (−3)
c (+3) − (−8)   d (−3) − (−8)
e (+9) − (−9)   f (−4) − (−4)
g (+6) − (−1)   h (−1) − (−2)
i −7 − (−6)   j −30 − (−80)
k 20 − (−10)   l −40 − (−60)
m −41 − (−26)   n −59 − (−37)
o 76 − (−74)   p 7 − (−8) + (−5)
q −3 − (−21) − 18

Exercise 12j (Practice)

① Which is greater?
a −3 or 4   b −4 or −7
c −5 or 3   d 0 or −5
e 2 or −15   f −7 or −10

② The temperature during the day in a cold country is 9 °C. At night the temperature falls by 13 °C. What is the night temperature?

③ Abudu and Baba have no money, but Abudu owes ₦450 to Baba. When Friday comes they both get the same wages. Abudu repays his debt to Baba. Baba now has more money than Abudu. How much more?

4 What must be added to:
a 3 to make 8
b −1 to make 2
c 16 to make 4
d 3 to make −8
e −35 to make −27
f 26 to make −4?

5 What must be subtracted from:
a 12 to make 8
b 6 to make −10
c −2 to make −7
d 8 to make 12
e −3 to make 4
f −10 to make −3?

6 A woman has ₦23 467 in her bank account. She writes a cheque for ₦39 500. How much will she be overdrawn?

7 In the year AD 45 a man was 63 years old. In what year was he 5 years old?

8 Copy and complete the tables in Fig. 12.23.
For example, in
a $(-1) + (+3) = +2$
enter +2 across from −1 and under +3.
b $(-1) - (+3) = -4$
enter −4 across from −1 and under +3.

9 Simplify the following.
a $-7 - (-16) - 3$
b $1 + (-4) - (-3)$
c $800 - (+500) - (-150)$
d $-50 + (-25) - (+45)$
e $6x - 9x - (-5x)$
f $-4y + 12y - (-10y)$

10 Simplify the following.
a $1\frac{3}{4} - 2\frac{1}{4}$
b $-2.8 + 6.3$
c $4.8 - (-3.9)$
d $-1\frac{1}{2} - (-3\frac{2}{3})$
e $7.2°C - 9.6°C$
f $-5.4°C + 8.6°C$

a

add First	−3	−2	−1	0	+1	+2	+3
−3							
−2							
−1						+2	
0							
+1							
+2							
+3							

(Second across top)

b

subtract First	−3	−2	−1	0	+1	+2	+3
−3							
−2							
−1							−4
0							
+1							
+2							
+3							

(Second across top)

Fig. 12.23

SUMMARY

1 The *number line* can be extended to numbers less than zero.

2 Numbers greater than zero are *positive*. Numbers less than zero are *negative*.

3 *Zero* is neither positive nor negative.

4 Positive and negative numbers are called *directed numbers*.

5 *Add and subtract directed numbers* on a horizontal number line as follows:
a to add a positive number, move to the right;
b to subtract a positive number, move to the left;
c adding a negative number is equivalent to subtracting a positive number (so move to the left);
d subtracting a negative number is equivalent to adding a positive number (so move to the right).

13 Plane shapes 2: Perimeter

OBJECTIVES

You should be able to:

1 Find the perimeter of regular and irregular shapes by direct measurement, using a ruler and thread/string where necessary
2 Derive and apply appropriate formulae to calculate the perimeter of rectangles, squares, parallelograms and circles
3 Find perimeters of shapes made up by combining basic shapes.

Teaching and learning materials

Teacher: Large regular and irregular cardboard shapes; large leaves; flat stones; rulers, tape measures (small, as used by tailors; and large, as used by surveyors); thread or string; tin cans or bottles

Students: Rulers, thread or string; large leaves, flat stones, tin cans or bottles

13-1 Measuring perimeters

Perimeter is the outside boundary or edge of a plane shape. For example, the boundary fence of your school compound is its perimeter. We also use the word *perimeter* to mean *the length of the boundary*. For example, if you take 240 paces to walk your school boundary, you could say its perimeter is 240 paces.

Perimeter of regular and irregular shapes

The simplest way to find a perimeter of any **regular** or **irregular shape** is to measure it directly with a ruler or tape measure. See Examples 1, 2 and 3.

Example 1

Measure the perimeter of the quadrilateral ABCD in Fig. 13.1.

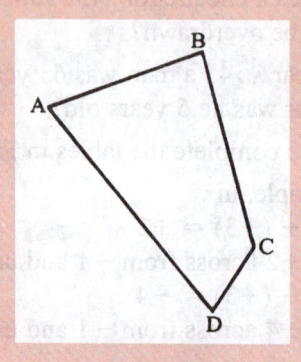

Fig. 13.1

By measurement, AB = 22 mm = 2·2 cm
BC = 27 mm = 2·7 cm
CD = 10 mm = 1·0 cm
DA = 35 mm = 3·5 cm
perimeter (total = 94 mm = 9·4 cm

In Example 1, ABCD is an **irregular** quadrilateral. It is necessary to measure every side, then add. Use this method for any irregular shape: triangles, quadrilaterals, pentagons and so on. Example 2 shows how to shorten the method when the given shape is **regular**.

Example 2

Find, in cm, the perimeter of the regular hexagon ABCDEF in Fig. 13.2.

Length of side AB = 1·6 cm.
There are 6 equal sides, so
  perimeter = 6 × 1·6 cm
       = 9·6 cm

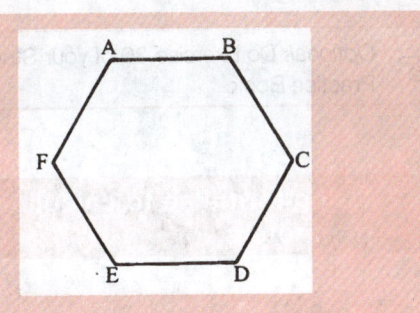

Fig. 13.2

If a shape has a curved side, use a piece of thread to get the shape of the curve. Make the thread straight and measure its length against a ruler.

Example 3

Measure the perimeter of the shape in Fig. 13.3.

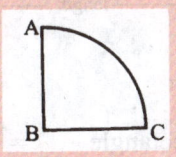

Fig. 13.3

straight edges: AB = 14 mm = 1·4 cm
BC = 14 mm = 1·4 cm
curved edge: CA = 22 mm approximately
= 2·2 cm
perimeter (total = 50 mm approximately
= 5·0 cm

Exercise 13a

① Use a ruler to measure the perimeters of the shapes in Fig. 13.4. Give your answers in cm.

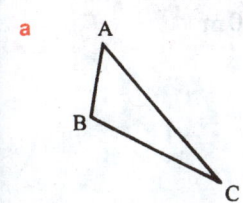

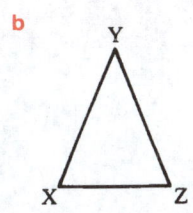

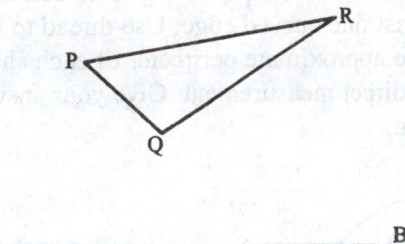

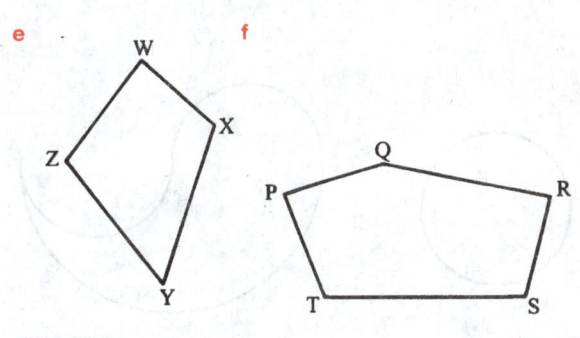

Fig. 13.4

② Each of the shapes in Fig. 13.5 is regular. Find the perimeter of each shape by measuring one side and multiplying by the number of sides. Give your answers in cm.

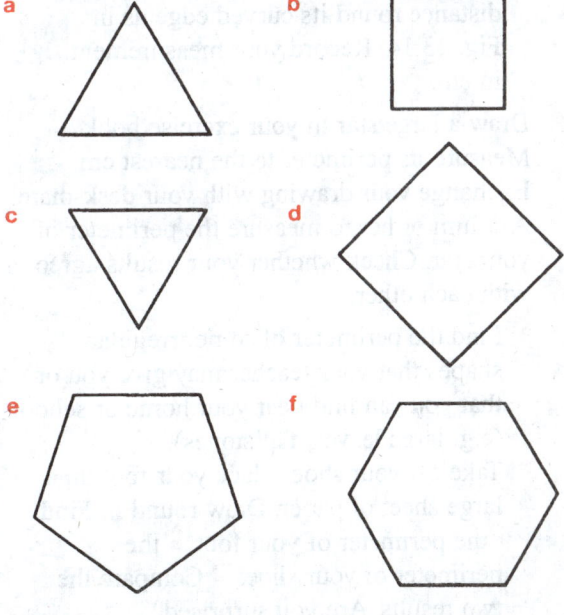

Fig. 13.5

103

3 Each of the shapes in Fig. 13.6 contains at least one curved edge. Use thread to find the approximate perimeter of each shape by indirect measurement. Give your answers in cm.

a   b

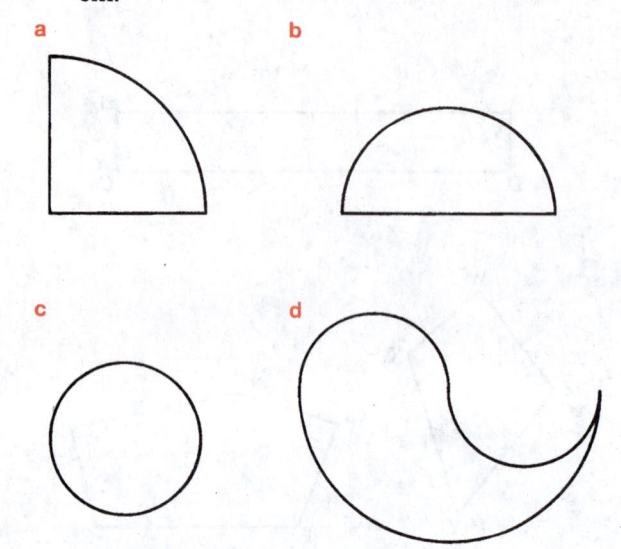

c   d

Fig. 13.6

Class activities

4 a Use a ruler to measure the perimeter of the top of your desk.
 b Place a tin can or a bottle on top of your desk. Using a string and ruler, measure the distance round its curved edge as in Fig. 13.14. Record your measurement in cm.

5 Draw a large star in your exercise book. Measure its perimeter to the nearest cm. Exchange your drawing with your desk-mate. Ask him or her to measure the perimeter of your star. Check whether your results agree with each other.

6 a Find the perimeter of some irregular shapes that your teacher may give you or that you can find near your home or school (e.g. large leaves, flat stones).
 b Take off your shoe. Place your foot on a large sheet of paper. Draw round it. Find **i** the perimeter of your foot, **ii** the perimeter of your shoe. **iii** Compare the two results. Are you surprised?

Optional: Do Exercise 30 of your Students' Practice Book.

13-2 Using formulae to calculate perimeters

Rectangles

We usually call the longer side of a rectangle the **length**, and the shorter side the **breadth**. We use the letters l and b to stand for the length and the breadth.

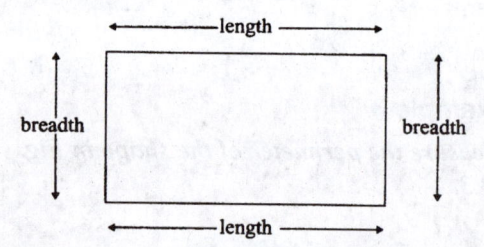

Fig. 13.7

In Fig 13.7:
$$\begin{aligned}\text{perimeter of rectangle} &= l + b + l + b \\ &= (l + b) + (l + b) \\ &= 2 \times (l + b) \\ &= 2(l + b)\end{aligned}$$

This **formula** can be used to calculate the perimeter of a rectangle.

Example 4

Calculate the perimeter of a football field which measures 80 m by 50 m.

$$\begin{aligned}\text{perimeter of field} &= 2(l + b) \\ &= 2 \times (80 + 50)\,\text{m} \\ &= 2 \times 130\,\text{m} \\ &= 260\,\text{m}\end{aligned}$$

Example 5

A rectangular piece of land measures 57 m by 42 m. What is the perimeter of the land?

perimeter of land $= 2(l + b)$
$= 2(57 + 42)$ m
$= 2 \times 99$ m
$= 198$ m

Since perimeter of rectangle $= 2(l + b)$,

length $= \frac{\text{perimeter of rectangle}}{2} -$ breadth.

Also

breadth $= \frac{\text{perimeter of rectangle}}{2} -$ length.

Example 6

A rectangle has a perimeter of 74 m. Find

a the length of the rectangle if its breadth is 17 m,

b the breadth of the rectangle if its length is 25 m.

a length $= \frac{74\,m}{2} - 17$ m
$= 37$ m $- 17$ m
$= 20$ m

b breadth $= \frac{74\,m}{2} - 25$ m
$= 37$ m $- 25$ m
$= 12$ m

Squares

A square is a regular four-sided shape. If the length of one side of a square is l, then,

perimeter of square $= l \times 4$
$= 4l$

As perimeter of square $= 4l$,

length of side of square $= \frac{\text{perimeter of square}}{4}$

Example 7

Calculate the perimeter of a square of side 12·3 cm.

perimeter $= 12\cdot3$ cm $\times 4$
perimeter $= 49\cdot2$ cm

Example 8

A square assembly area has a perimeter of 56 m. Find the length of the side of the assembly area.

length $= \frac{56\,m}{4}$
$= 14$ m

The formulae for perimeters of rectangles and squares can be useful. However, if you find it difficult to remember formulae, always sketch the given shape and work from that.

Parallelograms

The opposite sides of a parallelogram are equal. Fig. 13.8 shows a parallelogram with opposite sides of lengths a and b units.

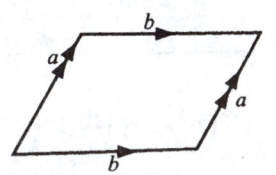

Fig. 13.8

In Fig. 13.8:
perimeter of parallelogram $= 2(a + b)$ units

Example 9

The perimeter of a parallelogram is 54 cm and one of its sides is 16 cm long. Find the lengths of the other three sides.

There are two sides of 16 cm. Let the other two sides be length k cm.

105

Then: $54 = 2(16 + k)$
       $27 = 16 + k$
       $k = 11$

The other three sides are of length 16 cm, 11 cm, 11 cm.
(Check: $16 + 16 + 11 + 11 = 54$)

Exercise 13b

1. Copy and complete the table of rectangles (Table 13.1).

	length	breadth	perimeter
a	3 cm	2 cm	
b	5 m	4 m	
c	16 cm	10 cm	
d	$2\frac{1}{2}$ m	1 m	
e	6 m	$2\frac{1}{2}$ m	
f	$8\frac{1}{2}$ cm	$4\frac{1}{2}$ cm	
g		3·2 cm	16·6 cm
h	4·3 cm		10·2 cm
i	7·35 cm	7·15 cm	
j	9 m	0·9 m	
k	8 m		36 m
l	14 cm		52 cm
m	17 cm		60 cm
n		7·5 m	45 m
o		6 m	33 m

Table 13.1

2. Copy and complete the table of squares (Table 13.2).

	length of side	perimeter
a	6 m	
b	14 cm	
c	$2\frac{1}{4}$ m	
d	8·3 cm	
e	7·25 m	
f	9·6 cm	
g		40 cm
h		360 cm
i		18 m
j		14·4 m
k		52 cm
l		49·2 m

Table 13.2

3. A rectangular field measures 400 m by 550 m. What is the perimeter of the field
   a in metres   b in kilometres?

4. A school compound is made up of a rectangle and a square as in Fig. 13.9. Find the perimeter of the compound.

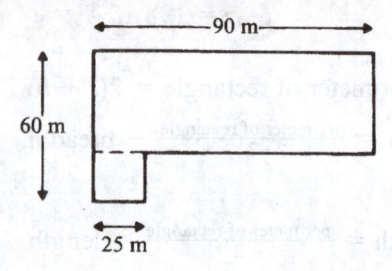

Fig. 13.9

5. A woman fences a 3 m by 4 m rectangular plot to keep her chickens in. The fencing costs ₦200 per metre. How much does it cost to fence the plot?

6. A length of wire is bent to make a square of side 3·2 cm.
   a What is the length of wire in the square?
   b If the wire is silver, costing ₦50 per centimetre, what is the cost of the square?
   c Twenty of these squares are linked together to make a necklace. What does it cost to make the necklace?

7. A rectangle has a perimeter of 60 m. Find the length of the rectangle if its breadth is
   a 10 m   b 5 m   c 12 m.

8. A man has 36 square tiles. Each tile measures 1 m by 1 m. He lays the tiles in the shape of a rectangle as in Fig. 13.10.

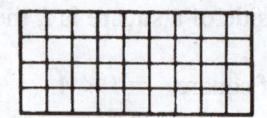

Fig. 13.10

   a Find the length, breadth and perimeter of this rectangle.
   b Use squared paper to show different rectangles the man can make using all 36 tiles. Find the perimeters of these rectangles. What do you notice?

106

9 Find the perimeter of the parallelograms and trapeziums in Fig. 13.11.

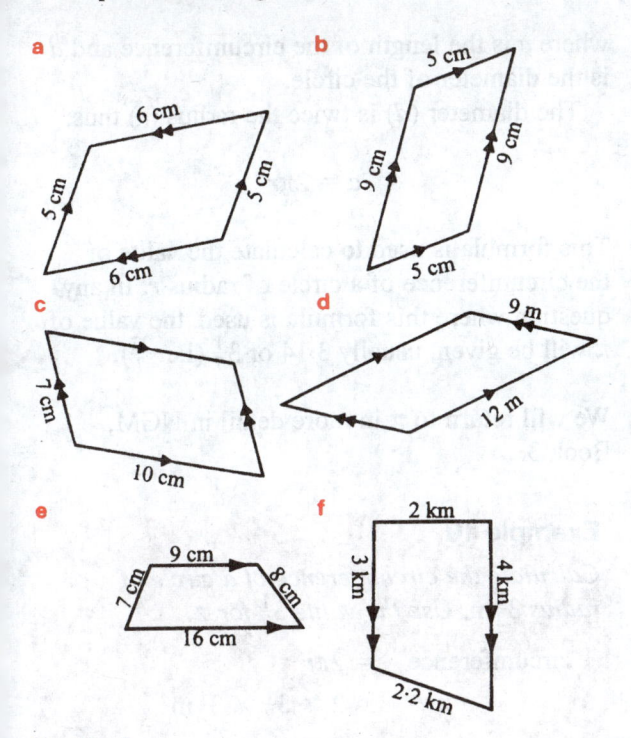

a 6 cm, 5 cm, 6 cm, 5 cm
b 5 cm, 6 cm, 5 cm, 6 cm
c 10 cm, 7 cm
d 9 m, 12 m, 5 cm
e 9 cm, 7 cm, 8 cm, 16 cm
f 2 km, 3 km, 4 km, 2·2 km

Fig. 13.11

10 Two sides of a parallelogram are of lengths 5 cm and 8 cm. Calculate the perimeter of the parallelogram.

11 The perimeter of a parallelogram is 38 cm and one of its sides is 14 cm long. Find the lengths of the other three sides.

12 In Fig. 13.12, a trapezium is made from three equilateral triangles. Find the perimeter of the trapezium if each side of the triangle is 6 cm long.

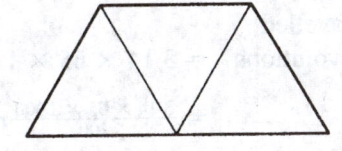

Fig. 13.12

13-3 Perimeter of circles

The perimeter of a circle is called the **circumference**.

Measuring circumference

Here are two ways of finding the circumference of a cylindrical tin can.

Rolling
a Make a mark on the circumference of the circular end-face (Fig. 13.13). Make a mark A on a long sheet of paper (e.g. newspaper). Start with the two marks opposite each other.
b Roll the tin along the paper.
c Stop when the mark is against the paper again. Make a mark B on the paper opposite the mark on the tin.

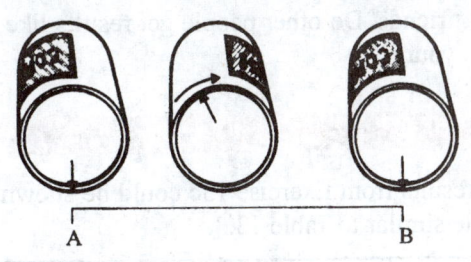

Fig. 13.13

The length AB will be the circumference of the circular end-face.

Winding thread
a Wind a piece of thread (or string) once around the tin (Fig. 13.14). Mark the thread at A and B where it crosses.

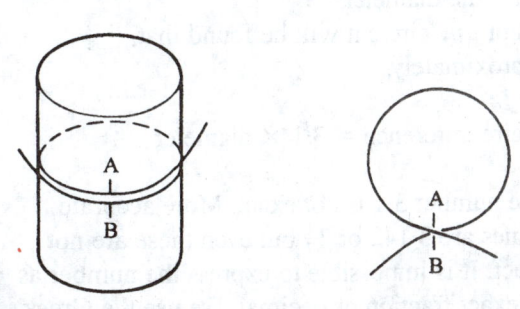

Fig. 13.14

107

b Remove the string from the tin. Pull the string straight and measure AB against a ruler. The length AB will be the circumference of the circle.

Exercise 13c (Class project)

Find three cylindrical objects, e.g. a cup, a tin can and a torch battery.

1. Use both of the above methods, rolling and winding thread, to find the circumference of the circular faces of the three objects.
2. Measure the diameters of the three objects. Compare the diameter of each object with its circumference.
   a Is the circumference greater than the diameter in each case?
   b If so, approximately how many times greater?
   c Is this true for all three objects?
   d Compare your results with those of your friends. Do other people get results like yours?

Formula for circumference

The results from Exercise 13c could be shown in a table similar to Table 13.3.

	circumference	diameter	$\dfrac{\text{circumference}}{\text{diameter}}$
battery	80 mm	25 mm	$\dfrac{80}{25} = 3\tfrac{1}{5}$
tin can	31·5 cm	10 cm	$\dfrac{31·5}{10} = 3·15$

Table 13.3

In each case, the circumference is just over 3 times the diameter.

For *any* circle it will be found that, approximately,

circumference = 3·1 × diameter

The number 3·1 is not exact. More accurate values are 3·142 or $3\tfrac{1}{7}$ but even these are not exact. It is impossible to express the number as an exact fraction or decimal. We use the Greek letter π (*pi*) to represent this number.

or
$$\text{circumference} = \pi \times \text{diameter}$$
$$c = \pi d$$

where *c* is the length of the circumference and *d* is the diameter of the circle.

The diameter (*d*) is twice the radius (*r*) thus:

$$c = 2\pi r$$

This formula is used to calculate the value of the circumference of a circle of radius *r*. In any question where this formula is used, the value of π will be given, usually 3·14 or $3\tfrac{1}{7}$ (i.e. $\tfrac{22}{7}$).

We will return to π in more detail in NGM, Book 3.

Example 10

Calculate the circumference of a circle of radius $3\tfrac{1}{2}$ m. Use the value $3\tfrac{1}{7}$ for π.

$$\begin{aligned}
\text{circumference} &= 2\pi r \\
&= 2 \times 3\tfrac{1}{7} \times 3\tfrac{1}{2}\,\text{m} \\
&= 2 \times \tfrac{22}{7} \times \tfrac{7}{2}\,\text{m} \\
&= 22\,\text{m}
\end{aligned}$$

Example 11

A bicycle wheel has a diameter of 65 cm. During a journey, the wheel makes 1 000 complete revolutions. How many metres does the bicycle travel? (Use the value 3·14 for π.)

circumference $= \pi d$

distance travelled
in one revolution $= 3·14 \times 65\,\text{cm}$

distance travelled
in 1 000 revolutions $= 3·14 \times 65 \times 1\,000\,\text{cm}$

$$= \tfrac{3·14 \times 65 \times 1\,000}{100}\,\text{m}$$

$$= 31·4 \times 65\,\text{m}$$

$$= 2\,041\,\text{m}$$

Exercise 13d

1. Copy and complete Table 13.4 for circles. (Use the value $\frac{22}{7}$ for π.)

	radius	diameter	circumference
a	7 m		
b		7 cm	
c	14 cm		
d		42 m	
e	35 cm		
f		63 cm	
g			5·6 m
h	4·9 m		
i		8·4 m	
j	3·85 m		

Table 13.4

2. Calculate the perimeter of a circle of radius 70 m. (Use the value $3\frac{1}{7}$ for π.)

3. A circular wire ring has a diameter of 20 cm. What is the length of the wire? (Use the value 3·14 for π.)

4. The diameter of the circular base of a round house is 14 m. What is the circumference of the base of the house? (Use the value $\frac{22}{7}$ for π.)

5. The minute hand of a clock is 10·5 cm long. How far does the tip of the hand travel in 1 hour? (Use the value $3\frac{1}{7}$ for π.)

6. A disc has a diameter of 30 cm and rotates at $33\frac{1}{3}$ revolutions per minute. How far does a point on the edge of the disc travel in a minute? Use the value 3·14 for π and give your answer in metres.

7. Fig. 13.15 shows a wire circle set inside a wire square of side 7 cm.

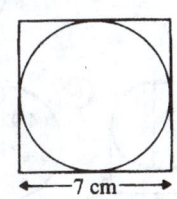

Fig. 13.15

   a Calculate the perimeter of the square.
   b Calculate the circumference of the circle. (Use $\frac{22}{7}$ for π.)
   c Calculate the total length of wire used.

8. A rope is wound 50 times round a cylinder of radius 25 cm (Fig. 13.16). How long is the rope? (Use the value 3·14 for π.)

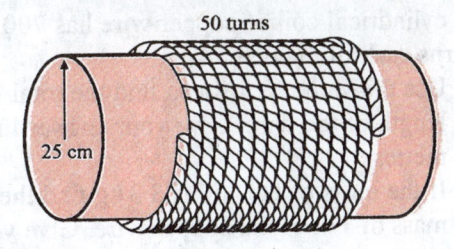

Fig. 13.16

9. A bicycle wheel has a diameter of 63 cm. How many metres does the bicycle travel for 100 revolutions of the wheel? (Use the value $\frac{22}{7}$ for π).

10. An arch of a bridge is made by bending a steel beam into the shape of a semi-circle. See Fig. 13.17.

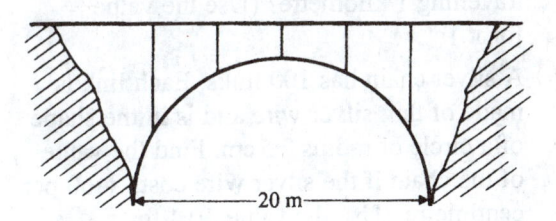

Fig. 13.17

If the span (diameter) of the arch is 20 m, use the value 3·14 for π to find the length of the steel beam to the nearest metre.

11. Fig. 13.18 shows the plan of a corner of a road.

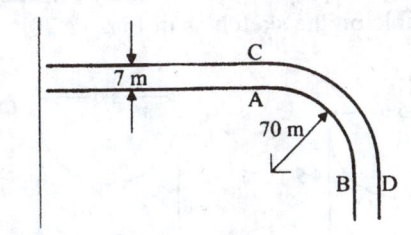

Fig. 13.18

The road is 7 m wide. The corner is in the shape of a quarter of a circle. The inside radius of the corner is 70 m. Ali walks round

109

the corner on the inside, from A to B. Obi walks round the corner on the outside, from C to D. How much further does Obi walk than Ali? Use the value $\frac{22}{7}$ for π.

12. A cylindrical coil of copper wire has 700 turns each of diameter 4 cm.
   a Use the value $\frac{22}{7}$ for π to find the total length of the wire. Give your answer in metres.
   b If the mass of the coil is 3·3 kg find the mass of 1 m of the copper wire. Give your answer in grammes.

13. Water is pulled up from a well in a bucket on a rope. The rope winds on a cylindrical drum 15 cm in diameter. It takes 28 turns of the drum to pull the bucket up from the bottom of the well. How deep is the well? (Use the value $\frac{22}{7}$ for π.)

14. A bicycle wheel is 56 cm in diameter. How many complete turns does it make in travelling 1 kilometre? (Use the value $\frac{22}{7}$ for π.)

15. A silver chain has 100 links. Each link is made of thin silver wire and is in the shape of a circle of radius 2·5 cm. Find the value of the chain if the silver wire costs ₦60 per centimetre. (Use the value 3·14 for π.)

Example 12

Calculate the perimeter of the shape in Fig. 13.19. All lengths are in centimetres. Use the value $\frac{22}{7}$ for π.

Sketch the shape and enter as many dimensions as possible on the sketch as in Fig. 13.20.

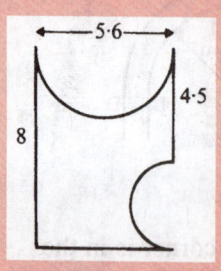

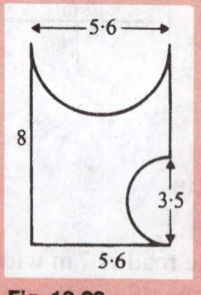

Fig. 13.19   Fig. 13.20

total length of straight edges
= 8 + 5·6 + 4·5 cm
= 18·1 cm

length of bigger semi-circle
= $\frac{1}{2}$ of $\pi \times 5\cdot6$ cm
= $\frac{1}{2} \times \frac{22}{7} \times \frac{5\cdot6}{1}$ cm
= 11 × 0·8 cm = 8·8 cm

length of smaller semi-circle
= $\frac{1}{2}$ of $\pi \times 3\cdot5$ cm
= $\frac{1}{2} \times \frac{22}{7} \times \frac{3\cdot5}{1}$ cm
= 11 × 0·5 cm = 5·5 cm

perimeter of shape
= 18·1 + 8·8 + 5·5 cm
= 32·4 cm

Exercise 13e

Find the perimeters of the shapes in Fig. 13.21. All measurements are in cm. (Use the value $\frac{22}{7}$ for π.)

(*Hint*: Make your own sketches and put in as many measurements as you can, especially diameters and radii of circular parts.)

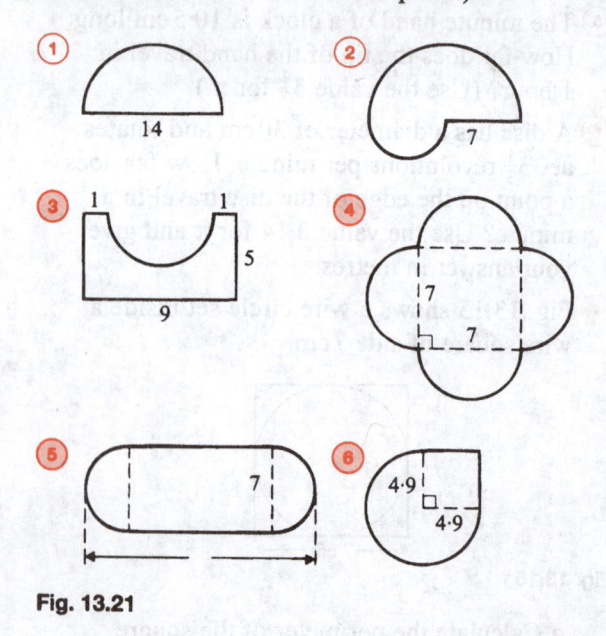

Fig. 13.21

☞ *Optional*: Do Exercise 31 of your Students' Practice Book.

SUMMARY

1. The *perimeter* of a shape is a measure of the distance round the boundary or edge of the shape.
2. With the usual lettering, the perimeter of a
   rectangle is $2(l + b)$,
   square is $4l$,
   circle is $2\pi r$ or πd.
3. The perimeter of a circle is called the *circumference*.

PUZZLE CORNER

Page Numbers

It takes 852 digits to number the pages of a book.

a) How many pages are there?
b) How many times does the digit 7 appear?

PUZZLE CORNER

Pentagon and triangles

These five points are the vertices of a regular pentagon →

How many different triangles can you make from 3 of the points?

What if we add a point at the centre? →

14 Plane shapes 3: Area

OBJECTIVES

You should be able to:

1 Find the area of regular and irregular shapes by drawing them on squared paper
2 Derive and apply appropriate formulae to calculate the area of rectangles, squares, parallelograms, triangles and trapeziums
3 Calculate the area of a circle using the formula $A = \pi r^2$
4 Calculate the areas of shapes made by combining other basic shapes.

Teaching and learning materials

Teacher: Regular and irregular cardboard shapes; large leaves; flat stones; squared paper; poster of Figure 14.31; tin cans or bottles

Students: Large leaves; flat stones; squared paper (graph exercise book); scissors; protractor; tin cans or bottles

14-1 Area

The **area** of a shape is a measure of its surface. The square is used as the shape for the basic unit of area. A square of side 1 m covers an area of **1 square metre** or **1 m²**. A square of side 1 cm (Fig. 14.1) covers an area of **1 square centimetre** or **1 cm²**.

Fig. 14.1 1 cm²

Exercise 14a

1 Measure the area of the shapes in Fig. 14.2 by counting the squares each contains. If bits are left over, try to estimate by adding them together to make whole squares. Each of the small squares represents 1 cm².

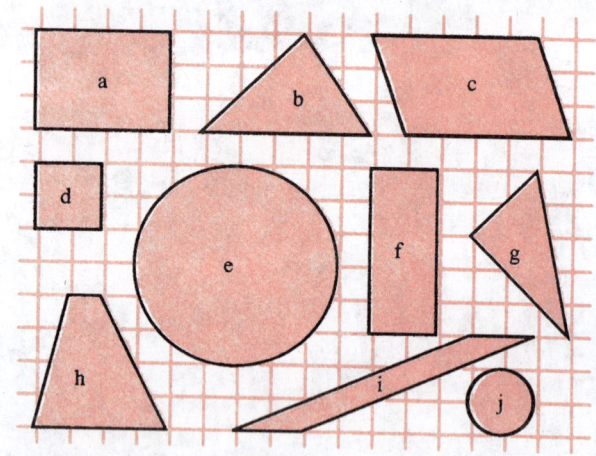

Fig. 14.2

2 Find a large leaf. Put the leaf on 1 cm² squared paper and draw round it. Measure the area of the leaf in cm² by counting squares. Estimate the total number of parts of squares as before.

3 On 1 cm² squared paper draw:
   a a circle of radius 3·5 cm;
   b a square of side 7 cm;
   c a rectangle of length 8 cm and breadth 5 cm.

In each case find the area of the shape by counting the squares each contains. When working on the circle, estimate squares as accurately as you can.

☞ *Optional:* Do Exercise 32 of your Students' Practice Book.

112

14-2 Area of rectangles and squares

A rectangle 5 cm long by 3 cm broad can be divided into squares of side 1 cm as shown in Fig. 14.3.

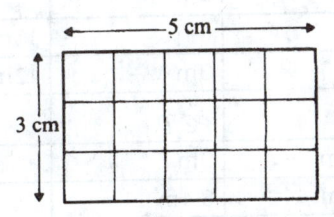

Fig. 14.3

By counting, the area of the rectangle = 15 cm². Notice also that 5 × 3 = 15; thus, in general:

area of rectangle = length × breadth.

Also notice that 5 = 15 ÷ 3 and 3 = 15 ÷ 5, thus:

length of rectangle = area ÷ breadth
breadth of rectangle = area ÷ length.

A square is a rectangle whose length and breadth are equal, thus:

area of square = (length of side)².

Therefore

length of side = √area of square.

Example 1
Calculate the area of a rectangle 6 cm by 3·5 cm.

area of rectangle = 6 cm × 3·5 cm = 21 cm²

Example 2
The area of a rectangle is 224 cm². If its length is 16 cm, calculate the breadth.

breadth = $\frac{224 \text{ cm}^3}{16 \text{ cm}}$
= 14 cm

Example 3
Calculate the area of a square advertising board of length 5 m.

area of square board = 5 m × 5 m = 25 m²

Example 4
The area of a square plot is 144 m². Calculate the length of a side of the plot.

length of side = √144 m² = 12 m

Example 5
An assembly area is in the shape of a 30 m by 30 m square. Part of the area is a concrete rectangle 25 m by 5 m; the rest is grass. Calculate the area of the grass.

Make a sketch of the assembly area as shown in Fig. 14.4.

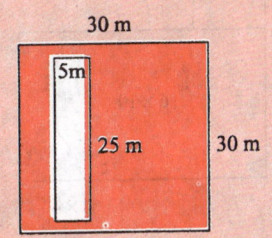

Fig. 14.4

area of assembly area = (30 m)² = 900 m²
area of concrete = 25 m × 5 m
= 125 m²
area of grass = 900 m² − 125 m²
= 775 m²

Example 6
The area of a rectangle is 24 cm² and one side is 6 cm in length. Find its breadth and perimeter.

breadth of rectangle = 24 cm² ÷ 6 cm = 4 cm

perimeter = 2(6 + 4) cm = 2 × 10 cm = 20 cm

Example 7

Calculate the area of the shape in Fig. 14.5. All measurements are in metres and all angles are right angles.

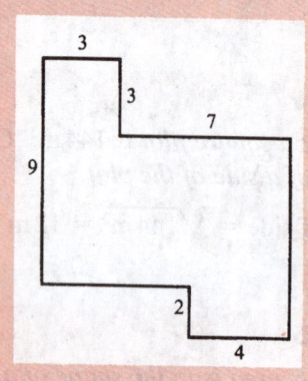

Fig. 14.5

The shape can be split into a 3 × 3 square and 6 × 10 and 2 × 4 rectangles, Fig. 14.6.

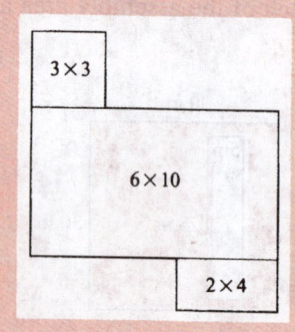

Fig. 14.6

area = area of square + area of the 2 rectangles.
= (3 × 3 + 6 × 10 + 2 × 4) m²
= (9 + 60 + 8) m²
= 77 m²

Exercise 14b

1. Copy and complete the table of rectangles (Table 14.1).

	length	breadth	area
a	3 cm	2 cm	
b	5 m	4 m	
c	5 m		15 m²
d		3 m	12 m²
e	6 m	$2\frac{1}{2}$ m	
f	5·2 m	3 m	
g	2·1 m	3·4 m	
h	4 m		18 m²
i	12 cm	9 cm	
j		6 m	48 m²
k	11 cm	8 cm	
l		5 m	31·5 m²
m	13 cm	7 cm	
n	7·5 m	4 m	
o	14 cm		84 cm²

Table 14.1

2. Copy and complete the table of squares (Table 14.2).

	length of side	area
a	6 cm	
b	9 m	
c		49 m²
d		16 cm²
e	1·2 m	
f	$2\frac{1}{2}$ cm	
g	8 cm	
h	12 cm	
i	14 cm	
j		100 m²
k		225 cm²
l	2·4 cm	

Table 14.2

3. Calculate the areas of the shapes in Fig. 14.7. All lengths are in metres and all angles are right angles.

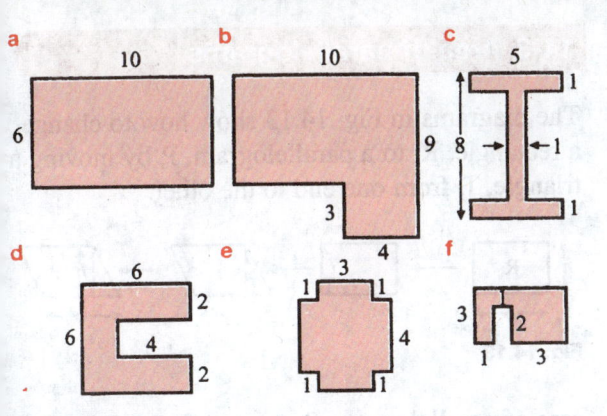

Fig. 14.7

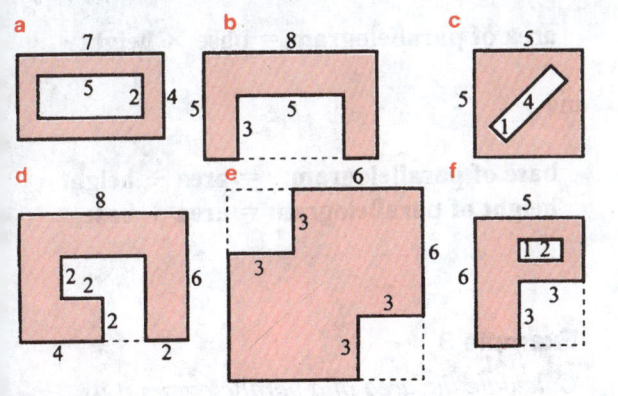

Fig. 14.8

4. Calculate the *shaded areas* in the diagrams in Fig. 14.8. All lengths are in metres and all angles are right angles.

5. A floor 4 m long and $3\frac{1}{2}$ m wide is to be concreted. Find
   a the area of the floor
   b the cost, if concrete costs ₦2 400 per m².

6. How many m² of floor are there in a hall 6 metres square? (6 metres square means 6 m by 6 m.)

7. A sheet is 2·15 m long and 1·6 m wide. What is the area of the sheet?

8. In a dining hall 25 m by 12 m, an area 8 m square is kept clear for cooking. What area is left over for dining?

9. A 12 m by 12 m square garden has a 1 m wide path through the centre, parallel to one side of the square. See Fig. 14.9. Calculate the area of garden left over for planting.

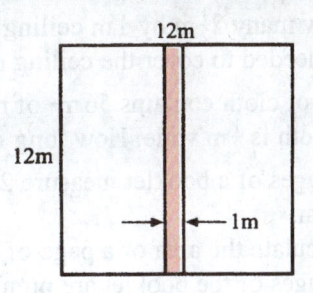

Fig. 14.9

10. An open cardboard box is 20 cm long, 12 cm wide and 8 cm deep (Fig. 14.10). Calculate the total area of cardboard in the box.

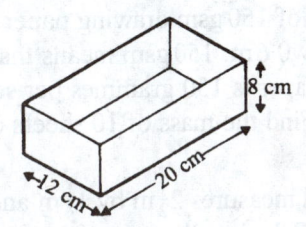

Fig. 14.10

11. The box in question 10 is cut down the edges and flattened as shown in Fig. 14.11a).

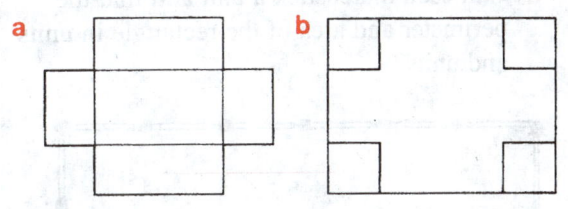

Fig. 14.11

   a Calculate the area of the smallest single rectangle from which the box could be made, i.e. calculate the area of the rectangle in Fig. 14.11b).
   b What area would be wasted?

12. Calculate the total area of the walls of a hospital ward 5 m long, 4 m wide and $2\frac{1}{2}$ m high. (Do not allow for doors and windows.)

13. 1 litre of paint covers 15 m². How many litres of paint will be needed to paint the inside walls of the ward in question 12?

14. a Calculate the area of the ceiling of the ward in question 12.

115

b How many $2\frac{1}{2}$ m by 1 m ceiling boards will be needed to cover the ceiling of the ward?

15. A roll of cloth contains 56 m² of material. The cloth is $\frac{1}{2}$ m wide. How long is the roll?

16. The pages of a booklet measure 20 cm by 12·5 cm.
    a Calculate the area of a page of the booklet. The pages of the booklet are numbered 1 to 36.
    b How many sheets of paper are needed for a booklet of 36 pages?
    c Calculate the total area of paper used in the booklet.

17. A sheet of 150 gsm drawing paper measures 0·8 m by 0·6 m. 150 gsm means that the mass of the paper is 150 grammes per square metre. Find the mass of 10 sheets of drawing paper.

18. A board measures $2\frac{1}{2}$ m by $1\frac{1}{4}$ m and costs ₦750. Calculate the cost of 1 m² of the board.

19. A boy has 16 matchsticks. He lays them in the shape of a rectangle (Fig. 14.12).
    a Call each matchstick a unit and find the perimeter and area of the rectangle in units and units².

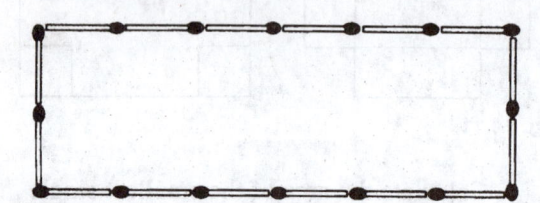

Fig. 14.12

   b Use matchsticks or squared paper to show the different rectangles which the boy can make using all 16 matchsticks.
   c Find the perimeters and areas of these rectangles.
   d What do you notice?

Optional: Do Exercise 33 of your Students' Practice Book.

14-3 Area of parallelograms

The diagrams in Fig. 14.13 show how to change a rectangle, R, to a parallelogram, P, by moving a triangle, T, from one end to the other.

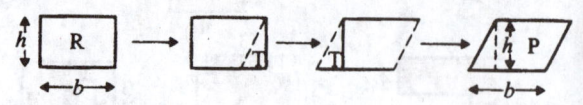

Fig. 14.13

area of parallelogram, P = area of rectangle, R
$$= b \times h$$

In the diagram, the height of the parallelogram is h and its base is b. In general:

area of parallelogram = base × height

and

base of parallelogram = area ÷ height
height of parallelogram = area ÷ base

Example 8
Calculate the area of a parallelogram if its base is 9·2 cm and its height is 6 cm.

area of parallelogram = 9·2 cm × 6 cm
= 55·2 cm²

Example 9
The area of a parallelogram is 99 cm² and its base is 11 cm. Calculate the corresponding height of the parallelogram.

height of parallelogram = 99 cm² ÷ 11 cm
= 9 cm

A parallelogram can have two bases and two corresponding heights as shown in Fig. 14.14.

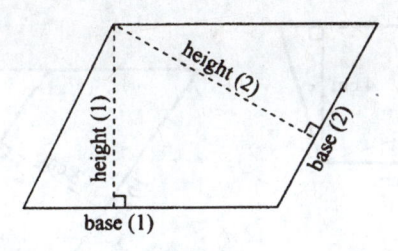

Fig. 14.14

area (A) = base(1) × height(1)
Also area (A) = base(2) × height(2)
Therefore: base(1) × height(1) = base(2) × height(2)

Example 10

In Fig. 14.15, the base of the parallelogram is 6 cm and its height is 4 cm. Calculate the area of the parallelogram. If the length of the other side of the parallelogram is 8 cm, calculate its corresponding height, h.

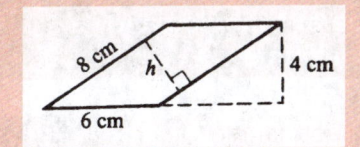

Fig. 14.15

area of parallelogram = 6 cm × 4 cm
   = 24 cm²

Also,
   area of parallelogram = 8 cm × height h

Therefore:
$$8 \text{ cm} \times h = 24 \text{ cm}^2$$
$$= 24 \text{ cm}^2 \div 8 \text{ cm}$$
$$= 3 \text{ cm}$$

Exercise 14c

① Calculate the areas of the parallelograms in Fig. 14.16. All dimensions are in centimetres. In each of the parallelograms in Fig. 14.17, calculate the height, h.

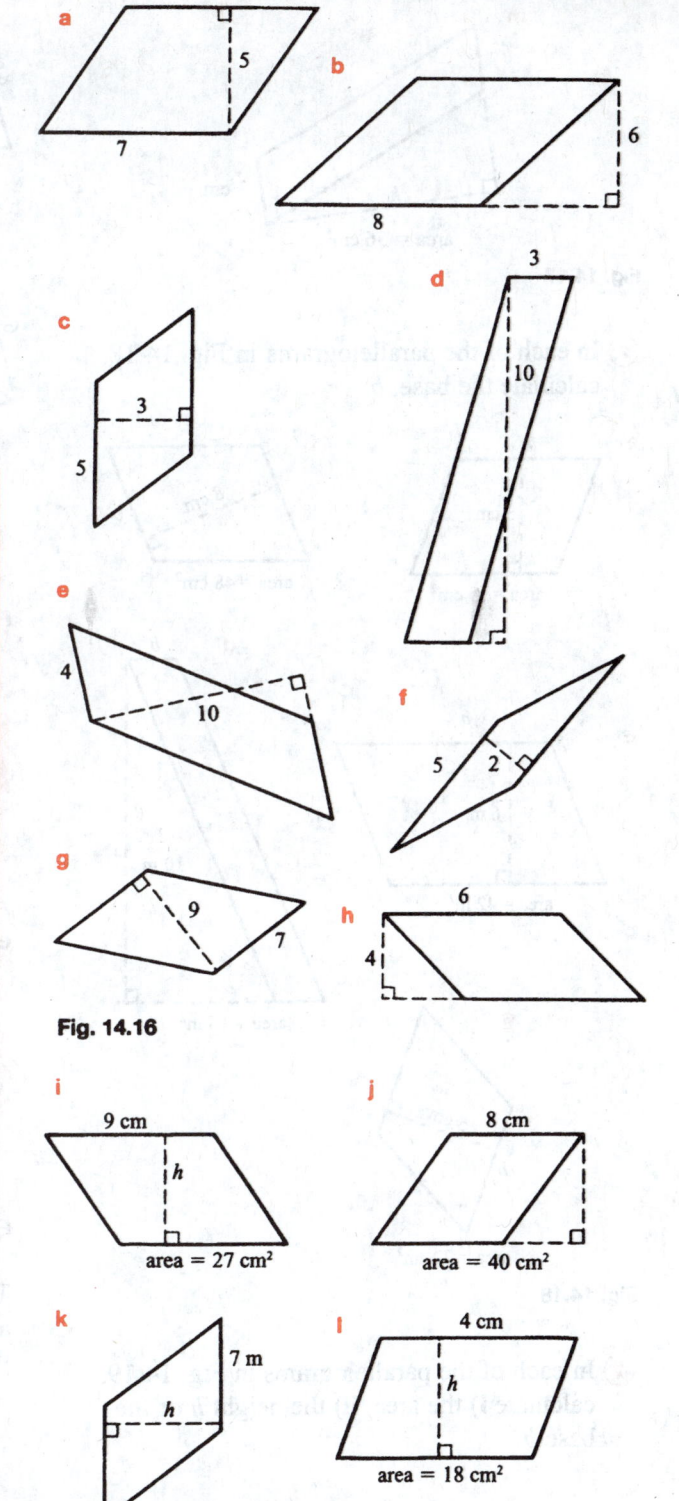

Fig. 14.16

a) 7, 5
b) 8, 6
c) 5, 3
d) 3, 10
e) 4, 10
f) 5, 2
g) 9, 7
h) 6, 4

i) 9 cm, h, area = 27 cm²
j) 8 cm, area = 40 cm²
k) 7 m, h, area = 28 cm²
l) 4 cm, h, area = 18 cm²

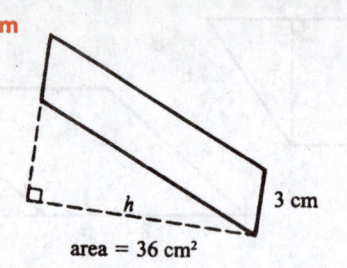

Fig. 14.17

② In each of the parallelograms in Fig. 14.18, calculate the base, b.

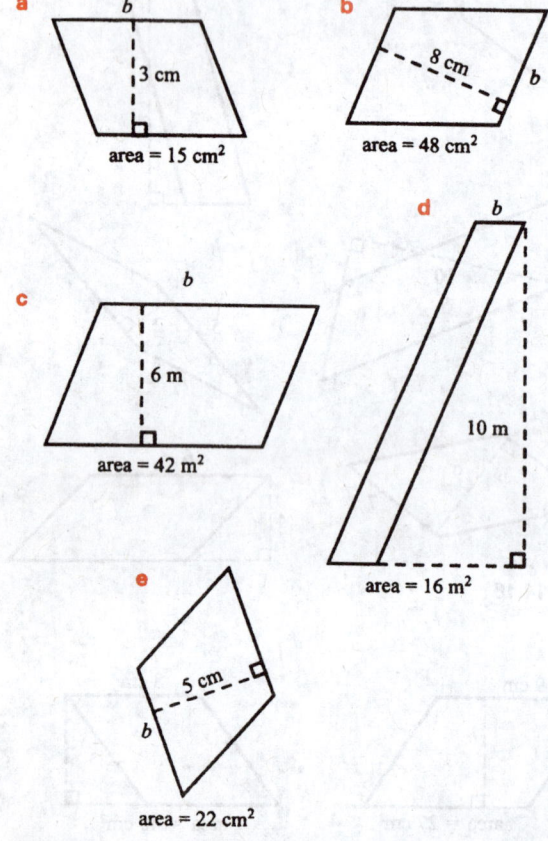

Fig. 14.18

③ In each of the parallelograms in Fig. 14.19, calculate i) the area, ii) the height h or the base b.

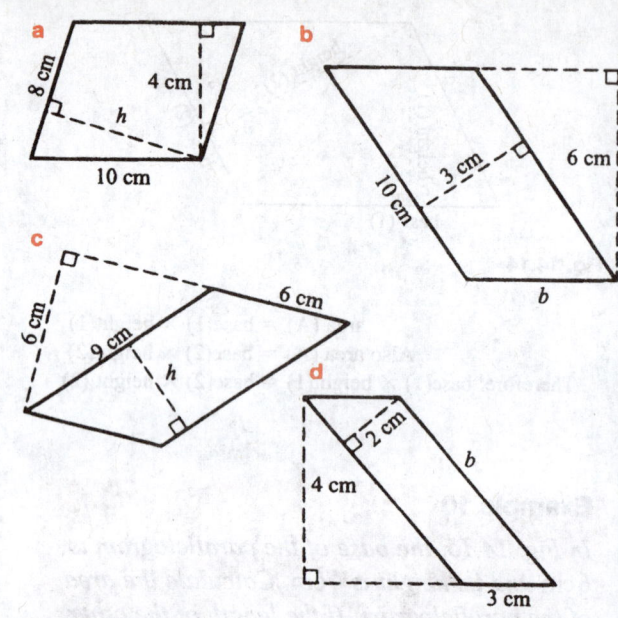

Fig. 14.19

14-4 Area of triangles and trapeziums

Right-angled triangle

Any diagonal of a rectangle divides it into two equal right-angled triangles (Fig. 14.20).

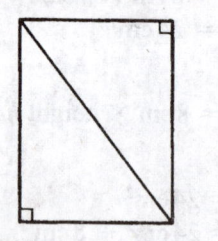

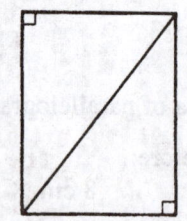

Fig. 14.20

Thus:
area of a right-angled triangle

$= \frac{1}{2} \times$ product of sides containing the right angle.

Any triangle

Any diagonal of a parallelogram divides it into two equal triangles (Fig. 14.21).

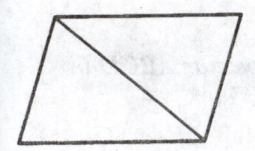

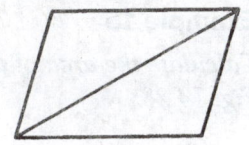

Fig. 14.21

Thus the area of each triangle is half the area of the containing parallelogram (Fig. 14.22).

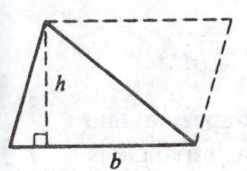

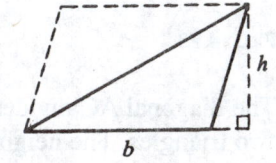

Fig. 14.22

Since
  area of parallelogram = base × height then:

  area of triangle = $\frac{1}{2}$ × **base** × **height**

Notice that any side of a triangle can be taken as base. Each base has its corresponding height.

Example 11
Calculate the area of the triangle shown in Fig. 14.23.

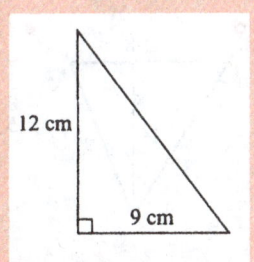

Fig. 14.23

The two sides containing the right angle measure 9 cm and 12 cm.

  area of triangle = $\frac{1}{2}$ × 9 cm × 12 cm
                   = 54 cm²

Example 12
Calculate the area of the triangle shown in Fig. 14.24.

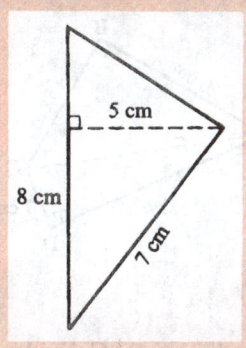

Fig. 14.24

The height is 5 cm. The corresponding base is 8 cm. We do not need the 7 cm side.

  area of triangle = $\frac{1}{2}$ × base × height
                   = $\frac{1}{2}$ × 8 cm × 5 cm
                   = 20 cm²

Example 13
Calculate the area of the triangle shown in Fig. 14.25.

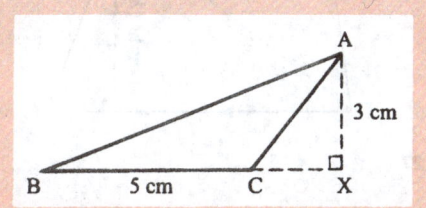

Fig. 14.25

Notice that the height from A to base BC falls outside the triangle.

  area of △ABC = $\frac{1}{2}$ × base BC × height AX
               = $\frac{1}{2}$ × 5 cm × 3 cm
               = $7\frac{1}{2}$ cm²

Example 14

Calculate the area of the quadrilateral ABCD in Fig. 14.26.

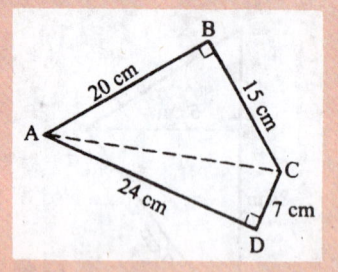

Fig. 14.26

Notice that the diagonal AC divides the quadrilateral into two right-angled triangles.

area of △ABC = $\frac{1}{2}$ × 20 cm × 15 cm = 150 cm^2

area of △ADC = $\frac{1}{2}$ × 24 cm × 7 cm = 84 cm^2

area of ABCD = 150 cm^2 + 84 cm^2 = 234 cm^2

Trapeziums

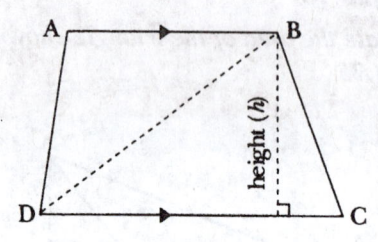

Fig. 14.27

ABCD is a trapezium in which AB is parallel to DC. The diagonal BD divides the trapezium into two triangles. The height, h, is the same for both triangles.

area of trapezium ABCD
 = area of △ABD + area of △BDC
 = $\frac{1}{2}$AB × h + $\frac{1}{2}$DC × h
 = $\frac{1}{2}$(AB + DC)h

Example 15

Calculate the area of the trapezium ABCD in Fig. 14.28.

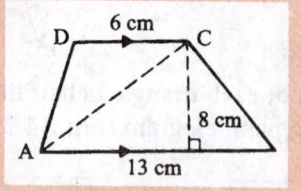

Fig. 14.28

The diagonal AC divides the trapezium into two triangles. The height of each triangle is 8 cm.

area of △ACB = $\frac{1}{2}$ × 13 cm × 8 cm = 52 cm^2

area of △ACD = $\frac{1}{2}$ × 6 cm × 8 cm = 24 cm^2

area of trapezium = 52 cm^2 + 24 cm^2 = 76 cm^2

Exercise 14d

1. Calculate the areas of the triangles in Fig. 14.29. All dimensions are in cm.

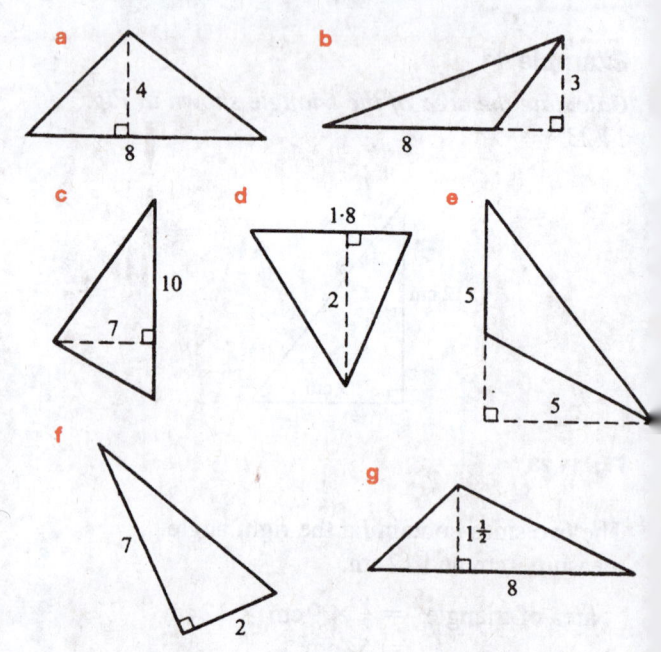

a
b
c
d
e
f
g

120

Fig. 14.29

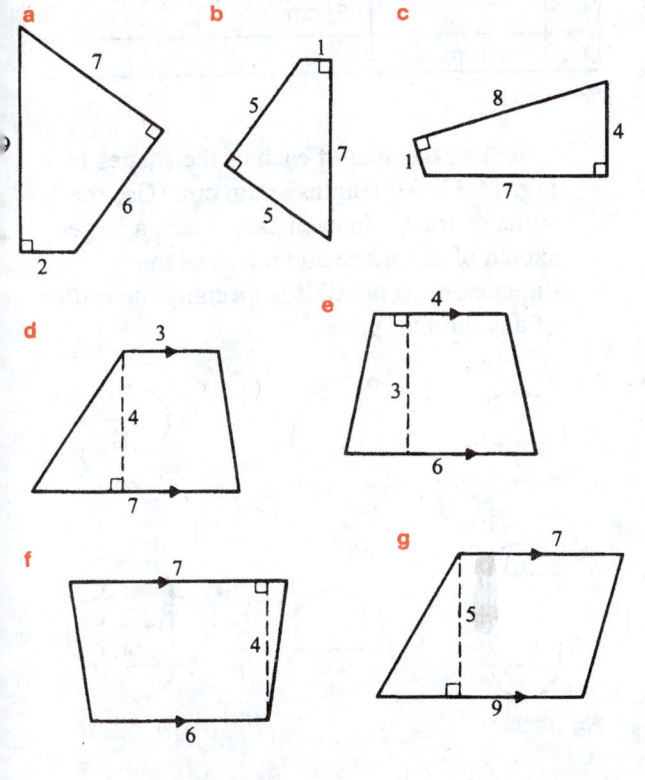

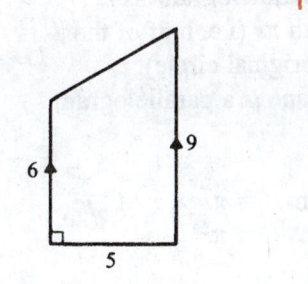

Fig. 14.30

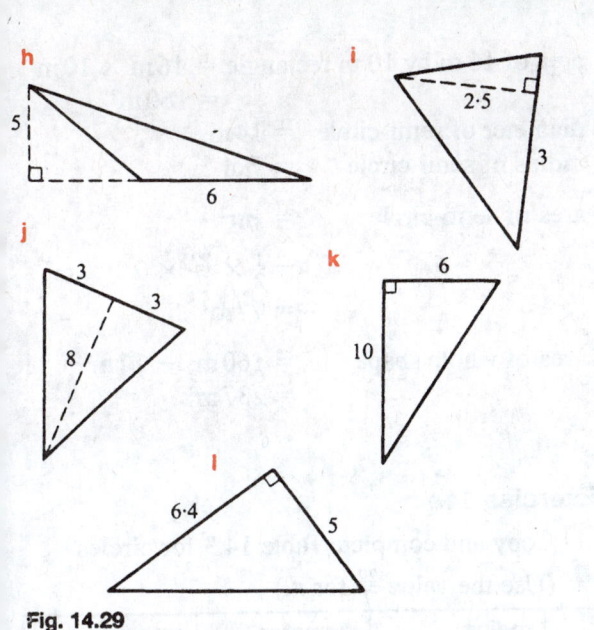

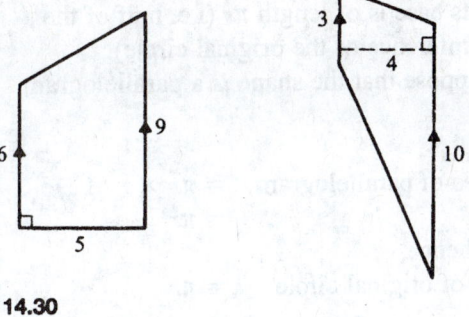

② Calculate the areas of the quadrilaterals in Fig. 14.30. In each case, make a sketch of the quadrilateral and draw a diagonal to divide it into two triangles. All dimensions are in cm.

Optional: Do Exercise 34 of your Students' Practice Book.

14-5 Area of circles

Optional: Do Exercise 35 of your Students' Practice Book.

For the following you will need paper, scissors and a protractor. Draw a circle of any radius, r. Divide it into 12 equal sectors. The angle of each sector is 30°. Cut out the 12 sectors and arrange them to make a 'parallelogram' as shown in Fig. 14.31.

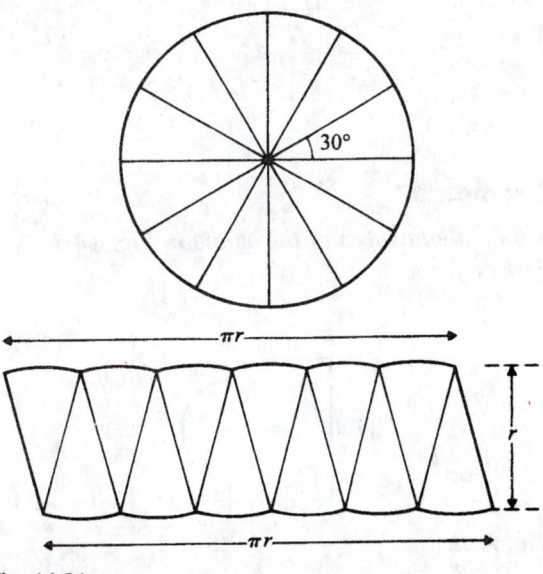

Fig. 14.31

121

The height of the 'parallelogram' is r and its base is of length πr (i.e. half of the circumference of the original circle).

Suppose that the shape *is* a parallelogram, then,

area of parallelogram $= \pi r \times r$
$= \pi r^2$

and, hence,
area of original circle $= \pi r^2$

When more sectors of the original circle are taken, the sides of the parallelogram become much straighter. (For example, try this activity with 36 sectors, each of 10°.) Thus, to calculate the area of any circle of radius r, use the formula:

area of circle $= \pi r^2$

Example 16
Find the area of a circle of radius $3\frac{1}{2}$ metres. Use the value $\frac{22}{7}$ for π.

area of circle $= \pi r^2$
$= \frac{22}{7} \times (3\frac{1}{2})^2 = \frac{22}{7} \times \frac{7}{2} \times \frac{7}{2}$ m²
$= \frac{11 \times 7}{2}$ m²
$= 38\frac{1}{2}$ m²

Example 17
Calculate the area of the shape in Fig. 14.32. Use $\frac{22}{7}$ for π.

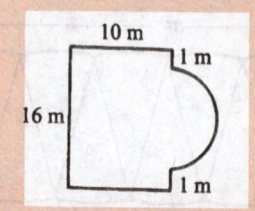

Fig. 14.32

area of 16 m by 10 m rectangle $= 16\,\text{m} \times 10\,\text{m}$
$= 160\,\text{m}^2$
diameter of semi-circle $= 14\,\text{m}$
radius of semi-circle $= 7\,\text{m}$
area of semi-circle $= \frac{1}{2}\pi r^2$
$= \frac{1}{2} \times \frac{22}{7} \times 7 \times 7\,\text{m}^2$
$= 77\,\text{m}^2$
area of whole shape $= 160\,\text{m}^2 + 77\,\text{m}^2$
$= 237\,\text{m}^2$

Exercise 14e
1. Copy and complete Table 14.3 for circles. (Use the value $\frac{22}{7}$ for π.)

	radius	diameter	area
a	7 m		
b		7 cm	
c	140 mm		
d		28 m	
e		$3\frac{1}{2}$ cm	
f	2·1 cm		

Table 14.3

2. Calculate the area of each of the shapes in Fig. 14.33. All lengths are in cm. (Use the value $\frac{22}{7}$ for π.) In each case, make a larger sketch of the shape and put in as many dimensions as possible, especially the *radius* of any circular parts.

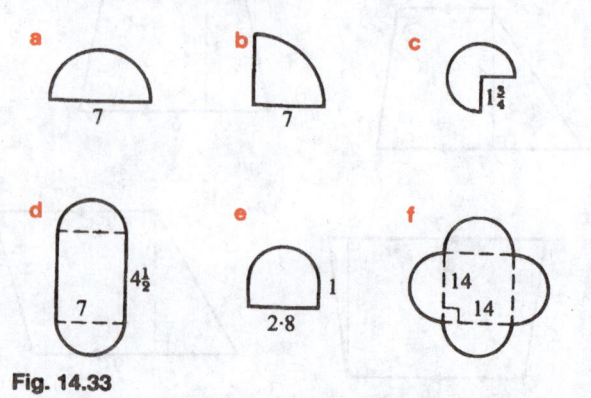

Fig. 14.33

3 Calculate the shaded areas in the shapes in Fig. 14.34. All dimensions are in centimetres. (Use the value $\frac{22}{7}$ for π.)

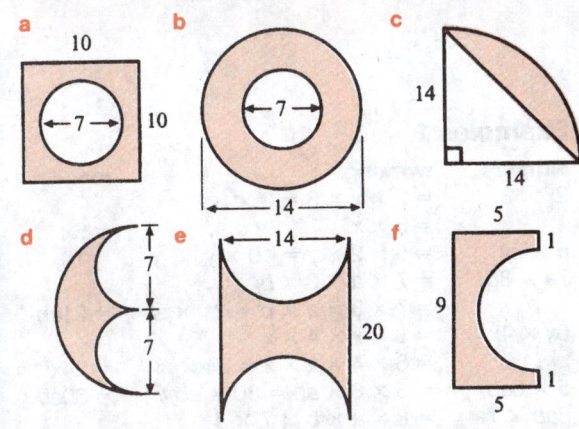

Fig. 14.34

4 A circular mat has a diameter of 20 cm. Find its radius and hence calculate the area of the mat. (Use the value 3·14 for π.)

5 A goat is tied to a peg in the ground. The rope is 3 m long. What area of grass can the goat eat? (Use the value 3·1 for π.)

6 A protractor is in the shape of a semi-circle of radius 5 cm. Calculate the area of the protractor. (Use the value 3·14 for π.)

7 There are two circles, one large and one small. The radius of the large circle is three times the radius of the small circle. Find the value of the fraction: $\frac{\text{area of small circle}}{\text{area of large circle}}$

8 The floor of a round house is 10 m in diameter. A weaver charges ₦15 500 to make a mat to fit the floor. Find the cost of the mat per square metre. (Use the value 3·1 for π.)

9 A design is made by drawing seven small circles inside one large circle as shown in Fig. 14.35.

If the diameter of the large circle is 30 cm, calculate
a the radius of the large circle,
b the radius of each small circle,
c the area shaded in the diagram.
   (Use the value 3·14 for π.)

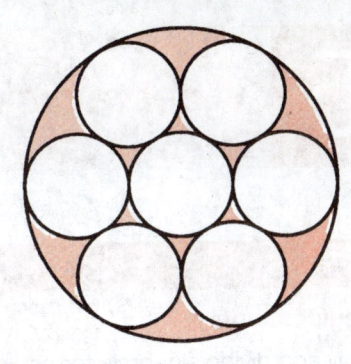

Fig. 14.35

10 The sports field shown in Fig. 14.36 has a 90 m by 70 m football field with a semi-circular area at each end. A track runs round the perimeter of the sports field.

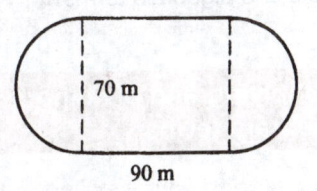

Fig. 14.36

Use the value $\frac{22}{7}$ for π to calculate
a the area of the sports field,
b the length of one lap of the track.

☞ *Optional:* Do Exercise 36 of your Students' Practice Book.

SUMMARY

1 The *area* of a shape is a measure of its surface.
2 Area is measured in units such as cm² or m² which are derived from the SI units of length. See the table on page 194.
3 The areas of common plane shapes are as follows.
rectangle = $l \times b$
square = l^2
parallelogram = base × height
triangle = $\frac{1}{2}$ × base × height
trapezium = $\frac{1}{2}h(a+b)$
circle = πr^2.

123

15 Algebraic simplification 2: Brackets

OBJECTIVES

You should be able to:
1. Multiply and divide algebraic terms
2. Simplify algebraic expressions by following an agreed order of operations
3. Remove brackets from simple numerical and algebraic expressions
4. Solve simple word problems that involve brackets and algebraic terms.

15-1 Multiplying and dividing algebraic terms

Examples 1

simplify	working	result
$2x \times 3$	$= 2 \times x \times 3 = 2 \times 3 \times x$	
	$= 6 \times x$	$= 6x$
$5 \times 2y$	$= 5 \times 2 \times y = 10 \times y$	$= 10y$
$7a \times 3b$	$= 7 \times a \times 3 \times b$	
	$= 7 \times 3 \times a \times b = 21 \times ab$	$= 21ab$
$6x \times 4x$	$= 6 \times x \times 4 \times x$	
	$= 6 \times 4 \times x \times x = 24 \times x^2$	$= 24x^2$
$5 \times 6ab$	$= 5 \times 6 \times ab = 30 \times ab$	$= 30ab$
$8ab \times 7a$	$= 8 \times a \times b \times 7 \times a$	
	$= 8 \times 7 \times a \times a \times b$	
	$= 56 \times a^2 \times b$	$= 56a^2b$
$y \times 11xy$	$= y \times 11 \times x \times y$	
	$= 11 \times x \times y \times y$	
	$= 11 \times xy^2$	$= 11xy^2$

Multiplication

a Just as $5a$ is short for $5 \times a$, so ab is short for $a \times b$.

b Just as $3 \times 5 = 5 \times 3 = 15$,
so $a \times b = b \times a = ab$.
It is usual to write the letters in alphabetical order, but ba would be just as correct as ab.

c Just as 5^2 is short for 5×5, so a^2 is short for $a \times a$ and x^3 is short for $x \times x \times x$.

d
$$4x + 4x + 4x = 12x$$
$$3 \times 4x = 12x$$
and
$$3x + 3x + 3x + 3x = 12x$$
$$4 \times 3x = 12x$$
Thus: $3 \times 4x = 4 \times 3x = 12x$
The terms 3, 4 and x can be multiplied in any order.
$$3 \times 4x = 4 \times 3x = 3x \times 4 = 4x \times 3$$
$$= 4 \times x \times 3 = x \times 3 \times 4 = 12x$$

It is usual to write the numbers before the letters. Look at Examples 1 before doing Exercise 15a.

Exercise 15a
Simplify the following.

1. $5 \times a$
2. $x \times 4$
3. $x \times y$
4. $y \times x$
5. $a \times a$
6. $1 \times x2$
7. $2a \times 3$
8. $3 \times 2a$
9. $3a \times 2$
10. $2 \times 3a$
11. $4x \times 7$
12. $5 \times 8n$
13. $2 \times x^2$
14. $3y^2 \times 4$
15. $16 \times 2x^2$
16. $4ab \times 5$
17. $7 \times 5pq$
18. $9ab \times 3$
19. $6x \times x$
20. $y \times 8y$
21. $3x \times x$
22. $p \times 2q$
23. $6a \times b$
24. $m \times 7n$
25. $4a \times 3a$
26. $5n \times 7n$
27. $3x \times 10x$
28. $9n \times 4n$
29. $10q \times 5p$
30. $4a \times 5b$
31. $4ab \times 7a$
32. $3b \times 11ab$
33. $2xy \times 9y$
34. $6y \times 5xy$
35. $14pq \times p$
36. $3a \times 8ab$

Division

In algebra, letters stand for numbers. Just as fractions can be reduced to their lowest terms by equal division of the numerator and denominator, so a letter can be divided by the same letter. For example $x \div x = 1$, just as $3 \div 3 = 1$.

Look at Examples 2 and 3 before doing Exercise 15b.

Examples 2

simplify	working	result
$\frac{14a}{7}$	$= \frac{7 \times 2a}{7} = \frac{1 \times 2a}{1}$	$= 2a$
$\frac{1}{3}$ of $36x$	$= \frac{36 \times x}{3} = \frac{3 \times 12x}{3}$	
	$= \frac{1 \times 12x}{1}$	$= 12x$
$\frac{1}{5}$ of y	does not simplify	$= \frac{1}{5}y$ or $\frac{y}{5}$

Examples 3

simplify	working	result
$5ab \div a$	$= \frac{5 \times a \times b}{a}$	
	$= \frac{5 \times 1 \times b}{1} = 5 \times b$	$= 5b$
$\frac{6xy}{2y}$	$= \frac{6 \times x \times y}{2 \times y} = \frac{3 \times x \times 1}{1 \times 1}$	
	$= 3 \times x$	$= 3x$
$x^2 \div x$	$= \frac{x \times x}{x} = \frac{1 \times x}{1}$	$= x$
$24x^2y \div 3xy$	$= \frac{24 \times x^2 \times y}{3 \times x \times y}$	
	$= \frac{3 \times 8 \times x \times 1}{3 \times 1 \times 1} = 8 \times x$	$= 8x$

Exercise 15b
Simplify the following.

1. $\frac{6a}{3}$
2. $12a \div 2$
3. $\frac{1}{4}$ of $24x$
4. $18y \div 6$
5. $\frac{1}{5}$ of $15x$
6. $\frac{32c}{8}$
7. $\frac{1}{8}$ of $32x$
8. $\frac{21y}{3}$
9. $\frac{1}{7} \times 35y$
10. $\frac{1}{9} \times x$
11. $\frac{1}{4}$ of d
12. $x \times \frac{1}{2}$
13. $28ab \div 4$
14. $16xy \div x$
15. $30pq \div 6$
16. $17mn \div n$
17. $22kl \div 11$
18. $6ab \div b$
19. $d^2 \div d$
20. $a \div a^2$
21. $\frac{z^2}{z}$
22. $\frac{3x^2}{x}$
23. $6x^2 \div x$
24. $\frac{5c^2}{c}$
25. $\frac{7x^3}{x}$
26. $\frac{2x^3}{x}$
27. $\frac{5x^3}{x^2}$
28. $\frac{12x^2}{3x}$
29. $\frac{18a^3}{3a}$
30. $\frac{26x^2}{2x}$
31. $\frac{33mn}{8a}$
32. $\frac{42xy}{7y}$
33. $\frac{54ab}{9b}$
34. $\frac{72a^2b}{8a}$
35. $\frac{48x^2y}{12xy}$
36. $\frac{40pq^2}{8pq}$

An algebra puzzle [QR]

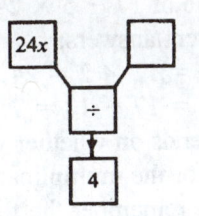

Fig. 15.1

Fig. 15.1 represents $\boxed{24x} \div \boxed{} = \boxed{4}$

What should go in the empty box?

If the contents of the box are y, then,

$24x \div y = 4 \rightarrow y = 24x \div 4 = 6x$

$6x$ should go in the box: $\boxed{6x}$

See if you can fill the boxes in Fig. 15.2.

a. $18k \div \boxed{} \rightarrow 9$

b. $3n \times \boxed{} \rightarrow 15n^2$

c. $30p^2 \div 2p \rightarrow \boxed{}$

d. $\boxed{} \times 4s \rightarrow 20s^2$

e. $\boxed{} \div 9 \rightarrow 2t^2$

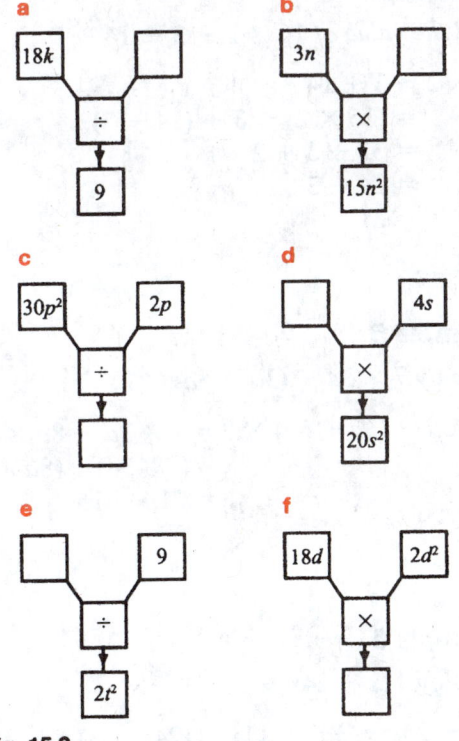

f. $18d \times 2d^2 \rightarrow \boxed{}$

Fig. 15.2

Make up some puzzles like this for your friends.

125

15-2 Order of operations

What is the value of $17 - 5 \times 2$? It is possible to get two different answers:

a $(17 - 5) \times 2 = 12 \times 2 = 24$
b $17 - (5 \times 2) = 17 - 10 = 7$

The answer depends on whether we do the subtraction first or the multiplication first. To avoid confusion, remember the following rules.

a If there are no brackets, do multiplication or division before addition or subtraction.
b If there are brackets, do the operations inside the brackets first.

Usually operations involving multiplication and division are enclosed in brackets and done before addition and subtraction.

Use the 'word' BODMAS to remember the correct order: **Brackets, Of, Division, Multiplication, Addition, Subtraction.**

Example 4

Find the value of $16 \times 2 - 3 + 14 \div 7$.

$16 \times 2 - 3 + 14 \div 7$
$= (16 \times 2) - 3 + (14 \div 7)$
$= 32 - 3 + 2$
$= 34 - 3$
$= 31$

Example 5

Simplify $7 \times 3a - (3a + 5a) \times 2$.

$7 \times 3a - (3a + 5a) \times 2 = 7 \times 3a - 8a \times 2$
$= (7 \times 3a) - (8a \times 2)$
$= 21a - 16a$
$= 5a$

Example 6

Simplify $11x + 24x \div 3$.

$11x + 24x \div 3 = 11x + (24x \div 3)$
$= 11x + 8x$
$= 19x$

Example 7

Simplify $18y \div 9 + 5y + 3 \times 4y$.

$18y \div 9 + 5y + 3 \times 4y$
$= (18y \div 9) + 5y + (3 \times 4y)$
$= 2y + 5y + 12y$
$= 19y$

Exercise 15c

Find the value of the following.

1. $18 - 6 \times 2$
2. $12 \div 4 + 2$
3. $6 - 18 \div 3$
4. $4 \times 5 + 8 \div 4$
5. $16 \div 2 - 3 \times 2$
6. $7 \times 3 + 27 \div 9$
7. $(5 + 3) + 3 \times 5$
8. $5 + (3 + 3) \times 5$
9. $4 \times 6 - (7 - 3)$
10. $8 \times 3 - 17 + 15 \div 5$
11. $28 \div 4 + 2 - 2 \times 4$
12. $6 \times 2 - 2 - 40 \div 4$

Exercise 15d

Simplify the following as far as possible.

1. $3x \times 2 + 5x$
2. $4 \times 5p - 3p$
3. $4n + 3n \times 10$
4. $2 \times 7b - 3$
5. $6 + 2 \times 5m$
6. $4a \times 3 + 5$
7. $17y - 5y \times 2$
8. $21a - 2 \times 7a$
9. $3x + 8x \div 2$
10. $n + 12n \div 4$
11. $15 \div 5 + 6y$
12. $7x \div x + 5$
13. $5a + 21a \div 7$
14. $4x - 6 \div 3$
15. $1 - x \times 0$
16. $6a \times 4 - 2 \times 7a$
17. $3 \times 5x + 4x \div 2$
18. $4 \times 8x + 7x \times 3$
19. $6u \times 5 - 3 \times 4u - 2u$
20. $24x \div 6 + x + 1 \times 5x$
21. $7x - 3 \times 4x + 5x \times 2$
22. $8v \times 2 + 5v \div 5 - 12v$
23. $7a \times 2 + 5 \times 8a - 6a \times 9$
24. $5 \times 6x - 4x \times 0 - 7x \times 4$

15-3 Removing brackets

Always try to simplify the terms inside brackets first. If they will not simplify, remove the brackets.

Positive sign before a bracket

a $9 + (5 + 2) = 9 + 7 = 16$
 also $9 + 5 + 2 = 14 + 2 = 16$
 thus $9 + (5 + 2) = 9 + 5 + 2$
 Similarly with letters,
  $a + (b + c) = a + b + c$

b $9 + (5 - 2) = 9 + 3 = 12$
 also $9 + 5 - 2 = 14 - 2 = 12$
 thus $9 + (5 - 2) = 9 + 5 - 2$
 Similarly with letters,
  $a + (b - c) = a + b - c$

When there is a positive sign before a bracket: the signs of the terms inside the bracket stay the same when it is removed.

Example 8
Simplify $7g + (3g + 4h)$.

$7g + (3g + 4h) = 7g + 3g + 4h = 10g + 4h$

Example 9
Simplify $13p + (6p - 3q)$.

$13p + (6p - 3q) = 13p + 6p - 3q = 19p - 3q$

Example 10
Simplify $(6x - 5y) + (3y + 4x)$.

$(6x - 5y) + (3y + 4x) = 6x - 5y + 3y + 4x$
$= 6x + 4x + 3y - 5y$
$= 10x - 2y$

Note: There is no sign before the first bracket. We take it to be positive.

Exercise 15e
Simplify each of the following in *two* ways. The first example shows you how to do this.

① $9 + (7 - 3)$
 a $9 + (7 - 3) = 9 + 4 = 13$
 b $9 + (7 - 3) = 9 + 7 - 3 = 16 - 3 = 13$

② $3 + (7 + 2)$ ③ $13 + (6 - 4)$
④ $3 + (9 - 4)$ ⑤ $6 + (4 - 2)$
⑥ $7 + (13 + 9)$ ⑦ $3 + (8 - 2)$
⑧ $3 + (2 - 8)$ ⑨ $4 + (3 - 11)$
⑩ $5 + (2 - 10)$

Exercise 15f
Write the following without brackets.

① $a + (b + c)$ ② $(a + b) + c$
③ $a + (b - c)$ ④ $(a + 3b) - 2c$
⑤ $2a + (b - 4c)$ ⑥ $(a - 5b) - 5c$
⑦ $(a + b) + (c + d)$ ⑧ $(a - b) + (c - d)$
⑨ $a + (b - c) - d$ ⑩ $7a + (2b - c) - 3d$
⑪ $5a + (b + 3c) - 3d$ ⑫ $(6a - b) + (c - 4d)$

Exercise 15g
Remove the brackets in the following and then simplify.

① $a + (a - b)$ ② $(a + 7) + 5$
③ $6x + (3 - x)$ ④ $(4m + 5n) - 3n$
⑤ $6a + (3a - 2b)$ ⑥ $(3a + 8b) + 8a$
⑦ $2 + (5a - 9)$ ⑧ $(4x - 5y) + 11y$
⑨ $(2p - 6q) - q$ ⑩ $(3a + 2) + (5a + 9)$
⑪ $(7 + 3n) + (1 - n)$
⑫ $(2x + 4) + (1 - x)$
⑬ $(x - 3y) + (x - 3y)$
⑭ $(12a - 7) + (4 - 5a)$
⑮ $(3x - 4y) + (5x - 8y)$

Negative sign before a bracket

a $9 - (5 + 2) = 9 - 7 = 2$
 The result is the same as first taking away 5, then taking away 2:
 i.e. $9 - 5 - 2 = 4 - 2 = 2$
 thus $9 - (5 + 2) = 9 - 5 - 2 = 2$.

127

Similarly with letters,
$a - (b + c) = a - b - c$.

b $9 - (5 - 2) = 9 - 3 = 6$

The result is the same as first taking away 5 and then *adding* 2:
i.e. $9 - 5 + 2 = 4 + 2 = 6$
thus $9 - (5 - 2) = 9 - 5 + 2$.
Similarly with letters,
$a - (b - c) = a - b + c$.

When there is a negative sign before a bracket:
the signs of the terms inside the bracket are changed when the bracket is removed.

Example 11
Simplify $5a - (2a + 8)$.

$5a - (2a + 8) = 5a - 2a - 8 = 3a - 8$

Example 12
Simplify $10d - (9c - 4d)$.

$10d - (9c - 4d) = 10d - 9c + 4d = 14d - 9c$

Example 13
Simplify $(6x - y) - (7x - 2y)$.

$(6x - y) - (7x - 2y) = 6x - y - 7x + 2y$
$\qquad = 6x - 7x + 2y - y$
$\qquad = -x + y \text{ (or } y - x\text{)}$

Exercise 15h
Simplify each of the following in *two* ways. The first example shows you how to do this.

1. $9 - (7 - 3)$
   a $9 - (7 - 3) = 9 - 4 = 5$
   b $9 - (7 - 3) = 9 - 7 + 3 = 2 + 3 = 5$
2. $9 - (5 + 2)$
3. $16 - (4 - 1)$
4. $24 - (15 + 8)$
5. $12 - (9 - 5)$
6. $15 - (10 + 2)$
7. $11 - (2 - 1)$
8. $4 - (6 + 3)$
9. $5 - (14 - 5)$
10. $8 - (2 + 6)$

Exercise 15i
Write the following without brackets.
1. $a - (b + c)$
2. $a - (b - c)$
3. $-(b + c) + a$
4. $2a - (3b - c)$
5. $-(b - 2c) - 5a$
6. $5x - (3y + z)$
7. $(a + b) - (c + d)$
8. $(a - b) - (c - d)$
9. $a - (b + c) - d$
10. $3a - (5b - 2c) + 4d$
11. $8a - (b + 5c) - 2d$
12. $-(2a + b) + (4c - 3d)$

Exercise 15j
Remove the brackets in the following and then simplify.
1. $3a - (a + 5)$
2. $5x - (2 - x)$
3. $6x - (x + 11y)$
4. $2 - (4n - 5)$
5. $7n - (m + n)$
6. $4a - (3 - a)$
7. $(8x + 3y) - (4x + y)$
8. $(9 - 2a) - (4 + 3a)$
9. $(14x + 5y) - (7x - 6y)$
10. $(6x - y) - (4x - 5y)$
11. $(4x - 2) - (3 - 2x)$
12. $(3a + 5b) - (7a + 10b)$

Example 14
A pen costs h naira and a pencil costs 30 naira less than a pen. Find the cost of a pen and a pencil.

$\qquad$ cost of a pen $\;= ₦h$
$\qquad$ cost of a pencil $= ₦(h - 30)$
$\qquad$ cost of both $\;\;\;= ₦h + ₦(h - 30)$
$\qquad\qquad\qquad\qquad\;\; = ₦h + ₦h - ₦30$
$\qquad\qquad\qquad\qquad\;\; = ₦(2h - 30)$

Example 15
The greater of two consecutive numbers* is x.

a *Find the sum of the two numbers.*

b *Subtract the sum of the two numbers from 5x.*

*(Two whole numbers are consecutive when their difference is 1. For example 5 and 6 are consecutive numbers; 49 and 50 are also consecutive. In algebra x and $x + 1$ or $y - 1$ and y are consecutive provided x and y are whole numbers.)

a If x is the greater of two consecutive numbers, the lower number is $x - 1$.

$$\text{sum of the two numbers} = x + (x - 1)$$
$$= x + x - 1$$
$$= 2x - 1$$

b $5x - (2x - 1) = 5x - 2x + 1$
$\qquad\qquad\qquad = 3x + 1$

Exercise 15k

1. A pen costs p naira and a pencil costs 15 naira less than a pen.
   a Find the cost of a pencil.
   b Find the cost of a pen and a pencil.

2. A pencil costs x naira and a rubber costs 40 naira more than a pencil.
   a Find the cost of a rubber.
   b Find the cost of a pencil and a rubber.

3. Envelopes cost d naira per pack. A notepad costs 20 naira more than a pack of envelopes. Find the total cost of a pack of envelopes and a notepad.

4. A pig costs ₦x and a goat costs ₦y less than a pig. Find the cost of two pigs and one goat.

5. Find the sum of the whole number n and the next whole number above it.

6. The greater of two consecutive numbers is m. Find the sum of the two numbers. (See Example 15 above.)

7. Audu buys three packets of sweets. John buys two packets of sweets and eats four sweets. Each packet contains x sweets.
   a How many sweets has Audu?
   b How many sweets has John?
   c How many more sweets has Audu than John?

8. A cup and a saucer together cost m naira. A cup alone costs n naira. Find the cost of
   a one saucer
   b three cups and one saucer.

9. The middle of three consecutive numbers is b. Find
   a the other two numbers
   b the sum of the three numbers.

10. A girl has x naira and her friend has ₦300 more than her.
    a How much money do they have altogether?
    b How much more money do they need so that they have ₦1 000 between them?

SUMMARY

1. a^2 is short for $a \times a$.

2. When simplifying arithmetic or algebraic expressions the *order of operations* is important.
   a If there are no brackets, do multiplication or division before addition and subtraction.
   b If there are brackets, first simplify the terms inside them.
   c Use BODMAS to remember the order (see page 126).

3. When removing brackets:
   a a positive sign outside the brackets *does not* change the signs of the terms inside the brackets;
   b a negative sign outside the brackets *does* change the signs of the terms inside the brackets.

16 Solids 2: Volume

OBJECTIVES

You should be able to:
1. Express the volume of solids in appropriate units
2. Calculate the volume of cuboids and cubes
3. Express the capacity of containers in appropriate units
4. Calculate the capacity of simple containers
5. Calculate the volume of triangular prisms.

Teaching and learning materials
Teacher: Unit cubes; cuboids (e.g. bricks, building blocks); empty packets (e.g. matchbox, chalk box)
Students: Empty packets

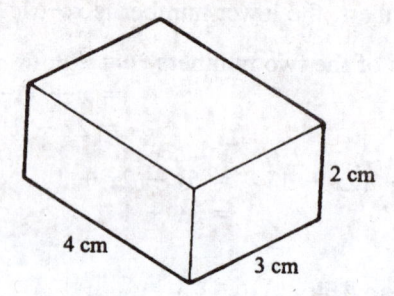

Fig. 16.2

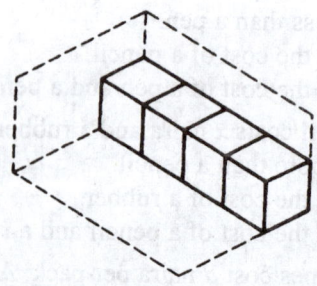

Fig. 16.3 1 row of 4 cubes.

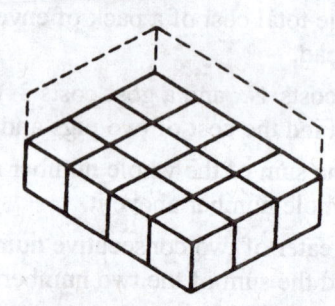

Fig. 16.4 3 rows of 4 cubes, i.e. 1 layer of 12 cubes.

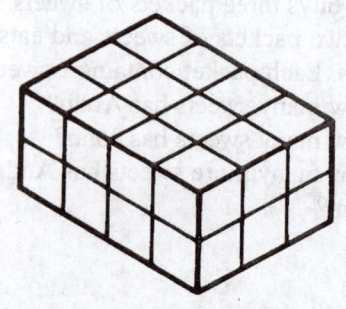

Fig. 16.5 2 layers of cubes, i.e. 24 cubes altogether.

16-1 Volume

The **volume** of a solid is a measure of the space it takes up. The cube is used as the shape for the basic unit of volume. A cube of edge 1 metre has a volume of **1 cubic metre** or **1 m³**. A cube of edge 1 centimetre has a volume of **1 cubic centimetre** or **1 cm³** (Fig. 16.1).

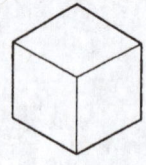

Fig. 16.1 1 cm³

It is difficult to measure volume directly. One way is to build a copy of the solid using basic units. For example, to measure the volume of the 4 cm by 3 cm by 2 cm cuboid in Fig. 16.2, a copy can be built from 1 cm³ cubes as in Figs 16.3, 16.4 and 16.5.

The volume of the cuboid is 24 cm³.

130

Units of volume

The **cubic metre, m³**, is the basic unit of volume.

$$1\,m = 100\,cm$$
$$1\,m^3 = (100 \times 100 \times 100)\,cm^3 = 1\,000\,000\,cm^3$$

Similarly

$$1\,cm = 10\,mm$$
$$1\,cm^3 = (10 \times 10 \times 10)\,mm^3 = 1\,000\,mm^3$$

When calculating problems about volume, make sure that all dimensions are in the same units.

16-2 Volume of cuboids and cubes

Cuboid

Notice that
a the 4 cm by 3 cm by 2 cm cuboid in Fig. 16.2 has a volume of 24 cm³ (as shown in Fig. 16.5); and
b $4 \times 3 \times 2 = 24$.
We can find the volume of any cuboid by finding the product of its length, breadth and height:
volume of cuboid = length × breadth × height
  = area of base × height
  = area of end face × length
  = area of side face × breadth

Cube

Similarly, for a cube of side s,

Volume of cube = (side) × (side) × (side)
  = $s \times s \times s$
  = s^3

Example 1

Calculate the volume of a rectangular box which measures 30 cm × 15 cm × 10 cm.

Volume of box = $(30 \times 15 \times 10)\,cm^3$
  = $4\,500\,cm^3$

Example 2

A rectangular room 4 m long by 3 m wide contains 30 m³ *of air.*
Calculate the height of the room.

volume of room = $30\,m^3$
area of floor (base) = $4\,m \times 3\,m = 12\,m^2$
height of room = $\frac{30}{12}\,m = 2\frac{1}{2}\,m$

Example 3

A concrete beam is 20 m *long. Its end face is a rectangle* 60 cm *by* 40 cm. *Calculate the volume of the beam. Find the mass of the beam if* 1 m³ *of concrete has a mass of* 2·5 *tonnes.*

Working in metres:
volume of beam = $20\,m \times 0·6\,m \times 0·4\,m$
  = $4·8\,m^3$
mass of beam = $4·8 \times 2·5\,t = 12\,t$

Exercise 16a

1. Copy and complete the table of cuboids (Table 16.1).

	length	breadth	height	volume
a	5 m	2 m	3 m	
b	4 m	5 m	3 m	
c	3 cm	2 cm	8 cm	
d	5 m	2 m	$2\frac{1}{2}$ m	
e	3 cm	3 cm	3 cm	
f	6 cm	2 cm		24 cm³
g	10 m	5 m		100 m³
h		4 m	3 m	36 m³
i	5 cm		4 cm	120 cm³
j	$5\frac{1}{3}$ m	3 m	$2\frac{1}{8}$ m	

Table 16.1

2. How many cm³ are in a cube of edge 2 cm?
3. A box has a square base of side 9 cm. Calculate the volume of the box if it is 10 cm deep.

131

4. A rectangular room 8 m long by 5 m wide contains 120 m³ of air. Calculate the height of the room.

5. A rectangular tank 6 m long by 2 m wide holds 36 m³ of water. How deep is the water in the tank?

6. Which has the greater volume, a 4 cm × 4 cm × 4 cm cube or a 3 cm × 7 cm × 3 cm cuboid?

7. Calculate the volume of air in a dormitory 10 m long, 5 m wide and 3 m high. If each person should have 15 m³ of air space, how many people can sleep in the dormitory?

8. A room is 3 m high and has a volume of 60 m³. Calculate the area of the floor of the room.

9. During a storm, rain falls to a depth of 1·5 cm. What volume of water will collect in a rectangular tank 30 cm by 10 cm?

10. A concrete block is made by pouring 1 000 cm³ of concrete into a 10 cm by 25 cm rectangular tray. How thick is the block?

11. A wooden beam has a rectangular cross face, 24 cm by 15 cm, and is 8 m long.
    a Calculate the volume of the beam. Express your answer in **i** cm³ and **ii** m³.
    b If the wood has a mass of 700 kg per m³, find the mass of the beam.

12. A flat rectangular roof measures 7·5 m by 4 m; 12 mm of rain falls on the roof.
    a Find the volume of water on the roof. Express your answer in **i** cm³ and **ii** m³.
    b Find the mass of water that falls on the roof if 1 cm³ of water has a mass of 1 gramme. Express your answer in kilogrammes.

13. A block of concrete is 1 m long, 50 cm wide and 4 cm thick.
    a Calculate the volume of the block in cm³.
    b If 1 cm³ has a mass of 2·7 g, find the mass of the block in kg.

14. A block measure 22 cm by 11 cm by 7 cm. How many of these blocks will be needed to build a wall $5\frac{1}{2}$ m long, 22 cm thick and $3\frac{1}{2}$ m high?

15. How many 2 cm × 2 cm × 2 cm cubes can be packed in a box 1 m long, 20 cm wide and 4 cm deep?

16-3 Capacity of containers

The **capacity** of a container is a measure of the space inside it. The basic unit of capacity is the **litre**. 1 litre of water will just fill a 10 cm by 10 cm by 10 cm cubic container (Fig. 16.6).

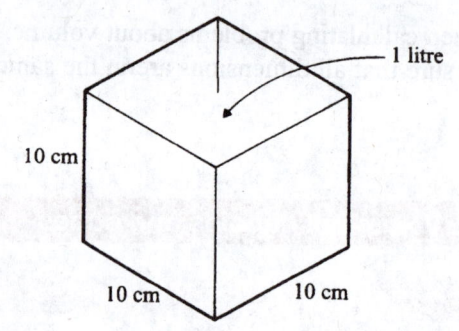

Fig. 16.6

Therefore in practice,

1 litre = (10 × 10 × 10) cm³ = 1 000 cm³

Table 16.2 shows the relation between units of capacity and units of volume.

	capacity	volume
kilolitre	1 kℓ = 1 000 ℓ	= 1 000 000 cm³ = 1 m³
litre	1 ℓ	= 1 000 cm³
millilitre	1 mℓ = 0·001 ℓ	= 1 cm³

Table 16.2

Example 4

How many litres of water does a 5 m × 4 m × 3 m tank hold?

volume of tank = (5 × 4 × 3) m³ = 60 m³
but, 1 m³ = 1 000 litres
capacity of tank = 60 × 1 000 litres
= 60 000 litres

Exercise 16b

1. A rectangluar tin measures 10 cm by 10 cm by 20 cm. What is its capacity in litres?
2. Calculate the capacity in litres of a tin 20 cm by 20 cm by 10 cm.
3. A rectangular tank, $1\frac{1}{2}$ m long and 1 m wide, contains water to a depth of 50 cm. How many litres does it contain?
4. How many kilolitres of water are there in a full tank, $5\frac{1}{2}$ m long, 4 m wide and $2\frac{1}{4}$ m deep?
5. A school's water tank measures 4 m by 3 m by 2 m.
   a How many litres does it contain when full?
   b If the school uses about 5 000 litres of water a day, approximately how many days will a full tank last?
6. Measure the length, breadth and height of a 1 litre juice packet. Use $V = l \times b \times h$ to check that 1 litre = 1 000 cm³.

16-4 Volume of right-angled triangular prism

Figure 16.7 shows how to cut a cuboid into two equal right-angled triangular prisms.

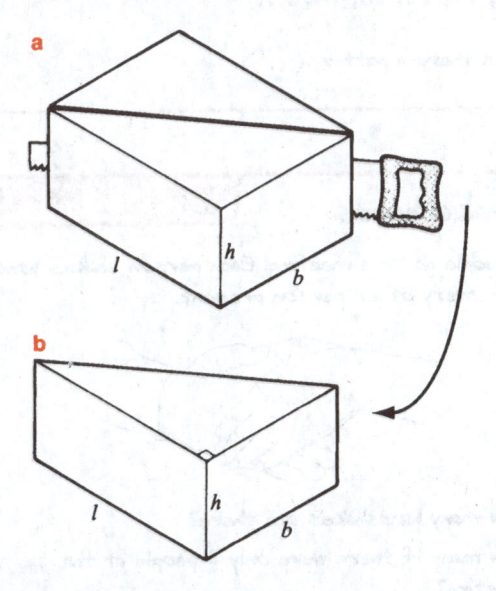

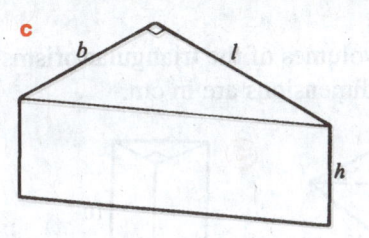

Fig. 16.7 a Volume = *lbh*.
b Volume = $\frac{1}{2}$ *lbh*.
c Volume = $\frac{1}{2}$ *lbh*.

For each prism:

volume of prism = $\frac{1}{2}lbh = (\frac{1}{2}lb) \times h$.

But, $\frac{1}{2}lb$ = area of end-face because the end-face is a right-angled triangle.

volume of prism = area of end-face × height

Example 5

Calculate the volume of the prism shown in Fig. 16.8.

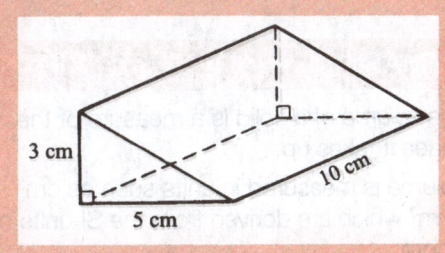

Fig. 16.8

area of triangular face = $\frac{1}{2} \times 5 \times 3$ cm²
volume of prism = $\frac{1}{2} \times 5 \times 3 \times 10$ cm³
= 75 cm³

In general, for any right-angled triangular prism:

**volume of prism =
area of end-face × distance between end-faces**

This is also true for some other types of prisms, such as cuboids and cubes.

Exercise 16c
Calculate the volumes of the triangular prisms in Fig. 16.9. All dimensions are in cm.

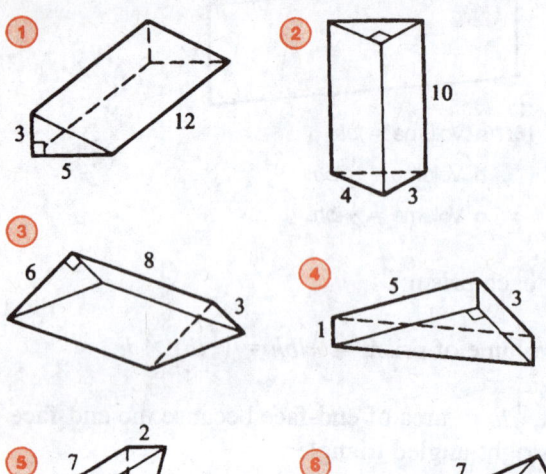

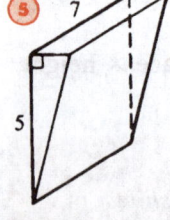

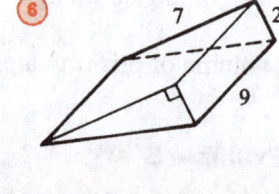

① (3, 5, 12)
② (10, 4, 3)
③ (6, 8, 3)
④ (5, 3, 1)
⑤ (7, 2, 5)
⑥ (7, 2, 9)

Fig. 16.9

SUMMARY

1. The *volume* of a solid is a measure of the space it takes up.
2. Volume is measured in units such as cm³ or m³ which are derived from the SI units of length.
3. The *capacity* of a container is a measure of the space inside it. The basic unit of capacity is the litre. Liquids and gases are usually measured in litres and mℓ.
4. 1 mℓ = 1 cm³. Also see the tables on pages 194 and 195.
5. The volume of a
   cuboid = length × breadth × height
   cube = (length of edge)³
   prism = area of end-face × height

PUZZLE CORNER
Sums and Products

10 = 5 + 5   &   5 × 5 = 25
   = 7 + 3   &   7 × 3 = 21
   = 5 + 3 + 2 &   5 × 3 × 2 = 30

What is the greatest product you can make from numbers that add to 10?

What about other numbers, e.g. 9, 11, 12, 13, 14, ...?

Is there a pattern?

PUZZLE CORNER
Shake hands

9 people go to a meeting. Each person shakes hands with every other person present.

How many handshakes are there?

How many if there were only 5 people at the meeting?

What if there were 500 people?

Chapters 9–16 Revision exercises and tests

Revision exercise 5 (Chapter 9)

1. Simplify the following.
   a $9 \cdot 04 + 6 \cdot 7$
   b $9 \cdot 04 - 6 \cdot 7$

2. Simplify the following.
   a $3 \cdot 46 \times 1000$
   b 80×10^2
   c $5 \cdot 15 \div 100$
   d $247 \div 10^3$

3. Simplify the following.
   a $8 \times 0 \cdot 5$
   b $0 \cdot 6 \times 0 \cdot 04$
   c $3 \cdot 2 \times 0 \cdot 002$

4. Simplify the following.
   a $\frac{0 \cdot 42}{7}$
   b $36 \div 0 \cdot 0004$
   c $5 \cdot 8 \div 0 \cdot 058$

5. Express $2\frac{5}{8}$ as a terminating decimal.

6. Express $0 \cdot 275$
   a as a fraction in its lowest terms,
   b as a percentage.

7. Divide $4 \cdot 914$ by $0 \cdot 091$.

8. Find the cost of $8 \cdot 5$ metres of cloth at ₦660 per metre.

9. Some copies of a textbook are put on a shelf $2 \cdot 66$ m long. Each book is $2 \cdot 8$ cm thick. How many books can be put on the shelf?

10. A trader bought a pair of sandals for ₦1 240 and sold them at a profit of 35%. What was the selling price of the sandals?

Revision test 5 (Chapter 9)

1. Select the correct answer to the following.
   $0 \cdot 017 \times 100 =$
   A $0 \cdot 00017$ B $0 \cdot 0017$ C $0 \cdot 17$
   D $1 \cdot 7$ E 17

2. Select the correct answer to the following.
   $0 \cdot 5 \times 0 \cdot 2 =$
   A $0 \cdot 001$ B $0 \cdot 01$ C $0 \cdot 1$ D 1 E 10

3. Select the correct answer to the following.
   $24 \div 10 000 =$
   A $0 \cdot 000024$ B $0 \cdot 00024$ C $0 \cdot 0024$
   D $0 \cdot 024$ E $0 \cdot 24$

4. Select the correct answer to the following.
   $1200 \div 0 \cdot 04 =$
   A $30 000$ B $3 000$ C 300 D 30 E 3

5. If $23 \times 54 = 1 242$, then $1 \cdot 242 \div 0 \cdot 54 =$
   A $0 \cdot 023$ B $0 \cdot 23$ C $2 \cdot 3$ D 23 E 230

6. A piece of string $1 \cdot 82$ metres long is cut from a string $6 \cdot 58$ metres long. What length of string is left?

7. Find the product of $0 \cdot 17$ and $5 \cdot 2$.

8. What percentage of 2 km is 800 m?

9. How many cans, each $1 \cdot 8$ litres in capacity, can be filled from a tank containing 54 litres of water?

10. The value of a house when new was ₦25 350 000. After 5 years its value had increased by $33\frac{1}{3}\%$. Calculate its value after 5 years.

Revision exercise 6 (Chapters 10, 11)

1. A baby is b weeks old. How old will it be in five weeks time?

2. What number is 8 less than a?

3. How many seconds are there in m minutes?

4. A loaf has a mass of x grammes. If it is cut into four equal pieces, what is the mass of each piece?

5. Find the sum of n metres and $5n$ cm. Give the answer in cm.

6. What is the sum of the angles of a square?

7. Two sides of an isosceles triangle are 3 cm and 10 cm. What must be the length of the third side?

8. The diameter of a circle is $13 \cdot 8$ cm long. Find the length of its radius.

9. Write down three differences between a rectangle and a square.

10. How many lines of symmetry do the following have?
   a a rectangle
   b a square
   c an equilateral triangle
   d an isosceles triangle

Revision test 6 (Chapters 10, 11).

1. The number which is 5 times greater than a is
   A $5 - a$ B $\frac{a}{5}$ C $5 + a$
   D $5a$ E $a - 5$

2. The sum of a minutes and b seconds, expressed in minutes, is
   A $60a + b$ B $a + 60b$ C $a + b$
   D $\frac{a}{60} + b$ E $a + \frac{b}{60}$

3. The number of years in x calendar months is
   A $12 + x$ B $\frac{x}{12}$ C $12x$
   D $\frac{12}{x}$ E $12 - x$

4. Which one of the following has *no* lines of symmetry?
   A circle   B regular hexagon
   C isosceles triangle   D equilateral triangle
   E scalene triangle

5. The diagonals of one of the following *always* cross at right angles. Which one?
   A rectangle B square C parallelogram
   D trapezium E regular pentagon

6. How many sweets at 50 kobo each can be bought for ₦r?

7. Express:
   a w kilogrammes in grammes,
   b h centimetres in millimetres,
   c d kobo in naira.

8. Name four quadrilaterals which have at least one pair of parallel sides.

9. What angle does the diagonal of a square make with its sides?

10. A girl is c years old. Her brother is twice as old. How old will the brother be in d years' time?

Revision exercise 7 (Chapters 12, 15)

1. Simplify the following.
   a $(-3) + (+8)$ b $(+5) - (+14)$
   c $(-7) - (+7)$

2. Simplify the following.
   a $-4 + (-7)$ b $-2 - (-10)$
   c $6 + (-9)$

3. In the year AD 21 a man was 36 years old. In what year was he 12 years old?

4. Simplify the following.
   a $2\frac{2}{3} - 4\frac{1}{2}$ b $9.8°C - 18°C$

5. Simplify the following.
   a $4x \times 5$ b $24y \div 3$
   c $b \times 3 + b$ d $\frac{1}{2}$ of $8c$

6. Simplify the following.
   a $3m \times 4n$ b $18ab \times \frac{1}{3}a$
   c $15am \div 25bm$ d $\frac{14x^2}{2x}$

7. Simplify the following.
   a $18x \div 6 - 4x + 3 \times 2x$
   b $3x - 8 \times 3x + 15x \div 5$

8. Simplify the following.
   a $3 + (4a - 7)$
   b $(5x - 8y) + 3y$
   c $(2x - 5y) + (3x - 6y)$

9. Simplify the following.
   a $4x - (3 - x)$
   b $9x - (8x + 7y)$
   c $(a - 3b) - (5a - 8b)$

10. A chair costs ₦x and a table costs ₦a more than a chair. Find the difference in cost between four chairs and one table.

Revision test 7 (Chapters 12, 15)

1. Which one of the following numbers is the greatest?
   A -2 B -30 C -100 D -50 E -3

2. Select the correct answer to the following.
   $-20 - (-70) =$
   A -90 B -50 C $+50$ D $+90$
   E None of these

3. Select the correct answer to the following.
   $3 - (-8) - 5 =$
   A -12 B -2 C $+6$ D $+12$ E $+16$

4. Select the correct answer to the following.
   $9 \times 2 - 12 \div 2 + 2 =$
   A -43 B -18 C 5 D 14 E 15

5. Daudu is n years old. His twin sisters are two years younger than he is. The sum of his sisters' ages, in years, is
   A $n-2$ B $n-4$ C $2n$ D $2n-2$
   E $n-4$

6. The temperature inside a refrigerator is 2·4°C. What will be the temperature if it falls by 3·9°C?

7. Simplify the following.
   a $3xy \times 9y$ b $2n \times 5an^2$
   c $36a^2b \div 12ab$ d $\frac{5x^2}{x}$

8. Simplify the following.
   a $3-11$ b $-9+4$
   c $8-(-15)$ d $-6+(-6)$

9. Simplify the following.
   a $-3a+(6y-8a)+y$
   b $-2x-5b-(8b-5x)$

10. Find the sum of the whole number n and the next two whole numbers greater than n.

Revision exercise 8 (Chapters 13, 14, 16)

1. The perimeter of a rectangle is 36 cm. Find the breadth of the rectangle if its length is
   a 17 cm   b 12 cm   c 9 cm

2. A wire ring has a diameter of 1 m. Use 3·14 for π to calculate the length of the wire.

3. Find the perimeter and area of a rectangle which measures 8 cm by 10 cm.

4. Find the circumference and area of a circle of diameter 56 cm. (Use $\frac{22}{7}$ for π.)

5. Calculate the area of a parallelogram of height 6 cm and base 9 cm.

6. Two sides of a triangle are 7 cm and 4 cm and the angle between them is a right angle. Calculate the area of the triangle.

7. A window is in the shape of a semi-circle of diameter 70 cm. Use the value $\frac{22}{7}$ for π to calculate the area of glass in the window.

8. Calculate the volume of a cuboid measuring 12 cm by 10 cm by 6 cm. How many 2 cm by 2 cm by 2 cm cubes would this cuboid contain?

9. How many litres of water does a 5 m by 10 m by 2 m tank hold?

10. The area of the end-face of a beam is 24 cm². Calculate the volume of a 5 m length of the beam.

Revision test 8 (Chapters 13, 14, 16)

1. The perimeter of a rectangle is 26 cm. Its breadth is 4 cm. Its length is
   A 9 cm   B 11 cm   C 13 cm
   D 17 cm   E 22 cm

2. The exact value of π is
   A 3·142   B $3\frac{1}{7}$ C 3·14
   D 3·1   E impossible to find.

3. The area of a floor 3 metres square (3 m by 3 m) is
   A 3 m²   B 6 m²   C 9 m²
   D 300 m²   E 90 000 m²

4. A triangle and a parallelogram have the same base and same area. If the height of the triangle is 5 cm, the height of the parallelogram is
   A 1·25 cm   B 2·5 cm   C 5 cm
   D 10 cm   E 25 cm

5. Which of the following is the number of cm³ in 1 m³?
   A 100   B 1000   C 10 000
   D 100 000   E 1 000 000

6. Calculate the area of a rectangle which measures 11 cm by 3 cm. Calculate the area of a square with the same perimeter.

7. Use 3·14 for π to calculate the area of a circle of radius 3 m.

8. Calculate the area of the triangle in Fig. R8. Calculate the height h shown in the diagram.

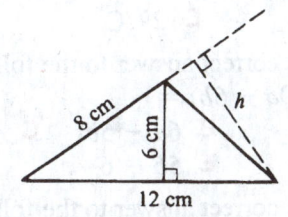

Fig. R8

9. A floor 4 m long by $2\frac{1}{2}$ m wide is concreted to a thickness of 10 cm. Calculate the volume of the concrete.

10. Calculate the area of the shape shown in Fig. R9. Use $\frac{22}{7}$ for π.

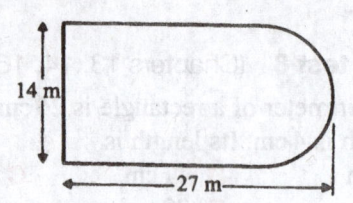

Fig. R9

General revision test B (Chapters 9–16)

1. Select the correct answer to the following.
   $3 \cdot 2 \div 8\,000 =$
   A 0·0004 B 0·004 C 0·04
   D 4 E 400

2. Which of the following is 20% of 1 hour?
   A 5 min B 6 min C 12 min
   D 20 min E 30 min

3. The difference, in grammes, between x kg and $50x$ grammes is
   A $x - 50x$ B $49x$ C $50x$
   D $950x$ E $9050x$

4. Which one of the following has two (and only two) lines of symmetry?
   A square
   B rectangle
   C isosceles triangle
   D regular pentagon
   E equilateral triangle

5. If $3 \cdot 4 \times 1 \cdot 8 = 6 \cdot 12$, then $61 \cdot 2 \div 0 \cdot 18 =$
   A 0·34 B 3·4 C 34
   D 340 E 3 400

6. Which of the following is the difference between temperatures of 17 °C above zero and 12 °C below zero?
   A 5 °C B 12 °C C 17 °C
   D 22 °C E 29 °C

7. Select the correct answer to the following.
   $3a - (9a - 5b) =$
   A $a + 5b$ B $6a - 5b$ C $-6a - 5b$
   D $b - 6a$ E $5b - 6$

8. Select the correct answer to the following.
   $12x^2y \div 3x =$
   A $4xy$ B $8y$ C $9xy$
   D $12xy$ E $16y$

9. A farmer buys n sheep at ₦a each and sells them at ₦b each. Which of the following is his profit in naira?
   A $an - bn$ B $bn - an$ C $a - b$
   D $b - a$ E $\frac{b-a}{n}$

10. A square has the same perimeter as a 5 cm by 7 cm rectangle. Which of the following is the area of the square?
    A 9 cm^2 B 25 cm^2 C 35 cm^2
    D 36 cm^2 E 49 cm^2

11. A thread is wound 100 times round a reel of diameter 3 cm. Calculate the length of the thread. (Use 3·14 for π.)

12. A student walks at the rate of 88 paces to the minute. If each pace is 0·85 m long, how far does the student walk in 10 minutes?

13. A price of ₦1 250 is marked down by ₦50. By what percentage is the price reduced?

14. What fraction of $1.75 is 77c? Express this fraction as a percentage.

15. From a piece of string $3\frac{1}{2}x$ m long, a length of $55x$ cm is cut off. Find the length of the remaining string in cm.

16. A boy is half his mother's age. If the boy is y years old, what will be the sum of their ages in z years' time?

17. Simplify the following.
    a $-4 - 9$ b $5 - (-12)$
    c $-8 - (-3)$ d $10 + (-9)$

18. Simplify the following.
    a $21 - (7x + 5)$ b $3a + 8 - (8 - 3a)$
    c $6 - (9x - 7) + 2x$

19. 4 discs, each of radius 1 cm, are cut from a 5 cm by 5 cm cardboard square. Use the value 3·14 for π to find the area of cardboard left over.

20. 1 litre of water is poured into a rectangular container. Find the height that the water will rise if the area of the base of the container is 80 cm^2.

17 Statistics 1: Purpose and data collection

OBJECTIVES

You should be able to:
1. Analyse and interpret statistical data presented in tables
2. Use statistical data for planning purposes
3. Collect and record statistical data in a systematic fashion.

Teaching and learning materials

Teacher: Data, tables, charts, graphs from newspapers, magazines and other relevant sources (to include data on drug abuse, population trends, election results, HIV&AIDS and other emerging issues); metre rule; bathroom scales

Students: Every student to bring a newspaper that contains some numerical or graphical information

17-1 The need for statistics

Statistical data

Suppose a stranger asks you for **information** about yourself. You could say lots of things. For example: your name; the town you live in; the school you go to; what you ate last night; the things you like; the things you don't like; etc.

You might also use numbers. For example: I am 12 years old; I have 4 brothers and 2 sisters; I am 171 cm tall and my mass is 48 kg; I wear size 6 shoes; my village is 5 km from the school; etc.

We use the word **data** for basic information like this. When we use numbers, the information is called **statistical data**, or just **statistics**. Table 17.1 contains statistical data about two teams.

	games played	won	lost
Eagles	18	10	5
Falcons	15	2	8

	drawn	goals for	goals against
Eagles	3	60	21
Falcons	5	19	37

Table 17.1

The statistics in the table give a lot of information about the two teams. Eagles seem to be more successful than Falcons. A good player, looking at the statistics, might prefer to play for Eagles than to play for Falcons. Thus statistics can help when making decisions.

Purposes of statistics

There are many more serious reasons for gathering statistics than selecting which team to play for. For example, statistics about population trends can inform the Government whether they need to encourage people to have smaller families; statistics about the availability of potable (drinkable) water can inform State and District planners whether or not to budget for pumps and pipelines. Table 17.2 shows the leading causes of death by age group in 2002 in a country in East Africa.

cause of death	age group (years)			
	0–4	5–14	15–59	60+
Malaria/Fever	40%	61%	16%	26%
HIV&AIDS/TB	4%	13%	56%	17%
Heart Disease	n/s	n/s	6%	23%
Injury/Accident	32%*	17%	5%	n/s

n/s means *not significant*
* Most of these deaths are linked to childbirth
Table 17.2 Leading causes of death by age group

139

Data like those[1] in Table 17.2 might tell a Health Minister that more needs to be done about malaria for young people aged 0 to 14 and that HIV&AIDS and TB need to be reduced in the 15–59 age range.

[1] Note that data is a plural word.

Exercise 17a   (Oral)

1. Refer to the statistics in Table 17.1 about the Eagles and Falcons.
   a Which team has played more games?
   b Which team has drawn more games?
   c Do the games won, lost and drawn add up to the games played?
   d How many goals have the two teams scored altogether?
   e How many goals have been scored against the two teams altogether?
   f How many games have the two teams lost altogether?
   g For every game that Eagles have lost, how many have they won?
   h For every game that Falcons have lost, how many have they won?
   i For every goal that Falcons have scored, approximately how many goals have been scored against them?
   j 'Goal average' means goals for, divided by goals against. Find the goal average for Eagles to the nearest whole number.
   k If a team gets 3 points for a win and 1 point for a draw, how many points do Eagles have?
   l Similarly, how many points do Falcons have?

2. Refer to Table 17.2.
   a What percentage of deaths are caused by heart disease in the 60+ age range?
   b Name the two biggest causes of death in the 5–14 age range.
   c What is the greatest cause of death among 15–59 year olds?
   d Which one of the following statements is correct?
      i *40% of children in the 0–4 age range die of malaria.*
      ii *40% of deaths in the 0–4 age range are caused by malaria.*
   e A newspaper reported these statistics as **Malaria still the biggest killer!**
   Do you agree with this headline? Discuss with your friends and teacher.
   f If you were the Health Minister, what would be your priority? Discuss with your friends and teacher.

3. Table 17.3 gives the statistics for the numbers of students at a Secondary School for the years 2003 to 2008.

	2003	2004	2005	2006	2007	2008
number of students	361	364	399	435	470	506

Table 17.3

   a Is the school growing in size?
   b What is the difference in the number of students in 2008 and 2003?
   c If there are about 36 students in each class, how many classes did the school have in 2003 and 2004?
   d In one year the school started a new JS 1 class. Which year?
   e In which year will that JS 1 class be a SS3 class?
   f Estimate the number of students that the school has in 2009.

4. A student made a note of the first 100 vehicles that passed on a road. The numbers of each type of vehicle are given in Table 17.4.

vehicle	lorry	bus	car	taxi	motor bike	bicycle
number	7	0	28	2	15	48

Table 17.4

   a Nearly half of the vehicles were of one kind. What were they?
   b How many vehicles had only two wheels?
   c How many cars were there for every one lorry?
   d Which was the third most common type of vehicle?
   e How many buses did the student see?

f Is it true to say that buses never go on the road?
g Is this road more likely to be in a big city or in a small village? Give reasons for your answer.

5. Table 17.5 shows how much a family spends on food, rent and entertainment for each of four weeks.

	week 1	week 2	week 3	week 4
food	₦8 900	₦7 500	₦10 200	₦8 400
rent	₦4 800	₦4 800	₦4 800	₦4 800
entertainment	₦3 600	₦4 000	₦2 900	₦3 400

Table 17.5

a Which item always costs the same?
b Which item is always the most expensive?
c What is the total money spent on rent?
d What is the total money spent on entertainment?
e What is the total money spent on food?
f During which week does the family spend most money?
g During which week does the family spend least money?
h The total income of the family is ₦28 000 per week. Approximately what fraction of this is spent on entertainment?

6. Discuss some statistics reported in newspapers with your friends and teachers. Do the statistics give you useful information? How would you use the data if you had the power?

Optional: Do Exercise 38 of your Students' Practice Book.

17-2 Data collection

It would be impossible to give statistics unless data were collected beforehand. To be able to collect data, you need to be able to count. You also need to be able to write down, or **record**, the data clearly. The examples in Fig. 17.1 show the same data collected in two different ways by two students.

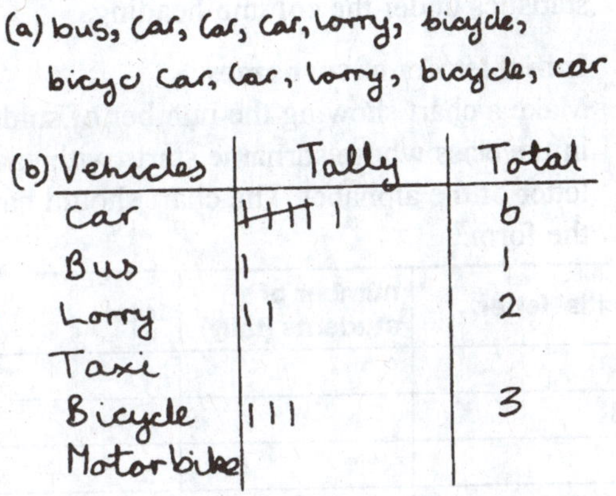

(a) bus, car, car, car, lorry, bicycle, bicyc car, car, lorry, bicycle, car

(b)
Vehicles	Tally	Total
Car	ⵑⵑⵑⵑ I	6
Bus	I	1
Lorry	I I	2
Taxi		
Bicycle	I I I	3
Motorbike		

Fig. 17.1 a First student b Second student

The first student tried to write down every vehicle as it came by. When two bicycles came by she did not have time to write them down properly. It is easy to make mistakes when counting this student's totals.

The second student spent some time before beginning to record. He wrote down all the vehicles he could think of in a column. When a vehicle came by he made a tally. It is easy to count his totals.

Work through the assignments in Exercise 17b; they show how to collect data systematically.

Class:	Date:				
Name	Age (years)	Height (cm)	Mass (kg)	Number of brothers	Number of sisters
Audu Abadu	14	169	47	1	4

Fig. 17.2

Exercise 17b

Keep the data you collect in the following assignments. You will use the data in Chapters 18 and 22.

1. **Class statistics**

   Make a large chart showing the full name of everyone in your class. The chart should contain the columns given in Fig. 17.2 on page 141. Pin the chart on the classroom wall. Find your name and enter your personal statistics under the column headings.

2. **Initial letters of surnames**

   Make a chart showing the number of students in the class whose surname starts with each letter of the alphabet. The chart should have the form:

initial letter	number of students (tally)	total
A		
B		
C		
.		
.		
Y		
Z		

3. **Preferred subjects**

   Make a chart showing the following four major subjects taught at Junior Secondary level: English Language, Mathematics, Science, and Social Studies. Record each student's most preferred subject on a copy of the following chart:

preferred subject	number of students (tally)	total
English language		
Mathematics		
Science		
Social studies		

4. **Traffic survey: Types of vehicle**

   Make a table in your exercise book as in Table 17.6 (or turn to Exercise 38 of your Students' Practice Book). Go to a place where traffic passes. Make a tally of the different kinds of vehicle that pass in one hour. (The time may be longer or shorter. Try to get between 50 and 100 vehicles.)

Name:		
Place:	Date:	
Direction of traffic: towards		
Vehicle	Tally	Total
Car		
Bicycle		
Motorbike		
Lorry		
Taxi		
Bus		
Others		

   Table 17.6

5. **Traffic survey: Traffic density**

   Make out a page of your exercise book as shown in Table 17.7 (or turn to Exercise 38 of your Students' Practice Book). Go to a place where traffic passes. Make a tally of the number of vehicles that pass during each hour for the 12 hours from 8 am to 8 pm. Work in groups. Change groups each hour.

   Note: If a vehicle passes at, say, 1 100 hours, count it in the 1 000 to 1 100 period.

Name:	Date:	
Place:		
Time	Number of vehicles (tally)	Total
0800–0900		
0900–1000		
1000–1100		
.		
.		
1900–2000		

   Table 17.7

   Note to teacher: The times available for the survey will depend on the school day. It may be necessary to obtain permission for groups to leave other lessons. At boarding schools weekend days could be used for the survey.

6. **Nature study**

   Mark out a small plot of land (about 1 m²). Count all the things you find growing, living or lying in the plot. Record the numbers of things you find. Some examples are given in Table 17.8, but you may find others. (See Exercise 38 of your Students' Practice Book.)

Things	Tally	Things	Tally
Stones (> 2 cm)		Insects	
Stick (> 2 cm)			
Seeds			
Flowers			
Bits of paper			

   Table 17.8

7. **Questionnaire**

   A **questionnaire** is a set of questions. Make a copy of the questionnaire in Table 17.9. (See Exercise 38 of your Students' Practice Book.) Leave enough spaces for tally marks. Ask the questions of 10 or 20 working adults, e.g. shop or market traders, office workers, farmers, mechanics, etc. Be sure that each person does not mind answering the questions. Be polite.

Questionnaire	Date			
How many languages can you speak	1	2	3	4
	5	6	> 7	
Which schools (if any) did you go to?	Primary	Secondary	Other	None
How many children do you have?	0	1	2	3
	4	5	6	> 6
Which vehicles have you travelled in?	Car	Lorry	Train	Aeroplane
Have you ever been to Lagos?	Yes			
	No			
Have you ever been to Kano?	Yes			
	No			
Do you own any cattle, sheep or goats?	Yes			
	No			

   Table 17.9

SUMMARY

1. *Statistics* is the study of information, usually numerical information.
2. *Data* means basic information, usually numerical.
3. It is most convenient to record data in tables.

PUZZLE CORNER

Two dice

If you throw two dice at the same time, what is the probability that neither die shows a 5 or a 6?

PUZZLE CORNER

Roman numerals

a) Which letters of the alphabet did the Romans use for numbers up to one thousand?
b) Arrange these in numerical order.
c) Arrange the letters to form the biggest possible number. What is that number in ordinary numeration?

18 Statistics 2: Presentation of data

OBJECTIVES

You should be able to:
1. Present statistical data in rank order
2. Construct a frequency table from given data
3. Present statistical data graphically in pictograms, bar charts and/or pie charts
4. Interpret statistical data presented numerically and graphically.

Teaching and learning materials

Teacher: Chalk board instruments (ruler, protractor, compasses); make sure students have the data they collected for Exercise 17b

Students: Mathematical set (ruler, protractor, compasses); data from Exercise 17b

18-1 Types of presentation

Good **presentation** can make statistical data easy to read, understand and interpret. Therefore it is important to present data clearly.

There are two main ways of presenting data:
i presentation of numbers or values in **lists** and **tables**;
ii presentation using **graphs**, i.e. pictures.
We use the following example to show the various kinds of presentation.

> *An English teacher gave an essay to 15 students.*
> *She graded the essays from A (very good), through B, C, D, E to F (very poor). The grades of the students were:*
> *B, C, A, B, A, D, F, E, C, C, A, B, B, E, B*

18-2 Lists and tables

Rank order list

Rank order means in order from highest to lowest. The 15 grades are given in rank order below:

A, A, A, B, B, B, B, B, C, C, C, D, E, E, F

Notice that *all* the grades are put in the list even though most of them appear more than once.

The ordered list makes it easier to find the following: the highest and lowest grades; the number of students who got each grade; the most common grade; the number of students above and below each grade; and so on.

Frequency table

Frequency means the number of times something happens. For example, three students got grade A.

The frequency of grade A is three. Table 18.1, a **frequency table**, gives the frequency of each grade.

grade	A	B	C	D	E	F
frequency	3	5	3	1	2	1

Table 18.1

18-3 Graphical presentation

In most cases, a picture will show the meaning of statistical data more clearly than a list or table or numbers. The following methods of presentation give the data of the example in picture, or **graph**, form.

Pictogram

A **pictogram** uses pictures or drawings to give a quick and easy meaning to statistical data. In the pictogram in Fig. 18.1 each pin figure represents a student who gets the grade shown.

Grade A	🚶 🚶 🚶
Grade B	🚶 🚶 🚶 🚶 🚶
Grade C	🚶 🚶 🚶
Grade D	🚶
Grade E	🚶 🚶
Grade F	🚶

Fig. 18.1

Bar chart

A **bar chart** is very like a pictogram. The number of students who get each grade is represented by a bar instead of a picture. The bars have the same width and usually have equal spaces between them. The height of each bar in Fig. 18.2 represents the frequency of that grade.

The scale at the left-hand side of the bar chart shows the frequency.

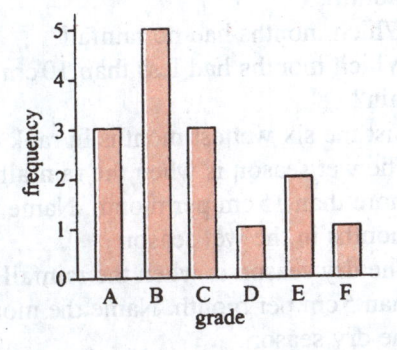

Fig. 18.2

Pie chart

A **pie chart** is a graph in the shape of a circular 'pie'. In Fig. 18.3, the total number of students (15) make up the whole pie of 360°. Each piece of the pie is a sector of the circle.

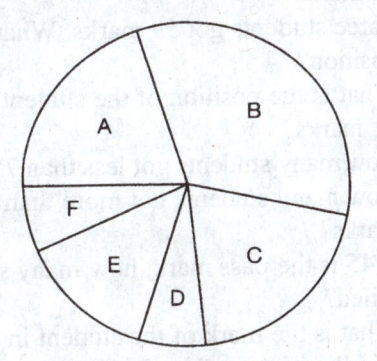

Fig. 18.3

The size of each sector in Figure 18.3 represents the number of students who get the grade shown in that sector. See Table 18.2.

grade	A	B	C	D	E	F	total
no. of students	3	5	3	1	2	1	15
angle at centre	72°	120°	72°	24°	48°	24°	360°

Table 18.2

The angles in Table 18.2 are calculated on the basis of simple ratio. For example:

angle for grade A = $\frac{3}{15}$ of 360° = 72°

angle for grade B = $\frac{5}{15}$ of 360° = 120°

The angles are used to draw the pie chart in Fig. 18.3. Usually there are *no* numbers on a pie chart. The sizes of the sectors give a quick comparison between the numbers of students getting each grade.

Exercise 18a (Oral)

1. The following is a rank order list of an exam result: 87, 82, 78, 76, 75, 70, 66, 64, 59, 59, 59, 51, 49, 48, 41.

a How many students took the exam?
b What was the highest mark?
c What was the lowest mark?
d What is the mark of the student who came 6th?
e What is the position of the student who got 76 marks?
f Three students got 59 marks. What is their position?
g What is the position of the student who got 51 marks?
h How many students got less than 75 marks?
i How many students got more than 45 marks?
j If 45 is the pass mark, how many students failed?
k What is the mark of the student in the middle of the rank order?

2 Table 18.3 shows a tally of types of vehicles that were wrecked in serious accidents during a month on a busy road.

vehicle	car	lorry	bus	taxi	others
frequency	⊬⊬⊬	⊬⊬⊬ ⊬⊬⊬⊬	⊬	⊬⊬	⊬⊬

Table 18.3

a Read the frequencies as numbers instead of tallies.
b Which type of vehicle had the biggest number of serious accidents?
c How many vehicles were wrecked altogether?
d Name some types of vehicles that might be included in 'others'.
e Is it true that cars and lorries together had nearly three times as many serious accidents as all the other vehicles?

3 The pictogram in Fig. 18.4 represents the number of people in the army, navy and airforce of a country.

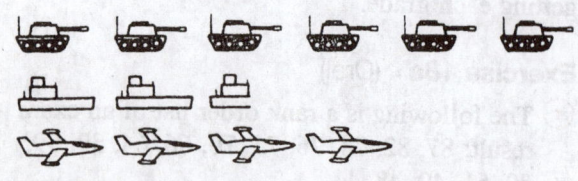

Fig. 18.4

a The pictogram shows tanks, ships and aircraft. Which of these represents the navy?
b Which has the most people, the army, the navy or the airforce?
c Which has the least people?
d Does the fact that there are six tanks mean that the army only has six people?
e Each tank, ship and aircraft represents 10 000 people. How many people are in the army?
f How many people are in the airforce?
g Approximately how many ships are there?
h Approximately how many people are in the navy?

4 The bar chart in Fig. 18.5 shows the rainfall (cm) in Kano for each month in a year.

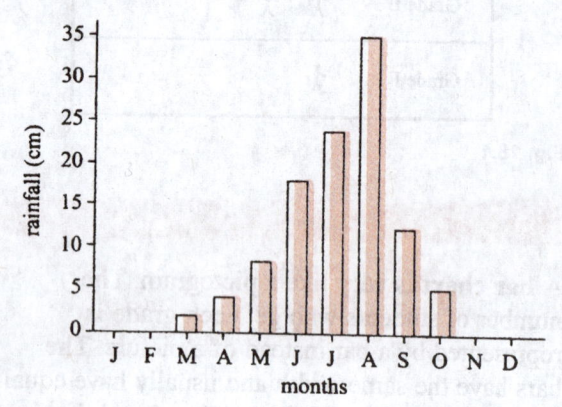

Fig. 18.5

a Which month had most rainfall?
b How many cm of rain fell in the wettest month?
c Which months had no rainfall?
d Which months had less than 10 cm of rain?
e List the six wettest months in rank order.
f The wet season is when the rainfall is more than 15 cm per month. Name the months in the wet season.
g The dry season is when the rainfall is less than 5 cm per month. Name the months in the dry season.
h Find, in cm, the total rainfall for the year.
i Is it true that over half the rainfall for the year fell in just two months?

5 The pie chart in Fig. 18.6 shows the division of money that a government spends on Universities, Teacher Training Colleges, Secondary Schools and Primary Schools.

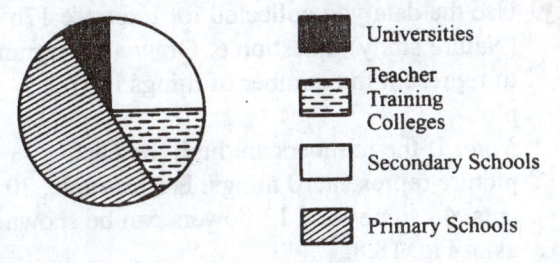

Fig. 18.6

a Does the pie chart tell you how much money the government spent?
b Which of the four gets least money?
c Which of the four gets most money?
d Can you think of reasons for your answers to b and c?
e What fraction of the money is spent on Primary Schools?
f What fraction of the money is spent on Secondary Schools?
g Approximately what fraction of the money is spent on Teacher Training Colleges?

6 As part of its policy to promote HIV&AIDS education in schools, in 2005 the Government decided to train every State HIV&AIDS Education Officer in HIV&AIDS strategic planning. The pie chart in Fig. 18.7 shows the proportion of the 36 States that had received training by April 2006.

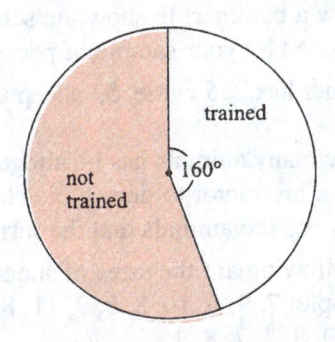

Fig. 18.7

a What size of sector represents one State?
b How many States had received training?
c How many States remained to receive training after April 2006?
d Should the FCT (Federal Capital Territory) be included in Fig. 18.7?

☞ *Optional:* Do Exercises 39 and 40 of your Students' Practice Book.

Exercise 18b (Class activity)
Use squared paper to draw pictograms and bar charts.

1 A History test was graded from A to D. The results of 10 students are given below:

B, A, C, C, B, C, D, B, A, B

a List the grades in rank order.
b Which grade did most students get?
c How many students got above grade C?
d Make a frequency table of the results.
e Draw a pictogram to show the results of the test.

2 The dress sizes of 20 women are given in Table 18.4.

size	10	12	14	16	18
frequency	1	6	8	4	1

Table 18.4

a Draw a bar chart to show the frequencies of the dress sizes.
b If you were a trader selling dresses, which three sizes would you order most of?

3 A transport company has six lorries, four vans and two cars.
a How many vehicles does the transport company have?
b Draw a pie chart to show how the vehicles are divided.

4 15 people were asked to name their favourite colour. Their answers are shown in Table 18.5.

colour	blue	red	green	yellow	black
frequency	3	4	5	1	2

Table 18.5

147

a Which is the most popular colour?
b Draw a bar chart to show the results in the table. If possible, use the given colours to colour the bars.

5. Every 800 g of dried fish contains about 300 g of water, 100 g of fats, 300 g of protein and 100 g of other substances.
   a What is 100 g as a fraction of 800 g?
   b What is 300 g as a fraction of 800 g?
   c What is $\frac{1}{8}$ of 360°?
   d What is $\frac{3}{8}$ of 360°?
   e Draw a pie chart to show the contents of dried fish.

6. Use the data you collected for Exercise 17b
   a Copy and complete Table 18.6 with the ages of students in your class.

	≤ 12 years	13 years	14 years	15 years	≥ 16 years
frequency					

Table 18.6

   b What is the most common age?
   c Draw a bar chart to show the frequency of ages of students in your class.

7. Use the data you collected for Exercise 17b (Types of vehicle), question 4.
   Either a draw a pictogram to represent the types and numbers of vehicles,
   Or b draw a bar chart to show the types and frequencies of vehicles.

8. Use the data you collected for Exercise 17b (Traffic density), question 5.
   a Copy and complete Table 18.7. (Note that times are in two-hour intervals.)

time of day	0800–1000 hours	1000–1200 hours	1200–1400 hours
number of vehicles			
time of day	1400–1600 hours	1600–1800 hours	1800–2000 hours
number of vehicles			

Table 18.7

b Draw a bar chart to show the numbers of vehicles at different times of day.
c Which are the busiest times of the day for traffic?

9. Use the data you collected for Exercise 17b (Nature study), question 6. Draw a pictogram to represent the number of things in your plot.
   Note: If the numbers are high, let each picture represent 10 things. For example, 30 ants, 45 stones and 12 flowers can be shown as in Fig. 18.8.

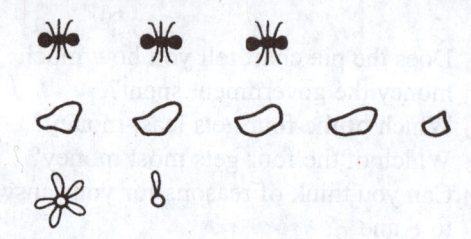

Fig. 18.8

10. Use the data you collected for Exercise 17b (Questionnaire), question 7.
    a Combine your results with those of your classmates to get the replies of about 300 people.
    b Make a frequency table as shown in Table 18.8.

schools	Primary	Secondary	other	none
frequency				

Table 18.8

    c Draw a bar chart to show the schools attended by your sample of people.

11. A farmer has 215 cattle, 53 sheep and 92 goats.
    a How many animals has he altogether?
    b Use a protractor to draw a pie chart showing the animals that the farmer has.

12. The following are the sizes of shoes worn by 20 people: 7, 9, 6, 10, 8, 8, 9, 11, 8, 7, 9, 6, 8, 10, 9, 8, 7, 7, 8, 9.
    a Copy and complete Table 18.9.

size	frequency
6	
7	
8	
9	
10	
11	

Table 18.9

   b Draw a bar chart showing the frequency of shoe size.
   c A trader sells shoes. Which sizes do you think he sells most of?

13 The scores of some students in a mathematics test were as follows:

10 7 7 8 6 10 8 8 9 6 5
9 9 8 8 5 5 10 9 8 9 7
5 9 7 10 8 6 9 7 7 8 10

   a Copy and complete frequency Table 18.10.

score	frequency
5	
6	
7	
8	
9	
10	

Table 18.10

   b How many students took the test?
   c How many students scored less than seven?
   d Which score occurred most often?

14 The ages of students in a JSS 1 class of a school are:

11 9 10 10 13 11 10 10 9 12
10 9 13 9 10 9 10 10 11 11
10 12 12 10 10

   a Represent the data in a frequency table.
   b How many students are in the class?
   c What is the difference between the ages of the youngest and oldest students?

15 A die is tossed 25 times and the following numbers are obtained.

4 6 4 3 2 5 5 5 1 3
3 4 3 5 1 2 3 3 4 5
5 2 4 3 5

   a Represent the information in a frequency table.
   b Which numbers occur most often?

Optional: Do Exercises 41 and 42 of your Students' Practice Book.

SUMMARY

1 Data can be organised and clearly presented in many ways. These include the following.
   a *Rank order list* – where data is placed in numerical order from highest to lowest.
   b *Frequency table* – where the number of times a particular event happens is recorded in a table. (*Frequency* means the number of times something happens.)

2 Data can also be represented in a *graph*, or picture. Examples include the following.
   a *Pictogram* – where pictures or drawings represent data.
   b *Bar chart* – where the length or height of a bar is proportional to the data.
   c *Pie chart* – where the size of the sector of a circle is proportional to the data.

19 Simple equations

OBJECTIVES

You should be able to:
1. Identify an equation as an algebraic sentence involving equality
2. Distinguish between true and false open sentences
3. Solve simple equations using the balance method
4. Check your solution to an equation.

Teaching and learning materials
Teacher: Flash cards of open sentences such as $3 \times \square - 5 = 13$

19-1 Equations

The expression $3 \times \square = 18$ is an **algebraic sentence**. It means 'three times an unknown number is equal to eighteen'. As we saw in Chapter 5, we can also write this as $3x = 18$. An algebraic sentence with an equals sign is called an **equation**.

$3x = 18$ is **an equation in x**.

Other examples of equations are
$y + 2 = 5$
$a = 7$
$17 - \square = 0$
$1 = 16 - 3n$

The letter, or empty box, in an equation is the **unknown**.

True and false open sentences

A sentence like $3 \times \square = 18$ or $3x = 18$ may be *true* or *false*. It depends on the value of the unknown. For example,

if 2 goes in the box, then $3 \times \square = 18$ is false,
if $x = 6$, then $3x = 18$ is true.
A sentence which may be true or false is called an **open sentence**.

Example 1

Say whether the following are true or false:

a $\square + 2 = 5$, when 3 goes in the box
b $3x + 1 = 10$, when $x = 2$.

a When 3 goes in the box:
$\square + 2 \rightarrow \boxed{3} + 2 \rightarrow 5$.
Thus
$\square + 2 = 5$ is *true* when 3 goes in the box.

b When $x = 2$
$3x + 1 = 3 \times 2 + 1$
$= 6 + 1$
$= 7$.
$7 \neq 10$, thus
$3x + 1 = 10$ is *false* when $x = 2$.

(The symbol $\neq$ means: is not equal to.)

Example 2

Is the equation $\frac{x}{4} = 5$ true when $x = 24$?

When $x = 24$
$\frac{x}{4} = \frac{24}{4} = 6$
$6 \neq 5$, thus
$\frac{x}{4} = 5$ is *not true* when $x = 24$.

Exercise 19a (Oral/QR)
Say whether the following are true or false.
1. $\square + 3 = 7$ when 4 goes in the box
2. $5x = 15$ when $x = 3$
3. $x - 2 = 9$ when $x = 10$
4. $11 + \square = 16$ when 7 goes in the box

(5) $\frac{12}{x} = 4$ when $x = 3$

(6) $2x = 22$ when $x = 2$

(7) $23 - x = 20$ when $x = 3$

(8) $\frac{\Box}{2} = 2$ when 16 goes in the box

(9) $x - 5 = 7$ when $x = 2$

(10) $6x = 36$ when $x = 6$

(11) $4 = 3 + x$ when $x = 1$

(12) $25 = 2\frac{1}{2}x$ when $x = 10$

(13) $\frac{24}{x} = 4$ when $x = 4$

(14) $9 = 14 - \Box$ when 5 goes in the box

(15) $6 = \frac{x}{3}$ when $x = 12$

(16) $15 = x + 2$ when $x = 17$

(17) $19 = 19 + x$ when $x = 0$

(18) $1 = \frac{x}{2}$ when $x = 1$

(19) $10 \times \Box = 10$ when 1 goes in the box

(20) $12 = 12 - x$ when $x = 12$

In the rest of this chapter we will use letters for the unknowns, rather than boxes.

19-2 Solution of an equation

It is usually possible to find the value of the unknown which makes an equation true. We call this value the **solution** of the equation.
   $x = 6$ is the solution of $3x = 18$.
To **solve an equation** means to find its solution.

Example 3
Solve the equation $18 - x = 7$.

The problem is to find a number which when taken from 18 gives 7. The number is 11.
   $x = 11$ is the solution.

Example 4
Find the value of x which makes $x + 3 = -5$.

What is the number to add to 3 to make -5?

The number line in Fig. 19.1 can help to answer this question.

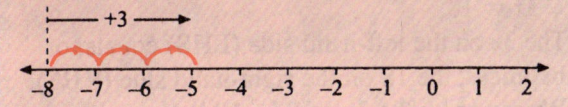

Fig. 19.1

From the number line, $-8 + 3 = -5$, thus $x = -8$.

Example 5
Find the solution of $3x = 15$.

Which number multiplied by 3 gives 15? The number is 5. Thus
   $x = 5$.

Example 6
Find the solution of $\frac{x}{6} = 5$.

The problem is to find a number which divided by 6 will give 5. The number is 30.
   $x = 30$ is the solution.

Exercise 19b (Oral/QR)
Solve the following equations.

(1) $x + 8 = 12$ (2) $x + 3 = 8$

(3) $20 + x = 28$ (4) $14 + x = 20$

(5) $14 - x = 11$ (6) $16 - x = 13$

(7) $x - 2 = 15$ (8) $x - 3 = 8$

(9) $4x = 20$ (10) $2x = 50$

(11) $12 = 3x$ (12) $72 = 9x$

(13) $\frac{x}{2} = 5$ (14) $4 = \frac{x}{9}$

(15) $\frac{28}{x} = 7$ (16) $3 = \frac{24}{x}$

(17) $14 = x + 8$ (18) $8 = 9 - x$

(19) $22 = 11 + x$ (20) $12 = x - 12$

(21) $7x = 7$ (22) $\frac{x}{6} = 1$

(23) $x + 5 = 5$ (24) $x - 3 = 0$

(25) $9 = x + 2$ (26) $15 = x + 9$

(27) $20 = 5x$ (28) $6 = \frac{x}{4}$

(29) $x - 5 = 0$ (30) $5x = 0$

The balance method of solving equations

Consider the equation
$3x = 18$.
The $3x$ on the left-hand side (LHS) equals, or **balances**, the 18 on the right-hand side (RHS). We can show the $3x$ and the 18 balancing on a pair of scales as in Fig. 19.2.

Fig. 19.2

Just as with real scales, the two sides will balance if we add equal amounts to both sides or if we subtract the same from both sides (Fig. 19.3).

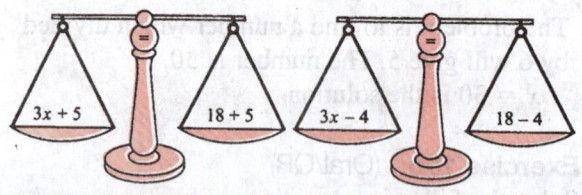

Fig. 19.3

The scales will also balance if we multiply or divide by the same amount on both sides (Fig. 19.4).

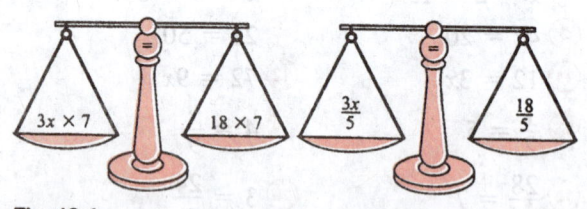

Fig. 19.4

The two sides will stay balanced if we **do the same to both sides**.

To solve $3x = 18$ by the balance method, first find which side the unknown, x, is on. $3x$ is on the LHS. If $3x$ is divided by 3 the result will be x. If we divide the LHS by 3, we must also divide the RHS by 3 to keep the balance.
$3x = 18$

Divide both sides by 3:
$$\frac{3x}{3} = \frac{18}{3}$$
$x = 6$

Example 7

Solve the following equations using the balance method.

a $x + 11 = 18$ **b** $\frac{1}{4}y = 7$ **c** $8 = x - 5$

a $x + 11 = 18$
The unknown x is on the LHS.
11 is added to x to give $x + 11$ on the LHS.
Subtract 11 from both sides.
$x + 11 - 11 = 18 - 11$
$x = 7$

b $\frac{1}{4}y = 7$
The unknown y is on the LHS.
It is divided by 4 to give $\frac{1}{4}y$ on the LHS.
Multiply both sides by 4.
$\frac{1}{4}y \times 4 = 7 \times 4$
$y = 28$

c $8 = x - 5$
The unknown x is on the RHS.
5 is subtracted from x to give $x - 5$ on the RHS. Add 5 to both sides.
$8 + 5 = x - 5 + 5$
$13 = x$
$x = 13$

Remember that the aim of solving equations is to find the number that the letter stands for.

Exercise 19c

Use the balance method to solve the following equations. Write down the steps and working as in the above examples.

1. $3x = 21$
2. $5x = 20$
3. $32 = 8x$
4. $27 = 9x$
5. $x + 3 = 8$
6. $x + 5 = 11$
7. $8 + x = 18$
8. $17 + x = 23$
9. $\frac{1}{2}x = 5$
10. $\frac{1}{4}x = 9$
11. $2 = \frac{1}{3}x$
12. $6 = \frac{1}{5}x$
13. $x - 1 = 20$
14. $x - 3 = 1$

(15) $13 = x - 7$
(16) $0 = x - 6$
(17) $9 = x + 2$
(18) $20 = x + 14$
(19) $15 = 13 + x$
(20) $7 = 1 + x$
(21) $6x = 6$
(22) $\frac{1}{4}x = 2\frac{1}{2}$
(23) $x - 10 = 10$
(24) $x - 16 = 1$
(25) $4x = 28$
(26) $27 = 3x$
(27) $3 + x = 3$
(28) $8 = x + 3$
(29) $8 = \frac{1}{6}x$
(30) $\frac{1}{10}x = 3\frac{1}{2}$

It is possible to solve the equations in the above exercise from knowledge of numbers. However, the balance method is very useful with more difficult equations. For example, the equation
$$4x + 5 = 17$$
is more difficult to solve directly. Figs 19.5–19.9 show how to solve this equation by the balance method.

Fig. 19.5

a The LHS of
$$4x + 5 = 17$$
contains the unknown. Subtract 5 to leave $4x$ on the LHS. Since 5 is taken from the LHS, 5 must also be taken from the RHS to keep the balance. Subtract 5 from both sides (Fig. 19.6).

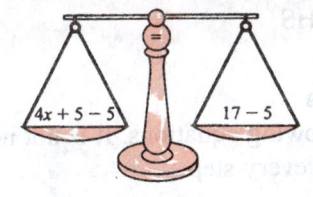

Fig. 19.6

Simplifying: $4x + 5 - 5 = 17 - 5$
$4x = 12$ (Fig. 19.7).

Fig. 19.7

b The equation is now easier. Divide the LHS by 4 to leave x. The RHS must also be divided by 4 to keep the balance.
Divide both sides by 4 (Fig. 19.8).

Fig. 19.8

$$\frac{4x}{4} = \frac{12}{4}$$

Simplifying: $x = 3$ (Fig. 19.9)

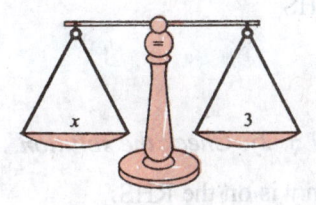

Fig. 19.9

$x = 3$ is the solution of $4x + 5 = 17$

Checking the solution

In the above example, we arrive at the result:
$x = 3$
is the solution of
$4x + 5 = 17$
How do we know that this is correct? One way is to replace x in the given equation by the value 3, then to compare the LHS and the RHS.
Check: When $x = 3$,
LHS $= 4 \times 3 + 5$
$= 12 + 5$
$= 17$
$=$ RHS
The following examples use the balance method. The solution is checked in each case.

Example 8

Solve $5x - 6 = 29$. Check the solution.

The unknown x is contained in the LHS.

153

Add 6 to both sides to leave $5x$ alone on the LHS.

$$5x - 6 = 29$$
$$5x - 6 + 6 = 29 + 6$$
i.e. $\quad 5x = 35$

The unknown x is on the LHS.
It is multiplied by 5.
Divide both sides by 5 to obtain x on the LHS.

$$5x \div 5 = 35 \div 5$$
i.e. $\quad x = 7$

Check: When $x = 7$,
$$\begin{aligned}\text{LHS} &= 5 \times 7 - 6 \\ &= 35 - 6 \\ &= 29 \\ &= \text{RHS}\end{aligned}$$

(7) $5t - 2 = 18$
(8) $8x - 9 = 7$
(9) $6 + 2a = 18$
(10) $8 + 5y = 23$
(11) $4 + 3d = 25$
(12) $1 + 7q = 22$
(13) $5 = 7b - 9$
(14) $16 = 2a - 4$
(15) $3 = 4a - 1$
(16) $9 = 5x - 1$
(17) $16 = 2a + 4$
(18) $17 = 5x + 2$
(19) $19 = 10 + 3x$
(20) $24 = 10 + 7x$
(21) $5x - 5 = 5$
(22) $6x - 11 = 19$
(23) $8x - 24 = 0$
(24) $3x + 7 = 7$
(25) $4a + 5 = 21$
(26) $25 = 11x - 8$
(27) $3 + 7b = 24$
(28) $6 = 3y - 15$
(29) $5p - 30 = 0$
(30) $4 = 4 + 8w$

The value of the unknown can be fractional.

Example 9

Solve $21 = 9 + 2y$. Check the solution.

The unknown y is on the RHS.
Subtract 9 from both sides to leave $2y$ alone.

$$21 = 9 + 2y$$
$$21 - 9 = 9 + 2y - 9$$
$$ = 2y + 9 - 9$$
$$12 = 2y$$

The unknown y is multiplied by 2.
Divide both sides by 2 to leave y on the RHS.

$$\frac{12}{2} = \frac{2y}{2}$$
$$6 = y$$

Check: When $y = 6$,
$$\begin{aligned}\text{RHS} &= 9 + 2 \times 6 \\ &= 9 + 12 \\ &= 21 \\ &= \text{LHS}\end{aligned}$$

Example 10

Solve the equation $2x + 7 = 12$.

Subtract 7 from both sides.
$$2x + 7 - 7 = 12 - 7$$
$$2x = 5$$

Divide both sides by 2.
$$\frac{2x}{2} = \frac{5}{2}$$
$$x = 2\tfrac{1}{2}$$

Check: When $x = 2\tfrac{1}{2}$,
$$\begin{aligned}\text{LHS} &= 2 \times 2\tfrac{1}{2} + 7 \\ &= 5 + 7 \\ &= 12 \\ &= \text{RHS}\end{aligned}$$

Exercise 19e

Solve the following equations. It is not necessary to write down every step.

(1) $3x + 4 = 17$
(2) $6x - 5 = 6$
(3) $5x + 8 = 11$
(4) $4x - 1 = 2$
(5) $3 + 2x = 10$
(6) $2 = 7x - 4$
(7) $19 = 6 + 9x$
(8) $8x + 3 = 4$
(9) $10x - 3 = 5$
(10) $12x + 3 = 21$
(11) $9 = 6x - 5$
(12) $6 + 14x = 41$
(13) $4a + 3 = 16$
(14) $8x - 3 = 17$
(15) $7p - 9 = 18$
(16) $21 = 8y - 4$

Exercise 19d

Solve the following equations by the balance method. Write down every step and show all working. Check each solution as in the above examples.

(1) $5y + 6 = 21$
(2) $4a + 3 = 15$
(3) $3x + 2 = 14$
(4) $6p + 2 = 20$
(5) $2n - 3 = 5$
(6) $3m - 4 = 26$

17 $10m - 11 = 12$ **18** $21 = 4 + 9n$
19 $6s - 5 = 16$ **20** $3x + 10 = 50$

Example 11

Solve the equation $3a - 7 = 8$.

Add 7 to both sides.
$$3a - 7 + 7 = 8 + 7$$
$$3a = 15$$

Divide both sides by 3.
$$a = 5$$

Check: When $a = 5$,
$$\text{LHS} = 3 \times 5 - 7$$
$$= 15 - 7$$
$$= 8$$
$$= \text{RHS}$$

You can shorten the work if you feel confident enough. However, do not cut out too many steps and always remember to do the same to both sides.

Exercise 19f (Further practice)

Solve the following equations. Write down as many steps as you need. Check each solution.

1 $4n + 3 = 19$ **2** $3y + 8 = 41$
3 $9c + 11 = 65$ **4** $5b - 12 = 3$
5 $2x - 19 = 5$ **6** $7s - 10 = 18$
7 $1 + 2u = 23$ **8** $5 + 6m = 29$
9 $3 + 8p = 51$ **10** $7 = 3a + 4$
11 $15 = 7t + 1$ **12** $29 = 5f + 4$
13 $47 = 10h - 33$ **14** $1 = 3y - 14$
15 $0 = 8d - 56$ **16** $32 = 6 + 13k$
17 $19 = 7 + 4q$ **18** $21 = 5 + 2n$
19 $2t + 3 = 14$ **20** $5a + 14 = 22$
21 $6z + 9 = 23$ **22** $4x - 5 = 5$
23 $9y - 4 = 0$ **24** $3b - 15 = 16$
25 $9 = 3h + 7$ **26** $11 = 10k + 4$
27 $5 = 4m + 4$ **28** $0 = 6z - 11$
29 $8 = 11y - 8$ **30** $19 = 16y - 21$

SUMMARY

1 An algebraic sentence with an equals sign is called an *equation*. For example, $x + 8 = 3$ is an equation in x.

2 The *unknown* in an equation is shown by a letter. For example, m is the unknown in the equation $2m + 3 = 17$.

3 If a value is substituted for an unknown, the equation may be *true* or *false*. For example, $2y = 6$ is true when $y = 3$ and is false when $y = 5$.

4 To *solve an equation* means to find the value of the unknown that makes the equation true.

5 You can solve an equation using the *balance method*. When using this method, always do the same to both sides of the equation.

6 When solving an equation, you may cut out steps in the method when you can do them mentally.

7 Check if your solution is correct by substituting the value to see if it makes the equation true.

PUZZLE CORNER

Snail in the Well

A snail is at the bottom of a well 5 m deep. It starts to climb out of the well. Every day it goes up 600 cm. But at night it slides down 400 cm.

How many days does it take to get out of the well?

20 Angles 2: Angles between lines; angles in a triangle

OBJECTIVES

You should be able to:

1. Calculate the sizes of angles between lines, using the properties of adjacent angles, vertically opposite angles and angles at a point
2. Calculate the sizes of angles between parallel lines and a transversal, using the properties of alternate and corresponding angles
3. Use the sum of the angles of a triangle to find unknown angles in a triangle.

Teaching and learning materials

Teacher: Chalk board instruments (ruler and protractor); cardboard, paper, scissors
Students: Mathematical set: protractor and ruler are essential for this topic

20-1 Angles between lines

Exercise 20a revises some of the work you did in Chapter 8. You will need a protractor, ruler and pencil.

Exercise 20a (Class activity)

1. Make a drawing like that in Fig. 20.1. BCA is a straight line. $A\hat{C}D$ can be any size.

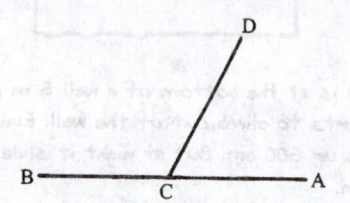

Fig. 20.1

  a Measure $A\hat{C}D$ and $B\hat{C}D$.
  b Find the sum of $A\hat{C}D$ and $B\hat{C}D$.

  c Compare your result with other students in your class. What do you notice?

2. Draw any two straight lines AB and CD to intersect at a point O (Fig. 20.2).

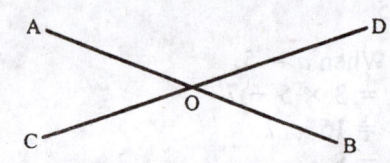

Fig. 20.2

  a Measure $A\hat{O}C$ and $D\hat{O}B$. What do you notice?
  b Measure $A\hat{O}C$ and $A\hat{O}D$ and add them together. What do you notice?
  c Guess the size of $C\hat{O}B$.
  d Measure $C\hat{O}B$ to see if your guess was correct.
  e Find the sum of the four angles at O.

3. Mark a point O on your paper. Draw any five lines each starting at O. This will give 5 angles at O (Fig. 20.3). Mark them a, b, c, d, e.

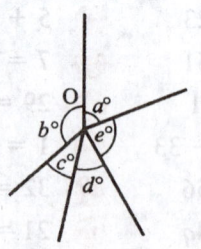

Fig. 20.3

  a Measure the 5 angles, a, b, c, d, e.
  b Find the sum of the five angles.
  c Compare your results with other students in your class. What do you notice?

While working through Exercise 20a you may have discovered some facts about the angles formed where lines meet or cross. These facts are discussed on the next page.

156

Adjacent angles on a straight line

When two angles lie beside each other and have a common vertex, we say they are **adjacent** to each other. In Fig. 20.4 AÔB is adjacent to BÔC. BÔC is adjacent to AÔB.

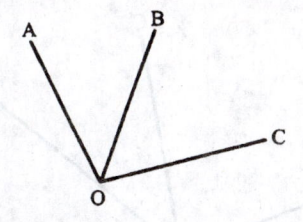

Fig. 20.4

When a straight line stands on another straight line, two adjacent angles are formed. The sum of the two adjacent angles is 180°. In Fig. 20.5
AÔC + BÔC = 180°

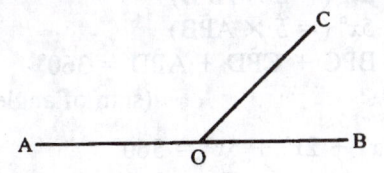

Fig. 20.5

Vertically opposite angles

When two straight lines intersect, they form four angles. The two angles opposite each other are said to be **vertically opposite**. In Fig. 20.6 AÔC is vertically opposite BÔD. AÔD is vertically opposite BÔC. Vertically opposite angles are equal.
AÔC = BÔD
AÔD = BÔC

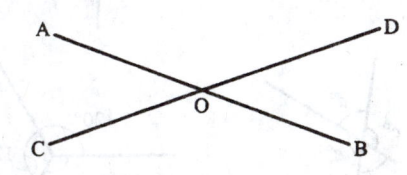

Fig. 20.6

Angles meeting at a point

When a number of lines meet at a point they will form the same number of angles. The sum of the angles at a point is 360°. In Fig. 20.7,
AÔB + BÔC + CÔD + DÔA = 360°

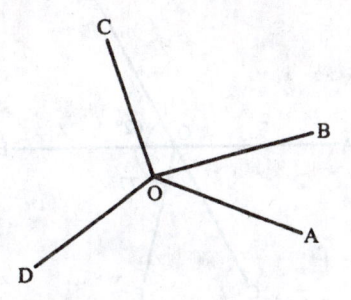

Fig. 20.7

20-2 Calculating the sizes of angles

The above facts make it possible to **calculate** the sizes of angles in given figures.

Example 1

In Fig. 20.8 AOB and COD are straight lines which meet at O.
BÔD = 53°
Find angles AOC and AOD.

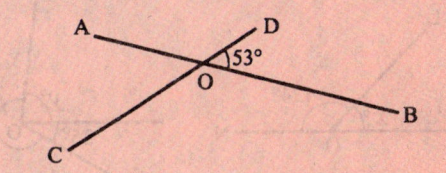

Fig. 20.8

AÔC = 53°   (vertically opposite to BÔD)
AÔD + 53° = 180°   (adjacent angles on
                    straight line AOB)
AÔD = 180° − 53°
    = 127°

Example 2

In Fig. 20.9 AOB and COD are straight lines. BÔD = 62° and BÔE = 77°.
Calculate the other angles in the figure.

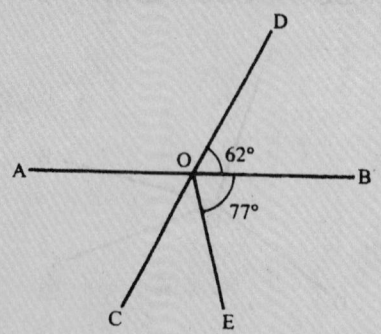

Fig. 20.9

AÔC = 62°   (vertically opposite to BÔD)
AÔD = 180° − 62°   (adjacent angles on
    = 118°   straight line AOB)
CÔE = 360° − (62° + 62° + 118° + 77°)
                      (sum of angles at O)
    = 360° − 319° = 41°

Example 3

Calculate the sizes of the lettered angles in Fig. 20.10.

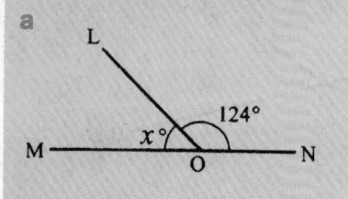

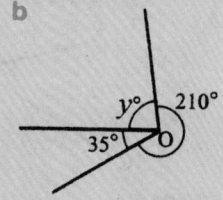

Fig. 20.10

a $x° + 124° = 180°$ (adjacent angles on
                           straight line MON)
    $x° = 180° − 124°$
       $= 56°$

b $y° + 35° + 210° = 360°$ (sum of angles
                                 at point O)
    $y° + 245° = 360°$
    $y° = 360° − 245°$
       $= 115°$

Example 4

In Fig. 20.11 AP̂B = x°, BP̂C = AP̂B, CP̂D is twice as big as AP̂B, and reflex AP̂D is five times as big as AP̂B. Make an equation in x. Solve the equation and find the four angles.

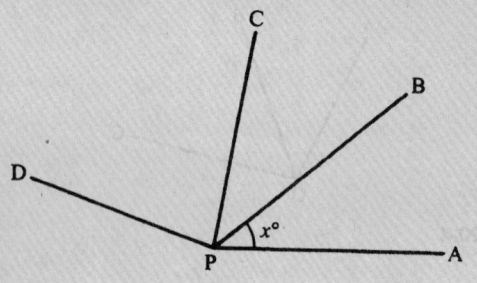

Fig. 20.11

AP̂B = x°
BP̂C = x° (= AP̂B)
CP̂D = 2x° (= 2 × AP̂B)
AP̂D = 5x° (= 5 × AP̂B)
AP̂B + BP̂C + CP̂D + AP̂D = 360°
                          (sum of angles at P)

$x° + x° + 2x° + 5x° = 360°$
$9x = 360°$
$x = \frac{360°}{9} = 40°$

The four angles are 40°, 40°, 80° and 200°.

Exercise 20b (Class activity/Oral/QR)

Find the size of the lettered angles in Fig. 20.12. Give reasons.

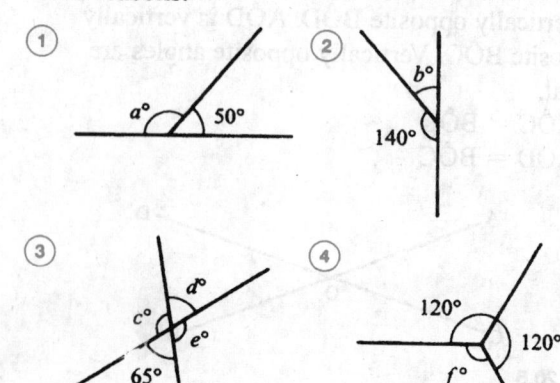

Fig. 20.12

158

③ In Fig. 20.14, calculate RX̂S, given that PX̂Q = 35° and RX̂Q = 98°.

④ In Fig. 20.14, calculate PX̂Q, if QX̂R is a right angle and RX̂S = 68°.

⑤ In Fig. 20.15, BX̂C = 36° and AX̂D = 126°.
  a If BX̂D is a right angle, calculate CX̂D and AX̂B.
  b Find the size of AX̂C.
  c In what way could the drawing be made better?

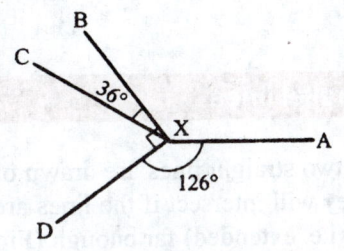

Fig. 20.15

⑥ In Fig. 20.16, the angles marked $x°$ are equal to each other and the angles marked $y°$ are equal to each other. Make an equation using the letters x and y. Hence calculate MÔN.

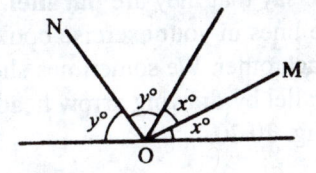

Fig. 20.16

⑦ In Fig. 20.17, EK̂F = $x°$, FK̂G is twice as big as EK̂F, GK̂H is three times as big as EK̂F and HK̂E is four times as big as EK̂F.

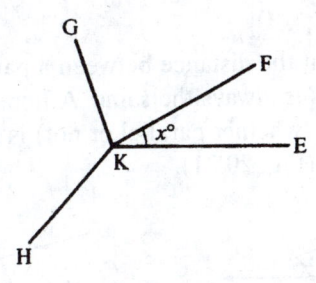

Fig. 20.17

  a Make an equation in x.
  b Solve the equation to find the four angles.
  c Check your answer by finding the sum of the four angles.

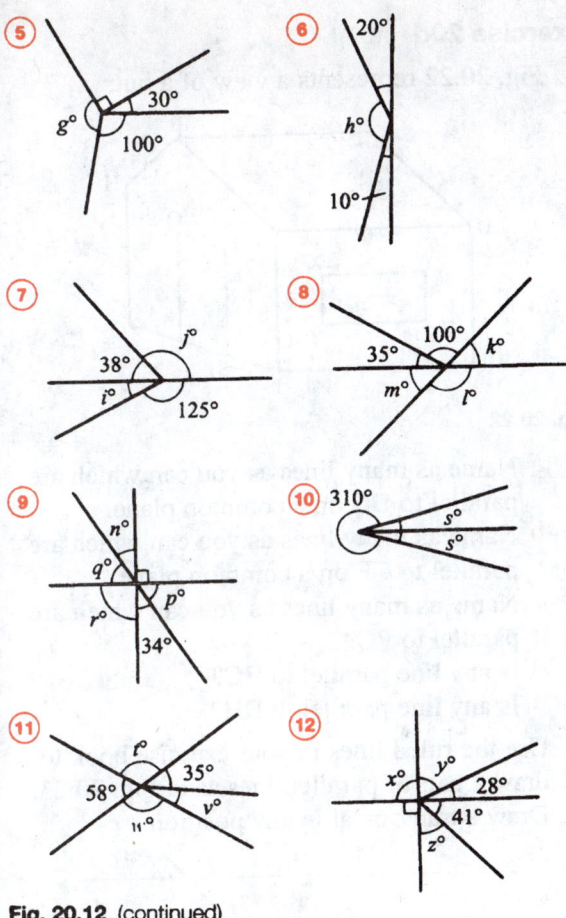

Fig. 20.12 (continued)

Exercise 20c

① In Fig. 20.13, PÔR = 37°. Calculate the other three angles. Give reasons.

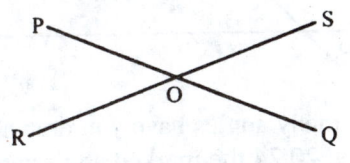

Fig. 20.13

② In Fig. 20.14, if PX̂Q = 61° and RX̂S = 84°, calculate QX̂R.

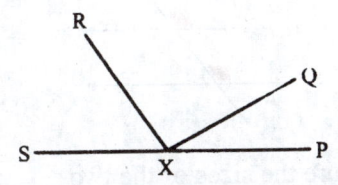

Fig. 20.14

159

8. In Fig. 20.18
   $V\hat{X}W = 2 \times U\hat{X}V$ and
   $W\hat{X}Y = 3 \times V\hat{X}W$.
   Calculate $U\hat{X}V$. (*Hint*: Let $U\hat{X}V = x°$. Form an equation in x and then solve it.)

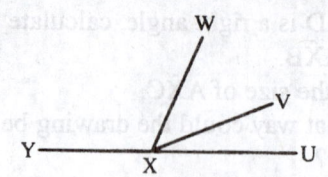

Fig. 20.18

20-3 Parallel lines

Usually, if two straight lines are drawn on a plane, they will intersect if the lines are **produced** (i.e. extended) far enough (Fig. 20.19).

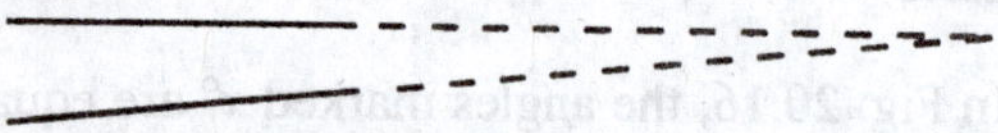

Fig. 20.19

If the lines never meet, however far they are produced, we say that they are **parallel**. For example, the lines in your exercise book are parallel to each other. We sometimes show that lines are parallel by drawing arrow heads on them as in Fig. 20.20.

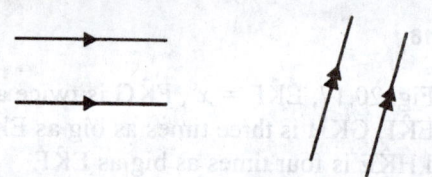

Fig. 20.20

Notice that the distance between a pair of parallel lines is always the same. A line cutting a pair of lines (whether parallel or not) is called a **transversal** (Fig. 20.21).

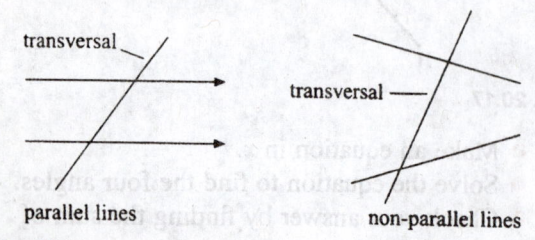

Fig. 20.21

Exercise 20d

1. Fig. 20.22 represents a view of a hut.

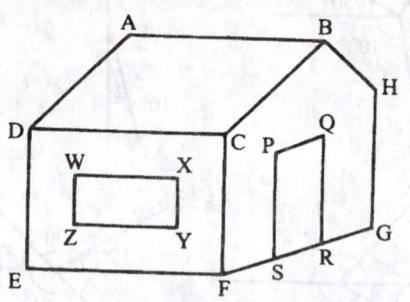

Fig. 20.22

a Name as many lines as you can which are parallel to DC on a common plane.
b Name as many lines as you can which are parallel to CF on a common plane.
c Name as many lines as you can which are parallel to PQ.
d Is any line parallel to BC?
e Is any line parallel to BH?

2. Use the ruled lines in your exercise book to draw a pair of parallel lines as in Fig. 20.23. Draw a transversal in any position.

Fig. 20.23

a How many angles have you drawn?
b In Fig. 20.24 the marked angles are called **corresponding angles**. They are in the same, or corresponding, positions at the two intersections.

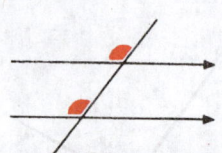

Fig. 20.24

Measure the sizes of the two corresponding angles on your diagram. What do you notice?

c Fig. 20.25 shows two other pairs of corresponding angles. Draw a sketch to show one more pair of corresponding angles.

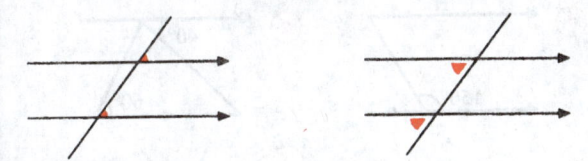

Fig. 20.25

Measure each pair of corresponding angles on your diagram. What do you notice? Corresponding angles are sometimes called **F angles**. Can you think why?

d In Fig. 20.26, the marked angles are called alternate angles. Measure the size of this pair of **alternate angles** on your diagram. What do you notice?

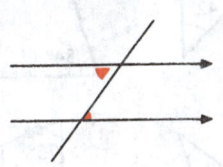

Fig. 20.26

e There is one other pair of alternate angles (Fig. 20.27). Measure these angles on your diagram. What do you notice? Alternate angles are sometimes called **Z angles**. Can you think why?

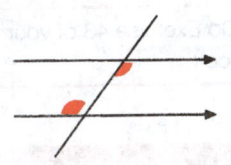

Fig. 20.27

In Fig. 20.28 name the angle that
a corresponds to $A\hat{X}P$, $B\hat{X}Y$, $Q\hat{Y}D$, $C\hat{Y}Q$;
b is alternate to $B\hat{X}Y$, $X\hat{Y}D$.

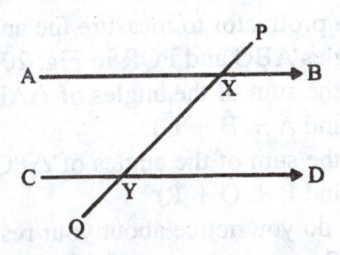

Fig. 20.28

In Fig. 20.29, which angle corresponds to
a $\hat{r}$ b $\hat{p}$ c $\hat{z}$ d $\hat{j}$?

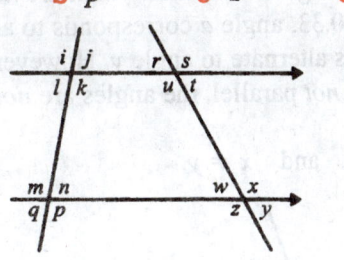

Fig. 20.29

Which angle is alternate to
e $\hat{t}$ f $\hat{m}$ g $\hat{w}$ h $\hat{l}$?

Fig. 20.30 shows a pair of parallel lines and a transversal intersecting at X and Y. One angle is given as 80°. Sketch a copy of the diagram. Fill in the sizes of all the angles at X. Try to fill in the sizes of the angles at Y.

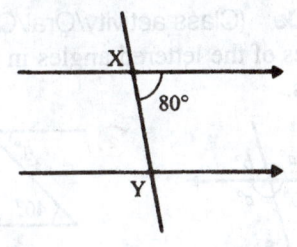

Fig. 20.30

While working through Exercise 20d you may have noticed the following facts about the angles formed when a transversal crosses parallel lines.

Corresponding angles

Corresponding angles are equal (Fig. 20.31).

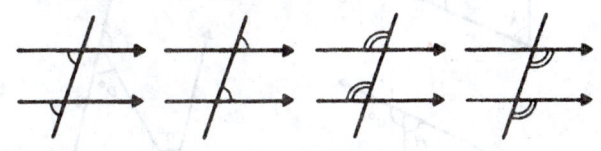

Fig. 20.31

Alternate angles

Alternate angles are equal (Fig. 20.32).

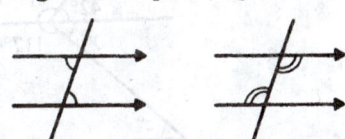

Fig. 20.32

Note: It is possible to have corresponding and alternate angles with lines which are *not* parallel. In Fig. 20.33, angle *a* corresponds to angle *b*; angle *x* is alternate to angle *y*. However, since the lines are *not* parallel, the angles are *not* equal, i.e.

$a \neq b$ and $x \neq y$.

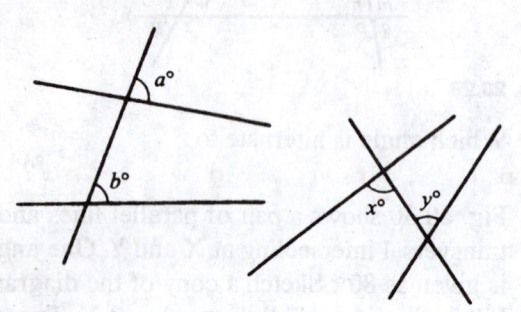

Fig. 20.33

Exercise 20e (Class activity/Oral/QR)

Find the sizes of the lettered angles in Fig. 20.34. Give reasons.

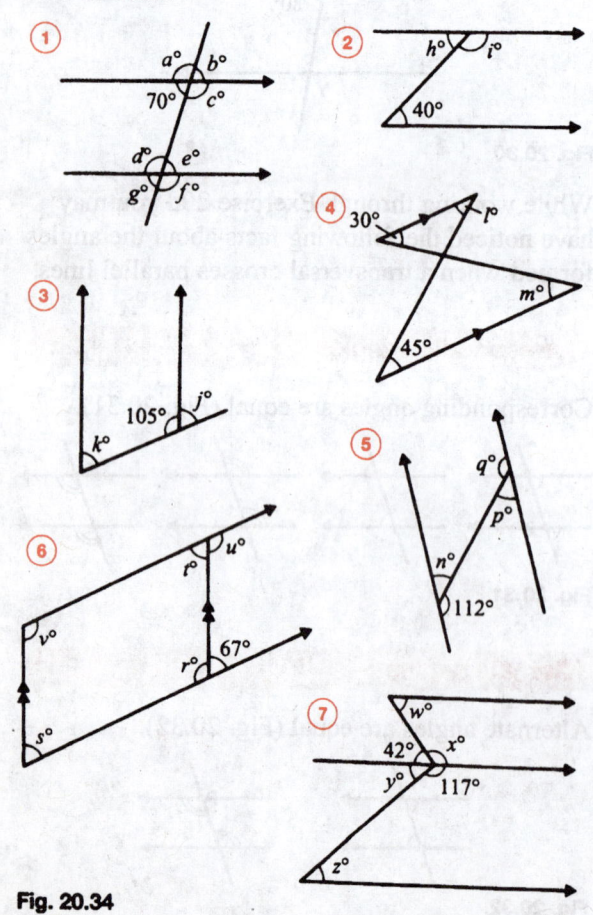

Fig. 20.34

Exercise 20f

Sketch a copy of each diagram in Fig. 20.35. Do not make an accurate drawing. Fill in the sizes of the missing angles.

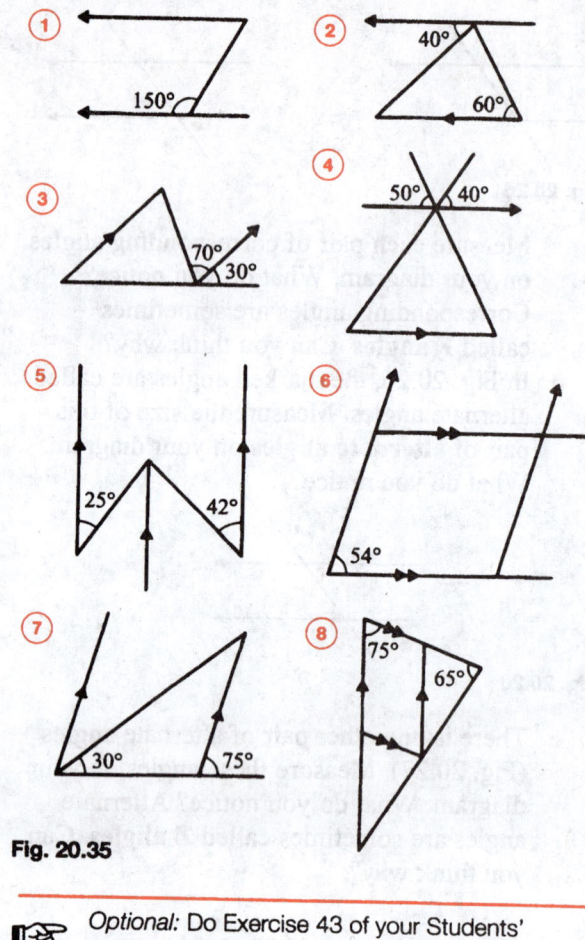

Fig. 20.35

👉 *Optional:* Do Exercise 43 of your Students' Practice Book.

20-4 Angles in a triangle

Tri-angle means *three* angles.

Exercise 20g

1. **a** Use a protractor to measure the angles in triangles ABC and PQR in Fig. 20.36.
   b Find the sum of the angles of △ABC (i.e. find $\hat{A} + \hat{B} + \hat{C}$).
   c Find the sum of the angles of △PQR (i.e. find $\hat{P} + \hat{Q} + \hat{R}$).
   d What do you notice about your results in **b** and **c**?

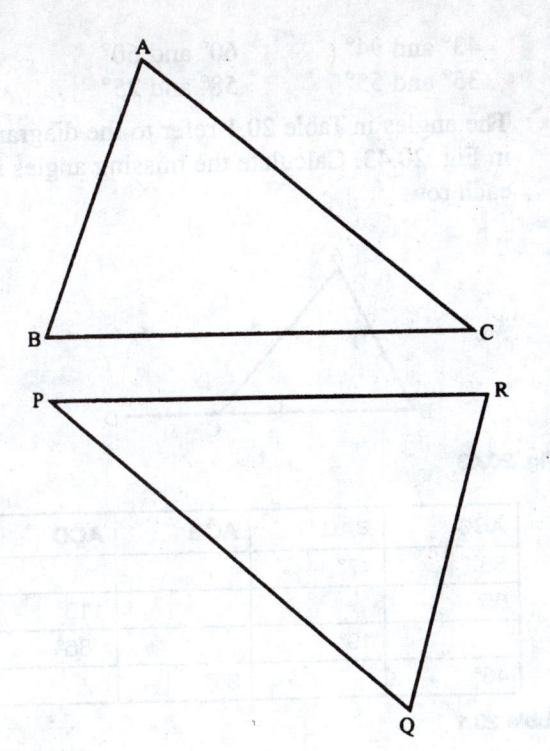

Fig. 20.36

2. Draw two large triangles. One of them should include an obtuse angle.
   a Measure the angles in each triangle.
   b Find the sum of the angles in each triangle.
   c What do you notice about your results in b? Do your friends get the same kinds of results?

3. a Draw any triangle. Cut it out carefully along its sides.
   b Tear off the three angles of the triangle as in Fig. 20.37.

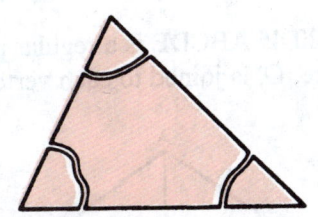

Fig. 20.37

   c Take the three angles and arrange them as in Fig. 20.38.

Fig. 20.38

d What do you notice? What is the sum of the angles on a straight line?

When working through Exercise 20g you may have noticed that the sum of the angles of a triangle is 180°. This is true for any triangle.

We can show this in the following way. In Fig. 20.39, ABC is any triangle. Its angles are $x°$, $y°$ and $z°$.

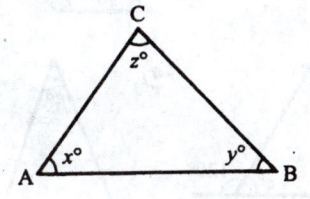

Fig. 20.39

In Fig. 20.40 PCQ is a line through C parallel to AB.

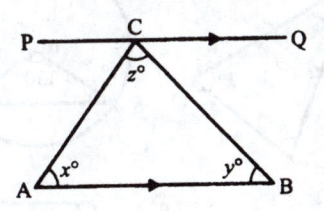

Fig. 20.40

We can use the alternate angles fact as in Fig. 20.41 to fill in the missing angles at C.

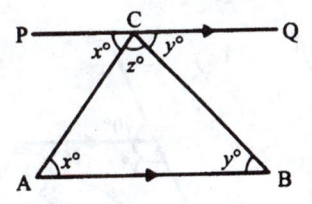

Fig. 20.41

At C, the three angles are adjacent on a straight line. Thus $x° + y° + z° = 180°$. But $x°$, $y°$ and $z°$ are also the sizes of the angles of the △ABC. Thus the sum of the angles of any triangle is 180°.

Use this fact in Exercise 20h.

Exercise 20h (Class activity/Oral/QR)

State the sizes of the lettered angles in Fig. 20.42. Give reasons.

Note: In any diagram, lines marked with a small line are equal in length.

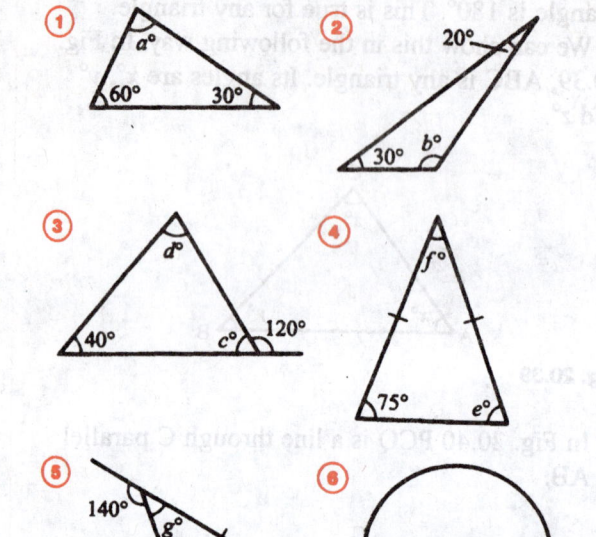

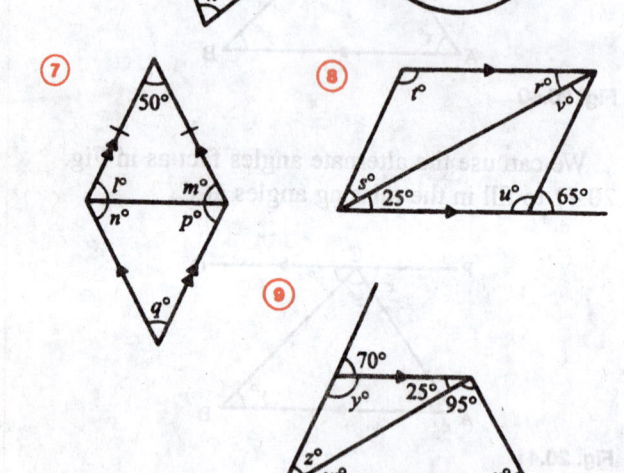

Fig. 20.42

Exercise 20i

1. Calculate the third angle of a triangle in which two of the angles are as follows.
   a 47° and 65° b 24° and 77°
   c 56° and 18° d 39° and 21°
   e each 58°
   f 103° and 42°
   g 69° and 46° h 38° and 71°
   i 43° and 94° j 60° and 60°
   k 35° and 55° l 58° and 25°

2. The angles in Table 20.1 refer to the diagram in Fig. 20.43. Calculate the missing angles in each row.

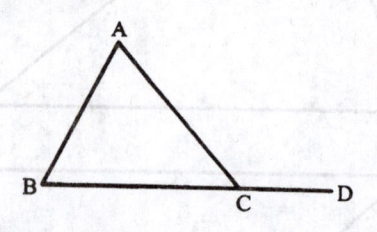

Fig. 20.43

	AB̂C	BÂC	AĈB	AĈD
a	58°	47°		
b	65°			118°
c		19°		86°
d	46°		35°	

Table 20.1

3. In Fig. 20.44, AB̂C = $x°$. BÂC is twice as big as AB̂C. AĈB is three times as big as AB̂C.
   a Make an equation in x. Solve the equation.
   b Find the three angles of the triangle.

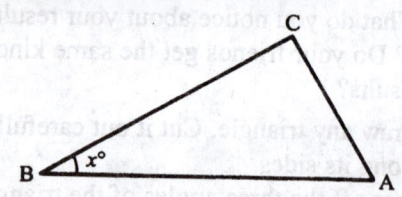

Fig. 20.44

4. In Fig. 20.45 ABCDE is a regular pentagon. Its centre, O, is joined to each vertex.

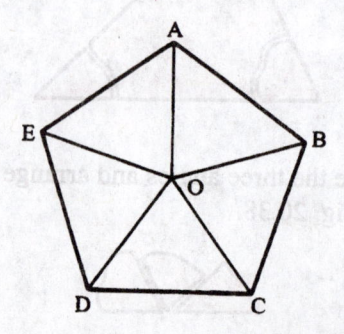

Fig. 20.45

a Calculate the size of each angle at O.
b What kind of triangle is △AOB?
c Calculate the angles of △AOB.

5 Sketch a copy of each diagram in Fig. 20.46. Fill in the missing angles.

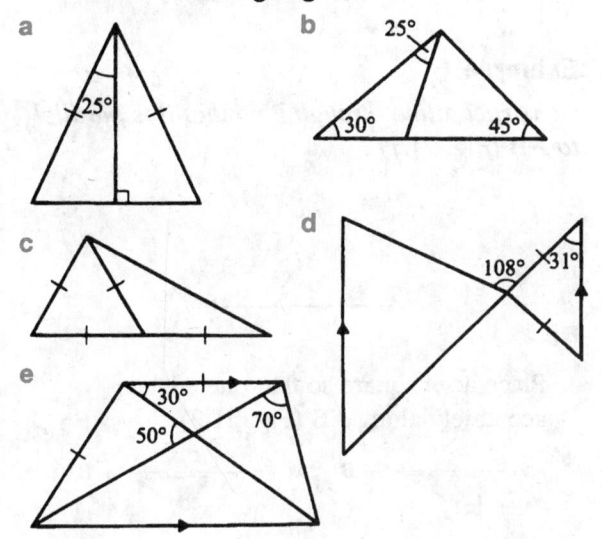

a
b
c
d
e

Fig. 20.46

☞ *Optional:* Do Exercise 44 of your Students' Practice Book.

SUMMARY

1 The sum of *adjacent angles* on a straight line is 180° (see Fig. 20.47).

$x° + y° = 180°$

adjacent angles

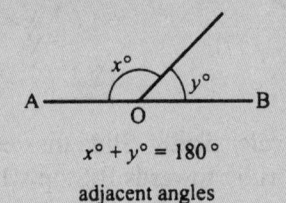

Fig. 20.47

2 *Vertically opposite* angles are equal (see Fig. 20.48).

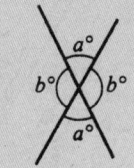

vertically opposite angles

Fig. 20.48

3 The sum of the *angles at a point* is 360° (see Fig. 20.49).

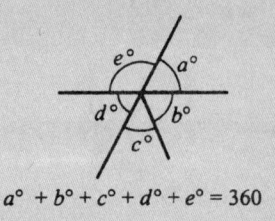

$a° + b° + c° + d° + e° = 360$

Fig. 20.49

4 Fig. 20.50 shows two *non-parallel* lines cut by a transversal. The corresponding and alternate angles formed are shown. In this case they are not equal.

transversal   transversal

non-parallel lines

corresponding angles   alternate angles

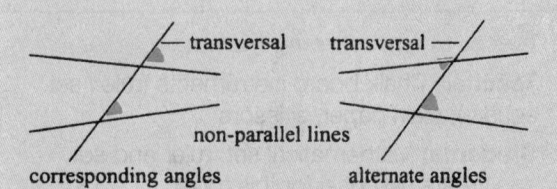

Fig. 20.50

5 If two *parallel* lines are cut by a transversal (Fig. 20.51), *alternate angles* are equal. *Corresponding angles* are also equal.

parallel lines

alternate angles equal   corresponding angles equal

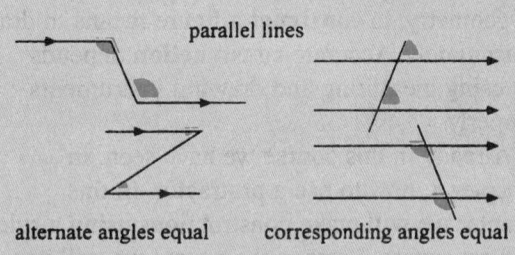

Fig. 20.51

Alternate angles are sometimes called Z angles.
Corresponding angles are sometimes called F angles.

6 A triangle has three angles. The sum of its angles is 180°.

165

21 Construction: Parallel and perpendicular lines

OBJECTIVES

You should be able to:
1 Construct parallel lines using ruler and set square
2 Construct perpendiculars to a line, or from a point to a line, using ruler and set square.

Teaching and learning materials
Teacher: Chalk board instruments (ruler, set square); plain paper, scissors
Students: Mathematical set: ruler and set square are essential for this topic

21-1 Construction

In geometry, to **construct** a figure means to draw it accurately. Accurate **construction** depends on using measuring and drawing instruments properly.

Already in this course we have seen, in Chapter 8, how to use a protractor. In this chapter we will make constructions using a ruler and set square. Later in the course we will use other instruments, such as compasses. Make sure that you have a pencil, a ruler and a set square before beginning work on this chapter. You will also need a protractor for some of the questions.

Before starting construction questions, make a **rough sketch** of what you are going to draw. This will help you when making the accurate construction.

21-2 Construction of parallel lines

Work on a blank sheet of paper. Follow Example 1 carefully.

Example 1

Construct a line through P so that it is parallel to AB (Fig. 21.1)

Fig. 21.1

a Place a set square so that one edge is accurately along AB (Fig. 21.2).

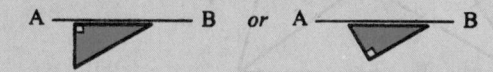

Fig. 21.2

b Place a ruler along one of the other edges of the set square (Fig. 21.3). (Use the left-hand edge if you are right handed.)

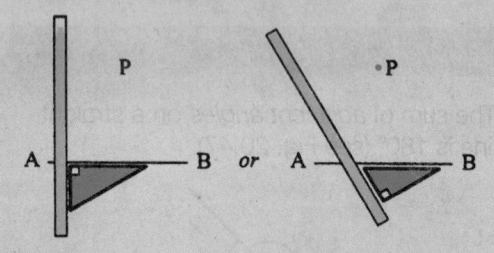

Fig. 21.3

c Hold the ruler firmly. Slide the set square along the ruler towards P. Stop when the edge that was on AB reaches P. Draw a line along this edge of the set square through P (Fig. 21.4).

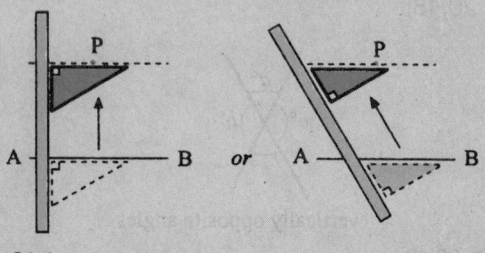

Fig. 21.4

166

Notice, in Example 1, that since corresponding angles are equal, the line through P and the line AB are parallel.

Exercise 21a

Work on blank (i.e. unruled) paper.

1. **a** Draw a straight line AB on a piece of unruled paper.
   b Mark a point P which is not on the line.
   c Use a ruler and set square to draw a line through P which is parallel to AB.

2. Use a ruler and set square to draw four lines that are parallel to each other.

3. **a** Draw any triangle near the centre of a sheet of paper.
   b Use a ruler and set square to draw another triangle with sides parallel to those of the first triangle.

4. **a** Draw angle ABC = 70° so that the arms BA and BC are 5 cm and 3 cm long. See the sketch in Fig. 21.5.

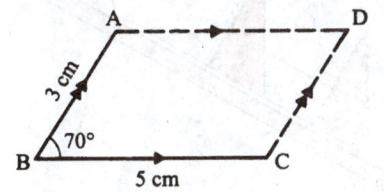

Fig. 21.5

   b Draw a line through A parallel to BC.
   c Draw a line through C parallel to BA to make parallelogram ABCD.
   d Measure the four sides of the parallelogram. What do you notice?
   e Measure the four angles of the parallelogram. What do you notice?

5. Use a ruler and set square to draw any parallelogram (*not* a rectangle or a square). Measure both obtuse angles. Measure both acute angles. What do you notice?

6. **a** Construct a parallelogram ABCD with AB = 3 cm, BC = 4 cm and $\hat{B}$ = 75°.
   b Draw the diagonals AC and BD to intersect at point X.
   c Measure XA and XC. Measure XB and XD.
   d What can you say about the point X?

7. **a** Draw two parallelograms of any size and shape.
   b Repeat the measurements of the diagonals as in question 6.
   c Does it seem to be true to say that the diagonals of a parallelogram **bisect** each other? (Bisect means: to cut in half.)

8. A **rhombus** is a parallelogram with all its sides the same length.
   a Construct a rhombus with one angle of 65° and each side 4 cm long.
   b Measure the angle between the diagonals.

9. **a** Construct the trapezium ABCD shown in Fig. 21.6.

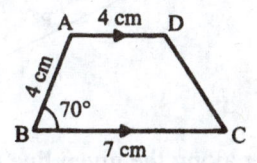

Fig. 21.6

   b Measure DC and the three unknown angles.

10. **a** Construct trapezium ABCD so that BC = 6 cm, AB = 3 cm, $\hat{B}$ = 80° and $\hat{C}$ = 70°.
    b Measure BD.

☞ *Optional:* Do Exercise 46 of your Students' Practice Book.

21-3 Constructing perpendiculars

Perpendicular lines

When two lines meet at right angles we say that they are **perpendicular** to each other.

In Fig. 21.7, XY is perpendicular to AB *and* AB is perpendicular to XY.

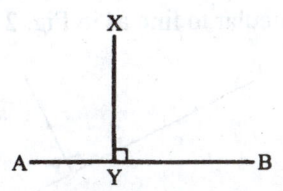

Fig. 21.7

167

Lines which meet perpendicularly are very common. Adjacent edges of a door frame are perpendicular to each other. The margin in an exercise book is perpendicular to the ruled lines. There are many other examples.

To construct a perpendicular from a point on a line

In Fig. 21.8, P is any point on a line l. It is required to construct a line through P perpendicular to line l.

Fig. 21.8

Method:
a Place a ruler along the given line (Fig. 21.9).

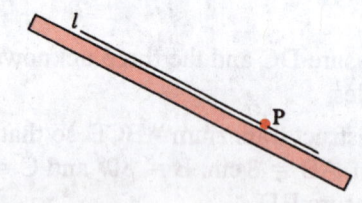

Fig. 21.9

b Use the two edges of the set square which contain its right angle. Place one of these edges along the ruler. Slide the set square along the ruler until the other edge reaches P (Fig. 21.10).

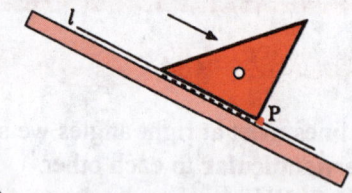

Fig. 21.10

c Hold the set square firm. Draw the line through P perpendicular to line as in Fig. 21.11.

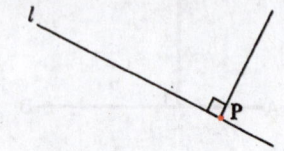

Fig. 21.11

To construct a perpendicular to a line from a point outside the line

In this case the point P is some distance away from the line l as in Fig. 21.12.

a Place a ruler along the given line (Fig. 21.12).

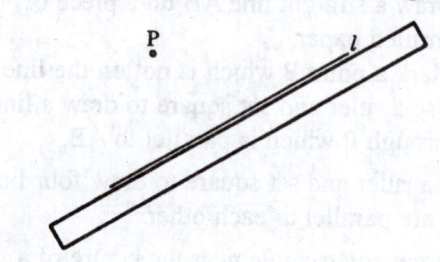

Fig. 21.12

b Use the two edges of a set square which are the arms of its right angle. Place one of these edges along the ruler. Slide the set square along the ruler until the other edge reaches P (Fig. 21.13).

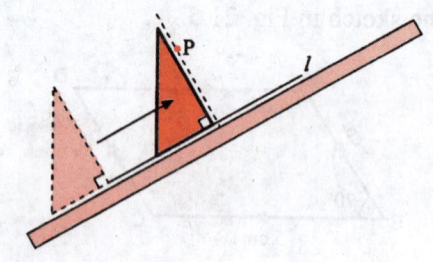

Fig. 21.13

c Hold the set square firm. Draw the line through P to meet the line perpendicularly (Fig. 21.14).

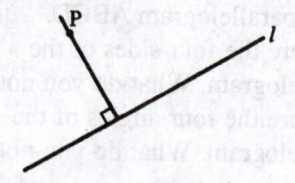

Fig. 21.14

The perpendicular distance of a point from a line

In Fig. 21.15 P is a point and l is any line.

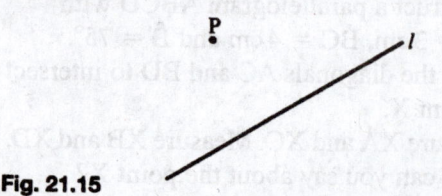

Fig. 21.15

P is different distances from different points D1, D2, D3, D4, ... on the line (Fig. 21.16).

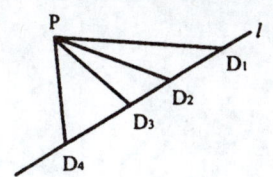

Fig. 21.16

One point on the line is nearest to P. This is the point D such that PD is perpendicular to *l* (Fig. 21.17).

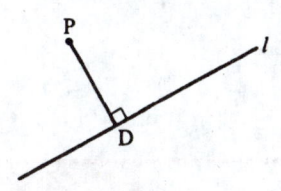

Fig. 21.17

The length PD is the **perpendicular distance** of P from line *l*.

Exercise 21b

1. Draw any line at an angle to the rules in your exercise book. Mark four points A, B, C and D on the line.
   a Use a ruler and set square to draw lines through A and B that are perpendicular to the line, and above it.
   b Use a ruler and set square to draw lines through C and D that are perpendicular to the line, and below it.
   See Fig. 21.18.

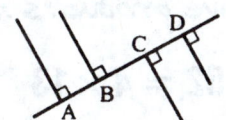

Fig. 21.18

   c What can you say about the four lines you have drawn?

2. Mark a point P near the middle of a page in your exercise book. Make sure that P is between two of the ruled lines in your exercise book. Use ruler and set square to draw and measure the perpendicular distance of P from
   a the line which is 4 lines above P,
   b the line which is 6 lines below P,
   c the left-hand margin.

3. Trace Fig. 21.19 into your exercise book. Draw and measure the perpendicular distances of P from the five sides of the pentagon.

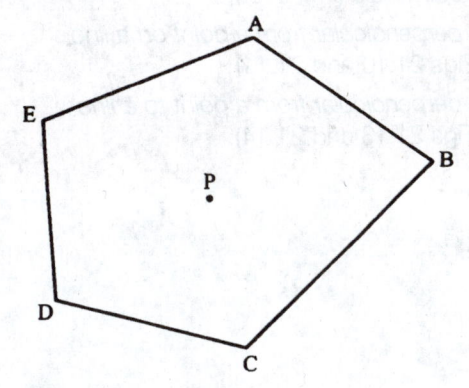

Fig. 21.19

4. Use ruler and set square to construct the following.
   a a square of side 3 cm
   b a square of side 5 cm
   c a rectangle 3 cm by 6 cm
   d a rectangle 4 cm by 5 cm

5. Use ruler and set square to construct a pair of parallel lines that are
   a 3 cm apart   b 5 cm apart
   c 4·2 cm apart   d 57 mm apart.

6. Turn back to the parallelograms you constructed in Exercise 21a, questions 4 and 6. In each case, measure the perpendicular distances between
   a parallel lines AD and BC,
   b parallel lines AB and DC.
   Hence calculate the area of each parallelogram in two ways.

Optional: Do Exercise 47 of your Students' Practice Book.

SUMMARY

1. In mathematics *to construct* a figure means to draw it accurately.
2. When constructing figures, first make a *freehand sketch*. Show all the measurements on your sketch.
3. A *ruler* and *set square* can be used to construct
   parallel lines (Fig. 21.4),
   a *perpendicular from a point on a line* (Figs 21.10 and 21.11)
   a *perpendicular from a point to a line* (Figs 21.13 and 21.14).

PUZZLE CORNER

Five past Five

What is the angle between the hands of a clock at five past five?

PUZZLE CORNER

Consecutive products

$$52 = 4 \times 13$$

In the multiplication above, the digits 1, 2, 3, 4, 5 and the signs = and × are arranged to give one number equal to another number times another.

Do the same with:

a) 1, 2, 3, 4 and = and × (easy),
b) 1, 2, 3, 4, 5, 6 and = and × (difficult).

22 Statistics 3: Averages

OBJECTIVES

You should be able to:
1 Calculate the mean of a given set of numbers
2 Obtain the median and mode of a given set of data
3 Find the mean, median and mode of statistical data based on studies of the environment.

22-1 Averages

The **average** of a set of numbers is a very important statistic. The average is typical of the set of numbers and gives information about them. For example:
a If a football team's **average score** is 5·2 goals, we know that the team is good at scoring goals.
b If two classes have **average ages** of 8·7 years and 16·9 years, we expect that the first is a Primary School class and the second is a Secondary School class.
c If the **average life** of a battery is 20 hours, we expect a new battery to last about 20 hours, maybe a little more or a little less.

There are many kinds of averages. In this chapter we will find out about three: the **mean**, the **median** and the **mode**.

22-2 The mean

The **mean**, sometimes called the **arithmetic mean**, is the most common average. The averages in **a**, **b** and **c** above are all examples of means. If there are n numbers in a set, then,

$$\text{mean} = \frac{\text{sum of numbers in the set}}{n}$$

Example 1

In five tests a student's marks were 13, 17, 18, 8 and 10.
What is the average mark?

$$\text{average (mean) mark} = \frac{13 + 17 + 18 + 8 + 10}{5}$$
$$= \frac{66}{5}$$
$$= 13\cdot2$$

Example 2

A hockey team has played eight games and has a mean score of 3·5 goals per game. How many goals has the team scored?

$$\text{mean score} = \frac{\text{total number of goals}}{\text{number of games}}$$

$$3\cdot5 = \frac{\text{total number of goals}}{8}$$

Multiply both sides by 8.
$$3\cdot5 \times 8 = \text{total number of goals}$$
$$28 = \text{total number of goals scored}$$

Exercise 22a

1 Calculate the mean of the following sets of numbers.
   a 9, 11, 13
   b 7, 8, 12
   c 1, 9, 4, 6
   d 15, 3, 5, 9
   e 1, 8, 6, 8, 7
   f 4, 6, 2, 1, 7
   g 5, 12, 3, 9, 10, 3
   h 8, 9, 11, 12, 15, 17
   i 3, 1, 9, 8, 2, 3, 0, 7, 2, 5
   j 8, 2, 3, 1, 7, 8, 8, 4, 1, 1

2 Calculate the mean of the following.
   a 4 cm, 7 cm, 1 cm, 6 cm
   b ₦60, ₦70, ₦70, ₦90, ₦120
   c 3·9 kg, 5·2 kg, 5·3 kg
   d $1\frac{1}{4}$, $3\frac{3}{4}$, $4\frac{3}{4}$
   e 0·9, 0·8, 0·6, 0·4, 0·9, 1·1, 0·2, 0·3, 0·5, 0·6

171

3. A street trader's profit after five days of trading was ₦6385. Calculate the mean profit per day.

4. On six working days a garage mended 6, 5, 2, 0, 3, 2 punctures.
Calculate the mean number of punctures per day mended by the garage.

5. In four successive days a market trader sold 24, 48, 12 and 60 oranges.
Calculate the mean daily sale of oranges.

6. The temperatures at midday during a week in Lagos were
23°, 25°, 24°, 26°, 25°, 26°, 26°C.
Find, to the nearest degree, the average midday temperature for the week.

7. In the first six days of the month of November, the rainfall was
39 mm, 21 mm, 17 mm, 11 mm, 0 mm, 2 mm.
It didn't rain on any of the other days of the month. Calculate
   a the mean daily rainfall for the first six days,
   b the mean daily rainfall for the whole month. (November has 30 days.)

8. After 15 matches a football team's goal average was 1·8. How many goals has the team scored?

9. The average age of a mother and her three children is 10 years. If the ages of the children are 1, 4 and 7 years, how old is the mother?

11. If the 'average man' has a mass of 77 kg, find, approximately, how many men together have a mass of 1 tonne.

10. In a test out of 40, the marks of 15 students were
31, 18, 6, 26, 36, 24, 23, 14, 29, 28, 32, 9, 11, 22, 21.
   a Calculate the mean mark for the test.
   b Express the mean mark as a percentage.

12. Ten *Atlas* batteries were tested to find their average life. The times, in hours, that the batteries lasted were as follows:
10·8, 10·6, 11·4, 8·9, 10·1, 10·6, 9·9, 12·6, 10·5, 11·9.
   a Find, to the nearest tenth of an hour, the average life of the ten batteries.
   b Which of the following advertisements is more accurate?
      i *Atlas* batteries are guaranteed to last 10 hours.
      ii *Atlas* batteries have an average life of over 10 hours.

22-3 The median

The **median** of a set of numbers is the *middle number* when the numbers are arranged in order of size.

Example 3

Find the median of
17, 34, 13, 22, 27, 44, 8, 31, 13.

Arrange the numbers in order of increasing size.
8, 13, 13, 17, 22, 27, 31, 34, 44
There are nine numbers. The 5th number is in the middle. The 5th number is 22.
Median = 22.

Note that the result would be the same if the numbers were arranged in order of decreasing size (i.e. rank order). Also notice that *every* number is written down even if some numbers appear more than once. In Example 3, there are two 13's; each is written down and counted.

If there is an even number of terms in the set, find the mean of the middle two terms. Take this to be the median.

Example 4

Find the median of
8·3, 11·3, 9·4, 13·8, 12·9, 10·5.

Arrange the set of numbers in order of size.
8·3, 9·4, 10·5, 11·3, 12·9, 13·8
There are six numbers. The median is the mean of the 3rd and 4th numbers.
$$\text{median} = \frac{10·5 + 11·3}{2} = \frac{21·8}{2} = 10·9$$

Exercise 22b

1. What is the median value of the following?
   a. 1, 2, 4, 5, 7
   b. 1, 3, 5, 6, 6, 7, 8
   c. 1, 2, 4, 4, 6
   d. 1, 2, 3, 4, 5, 6
   e. 12, 14, 15, 16, 17, 18, 19, 19, 20

2. Arrange each set of numbers in order of size and find the median.
   a. 3, 1, 6, 4, 2, 5, 5
   b. 7, 6, 1, 2, 6, 5
   c. 4, 8, 9, 12, 5, 7, 3, 4
   d. 1, 2, 3, 3, 5, 4, 8, 7
   e. 21, 25, 31, 28, 22, 29, 24, 30
   f. 3, 6, 6, 9, 16, 15, 15, 18, 21, 27

3. (Class Activity)
   a. Obtain the heights of the students in your class to the nearest cm.
   b. Find the median height for your class.

4. (Class Activity)
   a. Find the shoe sizes of the students in your class.
   b. Obtain the median shoe size.

22-4 The mode

In many examples of statistical data, some numbers appear more than once. The **mode** is the number that appears most often. In Example 3, the number 13 appears twice. 13 is the mode of this data.

Example 5

The following are the number of days absent during a term for a class of 21 students.

7, 5, 0, 5, 0, 3, 0, 15, 0, 2, 2, 0, 1, 3, 5, 32, 1, 0, 0, 1, 2

Find the mode, median and mean days absent.

Arrange the absences in order.

0, 0, 0, 0, 0, 0, 0, 1, 1, 1, 2, 2, 2, 3, 3, 5, 5, 5, 7, 15, 32

0 appears most often.

  mode = 0 days

The median is the 11th number.

median = 2 days

$$\text{mean} = \frac{\text{total number of days absent}}{\text{total number of students}}$$

$$= \frac{0 + 0 + \ldots + 15 + 32}{21}$$

$$= \frac{84}{21} = 4 \text{ days}$$

The frequency is the number of times that a piece of data appears (see Chapter 18). Thus the mode is the piece of data with the greatest frequency.

Example 6

In a class test the grades scored by 40 students are shown in Table 22.1.

Find the mode of the grades.

grade	A	B	C	D	E	F	G
frequency	2	7	8	6	7	8	2

Table 22.1

The greatest frequency is 8. Two grades have this frequency: C and F.
Thus there are two modes: C and F.
Such a distribution is said to be **bimodal**.

Exercise 22c

1. Find the mode (or modes) of the following sets of numbers.
   a. 6, 6, 8, 9, 9, 9, 10
   b. 7, 5, 6, 7, 5, 4, 3, 3, 4, 4
   c. 15, 14, 13, 11, 15, 14, 16, 15, 14, 14
   d. 33, 35, 36, 36, 36, 37, 38, 38, 38
   e. 3, 3, 3, 3, 3, 4, 4, 5, 5, 5, 5, 5, 6, 6, 7, 7

2. The grades obtained in an English test are as follows:
   A, E, B, D, D, E, E, B, B, D, E, C, B, C, D, A, B, A, F, E
   a. Copy and complete Table 22.2.

grade	A	B	C	D	E	F
frequency						

Table 22.2

   b. Find the mode, or modes.

173

3 Find the modal shoe size in the distribution shown in Table 22.3.

shoe size	5	6	7	8	9
frequency	2	3	5	3	1

Table 22.3

Example 7

The distribution of ages of a group of 30 Teacher Training College students is given in Table 22.4. Find **a** *the mode,* **b** *the median and* **c** *the mean ages of the students.*

age in years	20	21	22	23
frequency	4	11	9	6

Table 22.4

a The greatest frequency is eleven. Eleven students are aged 21. The mode is 21 years; we say that the **modal age** is 21 years.

b There are 30 students. The median age is the mean of the ages of the 15th and 16th students.

In this case it is not necessary to make an ordered list of all the ages. Since there are four students aged 20 years and eleven students aged 21 years, the 15th student is aged 21 years (4 + 11 = 15). The 16th student is the first of the 22 year age group.

median age = $\frac{21 + 22}{2}$ = 21·5 years

c mean age = $\frac{\text{total ages of all the students}}{\text{number of students}}$

Using the frequency table,
four students are aged 20.
  sum of their ages = 20 × 4 = 80 years
Eleven students are aged 21.
  sum of their ages = 21 × 11 = 231 years
Nine students are aged 22.
  sum of their ages = 22 × 9 = 198 years
Six students are aged 23.
  sum of their ages = 23 × 6 = 138 years

mean age = $\frac{80 + 231 + 198 + 138}{30}$

  = $\frac{647}{30}$

  = 21·57 years

Notice, in Example 7, that the mode, median and mean are quite close in value to each other. This usually happens when the frequency figures rise and fall fairly smoothly. It is possible for some or all of these averages to be equal to each other.

Exercise 22d

1 Find the mode, median and mean of the following sets of numbers.
  a 7, 7, 9, 12, 15
  b 4, 5, 5, 7, 8, 10
  c 4, 8, 11, 11, 12, 12, 12
  d 2, 3, 6, 6, 7, 7, 7, 8, 8, 9
  e 15, 13, 13, 12, 11, 11, 10, 10, 10, 10, 9, 9, 8, 8, 7

2 Arrange the following numbers in order of size. Find the mode, median and mean of each set.
  a 2, 4, 3, 4
  b 7, 5, 2, 9, 5, 8
  c 1, 0, 14, 0, 5, 10
  d 7, 5, 11, 7, 12, 8, 6, 9, 7
  e 6, 5, 3, 6, 3, 2, 4, 6, 4, 5, 6, 4

3 In a test, the grades go from A (best) to E (poorest). The bar chart in Fig. 22.1 shows the number of students getting each of these grades. Find
  a the number of students who took the test;
  b the mode for the test;
  c the median grade for the test.

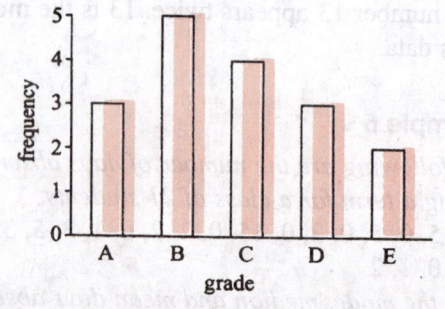

Fig. 22.1

4 Sixteen people were asked which size of shoe they took. Their answers are shown in Table 22.5. Find
  a the modal shoe size,
  b the median shoe size.

shoe size	5	6	7	8	9	10
Frequency	1	2	5	4	3	1

Table 22.5

5. Ten students walk to school each day. The distances they walk, to the nearest kilometre, are given in Table 22.6. Find
   a the mode,
   b the median and
   c the mean distances walked.

distance in km	1	2	3	4	5
frequency	4	2	2	1	1

Table 22.6

6. Table 22.7 gives the ages and frequencies of girls in a choir. Find
   a the number of girls in the choir;
   b the modal and median ages of the choir;
   c the mean age of the choir.

age in years	14	15	16	17
frequency	3	4	5	3

Table 22.7

7. Table 22.8 gives the marks and frequencies obtained in a test. Find
   a the number of students in the class;
   b the mode,
   c the median and
   d the mean marks for the test.

mark	11	12	13	14	15	16
frequency	2	1	3	6	5	3

Table 22.8

Exercise 22e
Use the data you collected for Exercise 17b.

1. **Class statistics**
   a Find the modal age in years of your class.
   b Find the median age of your class.
   c Calculate the mean age of your class.
   d Find the modal number of brothers for people in your class.
   e Find the modal number of sisters for people in your class.
   f Find the mean number of brothers for people in your class.
   g Find the mean number of sisters for people in your class.
   h Find the mean height of people in your class.
   i Find the mean body mass of people in your class.

2. **Traffic survey: Type of vehicle**
   Find the type of vehicle which is the mode.

3. **Traffic survey: Traffic density**
   a Calculate the mean number of vehicles per hour which passed between 0800 and 2000 hours.
   b How does your result in a) compare with the busiest hour?
   c Are there any hours in the day which you could say are 'average'?

4. **Questionnaire**
   a Find the mode and mean number of languages that people in your survey can speak.
   b Find the mode, median and mean number of children that people in your survey have.
   c What is the modal type of vehicle that people have travelled in?

SUMMARY

1. The *average* of a set of numbers is a number that is representative of the whole set of numbers.

2. There are three common averages: the *mean*, *median* and *mode*.

3. The *mean* is the sum of all the values divided by the number of values.

4. The *median* is the middle value when all the numbers are arranged in order of size. If there are two middle values, the median is the mean of the two numbers.

5. The *mode* is the value with the highest frequency. Some distributions (sets of values) may have more than one mode. A *bimodal* distribution has two modes.

23 Estimation and approximation

OBJECTIVES

You should be able to:
1 Estimate quantities
2 Decide which common units of measurement to use in a given situation
3 Use body measures and empty containers to estimate distances and quantities
4 Round off numbers to a given degree of accuracy
5 Use rounded numbers to approximate the answers to addition, subtraction, multiplication and division problems
6 Apply the principles of estimation and approximation to everyday situations and activities.

Teaching and learning materials

Teacher: Metre rule, measuring tape, 1 kg mass, scales, 1-litre container, containers, bottles, stones
Student: Empty bottles and juice packets, stones

23-1 Estimation

There are many advantages in being able to estimate quantities and distances. A quick estimate can prevent errors. It can tell you whether the answer to a problem is sensible or not. It can save you time. This section gives practice in estimating quantities.

Common measures

The most common units for length are millimetre (mm), centimetre (cm), metre (m) and kilometre (km). We use the lower units (millimetre and centimetre) for short lengths and the higher units (metre and kilometre) for larger distances.

The common units of mass are the gramme (g), kilogramme (kg) and tonne (t). The common units of capacity are the millilitre (mℓ), centilitre (cℓ) and litre (ℓ). As with length, we use the lower units for smaller quantities and the higher units for greater quantities.

Exercise 23a (Class Activity/Oral/QR)

1 State the units of length you would use to measure the following.
   a height of a desk
   b height of yourself
   c thickness of a book
   d distance from Lagos to Kano
   e diameter of a coin
   f distance of the classroom from the staffroom
   g length of your fingernail
   h thickness of a coin
   i distance round the earth
   j your waist

2 State the units of mass you would use to measure the mass of the following.
   a a parcel   b a lorry's load
   c a mango   d a book
   e yourself   f a letter
   g a car   h a packet of sugar
   i a table   j the liquid gas in a gas cylinder

3 State the units of capacity you would use to measure the capacity of the following.
   a cup   b car petrol tank
   c medicine bottle   d test-tube
   e bucket   f reservoir
   g teaspoon   h water storage tank
   i sink   j petrol tanker (lorry)

Body measures

You should know the sizes of parts of your body, such as your hand-span, the length of your foot, your waist measurement and your body mass. You can often use these to estimate other measures.

The following assignments show how to use body measurements to find other distances.

Exercise 23b (Class Activity – QR)
You will need a metre rule, a tape measure, an empty litre bottle or juice packet, a cup and a spring balance from the science laboratory.

1. a Use a metre rule to measure your hand-span in cm (Fig. 23.1).

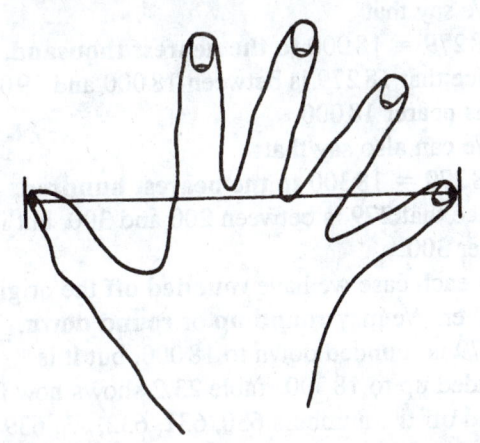

Fig. 23.1 Hand-span: distance between outstretched tips of small finger and thumb.

  b Does anyone in your class have a hand-span less than 15 cm?
  c Does anyone in your class have a hand-span greater than 24 cm?

  Use your hand-span to estimate
  d the width of your desk to the nearest 10 cm,
  e the width of the blackboard.
  f Use a metre rule to check your estimates in d and e.

2. a Measure the length of a new pencil.
  b Use the pencil to estimate the width of your desk.
  c Does your answer agree with that of question 1d?

3. Go outside and walk 10 paces (Fig. 23.2).
  a Use a measuring tape, or a metre rule, to measure the distance you have walked.
  b Calculate the length of one of your paces.

Fig. 23.2 Pace: length of a step in normal walking.

For example, if you walked 6·3 metres, then
$$1 \text{ pace} = 6·3 \text{ m} \div 10$$
$$= 0·63 \text{ m}$$
$$= 63 \text{ cm}$$

4. Measure the following distances in paces.
  a From the front of the classroom to the back of the classroom.
  b From the classroom door to the library.
  c The length of a football field or basketball court.
  d From the school gate to the Principal's office.
  e Another distance of your own choice.

5. Use your result in question 3 to estimate the distances in question 4.
  For example, if the football field is 126 paces long, then
  length of football field $\simeq$ 0·63 m $\times$ 126
  (rounding off) $\simeq$ 0·6 $\times$ 130
  length of football field $\simeq$ 78 m

6. Find an empty litre bottle or juice packet and a cup.
  a Fill the litre container full of water.
  b Find how many cups of water the litre container holds.
  c Calculate the approximate capacity, to the nearest 50 mℓ, of the cup.
  d Find how many cups of water it takes to fill an empty bucket (or large tin).

e Hence calculate the approximate capacity of the bucket (or tin).

7 Use a balance from the science laboratory.
a Find a stone which has a mass of about 1 kg.
b Using your hands as a balance, try to find three things which have the same mass as the stone.
c Check your estimate by measuring the three things on the balance.

8 Copy and complete Table 23.1 with your personal statistics.

name	
my height	cm
my mass	kg
my hand-span	cm
my pace	cm
my foot	cm

Table 23.1

Exercise 23c (Oral/QR)

The following are all answers that students gave to questions in a mathematics class. Which of these answers are *not* sensible? If you think an answer is not sensible, say what approximate size you think the answer could be.

a A girl walked 60 km in an hour.
b Five tins of milk cost ₦230 000.
c The mass of the dictionary is 1·2 kg.
d The height of the man is 181 cm.
e The mass of the woman is 558 kg.
f The pencil was 17 cm long.
g The cup holds 22 litres.
h The water tank has a capacity of 12 kilolitres.
i It took 15 seconds to drive from Ibadan to Lagos.
j The diameter of the tennis ball was 25 mm.
k The mass of the record player is 9·8 kg.
l The Principal's pay is ₦260 a year.
m The door was 80 cm wide.
n The car is 32 m long.
o The mass of the dog was 12 g.
p The candle was 26 m long.
q The area of the football field is 4000 cm².
r The diameter of the bicycle wheel is 60 cm.
s The new car cost ₦4 500.
t He used 2·6 m of string to tie the parcel.
u The mass of the ruler was 50 kg.
v The sun is 400 m from the earth.
w The boy put 224 cubes of sugar in his tea.
x It took 8 hours to fly from Lagos to London.
y The height of the flagpole is 3 mm.
z The bottle contained 48 mℓ of ink.

23-2 Rounding off numbers

Suppose that on a certain day the population of a town is exactly 18 279 people. What will be the population one week later? It is impossible to say. However, we will have a good idea of the population. It will be 18 000 **approximately**.
  We say that
18 279 = 18 000 **to the nearest thousand**.
Notice that 18 279 is between 18 000 and 19 000, but is nearer 18 000.
  We can also say that
18 279 = 18 300 **to the nearest hundred**.
Notice that 279 is between 200 and 300, but is nearer 300.
  In each case we have **rounded off** the original number. We may **round up** or **round down**. 18 279 is rounded down to 18 000, but it is rounded up to 18 300. Table 23.2 shows how to round off the numbers 630, 631, 632, ..., 639 **to the nearest ten**.

630	no need to round off
631 632 633 634	round *down* to 630 (these numbers are nearer 630 than 640)
635	halfway between 630 and 640: round up to 640*
636 637 638 639	round *up* to 640 (these numbers are nearer 640 than 630)

*There are other rules for rounding off a 5. However, the above rule will be used in this course.

Table 23.2

Example 1

Give 14 505 to the nearest
a thousand, **b** hundred, **c** ten.

a 14 505 = 15 000 to the nearest thousand
(14 505 is a little nearer 15 000 than 14 000)

b 14 505 = 14 500 to the nearest hundred

c 14 505 = 14 510 to the nearest ten
(the last digit of 14 505 is 5; round up)

Example 2

Approximate 79·75 to the nearest
a hundred, **b** ten, **c** whole number, **d** tenth.

Note: To approximate means to round off.

a 79·75 = 100 to the nearest hundred

b 79·75 = 80 to the nearest ten

c 79·75 = 80 to the nearest whole number
(the fraction 0·75 is nearer 1 than 0; thus 79 is rounded up to the nearest whole number, 80)

d 79·75 = 79·8 to the nearest tenth
(the last digit of 79·75 is 5; round up)

Exercise 23d (Oral/QR)

1. Approximate the following to the nearest
   i) thousand, **ii)** hundred, **iii)** ten.

a 18 624	b 25 246	c 32 781
d 7 163	e 2 968	f 9 476
g 14 939	h 26 888	i 45 072
j 5 616	k 16 065	l 12 505
m 9 895	n 30 097	o 8 350

2. Round off the following to the nearest ten.

   a 345   b 375   c 695
   d 705   e 715

3. Approximate the following to the nearest whole number.

   a 6·9   b 12·3   c 78·75
   d 29·6   e 9·5

4. Round off the following to the nearest tenth.

   a 0·71   b 0·09   c 0·15
   d 0·45   e 0·98

5. Approximate the following to the nearest hundredth.

   a 0·164   b 0·167   c 0·706
   d 0·702   e 0·295

6. Round off the following to the nearest
   i) whole number, **ii)** tenth.

   a 1·38   b 4·09   c 9·65

7. Round off the following to the nearest
   i) tenth, **ii)** hundredth.

   a 0·372   b 0·625   c 0·155

8. Approximate the following to the nearest
   i) ten, **ii)** whole number, **iii)** tenth.

   a 26·48   b 8·35   c 5·84

9. Round off 0·798 to the nearest
   a whole number   b tenth
   c hundredth.

10. Round off 69·65 to the nearest
    a hundred   b ten
    c whole number   d tenth.

23-3 Approximation

Approximation is the process of using rounded numbers, to estimate the outcome of calculations. As with the estimation of quantities, the ability to find approximate results is very useful. This section gives practice in approximating calculations.

Consider the following.

a A farmer is thinking of buying 220 week-old chickens at ₦170 each. He does a **rough calculation** first:
₦170 × 220 ≃ ₦200 × 200 = ₦40 000

The symbol ≃ means 'is approximately equal to'. ₦40 000 is an approximation of the cost of the chickens. The approximation is not accurate, but it gives the farmer a good idea of the true cost. He may think that ₦40 000 is too much money. However, he may think that he can buy at this price. He then does an accurate calculation:

₦170 × 200 = ₦37 400
         170
       × 220
       ─────
        3 400
       34 000
       ─────
       37 400

Notice that ₦37 400 ≃ ₦40 000.

b A student does the following problem.
'*Calculate the wage of a person who works a 48-hour week at ₦575 per hour.*'
She gets an answer of ₦276. She looks at the answer and thinks, '*₦276 is not much for a week's work. It is even less than one hour's wages!*' So she does a **rough check**.

$$₦575 \times 48 \simeq ₦600 \times 50 = ₦30\,000$$

This is very different from ₦276, so she looks at her working again. She sees that she was careless with the zeros. The correct answer is ₦27 600 which is close to her rough check, or *approximation*, of ₦30 000.

It is a good habit always to check calculations by making a rough check. A quick check can stop you making errors. It can also tell you whether your answer is sensible or not.

One significant figure/nearest whole number

When approximating, it is often enough to round off numbers, either **to one significant figure** or **to the nearest whole number**. For example:

$$713 = 700 \text{ to one significant figure}$$
$$0{\cdot}275 = 0{\cdot}3 \text{ to one significant figure}$$
$$75k = ₦1 \text{ to the nearest whole naira}$$
$$4{\cdot}82 = 5 \text{ to the nearest whole number}$$
$$2\tfrac{1}{4} = 2 \text{ to the nearest whole number.}$$

The following examples show how to approximate the answers to addition, subtraction, multiplication and division problems.

Addition

Example 3
Round off each number to one significant figure, then approximate the answers.
a 47 + 31   *b* 291 + 603

a 47 + 31 ≈ 50 + 30 = 80
b 291 + 603 ≈ 300 + 600 = 900

Subtraction

Example 4
Due to efficiency savings the cost of a new road was reduced from ₦8.8 billion per km to ₦7.9 billion per km. Round these values to the nearest billion. Hence find the approximate saving per km.

Saving = ₦(8.8 − 7.9) billion
≈ ₦(9 − 8) billion
= ₦1 billion

Multiplication

Example 5
a Find the rough value of $4\tfrac{1}{5} \times 1\tfrac{7}{8}$.
b Find the value of $4\tfrac{1}{5} \times 1\tfrac{7}{8}$ accurately.

a $4\tfrac{1}{5} \times 1\tfrac{7}{8} \simeq 4 \times 2 \simeq 8$
b $4\tfrac{1}{5} \times 1\tfrac{7}{8} = \dfrac{21}{5} \times \dfrac{15}{8} = \dfrac{21 \times 5 \times 3}{5 \times 8} = \dfrac{63}{8} = 7\tfrac{7}{8}$

Division

Example 6
A bottle of soda holds 330 ml. The factory fills the bottles from a container that holds 20 000 litres. Approximately how many bottles can be filled from the container?

20 000 litres = 20 000 × 1 000 ml

Number of bottles = $\dfrac{20\,000 \times 1\,000\,\text{ml}}{330}$
≈ 20 000 × 3
≈ 60 000

Notice, in Example 6:
a it is necessary to work in the same units (ml);
b 1 000 ÷ 330 ≈ 3.

Use methods like those above in Exercises 23e, 23f and 23g.

Exercise 23e   (Oral)
① [QR] Round off each number to one significant figure. Then approximate each answer.

1.
a 23 + 19   b 73 − 48
c 24 × 37   d 572 ÷ 22
e 17 + 58   f 92 − 26
g 69 × 52   h 817 ÷ 19
i 37 + 52   j 653 − 287
k 99 × 95   l 171 ÷ 18
m ₦470 + ₦610   n ₦510 − ₦170
o 9·6 × 5·8   p 43 ÷ 8·2
q 133g + 452g   r 943m − 482m
s ₦530 × 18   t ₦6720 ÷ 24

2. [QR] Round off each number to the nearest whole number. Then find the approximate answer.
a 6·2 + 3·7   b 12·3 + 8·7
c 3·4 × 5·8   d 14·07 ÷ 6·7
e 3·47 + 12·75   f $5\frac{2}{3} - 2\frac{3}{4}$
g 16·7 × 1·09   h $15\frac{3}{4} \div 4\frac{1}{5}$
i $6\frac{3}{4} + 5\frac{1}{8}$ j 7·55 − 3·45
k $8\frac{1}{2} \times 7\frac{4}{7}$ l 9·774 ÷ 3·64
m $\frac{5}{6} + 2\frac{3}{8}$ n $10\frac{1}{4} \times 3\frac{1}{3}$
o $17\frac{3}{4} - 6\frac{7}{8}$ p 12·48 ÷ 7·8
q 4·72m + 89cm   r $13·09 − $4·81
s 2·58kg × 4·5   t $19\frac{2}{3} \div 5\frac{1}{3}$

3. Round off each number to one significant figure. Then approximate each answer.
a 0·41 × 0·92   b 0·075 × 0·025
c 0·333 × 0·667   d 0·047 × 0·023
e 0·09 × 0·12   f 0·81 ÷ 0·22
g 0·617 ÷ 0·028   h 0·49 ÷ 0·12
i 0·067 ÷ 0·25   j 0·108 ÷ 0·027

Exercise 23f

1. Calculate the accurate answers to every fifth question in Exercise 23e, i.e. questions 1e), j), o), t); 2e), j), o), t); 3e), j). Use your approximations to check if your answers appear correct.

2. In 2008 the value of a plot of land was ₦238 000. Its value rises by about 10% each year. Estimate its value in 2009 to the nearest ₦1 000.

3. A bucket holds 10·5 litres. A cup holds about 320 mℓ. Estimate the number of cups of water that the bucket holds.

4. A farmer has ₦200 000 to spend on cattle. He wants to buy 9 calves. Each calf costs ₦18 500. Check, by approximation, that the farmer has enough money. Find, accurately, how much change he will get after buying the calves.

5. The populations of five towns are 15 600, 17 300, 62 800, 74 000 and 34 400, each to the nearest hundred. Find the total population of the 5 towns to the nearest thousand.

6. 36 teams meet at Kaduna stadium. Each team has 12 players. First estimate, then find accurately, the total number of players at Kaduna stadium.

7. $x = 0·176 \div 0·32$. By doing a rough calculation, decide which of the following is the value of x:
a 0·18   b 0·2   c 0·21   d 0·3   e 0·55

8. A student tries the following problem; 'Calculate the cost of 7·8 metres of cloth costing ₦215 per metre'. His answer is ₦16 770. Is his answer sensible? Find a rough answer by rounding off. Calculate the answer accurately. What error did the student make?

9. A shop sells about 340 magazines each week. The selling price of a magazine is ₦180. Estimate the amount of money the shop gets each week from selling magazines.

10. An aeroplane flies 2 783 km in $5\frac{3}{4}$ hours. First approximate, then calculate, the average distance it flies in 1 hour.

Exercise 23g

Round off all numbers to one significant figure before calculation.

1. A woman's pace is about 70 cm long. She takes 2 858 paces to walk from her home to the market. Find, roughly, distance from her home to the market.

2. A cup has a capacity of 290 mℓ. It takes 63 cups to fill a bucket. Find the approximate capacity of the bucket in litres.

181

3. A man's hand-span is 22 cm. He finds that the height of a door is about nine hand-spans. Find the approximate height of the door.

4. The total mass of eight mangoes is 965 g. Fatima bought 5 kg of mangoes. Approximately how many mangoes did she buy?

5. A textbook has a mass of 324 g. A school bought 96 copies of the textbook. Estimate the mass, in kg, of the parcel the books came in.

6. One block has a mass of 2·27 kg. A builder orders 5 800 blocks. Estimate the total mass, in tonnes, of the blocks.

7. A sum of ₦236 000 is divided equally among 54 members of a club. Approximately how much does each member get?

8. There are 96 exercise books in a pile. The height of the pile is 48 cm. Estimate the thickness of each exercise book in mm.

9. A packet of biscuits has a mass of 205 g. If there are 28 biscuits in the packet, what, roughly, is the mass of 1 biscuit?

10. The perimeter of a school compound is 1616 m. In the perimeter fence there are 203 fenceposts equally spaced. Find the approximate distance between any two posts.

SUMMARY

1. Always relate units of measurement to the quantities being measured. Use small units to measure small quantities, large units to measure large quantities.

2. Table 23.3 shows the *common small* and *large units* for length, mass and capacity.

measure	small (low) units	large (high) units
length/distance	millimetre (mm) centimetre (cm)	metre (m) kilometre (km)
mass	gramme (g)	kilogramme (kg) tonne (t)
capacity	millilitre (mℓ) centilitre (cℓ)	litre (ℓ) kilolitre (kℓ)

Table 23.3

3. You can use *body measures* such as the *hand-span*, *foot* or *pace* to estimate lengths and distances.

4. To *round off* a number means to find an approximate value. To approximate means to round off.

5. When *rounding off* numbers, round up or round down, depending on the digit being rounded. *Round down* 0, 1, 2, 3, 4 and *round up* 5, 6, 7, 8, 9.

6. *Approximation* of quantities helps:
to prevent errors in calculation;
to obtain correct answers to calculations.

7. To make a *rough approximation*, round off each number to the nearest whole number or to *one significant figure*.

PUZZLE CORNER

Prime Addition

$$P + Q = 99$$

In the above addition, P and Q are prime numbers.

What are P and Q?

How do you know that your answer is the only correct one?

24 Base two arithmetic

OBJECTIVES

You should be able to:
1. Expand numbers expressed in various bases
2. Express base ten numbers in base two
3. Convert binary (base two) numbers to base ten
4. Add, subtract and multiply binary numbers.

Teaching and learning materials

Teacher: Counters (e.g. matchsticks, bottle tops, pebbles)
Students: Matchsticks, bottle tops, pebbles

24-1 Number bases

As we saw in Chapter 1, some people traditionally count in 5's, others in 20's. When counting days in a week, we count in 7's, but when counting seconds in a minute, we count in 60's. However, for most purposes, people count in 10's.

The digits 0, 1, 2, 3, 4, 5, 6, 7, 8, 9 are used to represent numbers. The placing of the digits shows their value. For example, 3 706 means **3** thousands, **7** hundreds, **0** tens, **6** units.

$$3\,706 = 3 \times 1000 + 7 \times 100 + 0 \times 10 + 6 \times 1$$
$$= 3 \times 10^3 + 7 \times 10^2 + 0 \times 10^1 + 6 \times 1$$

Fig. 24.1 shows the place value of the digits in the number 3 706.

```
    thousands
     | hundreds
     |  | tens
     |  |  | units
     |  |  |  |
     3  7  0  6
```

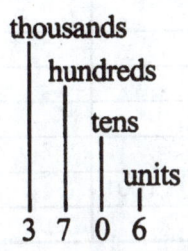

Fig. 24.1

Since this method is based on powers of ten, it is called the **base ten** system.

Other number systems are sometimes used. For example, the **base eight** system is based on powers of eight. In base eight, 25 means **2** eights, **5** units; 147 means **1** sixty-four, **4** eights, **7** units.

$$147_{eight} = 1 \text{ sixty-four, } 4 \text{ eights, } 7 \text{ units}$$
$$= 1 \times 64 + 4 \times 8 + 7 \times 1$$
$$= 1 \times 8^2 + 4 \times 8^1 + 7 \times 1$$

Notice that 147_{eight} is short for 147 in base eight.

Fig. 24.2 shows the place value of the digits in the number 147_{eight}.

```
  sixty-fours
    | eights
    |  | units
    |  |  |
    1  4  7
```

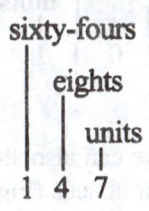

Fig. 24.2

Example 1

Expand a $25\,024_{six}$, *b* $1\,001_{two}$ *in powers of their bases.*

a $25\,024_{six}$
$= 2 \times 6^4 + 5 \times 6^3 + 0 \times 6^2 + 2 \times 6^1 + 4 \times 1$

b $1\,001_{two}$
$= 1 \times 2^3 + 0 \times 2^2 + 0 \times 2^1 + 1 \times 1$

Exercise 24a (Oral)

Expand the following in the powers of their bases.

1. $2\,389_{ten}$
2. 647_{eight}
3. $35\,154_{six}$
4. $4\,102_{five}$
5. $1\,001_{two}$
6. $33\,010_{four}$
7. $26\,523_{seven}$
8. $1\,100_{two}$

⑨ 2102_{three} ⑩ 81062_{nine}
⑪ 10110_{two} ⑫ 101101_{two}

24-2 Binary numbers

In Example 1b) and in Exercise 24a, questions 5, 8, 11 and 12, the numbers were in **base two**. The first thing to notice is that a base two number, or **binary number**, is made up of only two digits: 0 and 1 (just as in base ten there are ten digits: 0, 1, 2, 3, 4, 5, 6, 7, 8 and 9). Fig. 24.3 shows the place value of the digits in the binary number 1011_{two}.

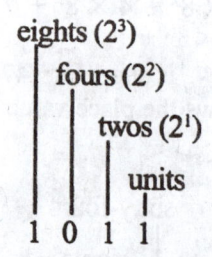

eights (2^3)
fours (2^2)
twos (2^1)
units
1 0 1 1

Fig 24.3

As in Chapter 1, we can also show this by using counters on a paper abacus (Fig. 24.4).

eights	fours	twos	units
●		●	●

Fig. 24.4

We can read Fig. 24.4 as
1 *eight*, 0 *fours*, 1 *two* and 1 *unit*.

Exercise 24b (Class activity – QR)
Work in pairs. Get a collection of about 25 counters (e.g. matchsticks, bottle tops, smooth pebbles). Make a paper abacus as in Fig. 24.4. Follow the example in question 1.

① **a** Count out nine counters.
   b Group them in twos (Fig. 24.5).

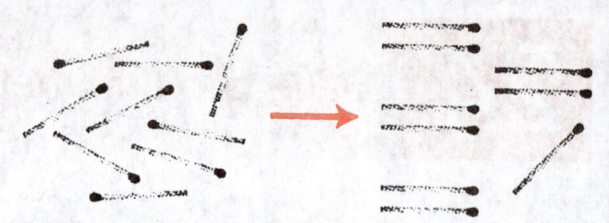

Fig. 24.5

   c Now group the pairs in *eights*, *fours*, *twos* and *units* as far as possible (Fig. 24.5).

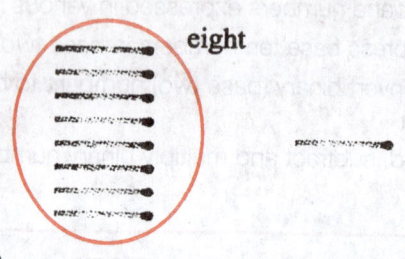

eight

Fig. 24.6

Fig. 24.6 shows that nine is made up of
1 *eight*, 0 *fours*, 0 *twos* and 1 *unit*.
   d Represent the binary number for 9 on your paper abacus (Fig. 24.7).

eights	fours	twos	units
●			●

Fig. 24.7

② Use the method in question 1 to represent the numbers from 1 to 20 in base two on a paper abacus.

③ Enter your results in a copy of Table 24.1.

base ten	binary	base ten	binary
1		11	
2		12	
3		13	
4		14	
5		15	
6		16	
7		17	
8		18	
9	1001	19	
10		20	

Table 24.1

The binary system is second in importance to our usual base ten system. It is important because it is used in computer programs. Binary numbers are made up of only two digits, 1 and 0. A computer contains a large number of switches. Each switch is either 'on' or 'off'. An 'on' switch represents 1; an 'off' switch represents 0.

Table 24.2 shows the first ten binary numbers.

binary number	value in powers of 2	base ten number
1	1×1	1
10	$1 \times 2^1 + 0 \times 1$	2
11	$1 \times 2^1 + 1 \times 1$	3
100	$1 \times 2^2 + 0 \times 2^1 + 0 \times 1$	4
101	$1 \times 2^2 + 0 \times 2^1 + 1 \times 1$	5
110	$1 \times 2^2 + 1 \times 2^1 + 0 \times 1$	6
111	$1 \times 2^2 + 1 \times 2^1 + 1 \times 1$	7
1000	$1 \times 2^3 + 0 \times 2^2 + 0 \times 2^1 + 0 \times 1$	8
1001	$1 \times 2^3 + 0 \times 2^2 + 0 \times 2^1 + 1 \times 1$	9
1010	$1 \times 2^3 + 0 \times 2^2 + 1 \times 2^1 + 0 \times 1$	10

Table 24.2

Converting between bases ten and two

To convert between bases, it is usually easiest to work in powers of the given base.

Example 2

Convert 30_{ten} to a base two number.

Express 30 as a sum of multiples of 2:

$30_{ten} = 16 + 8 + 4 + 2$

In powers of two:

$30_{ten} = 2^4 + 2^3 + 2^2 + 2^1$

In base two

$30_{ten} = 1 \times 2^4 + 1 \times 2^3 + 1 \times 2^2 + 1 \times 2^1$
$\phantom{30_{ten}} + 0 \times 1$
$\phantom{30_{ten}} = 11110_{two}$

Example 3

Convert 11001_{two} to a base ten number.

$11001_{two} = 1 \times 2^4 + 1 \times 2^3 + 0 \times 2^2 +$
$\phantom{11001_{two}} 0 \times 2^1 + 1 \times 1$
$\phantom{11001_{two}} = 16 + 8 + 0 + 0 + 1$
$\phantom{11001_{two}} = 25_{ten}$

Example 4

Find the value of $(111_{two})^2$ in base two.

$111_{two} = 1 \times 2^2 + 1 \times 2^1 + 1 \times 1$
$\phantom{111_{two}} = 4 + 2 + 1 = 7_{ten}$
$(111_{two})^2 = (7_{ten})^2$
$\phantom{(111_{two})^2} = 49_{ten}$
$\phantom{(111_{two})^2} = 32 + 16 + 1$
$\phantom{(111_{two})^2} = 2^5 + 2^4 + 1$
$\phantom{(111_{two})^2} = 1 \times 2^5 + 1 \times 2^4 + 0 \times 2^3 +$
$\phantom{(111_{two})^2} 0 \times 2^2 + 0 \times 2^1 + 1 \times 1$
$\phantom{(111_{two})^2} = 110001_{two}$

Note:
1 To use these methods successfully, it is important to have a good knowledge of the powers of two.
2 There are other methods for converting between bases. We will come across them later in the course. Meanwhile, use the above methods.

Exercise 24c

1. Write down the first 20 binary numbers.
2. Copy and complete Table 24.3.

2^1	2^2	2^3	2^4	2^5	2^6	2^7	2^8	2^9
2	4	8	16					

Table 24.3

3. In Fig. 24.8, to go from X to D, move along the arrowed paths. These paths are numbered 0, 1, 1 in order. The number 011 is written in box D.

185

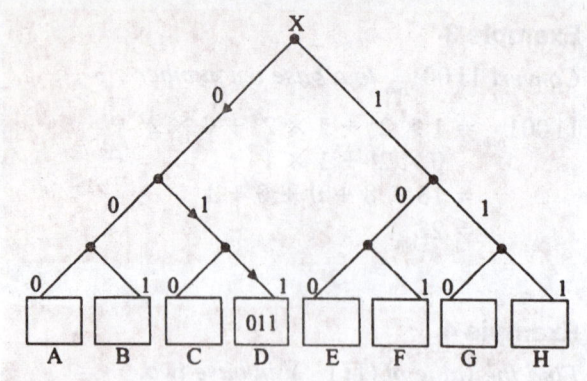

Fig. 24.8

a Start at X and find the numbers that go in boxes A, B, C, E, F, G, H.

b What do you notice about the numbers in the boxes?

4 Convert $(9_{ten})^2$ to a binary number. How many digits has your answer?

5 In Table 24.2 there is one number with 1 digit, two numbers with 2 digits and four numbers with 3 digits.

a How many 4-digit numbers does Table 24.2 contain?

b Use your answer to question 1 to state how many 4-digit binary numbers there are altogether.

c Hence guess how many binary numbers have 6 digits.

6 Convert the following base ten numbers into binary numbers.

a 26 **b** 32 **c** 39 **d** 47
e 52 **f** 60 **g** 65 **h** 71

7 Convert the following binary numbres into base ten numbers.

a 1101 **b** 1110
c 10000 **d** 10010
e 10101 **f** 11001
g 101001 **h** 111000

8 What is the last digit of **a** an even binary number, **b** an odd binary number?

9 Find the value of the following, leaving your answers in base two.

a the square of 110_{two} **b** $(1000_{two})^2$

10 Find the square roots of the following, leaving your answer in base two.

a 11001_{two} **b** 1010001_{two}

24-3 Operations with binary numbers

We can add, subtract and multiply binary numbers in much the same ways as we operate with base ten numbers. The main things to remember in base two are:

Addition:
$0 + 0 = 0 \qquad 1 + 0 = 1$
$0 + 1 = 1 \qquad 1 + 1 = 10$

Multiplication:
$0 \times 0 = 0 \qquad 1 \times 0 = 0$
$0 \times 1 = 0 \qquad 1 \times 1 = 1$

Addition

Example 5

Add the following.

a   1011
    + 1101

b   101
       101
     + 111

a   1011
    + 1101
    ─────
     11000

Note: 1st column: $1 + 1 = 10$, write down 0 and carry 1
2nd and 3rd columns: as above
4th column: $1 + 1 + 1$ (carried) = 11, write down 1 and carry 1

b   101
        101
      + 111
      ─────
      10001

Note: 1st column $1 + 1 + 1 = 11$, write down 1 and carry 1
2nd column: $0 + 0 + 1 + 1$ (carried) = 10, write down 0 and carry 1
3rd column: $1 + 1 + 1 + 1$ (carried) = 100 (i.e. four in binary)

Subtraction

Example 6
Subtract the following.

a)   1110
    − 1011

b) 10101
    − 111

a)   1110
    − 1001
    ─────
       101

Note: 1st column: 1 from 0 'won't go'.
Move the 1 in the 2nd column to the 1st column: 10 − 1 = 1 (or 2 − 1 = 1); write down 1
2nd column: the 1 has been removed to the 1st column, leaving 0: 0 − 0 = 0; write down 0
3rd column: 1 − 0 = 1, write down 1
4th column: 1 − 1 = 0 (no need to write anything)

b)   10011
    − 101
    ──────
      1110

Note: 1st and 2nd columns: straightforward
3rd column: do this as $100_{two} − 1$
One way is to think of this as $4_{ten} − 1 = 3_{ten} = 11_{two}$

Multiplication

Example 7
Calculate the following.

a)   101
    × 11

b)   1110
    × 101

Set these out as long multiplications, multiplying by 1 or 0 as necessary.

a)   101
     × 11
     ────
      101
     101.
     ────
     1111

b)   1110
     × 101
     ─────
      1110
     0000.
     1110..
     ──────
    1000110

Check the results of binary calculations by converting to base ten; e.g. check that Example 7b) is equivalent to 14 × 5 = 70.

Exercise 24d
In this exercise, all the numbers are binary.

1) Calculate in base two. Check your results in base ten

a)   111
    + 1

b)   11
    + 101

c)   101
    + 110

d)   101
    + 101

e)   111
    − 11

f)   110
    − 10

g)   111
    − 110

h)   100
    − 11

i)   11
    × 11

j)   10
    × 10

k)   10
    × 11

l)   1
      11
    + 111

2) Calculate in base two, checking your results in base ten.

a)   1110
    + 1001

b) 10101
    + 111

c) 11110
    − 1101

d) 10011
    − 110

e) 10101
    − 1101

f) 10111
    − 10111

g)   1011
    × 101

h)   1111
     1101
    + 101

i) 11011
    − 1101

j)   101
      101
    + 111

k)   1110
    × 110

l) 11101
    × 111

187

3. Use 'long multiplication' to check that $(101_{two})^3 = 1111101_{two}$.

4. Without converting to base ten, check your answers to question 9 of Exercise 24c.

5. Calculate
$110_{two} \times (1011_{two} + 1001_{two} - 101_{two})$.

SUMMARY

1. Most people count in tens, using the digits 1, 2, 3, 4, 5, 6, 7, 8, 9 and 0 (zero). This is called the *base ten* system.

2. It is possible to represent numbers using other systems, e.g. *base two*, *base five*, *base eight* and so on. Base two is called the *binary system*; it uses only two digits: 1 and 0.

3. The binary system is important because of its applications to computing.

4. When *converting between bases* ten and two, express the given numbers in powers of two. See Examples 2, 3 and 4.

5. When *adding*, *subtracting* and *multiplying* binary numbers, remember that:

   $0 + 0 = 0$ $1 + 0 = 1$
   $0 + 1 = 1$ $1 + 1 = 10$

   and

   $0 \times 0 = 0$ $1 \times 0 = 0$
   $0 \times 1 = 0$ $1 \times 1 = 1$

   See Examples 5, 6 and 7.

PUZZLE CORNER

Three Bags of Mangoes

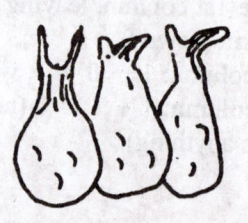

You have three bags. Each contains an odd number of mangoes. What is the smallest possible number of mangoes that there could be?
[Clue: bags can go inside bags!]

PUZZLE CORNER

Think of a Number

$5^2 0$
$7 2$

I asked my teacher to think of a number and then to multiply it by 9. I then asked him to remove one of the digits from his answer, to mix up the remaining digits and write them on the board. His result is shown above.

What digit did he remove?

Chapters 17–24: Revision exercises and tests

Revision exercise 9 (Chapters 17, 18, 22)

1. **a** Place the following distances in rank order: 5 km, 1 km, 6 km, 4 km, 9 km, 2 km, 15 km, 8 km, 10 km.
   b Find the fifth greatest distance.
2. In one year rain fell on 80 days. There was no rainfall on any of the other days. Take a year to be 360 days and draw a pie chart to show this information.

Table R1 shows the distribution of ages of a group of police cadets. Use the data in Table R1 to answer questions 3, 4, 5 and 6.

age in years	21	22	23	24
frequency	5	10	6	9

Table R1

3. Which age is the mode of the above data?
4. **a** How many cadets were in the group?
   b Find the median age of the cadets.
5. Calculate the mean age of the cadets.
6. Draw a bar chart to show the data in Table R1.
7. In a town, approximately half of the adults are farmers, one-third are traders, and the rest do other jobs. Draw a pie chart to show this information.
8. In Nigeria about 40% of the people live in towns and cities, and the rest live in rural areas. Taking the population of Nigeria to be 120 million, draw a pictogram to show this information. (Let one symbol represent 10 million people.)
9. The mean of eight numbers is 9. The mean of seven of the numbers is 10. What is the eighth number?
10. In a test the marks of four boys were 23, 18, 24, 27 and the marks of three girls were 21, 16, 29. Find the mean mark of
    a the boys, **b** the girls, **c** all seven students.

Revision test 9 (Chapters 17, 18, 22)

1. When recording data, the tally marks |||| |||| |||| ||| represent the number
   A 13   B 15   C 18   D 20   E 33
2. After five games a football team's goal average is 2·8. After one more game the goal average is 3. The number of goals scored in the 6th game was
   A 3   B 4   C 5   D 6   E 7

Use the following set of numbers in questions 3, 4 and 5.
2, 2, 2, 5, 5, 8, 9, 10, 11

3. The mode of the above set of numbers is
   A 2   B 3   C 5   D 6   E 9
4. The median of the above set of numbers is
   A 2   B 3   C 5   D 6   E 9
5. The mean of the above set of numbers is
   A 2   B 3   C 5   D 6   E 9
6. 100 people were asked their ages; the results are given in Table R2.

age	< 15	15–29	30–44
frequency	43	32	17
age	45–59	≥ 60	
frequency	5	3	

Table R2

   a What *fraction* of the people were under 30?
   b What *percentage* of the people were between 45 and 59?
7. Draw a bar chart to show the information in question 6.
8. A book has 120 pages of drawings, 72 pages of photographs and 168 pages of writing. Show this information on a pie chart.
9. Show the information from question 8 on a pictogram. (Let each symbol represent 24 pages.)

189

10 During a week, the midday temperatures were

28, 29, 29, 33, 28, 24, 25 °C.

Calculate the mean midday temperature.

Revision exercise 10 (Chapter 19)

1 Say whether each of the following is true or false.
  a $11 - x = 8$ when $x = 19$
  b $36 = 24x$ when $x = 1\frac{1}{2}$

2 Solve the following.
  a $5x = 35$ b $4x = 18$ c $6c - 2c = 12$

3 Solve the following.
  a $\frac{x}{5} = 20$ b $\frac{28}{x} = 7$ c $\frac{3}{4}w = 15$

4 Solve the following.
  a $x - 4 = 2$ b $8 = \frac{1}{2}x$ c $12 - x = 0$

5 Solve the following.
  a $3a + 5 = 23$ b $12 = 5b - 8$
  c $7 + 2c = 19$

6 Solve the following.
  a $2x - 8 = 1$ b $2 = 3x - 2$
  c $5x + 3 = 10$

7 What is the perimeter of a rectangle 3 m long and b m broad?

8 A rectangle is 3 m long and its perimeter is 11 m. The breadth of the rectangle is b m. Form an equation in b and solve it.

9 A number is multiplied by 4 and then 17 is added. The result is 41. Find the number.

10 A man was 24 years old when his son was born. Now he is three times as old as his son. Find the age of the son.

Revision test 10 (Chapter 19)

1 If $13 = x - 5$, then $x =$
  A 1   B 8   C 9   D 16   E 18

2 The value of x that makes $\frac{24}{x} = 8$ true is
  A 3   B 8   C 16   D 32   E 192

3 If $x - 10 = 10$, then $x =$
  A 0   B 1   C 10   D 20   E 100

4 If $6x + 7 = 55$, then $x =$
  A 7   B 8   C $10\frac{1}{3}$ D 42   E 48

5 The smaller of two consecutive numbers is doubled and added to the greater. If the smaller number is n, then the total will be
  A $2n$ B $2n + 1$ C $3n$
  D $3n + 1$ E $3n + 2$

6 Solve the following.
  a $13 - x = 10$ b $\frac{a}{3} = 3$ c $y + 8 = 20$

7 Solve the following.
  a $4n - 3 = 17$ b $50 = 7d + 1$
  c $12x + 8 = 20$

8 Two consecutive whole numbers are such that twice the smaller added to the greater make a total of 52. Find the numbers.

9 A packet of candles and a box of matches cost ₦420. The candles cost 20 times as much as the matches. Find the cost of the matches.

10 A number, x, is multiplied by 3; 5 is subtracted from the result. The final answer is 16. Make an equation in x and find the value of x.

Revision exercise 11 (Chapters 20, 21)

1 AÔB and BÔC are adjacent on a straight line AOC. If AÔB = 53°, calculate BÔC.

2 Two straight lines cross at a point X. If one of the angles at X is 160°, calculate the sizes of the other three angles at X.

3 If two angles of a triangle are 63° and 45°, calculate the size of the third angle.

4 Five lines meet at a point. The sum of three of the angles formed is 212°. Calculate the sum of the other two angles at the point.

5 Make a *freehand* sketch of △ABC in which AB = 6 cm, BÂC = 54° and AĈB = 69°. Calculate the third angle of the triangle and show this on your sketch. Make an accurate construction of △ABC.

6 Construct △ABC in which AB = 3·5 cm, BC = 4·5 cm and AC = 5·5 cm. Find the perpendicular distance of A from BC and hence calculate the area of the triangle.

7 In Fig. R10, find a, b, c, d.

190

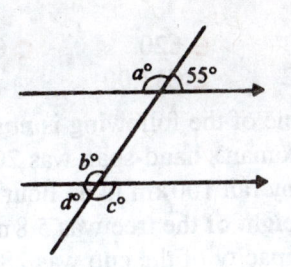

Fig. R10

(8) In Fig. R11, find a, b, c.

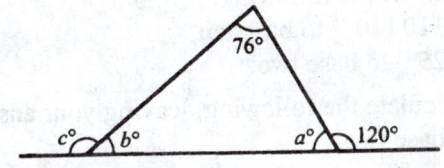

Fig. R11

(9) Use a ruler and set square to construct a rectangle 6 cm by 2·5 cm. Measure the length of one of its diagonals.

(10) In Fig. R12, find a, b, c, d, e.

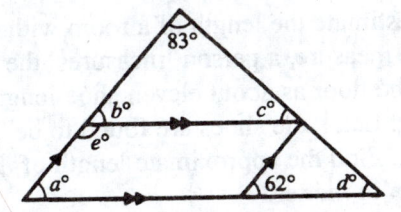

Fig. R12

Revision test 11 (Chapters 20, 21)

(1) XÔY and YÔZ are adjacent on a straight line XOZ. If XÔY = 58°, then YÔZ =
   A 32°   B 122°   C 132°   D 238°   E 302°

(2) Complete the following sentence correctly. Vertically opposite angles...
   A are alternate.   B add up to 180°.
   C are corresponding.   D are equal.
   E add up to 360°.

(3) Three lines meet at a point. If the sum of two of the angles formed is 163°, the other angle is
   A 17°   B 73°   C 163°   D 197°   E 343°

(4) Two angles of △ABC are 46° and 67°. Calculate the third angle of △ABC. Hence decide which one of the following kinds of triangle it is.
   A equilateral triangle   B isosceles triangle
   C right-angled triangle D scalene triangle
   E obtuse-angled triangle

(5) In △XYZ, XY = 5 cm, XŶZ = 40° and XẐY = 60°. Which one of the sketches in Fig. R13 shows this information correctly?

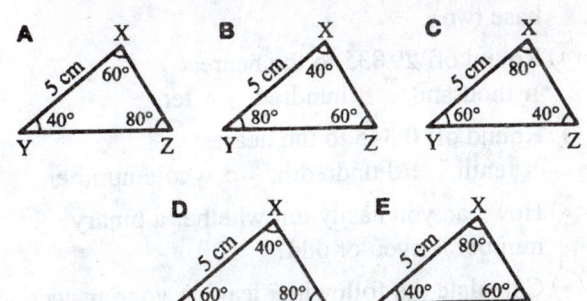

Fig. R13

(6) Construct △ABC in which BC = 4 cm, AB̂C = 50° and AB = 6 cm.

(7) In Fig. R14, find a, b, c.

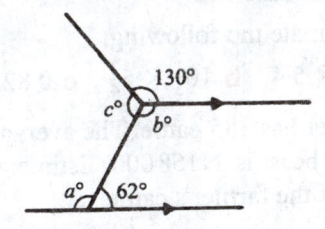

Fig. R14

(8) In Fig. R15, find a, b, c, d.

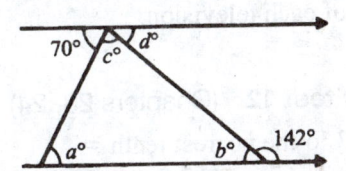

Fig. R15

(9) Construct a parallelogram ABCD in which AB = 4 cm, AB̂C = 70° and BC = 5 cm. Measure the distance between one pair of parallels and hence calculate the area of the parallelogram.

(10) In Fig. R16, find a, b, c, d.

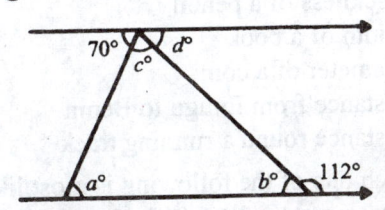

Fig. R16

191

Revision exercise 12 (Chapters 23, 24)

1. Give the binary number 11 101$_{two}$,
   a expand the number in powes of its base,
   b convert it to base ten.
2. Convert the base ten numbers 27 and 28 to base two.
3. Round off 29 835 to the nearest
   a thousand, b hundred, c ten.
4. Round off 0·845 to the nearest
   a tenth, b hundredth, c whole number.
5. How can you easily tell whether a binary number is even or odd?
6. Calculate the following, leaving your answer in base two.
   a 111
      + 111
   b 110
      − 11
7. Find the value of (110$_{two}$)^2, leaving your answer in base two.
8. Appoximate the following:
   a 8.6×5.4 b $10\frac{1}{3} \times 5\frac{3}{4}$ c $0.82 \div 0.39$
9. A farmer has 385 cattle. The average value of each beast is ₦158 000. Estimate the total value of the farmer's cattle.
10. A box contains eight identical televisions. If the mass of the box is 101·6 kg, estimate the mass of each television.

Revision test 12 (Chapters 23, 24)

1. 67·053 to the nearest tenth =
   A 70 B 67 C 67·0 D 67·1 E 67·05
2. 41 300 = 41 285 to the nearest
   A ten thousand   B thousand
   C hundred   D ten
   E whole number
3. Which one of the following is usually measured in metres?
   A thickness of a pencil
   B width of a book
   C diameter of a coin
   D distance from Enugu to Benin
   E distance round a running track
4. Which one of the following is most likely to be the correct value of €3.90 × 7·8?
   A 50c   B €20   C €21.50
   D €30.42 E €33.00
5. Which one of the following is not sensible?
   A The woman's hand-span was 20 cm.
   B The boy ran 100 km in an hour.
   C The height of the tree was 5·8 m.
   D The capacity of the cup was 280 mℓ.
   E It took a day to cycle from Lagos to Ibadan.
6. Convert the following:
   a 110110$_{two}$ to base ten,
   b 25$_{ten}$ to base two.
7. Calculate the following, leaving your answer in base two.
   a 101
      + 111
   b 111
      − 10
   c 101
      × 11
8. Estimate the cost of 20·5 hectares of land at ₦196 000 per hectare.
9. A hotel bill for nine days was ₦59 690. Estimate the daily cost.
10. To estimate the length of a room without a tape measure, a person 'measures' the room on the floor as about eleven shoe-lengths long. Later, the shoes are found to be 28 cm long. Find the approximate length of the room in metres.

General revision test C (Chapters 17–24)

1. The mean of 3, 5, 4, 8, 6, 4, 6, 2, 3, 6 is
   A 4·5 B 4·7 C 5 D 6 E 10
2. A number is trebled and then 17 is subtracted. If the result is 40, the original number is
   A $7\frac{2}{3}$ B 11 C 19 D 57 E 69
3. $16 - x = x$ is true when $x =$
   A 0 B 8 C 14 D 16 E 32
4. In Fig. R17, the value of x is
   A 28° B 31° C 33° D 56° E 62°

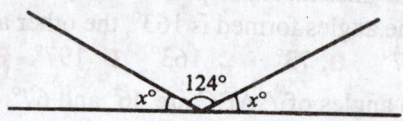

Fig. R17

5. The mass of which one of the following is usually measured in tonnes?

192

A a parcel B a packet of sugar
C a person's body D a packet of biscuits
E a lorry's load

6. The mean of three numbers is 6. The mode of the three numbers is 7. The lowest of the three numbers is
   A 2 B 3 C 4 D 6 E 7

7. If $\frac{x}{12} = 3$, then $x =$
   A $\frac{1}{4}$ B 3 C 4 D 9 E 36

8. In Fig. R18, $a =$
   A 21 B 24 C 42 D 48 E 69

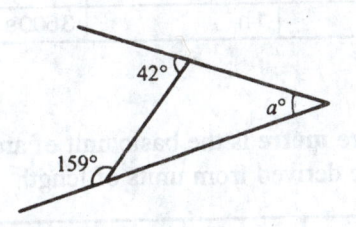

Fig. R18

9. In 2006 the estimated population of Nigeria was 131 000 000. The area of Nigeria is 923 768 square km. In 2006 Nigeria's population density (i.e. the number of people per square km) was approximately
   A 13 B 40 C 130 D 400 E 1 300

10. $x = 23\frac{4}{5} \div 8\frac{1}{2}$. Use estimation to decide which one of the following is the accurate value of x.
    A $2\frac{1}{2}$ B $2\frac{2}{3}$ C $1\frac{2}{5}$ D $2\frac{4}{5}$ E $3\frac{3}{5}$

11. Solve the following.
    a $5 + 8a = 37$ b $40 = 14a - 30$
    c $2a - 1 = 31$

12. A traffic survey gave the results shown in Table R3.

vehicles	car	lorry	bus	bicycle
frequency	12	10	5	23

Table R3

   a How many lorries were there for every one bus?
   b What percentage of the vehicles were bicycles?

13. Represent the data in question 12 on a bar chart.

14. Solve the following.
    a $3x - 4 = 1$ b $7 = 5 + 5x$
    c $7 + 8x = 9$

15. In Fig. R19, find a, b, c.

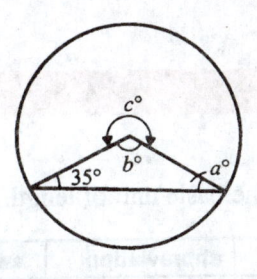

Fig. R19

16. Ten tomatoes have a mass of 628 g. A woman buys $2\frac{1}{2}$ kg of tomatoes. Approximately how many tomatoes will she get?

17. Find the mean, median and mode of 4 hours, 2 hours, 3 hours and 2 hours.

18. A plate costs twice as much as a saucer. Three plates and four saucers cost ₦1 800. How much does each cost?

19. Construct △ABC in which BC = 6 cm, AB̂C = 30° and BÂC = 100°. Measure the perpendicular distance of A from BC and hence calculate the area of the triangle.

20. Calculate the following, leaving your answer in base two.
    a   101
       + 11
       ____
    b   101
       − 11
       ____
    c   101
       × 11
       ____

PUZZLE CORNER

Two 2's

$$2 \div 2 = 1$$

The above example shows how to make the number 1 using two 2's and a mathematical symbol.

Use two 2's and any mathematical symbols to make
a) 4 (easy)
b) 2 (more tricky)
c) 10 (even more tricky)
d) 3, 5, 25 (big challenge!)
e) other numbers, e.g. fractions

Tables

SI units

Length
The **metre** is the basic unit of length.

unit	abbreviation	basic units
1 kilometre	1 km	1000 m
1 hectometre	1 hm	100 m
1 decametre	1 dam	10 m
1 metre	1 m	1 m
1 decimetre	1 dm	0·1 m
1 centimetre	1 cm	0·01 m
1 millimetre	1 mm	0·001 m

The most common measures are the millimetre, the metre and the kilometre.

1 m = 1000 mm
1 km = 1000 m = 1 000 000 mm

Mass
The **gramme** is the basic unit of mass.

unit	abbreviation	basic units
1 kilogramme	1 kg	1000 g
1 hectogramme	1 hg	100 g
1 decagramme	1 dag	10 g
1 gramme	1 g	1 g
1 decigramme	1 dg	0·1 g
1 centigramme	1 cg	0·01 g
1 milligramme	1 mg	0·001 g

The **tonne** (t) is used for large masses. The most common measures of mass are the milligramme, the gramme, the kilogramme and the tonne.

1 g = 1000 mg
1 kg = 1000 g = 1 000 000 mg
1 t = 1000 kg = 1 000 000 g

Time
The **second** is the basic unit of time. Units of time are not in powers of ten.

unit	abbreviation	basic units
1 second	1 s	1 s
1 minute	1 min	60 s
1 hour	1 h	3600 s

Area
The **square metre** is the basic unit of area. Units of area are derived from units of length.

unit	abbreviation	relation to other units of area
square millimetre	mm²	
square centimetre	cm²	1 cm² = 100 mm²
square metre	m²	1 m² = 10 000 cm²
square kilometre	km²	1 km² = 1 000 000 m²
hectare (for land measure)	ha	1 ha = 10 000 m²

Volume
The **cubic metre** is the basic unit of volume. Units of volume are derived from units of length.

unit	abbreviation	relation to other units of volume
cubic millimetre	mm³	
cubic centimetre	cm³	1 cm³ = 1000 mm³
cubic metre	m³	1 m³ = 1 000 000 cm³

Capacity

The **litre** is the basic unit of capacity. 1 litre takes up the same space as $1\,000\,cm^3$.

unit	abbreviation	relation to other units of capacity	relation to units of volume
millilitre	mℓ		$1\,mℓ = 1\,cm^3$
litre	ℓ	$1\,ℓ = 1\,000\,mℓ$	$1\,ℓ = 1\,000\,cm^3$
kilolitre	kℓ	$1\,kℓ = 1\,000\,ℓ$	$1\,kℓ = 1\,m^3$

Money

Some divided currencies

Europe	100 cents (c)	= 1 Euro (€)
Ghana	100 pesewas (p)	= 1 Cedi (₵)
South Africa	100 cents (c)	= 1 rand (R)
UK	100 pence (p)	= 1 pound (£)
USA	100 cents (c)	= 1 dollar ($)

Some undivided currencies

Japan	yen (¥)
Nigeria	naira (₦)
Uganda	shilling (USh)
Francophone countries	franc (CFA)

The calendar

Remember this poem:

Thirty days have September,
April, June and November.
All the rest have thirty-one,
Excepting February alone;
This has twenty-eight days clear,
And twenty-nine in each Leap Year.

For a Leap Year, the year date must be divisible by four. Thus 1996 was a Leap Year. Century year dates, such as 1900 and 2000, are Leap Years only if they are divisible by 400. Thus
  1900: not a Leap Year
  2000: a Leap Year.
  2100: not a Leap Year

Multiplication table

×	1	2	3	4	5	6	7	8	9	10
1	1	2	3	4	5	6	7	8	9	10
2	2	4	6	8	10	12	14	16	18	20
3	3	6	9	12	15	18	21	24	27	30
4	4	8	12	16	20	24	28	32	36	40
5	5	10	15	20	25	30	35	40	45	50
6	6	12	18	24	30	36	42	48	54	60
7	7	14	21	28	35	42	49	56	63	70
8	8	16	24	32	40	48	56	64	72	80
9	9	18	27	36	45	54	63	72	81	90
10	10	20	30	40	50	60	70	80	90	100

Divisibility tests

Any whole number is exactly divisible by
2 if its last digit is even or 0
3 if the sum of its digits is divisible by 3
4 if its last two digits form a number divisible by 4
5 if its last digit is 5 or 0
6 if its last digit is even and the sum of its digits is divisible by 3
8 if its last three digits form a number divisible by 8
9 if the sum of its digits is divisible by 9
10 if its last digit is 0

Mensuration formulae

	perimeter	area	volume
square side s	$4s$	s^2	
rectangle length l, breadth b	$2(l + b)$	lb	
circle radius r	$2\pi r$	πr^2	
triangle base b, height h		$\frac{1}{2}bh$	
parallelogram base b, height h		bh	
cube edge s		$6s^2$	s^3
cuboid length l, breadth b, height h			lbh
right-triangular prism length l, breadth b, height h			$\frac{1}{2}lbh$

Symbols

symbol	meaning
=	is equal to
≠	is not equal to
≃ (or ≈)	is approximately equal to
>	is greater than
<	is less than
≥	is greater than or equal to
≤	is less than or equal to
°	degrees (size of angle)
°C	degrees Celsius (temperature)
A, B, C, …	points
AB	line joining point A and point B, *or* distance between points A and B
△ABC	triangle ABC
AB̂C	angle ABC
⊥	lines meeting at right angles
π	pi (3·14………)
%	per cent

Answers

Preliminary chapter

Addition (page 3)

	Test A	Test B	Test C	Test D	Test E
1	8	9	9	7	5
2	17	16	19	19	18
3	15	13	13	11	12
4	48	37	45	77	89
5	13	15	19	18	16
6	51	37	71	90	40
7	64	99	89	98	48
8	54	117	80	91	146
9	133	120	104	136	131
10	831	1 133	1 798	932	971
11	820	1 505	501	1 041	1 601
12	1 052	2 091	390	8 054	928

	Test F	Test G	Test H	Test I	Test J
1	9	10	2	9	10
2	17	16	18	20	19
3	14	17	11	11	12
4	96	79	67	59	29
5	17	18	16	19	15
6	63	52	81	63	45
7	78	77	89	94	58
8	104	168	88	119	93
9	100	118	140	121	191
10	1 434	1 431	1 145	1 555	713
11	700	1 013	1 102	802	1 004
12	1 469	507	1 576	220	2 000

Subtraction (page 4)

	Test A	Test B	Test C	Test D	Test E
1	4	3	4	8	2
2	13	3	12	4	10

197

③	7	15	2	9	5
④	8	4	9	8	9
⑤	24	91	34	44	63
⑥	26	14	11	53	63
⑦	4	8	8	8	9
⑧	16	49	25	67	27
⑨	178	268	767	368	498
⑩	258	58	490	197	306
⑪	58	129	344	198	179
⑫	1188	1906	588	2104	776

	Test F	Test G	Test H	Test I	Test J
①	1	5	2	0	6
②	7	12	3	15	7
③	14	1	8	3	3
④	7	9	9	5	7
⑤	61	40	82	73	35
⑥	34	22	15	40	31
⑦	2	9	8	9	9
⑧	16	34	25	15	23
⑨	687	539	139	85	279
⑩	684	395	209	273	288
⑪	207	169	36	19	106
⑫	4725	1007	4507	1047	5279

Multiplication (page 5)

	Test A	Test B	Test C	Test D	Test E
①	42	72	54	28	56
②	32	60	64	80	36
③	84	86	55	61	36
④	117	84	34	128	90
⑤	312	312	441	345	234
⑥	3600	52000	8600	400	7000
⑦	2996	42155	2925	11343	2832
⑧	12504	2010	23205	1204	17098
⑨	340	380	780	2600	3240
⑩	4720	1710	5740	3120	5490
⑪	2236	14478	4514	23780	1581
⑫	173096	173825	213310	211761	113278

	Test F	Test G	Test H	Test I	Test J
①	36	48	63	49	81
②	48	63	48	45	42
③	0	46	90	88	69
④	112	56	45	114	91
⑤	144	196	498	216	148
⑥	600	50 800	90 000	10 000	30 000
⑦	16 614	7 232	15 764	6 888	31 375
⑧	1 404	7 107	1 104	30 705	2 768
⑨	2 340	3 350	570	2 320	2 220
⑩	1 860	2 320	1 900	5 220	1 860
⑪	24 955	6 177	6 613	2 232	4 935
⑫	81 480	253 624	363 780	135 360	98 988

Division (page 6)

	Test A	Test B	Test C	Test D	Test E
①	3	2	4	2	3
②	8	8	7	9	6
③	36	40	45	26	43
④	13	14	12	13	17
⑤	28	25	22	23	27
⑥	620	44	50	6	800
⑦	43	65	138	957	58
⑧	203	309	508	107	602
⑨	134	1 201	578	1 002	3 603
⑩	102	301	207	56	203
⑪	29	306	86	115	63
⑫	307	823	290	787	838

	Test F	Test G	Test H	Test I	Test J
①	1	5	2	1	0
②	5	9	7	6	10
③	29	49	18	38	17
④	14	12	13	17	16
⑤	24	21	27	26	29
⑥	405	10	6 200	1	700
⑦	759	567	149	233	761
⑧	130	1 002	206	704	108
⑨	203	301	572	1 540	2 669

⑩	106	307	308	305	103
⑪	208	213	874	94	507
⑫	965	808	915	725	908

Fractions and decimals (page 7)

	Test A	Test B	Test C	Test D	Test E
①	$\frac{1}{2}$	$\frac{3}{4}$	$\frac{2}{3}$	$\frac{1}{4}$	$\frac{3}{4}$
②	$\frac{1}{4}$	$\frac{7}{8}$	$\frac{1}{2}$	$\frac{2}{3}$	$\frac{5}{28}$
③	$\frac{4}{5}, \frac{9}{10}, \frac{19}{20}$	$\frac{4}{9}, \frac{7}{15}, \frac{2}{3}$	$\frac{4}{5}, \frac{5}{6}, \frac{6}{5}$	$\frac{1}{3}, \frac{3}{8}, \frac{5}{12}$	$\frac{11}{36}, \frac{1}{3}, \frac{13}{36}$
④	0·75	0·2	0·1	0·5	0·4
⑤	$\frac{7}{10}$	$\frac{13}{20}$	$\frac{9}{50}$	$\frac{2}{5}$	$\frac{8}{25}$
⑥	25%	55%	90%	62%	51%
⑦	$\frac{5}{6}$	0·66	$\frac{3}{8}$	75%	1·28
⑧	$\frac{3}{8}$	1·11	$\frac{1}{5}$	4·43	4·38
⑨	$\frac{2}{15}$	0·16	$\frac{5}{12}$	0·0084	0·24
⑩	$\frac{1}{4}$	2	$\frac{5}{6}$	15	0·9
⑪	60%	2	$\frac{3}{10}$	1·03	0·9
⑫	9	10	$\frac{3}{20}$	8·7	4

	Test F	Test G	Test H	Test I	Test J
①	$\frac{1}{2}$	$\frac{1}{8}$	$\frac{1}{3}$	$\frac{1}{3}$	$\frac{3}{4}$
②	$\frac{11}{12}$	$\frac{11}{24}$	$\frac{3}{4}$	$\frac{1}{2}$	$\frac{2}{9}$
③	$\frac{1}{4}, \frac{1}{3}, \frac{1}{2}$	$\frac{7}{12}, \frac{7}{11}, \frac{7}{10}$	$\frac{2}{5}, \frac{5}{4}, \frac{5}{2}$	$\frac{3}{10}, \frac{1}{3}, \frac{2}{5}$	$\frac{3}{4}, \frac{4}{3}, \frac{3}{2}$
④	0·25	0·15	0·03	0·8	0·85
⑤	$\frac{11}{25}$	$\frac{3}{20}$	$\frac{21}{25}$	$\frac{27}{100}$	$\frac{1}{4}$
⑥	20%	25%	50%	9%	75%
⑦	$\frac{5}{8}$	75%	1	1·1	$\frac{7}{9}$
⑧	$\frac{1}{4}$	0·33	$\frac{1}{12}$	0·5	$\frac{3}{8}$
⑨	$\frac{1}{12}$	0·0657	$\frac{9}{16}$	0·09	$\frac{3}{14}$
⑩	$\frac{3}{10}$	30	$\frac{1}{12}$	7	8
⑪	15%	$\frac{1}{30}$	6·3	6·4	$\frac{3}{10}$
⑫	$\frac{10}{3}$	$\frac{1}{3}$	0·11	$\frac{1}{12}$	0·99

Exercise Pa (page 9)

1. a 3000 b 5000 c 8000 d 2000
   e 6000 f 10000 g 9000 h 13000
   i 7000 j 4000 k 3500 l 4200
   m 6800 n 8100 o 5900 p 10400
   q 2700 r 9300

2. a 3850 b 2440 c 8390 d 6050
   e 9140 f 1070 g 4124 h 2993
   i 7625 j 5704 k 3009 l 2058
   m 9400 n 4620 o 3315 p 1082
   q 5050 r 6108 s 7008 t 1004

3. a 5 b 8 c 10 d 1·5
   e 2·4 f 9·5 g 6·52 h 4·35
   i 7·33 j 3·748 k 1·375 l 5·822
   m 2·056 n 9·04 o 4·007 p 3·416
   q 7·502 r 6·847 s 10·5 t 8·42
   u 1·44 v 9·025 w 5·005 x 2·009

4. a 1·73 b 4·58 c 8·43 d 1·5
   e 1·05 f 2·8 g 1·01 h 1
   i 0·99 j 0·53 k 0·4 l 0·08
   m 0·19 n 0·05 o 0·5

5. a 1 b 2 c 7 d 6·8
   e 4·1 f 1·4 g 3·726 h 9·504
   i 8·119 j 0·6 k 0·3 l 0·2
   m 0·051 n 0·06 o 0·003

Exercise Pb (page 10)

1. a 10·2 kg b 1·487 kg
   c 2·885 kg d 4620 kg

2. a 7·9 litres b 1·28 litres
   c 4·077 litres d 5150 litres

3. a ₦2980
   b ₦3175
   c ₦707
   d ₦875

4. a i $1.39 ii 139 c
   b i $2.50 ii 250 c
   c i $19.53 ii 1953 c
   d i $17.76 ii 1776 c

5. a 150 b 75 c 100 d 3 e $2\frac{1}{2}$

6. a 300 b 80 c 900 d 1800 e 10800

Exercise 1a (page 11)

4. from using fingers and toes to count

5. a base ten b *sha*
6. a base ten b *na*
7. 70 years
8. a the word for sixteen means: four before twenty
   b the words for 11, 12, 13, 14 contain the basic words for 1, 2, 3, 4; these words seem to be based on grouping in tens
   d the Yoruba system is a mixture of grouping in tens and grouping in twenties; mixing of bases is quite common in many languages

Exercise 1b (page 12)

1. 25 days
2. 18 wk 2 d
3. a 5 wk 6 d b 4 wk 4 d c 3 wk 1 d
   d 6 wk
4. a Wednesday b Friday c Thursday
   d Saturday
5. a 120 b 654 s c 202 s
   d 3600 s
6. a 4 min b 300 min c 154 min
   d 1440 min
7. a 2 min 19 s b 30 min c 4 h 1 min
   d 2 h 20 min 18 s
8. 7 days in a week came from religious tradition where man was to spend every seventh day in prayer; the ancient Babylonians used base sixty in their calculations: Babylonian mathematics was among the first written mathematics and their base sixty has survived to the present day; 60 is a useful number, it is divisible by many other numbers: 2, 3, 4, 5, 6, 10, 12, 15, 20, 30

Exercise 1c (page 13)

1. 14 2. 8 3. 16 4. 20 5. 37
6. 22 7. 48 8. 35 9. 48 10. 4

Exercise 1d (page 14)

1. a 25 b 26 c 24 d 57
   e 47 f 298 g 705 h 1312
   i 1471 j 1844 k 1900 l 1984

201

2
a XII b XVIII c XIX
d XXVI e XXXIX f XLI
g CC h CLXXV i CCXCIV
j DXII k MCDXXII
l MDCDXCIX or MCMXCIX (MIM would be a good guess)

Exercise 1e (page 15)

1
a NIGERIA
b ABUJA
c THE MARKET
d MEET ME TOMORROW
e ALL IS WELL
f HALF PAST SEVEN

3
a (19, 1, 22, 5) (6, 21, 5, 12)
b (7, 15) (20, 15) (2, 5, 14, 9, 14)
c (8, 5, 12, 16) (14, 5, 5, 4, 5, 4)
d (12, 5, 1, 22, 9, 14, 7)
   (20, 15, 14, 9, 7, 8, 20)
e (14, 15, 20, 8, 9, 14, 7) (9, 19)
   (16, 5, 18, 13, 1, 14, 5, 14, 20)
f (6, 9, 22, 5) (15) (3, 12, 15, 3, 11)

4
a A FUNNY DAY
b HAND IT IN
c DUTY DAY
d INFINITY
e TIN HAT

Exercise 1f (page 16)

1) 378 2) 699 3) 464 4) 758
5) 423 6) 374 7) 253 8) 571
9) 26 10) 42 11) 83 12) 178

Exercise 1g (page 17)

1 a 12 b 651 c 907 d 550 e 80 040

2
a four hundred b four units
c two units d two thousand
e two hundred f nine hundred
g nine units h six thousand
i six tens j no tens
k no thousands l one ten thousand

3 The units and tens are under the tens and hundreds

   352
 + 79

4
a 3107   b 6203   c 1429   d 6700
   26   − 97   + 6580   − 34
 + 147

5
a i 632, ii 236   b i 872, ii 278
c i 650, ii 056   d i 8521, ii 1258
e i 7421, ii 1247
f i 543 210, ii 012 345

Exercise 1h (page 18)

1
a eight tenths b eight hundredths
c five hundredths d five units
e six tenths f six units
g one unit h one thousandth
i one ten j zero (tenths) = zero

2
a 60·91   b 26·3
 + 3·2   − 1·7

c 4.50   d 42·50
+ 56.50   − 9·65

Exercise 2a (page 20)

1 a million b billion c trillion
2 a 40 000 000 cm² b 1 million
3 1 million
4 just over 11½ days
5 d (there are over 31½ million seconds in a year)

Exercise 2b (page 20)

1) 1 000 000 2) 59 244
3) 721 568 397 4) 2 312 400
5) 8 000 000 000 000 6) 3 000 000 000
7) 9215 8) 14 682 053
9) 108 412 10) 12 345
11) 100 000 000 12) 987 654
13) 923 006 110 317 14) 21 000 000 000
15) 6 006 006 006 16) 727 744
17) 6 401 000 000 000 18) 58 974 308

Exercise 2c (page 21)

1
a ₦2 000 000 b 150 000 000 km
c 3 000 000 000 d 5 500 000
e ₦2 100 000 000 000 f 4 200 000 litres
g 400 000 000 h ₦1 250 000

i 700 000 tonnes
  j US$750 000
  k 450 000
  l ₦580 000 000
② a 8 million tonnes
  b ₦6 million
  c 2 billion
  d ₦3·7 billion
  e US$7·4 billion
  f ₦1$\frac{3}{4}$ million
  g 0·2 million litres
  h $\frac{1}{2}$ billion or 500 million
  i 0·3 million tonnes
  j $\frac{1}{4}$ million
  k 0·98 million barrels
  l 490 trillion

Exercise 2d (page 22)
① 0·06   ② 0·004
③ 0·9   ④ 0·000 008
⑤ 0·0004   ⑥ 0·000 06
⑦ 0·003   ⑧ 0·000 09
⑨ 0·0007   ⑩ 0·16
⑪ 0·034   ⑫ 0·0026
⑬ 0·000 28   ⑭ 0·084
⑮ 0·0756   ⑯ 2·7
⑰ 0·65   ⑱ 0·402
⑲ 0·2   ⑳ 0·000 24
㉑ 0·7   ㉒ 0·0062
㉓ 0·0033   ㉔ 0·0402
㉕ 0·9   ㉖ 0·9
㉗ 0·03   ㉘ 0·72
㉙ 0·072   ㉚ 0·0072

Exercise 3a (page 23)
① a 1, 2, 3, 4, 6, 12
  b 1, 2, 3, 6, 9, 18
  c 1, 2, 4, 5, 10, 20
  d 1, 2, 3, 4, 6, 8, 12, 24
  e 1, 2, 4, 7, 14, 28
  f 1, 2, 3, 5, 6, 10, 15, 30
  g 1, 2, 4, 8, 16, 32
  h 1, 2, 3, 4, 6, 8, 12, 16, 24, 48
  i 1, 3, 7, 9, 21, 63
  j 1, 2, 3, 4, 6, 8, 9, 12, 18, 24, 36, 72

② a 3, 9   b 2, 3, 4, 6, 9
  c 2, 3, 6, 9   d 2, 4, 7, 8
  e 2, 3, 4, 5, 6   f 2, 3, 5, 6, 9
  g 2, 3, 4, 5, 6, 8 h 2, 3, 4, 6, 8, 9
  i 2, 3, 4, 5, 6, 9 j 2, 3, 5, 6, 7

Exercise 3b (page 23)
① 2, 3, 5, 7, 11, 13, 17, 19, 23, 29

Exercise 3c (page 24)
① $2 \times 2 \times 3$ ② $2 \times 3 \times 3$
③ $2 \times 2 \times 7$ ④ $2 \times 3 \times 5$
⑤ $2 \times 2 \times 2 \times 3 \times 3$ ⑥ $2 \times 2 \times 3 \times 7$
⑦ $2 \times 2 \times 3 \times 3 \times 3$ ⑧ $3 \times 5 \times 7$
⑨ $2 \times 2 \times 3 \times 3 \times 5$
⑩ $2 \times 2 \times 2 \times 3 \times 3 \times 3$
⑪ $2 \times 2 \times 2 \times 2 \times 2 \times 3 \times 3$
⑫ $5 \times 5 \times 5 \times 7$
⑬ $2 \times 2 \times 3 \times 3 \times 5 \times 5$
⑭ $2 \times 2 \times 2 \times 2 \times 5 \times 11$
⑮ $2 \times 2 \times 2 \times 3 \times 3 \times 3 \times 7$
⑯ $3 \times 3 \times 5 \times 5 \times 7 \times 11$

Exercise 3d (page 25)
① a 7^3 b 3^5 c 10^4 d 2^2 e 6^7 f 8^{10}
② (1) $2^2 \times 3$ (2) 2×3^2 (3) $2^2 \times 7$
  (5) $2^3 \times 3^2$ (6) $2^2 \times 3 \times 7$ (7) $2^2 \times 3^3$
  (9) $2^2 \times 3^2 \times 5$ (10) $2^3 \times 3^3$
  (11) 25×3^2 (12) $5^3 \times 7$
  (13) $2^2 \times 3^2 \times 52$ (14) $2^4 \times 5 \times 11$
  (15) $2^3 \times 3^3 \times 7$ (16) $3^2 \times 5^2 \times 7 \times 11$
③ a $2^3 \times 3$ b $2^4 \times 3$ c $3^2 \times 7$
  d $2^2 \times 23$ e $2^3 \times 17$ f $3^2 \times 7^2$
  g $2^3 \times 3^2 \times 5$ h 54   i 2^9
  j $2^4 \times 3^2 \times 5$ k 36   l $2^3 \times 5^3$
  m $2^4 \times 7 \times 11$ n $2^2 \times 3^3 \times 13$
  o $5^2 \times 7^2$ $2 \times 3^6 \times 5$
④ a $36 \rightarrow 2^2.3^2$ $44 \rightarrow 2^2.11$
  c $50 \rightarrow 2.5^2$ $117 \rightarrow 3^2.13$
  e $72 \rightarrow 2^3.3^2$ $132 \rightarrow 2^2.3.11$
  g $100 \rightarrow 2^2.5^2$ $800 \rightarrow 2^5.5^2$

203

Exercise 3e (page 25)

1. 2
2. 3
3. 7
4. 3
5. 2
6. 3
7. 2, 3, 6
8. 2, 5, 10
9. 2, 3, 6
10. 3, 9
11. 2, 4
12. 2, 4, 8
13. 2
14. 7
15. 3
16. 2, 11, 22
17. 3, 5, 15
18. 2, 3, 4, 6, 12

Exercise 3f (page 26)

1. a 3×3 b 2×3 c 2×5
   d $2 \times 3 \times 3$ e $3 \times 5 \times 7$
2. a 3 b 2 c 6 d 8
   e 5 f 15 g 14 h 9
3. a $2^2 \times 3$ b 2×3^3 c $3^2 \times 5^2$
   d $2^3 \times 3 \times 5$ e 5
4. a 21 b 72 c 35 d 18
   e 32 f 27 g 36

Exercise 3g (page 26)

1. 4, 6, 8, 10, 12
2. 6, 9, 12, 15, 18
3. 10, 15, 20, 25, 30
4. 14, 21, 28, 35, 42
5. 16, 24, 32, 40, 48
6. 18, 27, 36, 45, 54
7. 20, 30, 40, 50, 60
8. 22, 33, 44, 55, 66
9. 24, 36, 48, 60, 72
10. 40, 60, 80, 100, 120

Exercise 3h (page 27)

1. 12, 24, 36
2. 10, 20, 30
3. 21, 42, 63
4. 30, 60, 90
5. 60, 120, 180
6. 42, 84, 126
7. 30, 60, 90
8. 24, 48, 72
9. 30, 60, 90
10. 30, 60, 90
11. 24, 48, 72
12. 30, 60, 90

Exercise 3i (page 27)

1. a $2 \times 2 \times 3 \times 3 \times 5$
   b $2 \times 2 \times 2 \times 3 \times 3 \times 5$
   c $2 \times 2 \times 2 \times 3 \times 3 \times 5 \times 5$
   d $2 \times 3 \times 3 \times 5 \times 5 \times 7$
   e $2 \times 3 \times 3 \times 3 \times 5 \times 5 \times 7$
2. a $2^2 \times 3 \times 5^2$ b $2^3 \times 3^2 \times 5^2 \times 7$
   c $2^2 \times 3^3 \times 5 \times 7^2$ d $2^3 \times 3^2 \times 5^3 \times 7^2$
   e $2^4 \times 3^2 \times 5^3 \times 7^3$

3. a 12 b 24 c 18 d 56
   e 24 f 36 g 12 h 12
   i 36 j 24
4. a 120 b 120 c 60 d 90
   e 168 f 180 g 720 h 180
   i 120 j 180

Exercise 4a (page 30)

1. a $1\frac{1}{3}$ b $2\frac{1}{2}$ c $2\frac{3}{4}$ d $1\frac{2}{5}$
   e $2\frac{1}{5}$ f $3\frac{4}{7}$ g $4\frac{1}{6}$ h $2\frac{3}{8}$
   i $2\frac{8}{9}$ j $8\frac{1}{5}$ k $8\frac{4}{7}$ l $9\frac{1}{6}$
   m $9\frac{8}{9}$ n $3\frac{7}{11}$ o $37\frac{2}{3}$ p $13\frac{2}{9}$
   q $17\frac{4}{7}$ r $5\frac{7}{10}$ s $4\frac{13}{20}$ t $1\frac{29}{100}$
2. a $\frac{7}{4}$ b $\frac{10}{3}$ c $\frac{13}{2}$ d $\frac{23}{5}$
   e $\frac{37}{4}$ f $\frac{23}{6}$ g $\frac{30}{7}$ h $\frac{38}{5}$
   i $\frac{43}{8}$ j $\frac{47}{7}$ k $\frac{38}{3}$ l $\frac{40}{3}$
   m $\frac{41}{7}$ n $\frac{49}{12}$ o $\frac{46}{13}$ p $\frac{77}{9}$
   q $\frac{15}{2}$ r $\frac{97}{10}$ s $\frac{127}{20}$ t $\frac{213}{100}$

Exercise 4b (page 31)

1. $\frac{6}{18} = \frac{8}{24} = \frac{50}{150} = \frac{300}{900} = \frac{100}{300}$
2. $\frac{3}{6} = \frac{4}{8} = \frac{5}{10} = \frac{50}{100} = \frac{25}{50}$
3. $\frac{20}{30} = \frac{4}{6} = \frac{600}{900} = \frac{16}{24} = \frac{10}{15}$
4. $\frac{2}{8} = \frac{3}{12} = \frac{15}{60} = \frac{25}{100} = \frac{7}{28}$
5. $\frac{15}{20} = \frac{24}{32} = \frac{21}{28} = \frac{75}{100} = \frac{18}{24}$
6. $\frac{2}{10} = \frac{4}{20} = \frac{20}{100} = \frac{24}{120} = \frac{5}{25}$

Exercise 4c (page 31)

1. a 12 b 24 c 9 d 18
   e 21 f 22 g 3 h 12
   i 40 j 49 k 18 l 20
2. a $\frac{7}{12}, \frac{2}{3}, \frac{3}{4}, \frac{5}{6}, (\frac{7}{12}, \frac{8}{12}, \frac{9}{12}, \frac{10}{12})$
   b $\frac{3}{4}, \frac{4}{5}, \frac{17}{20}, \frac{9}{10} (\frac{15}{20}, \frac{16}{20}, \frac{17}{20}, \frac{18}{20})$
   c $\frac{5}{9}, \frac{7}{12}, \frac{11}{18}, \frac{2}{3} (\frac{20}{36}, \frac{21}{36}, \frac{22}{36}, \frac{24}{36})$
3. a $\frac{2}{9}, \frac{5}{18}, \frac{1}{3} (\frac{4}{18}, \frac{5}{18}, \frac{6}{18})$
   b $\frac{1}{2}, \frac{8}{15}, \frac{17}{30}, \frac{3}{5} (\frac{15}{30}, \frac{16}{30}, \frac{17}{30}, \frac{18}{30})$
   c $\frac{3}{5}, \frac{5}{8}, \frac{13}{20}, \frac{7}{10} (\frac{24}{40}, \frac{25}{40}, \frac{26}{40}, \frac{28}{40})$

Exercise 4d (page 32)

① a 5, 3 b 3, 7 c 6, 4 d 10, 5
   e 5, 1 f 28, 4 g 3 h 5
   i 9 j 25 k 5 l 1

② a $\frac{1}{5}$ b $\frac{1}{6}$ c $\frac{1}{20}$ d $\frac{3}{8}$
   e $\frac{2}{3}$ f $\frac{3}{4}$ g $\frac{5}{6}$ h $\frac{4}{5}$
   i $\frac{4}{9}$ j $\frac{3}{7}$ k $\frac{5}{7}$ l $\frac{8}{11}$

Exercise 4e (page 33)

① $1\frac{5}{12}$ ② $\frac{1}{12}$ ③ $1\frac{1}{18}$ ④ $\frac{11}{18}$
⑤ $\frac{5}{24}$ ⑥ $\frac{23}{24}$ ⑦ $\frac{1}{3}$ ⑧ $\frac{14}{15}$
⑨ $2\frac{1}{4}$ ⑩ $1\frac{1}{4}$ ⑪ $3\frac{5}{6}$ ⑫ $\frac{7}{12}$
⑬ $6\frac{5}{8}$ ⑭ $8\frac{11}{18}$ ⑮ $2\frac{19}{20}$ ⑯ $2\frac{13}{24}$
⑰ $7\frac{1}{12}$ ⑱ $4\frac{3}{8}$ ⑲ $5\frac{1}{8}$ ⑳ $8\frac{1}{12}$

Exercise 4f (page 33)

① $5\frac{5}{24}$ ② $\frac{11}{24}$ ③ $5\frac{11}{20}, \frac{9}{20}$ ④ $\frac{3}{8}$
⑤ $\frac{1}{8}(\frac{3}{24})$ ⑥ $\frac{27}{40}$ ⑦ $\frac{1}{3}(\frac{8}{24})$ ⑧ $\frac{1}{30}$
⑨ $3\frac{3}{4}$h ⑩ $\frac{4}{5}(\frac{8}{10})$

Exercise 4g (page 34)

① $5\frac{1}{3}$ ② 9 ③ $1\frac{1}{2}$ ④ $\frac{4}{5}$
⑤ $4\frac{1}{2}$ ⑥ 10 ⑦ $6\frac{2}{3}$ ⑧ $7\frac{1}{2}$
⑨ $\frac{2}{3}$ ⑩ $7\frac{1}{2}$

Exercise 4h (page 35)

① $\frac{3}{8}$ ② $\frac{1}{2}$ ③ $\frac{1}{4}$ ④ $\frac{2}{5}$
⑤ $\frac{5}{16}$ ⑥ $\frac{4}{9}$ ⑦ $\frac{3}{4}$ ⑧ $1\frac{1}{2}$
⑨ 1 ⑩ $2\frac{1}{2}$ ⑪ $2\frac{1}{5}$ ⑫ $1\frac{1}{3}$
⑬ $4\frac{1}{2}$ ⑭ 12 ⑮ $\frac{1}{6}$ ⑯ $\frac{1}{2}$
⑰ $1\frac{2}{3}$ ⑱ $1\frac{5}{27}$ ⑲ 5 ⑳ 6
㉑ $6\frac{1}{4}$ ㉒ 2 ㉓ $2\frac{1}{2}$ ㉔ $\frac{3}{4}$

Exercise 4i (page 36)

① $\frac{1}{3}$ ② $\frac{3}{4}$ ③ $1\frac{2}{5}$ ④ $1\frac{2}{7}$
⑤ $\frac{4}{15}$ ⑥ $\frac{11}{12}$ ⑦ $1\frac{1}{2}$ ⑧ 11
⑨ 10 ⑩ 35 ⑪ $\frac{3}{5}$ ⑫ $1\frac{1}{4}$
⑬ $1\frac{1}{2}$ ⑭ $\frac{8}{15}$ ⑮ $\frac{2}{3}$ ⑯ 6
⑰ $1\frac{4}{5}$ ⑱ 4 ⑲ $\frac{12}{25}$ ⑳ $2\frac{1}{7}$
㉑ $\frac{1}{14}$ ㉒ $\frac{4}{5}$ ㉓ $\frac{2}{7}$ ㉔ $\frac{9}{28}$
㉕ $2\frac{1}{10}$ ㉖ $1\frac{5}{22}$ ㉗ $2\frac{8}{21}$ ㉘ $1\frac{1}{2}$
㉙ $\frac{5}{16}$ ㉚ $7\frac{17}{25}$ ㉛ $3\frac{1}{5}$ ㉜ $2\frac{2}{5}$
㉝ $2\frac{2}{3}$ ㉞ $\frac{1}{2}$ ㉟ $2\frac{1}{3}$

Exercise 4j (page 36)

① $7\frac{4}{5}$ ② $3\frac{3}{4}$ ③ $2\frac{4}{7}$
④ $1\frac{4}{5} \div 4\frac{1}{2}, 2\frac{1}{2}, \frac{2}{5}$ ⑤ 35 kg ⑥ 50
⑦ 800 ⑧ 20 ⑨ ₦340
⑩ $\frac{3}{5}$ ⑪ 6 ⑫ $\frac{9}{25}$ m (36 cm)
⑬ $\frac{1}{8}$ ⑭ $\frac{5}{22}$

Exercise 4k (page 37)

① $\frac{1}{20}$ ② $\frac{1}{2}$ ③ $\frac{1}{4}$ ④ $\frac{2}{5}$
⑤ $\frac{7}{10}$ ⑥ $\frac{1}{25}$ ⑦ $\frac{7}{20}$ ⑧ $\frac{3}{25}$
⑨ $\frac{4}{5}$ ⑩ $\frac{3}{4}$ ⑪ $\frac{6}{25}$ ⑫ $\frac{13}{20}$
⑬ $\frac{16}{25}$ ⑭ $\frac{3}{5}$ ⑮ $\frac{9}{20}$ ⑯ $\frac{21}{25}$

Exercise 4l (page 37)

① 50% ② 25% ③ $33\frac{1}{3}$% ④ 75%
⑤ 20% ⑥ 10% ⑦ 5% ⑧ 4%
⑨ 30% ⑩ 60% ⑪ $13\frac{1}{3}$% ⑫ 85%
⑬ $62\frac{1}{2}$% ⑭ $16\frac{2}{3}$% ⑮ 36% ⑯ $25\frac{1}{3}$%

Exercise 4m (page 37)

① $\frac{1}{4}$ ② $\frac{1}{12}$ ③ $\frac{1}{4}$ ④ $\frac{1}{7}$
⑤ $\frac{2}{5}$ ⑥ $\frac{2}{3}$ ⑦ $\frac{13}{20}$ ⑧ $\frac{3}{8}$
⑨ $\frac{1}{4}$ ⑩ $\frac{1}{25}$
⑪ a $\frac{3}{10}$ b $\frac{7}{40}$ c $\frac{3}{5}$ d $\frac{3}{40}$
   e $\frac{1}{3}$ f $\frac{1}{2}$6 g $\frac{9}{50}$ h $\frac{22}{75}$
   i $\frac{1}{11}$ j $\frac{4}{9}$

205

Exercise 4n (page 38)

1. a 10% b 25% c 40% d 80%
   e 30% f 12½% g 60% h 2½%
   i 20% j 40%
2. 75%
3. 12%
4. 20%
5. 9%, 91%
6. 12 cm, 25%
7. 16%, 84%
8. 6%
9. 20%
10. 15%
11. 11%

Exercise 5a (page 40)

1. 5
2. 1
3. 14
4. 0
5. 8
6. 4
7. 14
8. 7
9. 14
10. 6
11. 9
12. 3
13. 20
14. 10
15. 16
16. 6
17. 12
18. 5
19. 11
20. 8
21. 2
22. 6
23. 3
24. 1
25. 7
26. 4
27. 5
28. 0
29. 4
30. 4
31. 3
32. 7
33. 1
34. 4
35. 4
36. 11
37. 0
38. 6
39. 7
40. 12
41. 1
42. 2
43. 5
44. 3
45. 3
46. 4
47. 5
48. 10
49. 12
50. 12
51. 4
52. 7
53. 3
54. 16
55. 2
56. 8
57. 6
58. 19
59. 7
60. 17
61. 12
62. 18
63. 5
64. 3
65. 36
66. 0
67. 11
68. 0
69. 4
70. 5
71. 3
72. 2
73. 6
74. 80
75. 1
76. 9

Exercise 5b (page 40)

1. 2
2. 3
3. 5
4. 6
5. 4
6. 1
7. 2
8. 5
9. 7
10. 3
11. 6
12. 10
13. 5
14. 8
15. 7
16. 1
17. 7
18. 10
19. and 20. any number

Exercise 5c (page 41)

1. a 8 b 12 c 9 d 12
   e 1 f 5 g 4 h 1
   i 0 j 15 k 40 l 7

2. a 17 b 23 c 8 d 2
   e 8 f 14 g 19 h 1
   i 1 j 32 k 2 l 1
3. a 18 b 0 c 20 d 12
   e 25 f 15 g 23 h 8
   i 85 j 6

Exercise 5d (page 41)

1. $x = 9$
2. $x = 3$
3. $y = 14$
4. $y = 10$
5. $z = 29$
6. $z = 7$
7. $a = 21$
8. $a = 17$
9. $b = 26$
10. $b = 5$
11. $c = 9$
12. $c = 2$
13. $p = 20$
14. $p = 11$
15. $q = 16$
16. $q = 9$
17. $r = 22$
18. $r = 7$
19. $s = 23$
20. $s = 9$
21. $m = 3$
22. $m = 1$
23. $n = 3$
24. $n = 5$
25. $d = 8$
26. $d = 8$
27. $e = 11$
28. $e = 10$
29. $f = 15$
30. $f = 6$
31. $z = 4$
32. $z = 8$
33. $y = 10$
34. $y = 28$
35. $x = 23$
36. $x = 14$
37. $c = 19$
38. $c = 30$
39. $b = 14$
40. $b = 29$
41. $a = 1$
42. $a = 1$
43. $r = 5$
44. $r = 5$
45. $q = 8$
46. $q = 4$
47. $p = 14$
48. $p = 17$
49. $s = 7$
50. $s = 18$
51. $n = 2$
52. $n = 14$
53. $m = 7$
54. $m = 25$
55. $f = 23$
56. $f = 27$
57. $e = 15$
58. $e = 24$
59. $d = 7$
60. $d = 27$
61. $y = 28$
62. $z = 21$
63. $g = 4$
64. $h = 5$
65. $j = 24$
66. $k = 0$
67. $m = 14$
68. $n = 0$
69. $p = 8$
70. $q = 6$
71. $r = 7$
72. $s = 11$
73. $t = 3$
74. $v = 80$
75. $w = 1$
76. $a = 5$

Exercise 5e (page 42)

1. $x = 4$
2. $y = 6$
3. $z = 7$
4. $a = 2$
5. $b = 9$
6. $c = 8$
7. $e = 1$
8. $f = 4$
9. $g = 10$
10. $h = 2$
11. $j = 8$
12. $k = 9$
13. $m = 6$
14. $n = 10$
15. $p = 14$
16. $b = 8$
17. $q = 2$
18. $r = 5$
19. and 20. any number

Exercise 5f (page 42)

1. a 9   b 12   c 3   d 0
   e 13   f 4   g 6   h 15
   i 12   j 2   k 24   l 7
2. a 16   b 24   c 12   d 1
   e 20   f 28   g 7   h 0
   i 30   j 3   k 45   l 4
3. a 14   b 0   c 20   d 17
   e 19   f 12   g 23   h 16
   i 11   j 6   k 1   l 2
   m 42   n 10

Exercise 5g (page 42)

1. $x = 6000$
2. $a = 13$
3. $m = 2, (m + 5)$ kg
4. 24 cm
5. 34
6. $n = 18$
7. $n = 470$
8. $y = 14$
9. 9, 14
10. $m = 48$
11. $k = 4$
12. $n = 1000$

Exercise 6b (page 48)

1. most boxes, room, book, rubber, block (there are many more)
2. a 4   b 4   c 5   d 4
3. rectangle
4. square
5.
6. a 9   b 36   c 8   d 16
   e 10   f 2
7. a, c, d, f
8. 140 cm
9. a 3 faces   b 9 edges   c 7 vertices
   d Table A1

	vertices	faces	edges
cuboid	8	6	12
cube	8	6	12

Table A1

Exercise 6c (page 50)

1. most tin cans, cotton reel, coin, new round pencil, torch battery (there are many others)
2. new hexagonal pencil, any cuboid, part of roof building, nut (from nut and bolt), laboratory glass prism (there are many others)
3. a 4   b 3   c 3   d 5
4. circle
5. triangle, rectangle
6. hexagonal prism, triangular prism, cylinder
7. 5 faces, 9 edges, 6 vertices
8.

view	vertices	faces	edges
a	5	2	6
b	6	3	8

Exercise 6d (page 51)

1. sharp end of round pencil, mound of rice, some hats, Hausa trumpet, roof of round hut (there are many others)
2. sharp end of hexagonal pencil, top of groundnut pyramid, some hats, part of roof of building, corner of box
3. a 2 cones,
   b 2 hexagonal pyramids,
   c 3 square-based pyramids,
   d 2 cones
4. triangular-based pyramid (or tetrahedron)
5. 7, hexagon
6.

	number of vertices	number of faces	number of edges
triangular-based pyramid	4	4	6
square-based pyramid	5	5	8
hexagonal-based pyramid	7	7	12
triangular prism	6	5	9
cube	8	6	12
cuboid	8	6	12

Table A2

7. a square-based pyramid   b cone
   c tetrahedron
8. a DC   b CB   c GF   d HA   e C, E
9. 5 vertices, 3 faces, 7 edges

Exercise 6e (page 53)

1.
   a cone, hemisphere;
   b cone, cylinder;
   c hemisphere, cuboid, cylinder
   d two cuboids, triangular prism, square-based pyramid
3. cone, sphere, cylinder
4. 5 cm
5. square-based pyramid, triangular prism
7. a BC   b JK   c IJ   d AN
   e C, K   f F, J
8. hexagonal prism
9. cylinder, sphere, hemisphere
10. a triangular-based pyramid (tetrahedron)
    b cuboid   c cube

Exercise 6f (page 54)

1. a AB   b BG   c BG, FG, HG
   d DE, FE, HE   e EH   f F
2. a E   b D   c B   d D
   e edge AC   f edge BF
3. a isosceles triangle   b square
   c 4   d B
   e V   f V
   g edge DC

Exercise 7a (page 56)

1. $3a$ 2. $3x$ 3. $2p$ 4. $5r$
5. $8t$ 6. $4m$ 7. $10z$ 8. $2y$
9. $6c$ 10. $5k$

Exercise 7b (page 56)

1. a $4+4+4$ b $30+4$ c $6+6+6$
   d $30+6$ e $9+9$ f $20+9$
   g 5 h $50+1$ i $70+7$
   j $90+8$
2. a $a+a+a$ b $x+x+x+x+x$
   c $y+y$ d $n+n+n+n$
   e $m+m+m$
   f $d+d+d+d+d+d$
   g $f+f$
   h $e+e+e+e+e+e+e+e+e+e$
   i $r+r+r+r+r+r+r+r$
   j $s+s+s+s+s$

Exercise 7c (page 56)

1. 3   2. 7   3. 4   4. 8
5. 15   6. 9   7. 18   8. 2
9. 1   10. 10   11. $\frac{1}{3}$ 12. $\frac{1}{2}$
13. $\frac{1}{4}$ 14. $\frac{2}{3}$ 15. $\frac{3}{4}$ 16. $\frac{1}{5}$
17. $\frac{1}{10}$ 18. $\frac{2}{3}$ 19. $\frac{3}{4}$ 20. $\frac{3}{5}$

Exercise 7d (page 57)

1. $5a$ 2. $2x$ 3. $8b$ 4. $4y$
5. $5c$ 6. $6z$ 7. $3p$ 8. k
9. $10q$ 10. $3m$ 11. $2r$ 12. 0
13. d 14. $10x$ 15. $18x$

Exercise 7e (page 57)

1. a $7a$ b $3b$ c $10c$ d $5d$
   e $19e$ f $4f$ g $14g$ h $12h$
   i $25j$ j k k $23m$ l $14n$
   m $6p$ n 0 o r p $10s$
   q $30t$ r $9u$ s $12v$ t $9w$
   u $12x$ v $20y$ w $11z$ x $10a$
2. a $8b$ b 0 c $3d$ d $15e$
   e $7f$ f $7g$ g $11h$ h $2j$
   i $4k$ j $3m$ k n l $7p$
   m $5q$ n 0 o $12s$ p $11t$
   q $6u$ r $6v$ s $5w$ t $8x$
   u $4y$ v $10z$ w $15a$ x $5b$
   y $12c$ z $8d$
3. a $5e$ b 0 c $3g$ d $5h$
   e j f $4k$ g $2m$ h $5n$
   i $4p$ j $6q$

Exercise 7f (page 58)

1. $5x+7$ 2. $3x+2$ 3. $11x+8y$
4. $6x+1$ 5. $5x-2$ 6. $5x-2y$
7. $5y+9x$ 8. $3y+5x$ 9. $9y+12x$
10. $15+8x$ 11. $1+2x$ 12. $4y+4x$
13. $6x+8y$ 14. $6x+5$ 15. $14x-5$
16. $11y$ 17. $10x+2$ 18. $x-8$
19. $13y+12x$ 20. $y-x$ 21. $14x+17$
22. $3x+9$ 23. $11y-3x$ 24. $8y-9x$
25. $8a+13$ 26. $3a+8$ 27. $11x+5y$
28. $9x+8y$ 29. $3a+b$ 30. $9m+4$

(31) $20n + 9$
(32) $10p + 1$
(33) $7p + 10t$
(34) $12a + 7b$
(35) $7x - 11$
(36) $17x - 5y$
(37) $20 + 6x$
(38) $12n - 11p$
(39) $9c - 7$
(40) $y + 3x$

Exercise 7g (page 59)
(1) $9x$
(2) $7d$
(3) $9a$
(4) $12b$
(5) $3m + 5n$
(6) $10y$
(7) $25h$
(8) $2x + 6y$
(9) $3n$
(10) $8k$
(11) $6e$
(12) $6g$
(13) $15a - 2$
(14) $7b$
(15) 0
(16) $6d$
(17) m
(18) a
(19) $8b$
(20) $31p - 9q$
(21) $28f - 11$
(22) $3c$
(23) $2d$
(24) $4m$
(25) $6n$
(26) $5x$
(27) $7m + 11n$
(28) $4a + 6b$
(29) $3h + 6$
(30) $7x + 5y - 4$
(31) $4x + 9y$
(32) $4a + 9b$
(33) $f + 2g$
(34) $2m + 5n + 9$
(35) $x + 4$
(36) $3a + b + 3c$
(37) $3h + 5k + 2$
(38) $3n + 3$
(39) $a + 3b + 3c$
(40) $4p + 3q + 4r + 3s$

Exercise 7h (page 59)
(1) $4x$ cm
(2) $x + y + z$, ₦$(500x + 600y + 900z)$
(3) $180 - 2n$
(4) ₦$(19\,000 - 5x)$
(5) $\frac{9}{10}k$ kg
(6) $3x + 3y$
(7) $\frac{1}{4}x + 5, \frac{3}{4}x - 5$
(8) ₦$(5n - 1200)$
(9) $\frac{2}{3}x - 2$
(10) for: $3x + 4y$, against: $x + 4y$, difference: $2x$

Exercise 8a (page 62)
(1) Table A3

revs	degrees
1	360°
2	720°
3	1080°
10	3600°
$\frac{1}{2}$	180°

revs	degrees
$\frac{1}{3}$	120°
$\frac{1}{4}$	90°
$\frac{1}{10}$	36°
$\frac{1}{8}$	45°
$1\frac{1}{2}$	540°

Table A3

(2) a $\frac{1}{6}$ revolution 60° b $\frac{1}{4}$, 90°
c $\frac{1}{3}$, 120° d $\frac{5}{12}$, 150°
e $\frac{1}{2}$, 180° f $\frac{5}{12}$, 150° (or $\frac{7}{12}$, 210°)
g $\frac{1}{4}$, 90° (or $\frac{3}{4}$, 270°)
h $\frac{1}{6}$, 60° (or $\frac{5}{6}$, 300°)
i $\frac{1}{12}$, 30° (or $\frac{11}{12}$, 330°)

(3) a midway between 2 and 3 b 15° c 105°
(4) a 75° b 135° c 75° d 165°
e 15° f 15°
(5) a quarter-way between 2 and 3 (nearer 2)
b $7\frac{1}{2}$° c $22\frac{1}{2}$° d $22\frac{1}{2}$°
(6) a $112\frac{1}{2}$° b $172\frac{1}{2}$° c $7\frac{1}{2}$°
d $82\frac{1}{2}$° e $127\frac{1}{2}$° f $7\frac{1}{2}$°

Exercise 8b (page 65)
(1) a HÂB, AB̂C, BĈD, DÊF, FĜH
b CD̂E, EF̂G, GĤA
c HÂB, AB̂C, BĈD, CD̂E, DÊF, EF̂G, FĜH, GĤA
(2) a right b obtuse c acute
d acute e reflex f obtuse
g acute h straight k obtuse
l reflex m right n reflex
(3) a 30° b 43° c 62° d 79°
e 140° f 156° g 117° h 161°

Exercise 8c (page 66)
(1) 40° (2) 65° (3) 58° (4) 80°
(5) 28° (6) 110° (7) 135° (8) 147°
(9) 102° (10) 167°

209

Exercise 8d (page 67)

1. BĈD = 112°; BĈD + AĈD = 180°
4. HF̂G = 65°; HF̂G + EF̂H = 90°
5. ZÔW = 127°, WÔY = 53°, YÔX = 127°
   there are many things to notice:
   opposite angles are equal (e.g. ZÔX = WÔY); the sum of the four angles is 360°; the sum of adjacent angles (e.g. ZÔX and ZÔW) is 180°
6. the sum of the three angles of any triangle is 180°

Exercise 8e (page 68)

1. a obtuse   b obtuse   c acute
   d reflex   e reflex   f acute
   g acute   h obtuse   i acute
   j obtuse   k reflex   l obtuse
   m reflex   n acute   o obtuse
2. a 20°   b 130°   c 270°
   d 220° (really 218°)   e 60° (really 57°)
   f 330° (really 331°)
3. see answers to question 2 above
6. the sum of the four angles of any quadrilateral is 360°
7. the angles opposite the equal sides should be equal; the sum of the three angles is 180°
8. the sum of the three angles should be 180°

Revision exercise 1 (page 69)

1. a 5 tens (50)   b 7 units (7)
   c 2 thousands (2000)
2. a 6 tenths   b 8 thousandths
   c 1 hundredth
3. CCXLIII
4. a 2 × 3 × 3 or 2 × 32   b 2 × 13
   c 3 × 3 × 5 or 32 × 5
5. a 49   b 125   c 72
6. 9
7. 60
8. 0·458 km
9. 10·25 m
10. 630 s

Revision exercise 2 (page 69)

1. a 9   b 81   c 9
2. a $\frac{3}{5}$ b $\frac{2}{3}$ c $\frac{4}{5}$
3. $\frac{14}{3}$
4. a $\frac{7}{12}$ b $\frac{7}{20}$ c $\frac{1}{6}$ d $\frac{5}{4}$ $(1\frac{1}{4})$
5. a $4\frac{3}{8}$ $(\frac{35}{8})$ b $\frac{7}{10}$ c $\frac{4}{15}$
6. $\frac{1}{8}$
7. $\frac{3}{5}$
8. a $\frac{1}{4}$ b $\frac{7}{25}$ c $\frac{11}{20}$
9. $\frac{2}{7}$
10. 30%

Revision exercise 3 (page 70)

1. a 5   b 17   c 5   d 36
2. a $a = 1$ b $a = 5$ c $a = 7$
3. a $m + 5$ b $m - 5$ c $5m$
4. $x = 32$
5. a 6   b 5   c 7
6. $n = 140$
7. a $9a$ b $6x$ c $2n$
8. a $10n - 5$ b $5 - 6x$ c $2a + 6b$
9. $2x + 6$
10. ₦$(95x + 120y)$

Revision exercise 4 (page 70)

1. 12 edges
2. 5 faces, 3 rectangular faces
3. 5 vertices
4. 60 cm
5. a 90   b 60   c 900
6. a reflex   b acute   c obtuse
   d reflex   e acute
7. AÔB = 34°, BÔC = 56°
9. BÔC = 114°
10. 135°

Exercise 9a (page 73)

1. 0·38
2. 4·3
3. 0·5
4. 1·5
5. 1·7
6. 1·8
7. 0·75
8. 1·08

Exercise 9b (page 74)

1. a 0·8 b 0·1 c 2·1 d 1·5
   e 6·5 f 3·4 g 21·01 h 0·38
   i 12·53 j 10·08
2. a 0·8 b 0·5 c 2·7 d 1·4
   e 8·1 f 0·22 g 10·4 h 3·4
   i 47·8 j 10·95
3. a 0·9 b 0·3 c 2·3 d 0·3
   e 8·0 f 0·04 g 26·21 h 2·5
   i 12·04 j 1·78
4. a 0·5 b 0·2 c 1·4 d 2·7
   e 8·1 f 5·0 g 21·00 h 0·59
   i 12·72 j 10·04
5. a 0·8 b 0·1 c 2·0 d 0·2
   e 9·2 f 3·1 g 13·01 h 0·27
   i 76·923 j 36·45
6. a $7.56 b 2·72 m
7. a 11·37 m b 2·207 kg *or* 2207 g
8. a 5·62 m b 7·88 m
9. 0·59 kg (or 590 g) 10. 3·05

Exercise 9c (page 75)

1. 267 2. 45 500 3. 8 030
4. 0·005 6 5. 0·811 6. 0·070 4
7. 270 8. 36 9. 8·5
10. 0·052 11. 0·006 3 12. 4·23
13. 50 14. 65 000 15. 9 000 000
16. 4370 17. 245 000 18. 20·7
19. 45·02 20. 0·020 05 21. 0·000 000 36
22. 0·051 4 23. 0·6 24. 0·03
25. 0·026 26. 0·7 27. 0·08
28. 0·000 242 29. 4·007 30. 0·070 63
31. 620 c 32. $3.44 33. 241 cm
34. 5·92 m
35. a 6240 kg b 6 240 000 g
36. a 0·92 t b 920 000 g
37. a 0·42 kg b 0·000 42 t
38. a 0·504 litre b 0·000 504 kℓ
39. a 20 900 mm b 0·020 9 km
40. a 7·05 kℓ b 7 050 000 mℓ

Exercise 9d (page 76)

1. 5·6 2. 0·8 3. 1·2
4. 2·7 5. 4 6. 3·6
7. 4·9 8. 4·2 9. 3
10. 4 11. 0·18 12. 0·28
13. 0·06 14. 0·12 15. 0·09
16. 0·018 17. 0·042 18. 0·003 2
19. 0·003 20. 0·000 15

Exercise 9e (page 76)

1. a 1·08 b 0·579 c 0·002 5
   d 1·6 e 4·234 6
2. a 1·2 b 13·95 c 0·04
   d 21·08 e 1·051 2
3. a 0·56 b 1·02 c 0·64
   d 0·280 8 e 0·677 5
4. a 3 b 0·51 c 0·000 016
   d 0·943 e 0·266 22
5. a 2·7 b 0·91 c 0·09
   d 0·115 5 e 33·858
6. 1·59
7. 0·111 65
8. 6·72 cm
9. ₦1 680
10. a 259·44 g b 0·259 44 kg

Exercise 9f (page 77)

1. 3 2. 0·3 3. 0·03 4. 30
5. 300 6. 3 7. 300 8. 3
9. 30 000 10. 0·03 11. 6 12. 0·6
13. 60 14. 0·06 15. 600 16. 600
17. 600 18. 60 19. 0·006 20. 6

Exercise 9g (page 77)

1. a 0·03 b 9 c 0·7
   d 3650 e 3·4
2. a 0·2 b 0·3 c 0·03
   d 46 e 6·1
3. a 0·04 b 8 c 40
   d 2·05 e 35
4. a 0·2 b 9 c 60
   d 53 e 230

211

⑤ a 0·1 b 0·5 c 400
  d 1·08 e 780
⑥ 0·35
⑦ a 0·47 kg b 470 g
⑧ 45
⑨ ₦180
⑩ 13·6 km

Exercise 9h (page 78)
① 0·5 ② 0·2 ③ 0·25 ④ 0·6
⑤ 0·75 ⑥ 0·55 ⑦ 0·4 ⑧ 0·24
⑨ 0·05 ⑩ 0·15 ⑪ 0·35 ⑫ 0·8
⑬ 0·04 ⑭ 0·72 ⑮ 0·12 ⑯ 0·68
⑰ 0·625 ⑱ 0·375 ⑲ 0·26 ⑳ 0·66
㉑ 0·92 ㉒ 0·075 ㉓ 0·85 ㉔ 0·975
㉕ 0·36 ㉖ 0·48 ㉗ 0·86 ㉘ 0·048
㉙ 0·875 ㉚ 0·275 ㉛ 1·75 ㉜ 0·62
㉝ 3·125 ㉞ 0·95 ㉟ 9·6 ㊱ 2·425
㊲ 4·65 ㊳ 7·76 ㊴ 0·5625 ㊵ 0·4375

Exercise 9i (page 79)
① 0·$\dot{3}$ ② 0·$\dot{6}$ ③ 0·$\dot{2}$ ④ 0·$\dot{5}$
⑤ 0·$\dot{8}$ ⑥ 0·2$\dot{7}$ ⑦ 0·4$\dot{5}$ ⑧ 0·8$\dot{3}$
⑨ 0·58$\dot{3}$ ⑩ 0·$\dot{1}4285\dot{7}$

Exercise 9j (page 79)
① $\frac{4}{5}$ ② $\frac{7}{10}$ ③ $\frac{3}{4}$ ④ $\frac{3}{5}$ ⑤ $\frac{1}{5}$ ⑥ $\frac{7}{25}$
⑦ $\frac{9}{20}$ ⑧ $\frac{8}{25}$ ⑨ $\frac{11}{25}$ ⑩ $\frac{21}{50}$ ⑪ $\frac{27}{50}$ ⑫ $\frac{12}{25}$
⑬ $\frac{14}{25}$ ⑭ $\frac{13}{25}$ ⑮ $\frac{33}{50}$ ⑯ $\frac{49}{50}$ ⑰ $\frac{21}{25}$ ⑱ $\frac{27}{200}$
⑲ $\frac{51}{500}$ ⑳ $\frac{21}{40}$ ㉑ $\frac{21}{200}$ ㉒ $\frac{33}{40}$ ㉓ $\frac{3}{8}$ ㉔ $\frac{61}{125}$
㉕ $\frac{29}{40}$ ㉖ $7\frac{2}{5}$ ㉗ $\frac{5}{8}$ ㉘ $1\frac{1}{4}$ ㉙ $\frac{78}{125}$ ㉚ $4\frac{18}{25}$

Exercise 9k (page 79)
① a 0·05 b 0·5 c 0·25 d 0·4
  e 0·7 f 0·04 g 0·15 h 0·12
  i 0·8 j 0·75 k 0·24 l 0·35
  m 0·64 n 0·6 o 0·45
② a 25% b 85% c 36% d 81%
  e 8% f 12$\frac{1}{2}$% g 30·8% h 70%
  i 7% j 66$\frac{2}{3}$% k 50% l 2·2%
  m $\frac{1}{2}$% n 80% o 13$\frac{1}{3}$%

Exercise 9l (page 80)
① a 30·98 b 11·39 kg
  c 12·00 kg d 84·61
  e 38·50 m f 1·85 kg
  g 38·9 cm (389 mm) h 773·75 km
  i 45·36 j $13.86
  k 3·5 l 0·16
  m 0·056 n 9·92
  o 15·914 p 0·0125
  q 0·075 r 62
  s 3·09 t 256
② a 0·59, $\frac{59}{100}$ b 0·26, $\frac{4}{15}$
  c 8·55, 8$\frac{11}{20}$ d 3·44, 3$\frac{11}{25}$
  e 0·24, $\frac{6}{25}$ f 2·1, 2$\frac{1}{10}$
  g 13·5, 13$\frac{1}{2}$ h 0·785, $\frac{157}{200}$
  i 4 j 0·8, $\frac{4}{5}$
  k 2·5, 2$\frac{1}{2}$ l 0·13, $\frac{2}{15}$
③ 18·75% ④ 25%
⑤ $54.27, $235.17 ⑥ 150·4
⑦ ₦151 800
⑧ a 8 705 mm b 0·008 705 km
⑨ ₦86 ⑩ ₦24 180

Exercise 10a (page 82)
① 21 years, 13 + y years ② 7, n + 4, x + 7
③ 6 + z cattle ④ (48 + m) kg
⑤ k + 1 kola nuts
⑥ (6 + n)th of September
⑦ 4d cm
⑧ a (x + 7) marks b (x + 7 + y) marks

Exercise 10b (page 82)
① 7, n − 2, r − 5
② 20 years, (30 − y) years
③ (x − 30) pages ④ (m − 5) mangoes
⑤ (15 − x) cm ⑥ ₦(165 500 − x)
⑦ (20 − x) km ⑧ ₦(s − t)

Exercise 10c (page 82)
① a 1000 m b 4000 m c 1000x m
② a 7 days b 35 days c 7w days

212

3 $12x$ months **4** $9d$
5 a ₦3 200 **b** ₦400x **c** ₦5t
6 $1000x$ g **7** $3x$ mm **8** $10m$ naira

Exercise 10d (page 83)
1 a 2 weeks **b** $\frac{d}{7}$ (or $\frac{1}{7}d$) weeks
2 a 3 m **b** $\frac{k}{1000}$ m
3 $\frac{b}{6}$ (or $\frac{1}{6}b$) kg **4 a** ₦80 **b** ₦$\frac{p}{5}$ or ₦$\frac{1}{5}p$
5 $\frac{h}{9}$ eggs per day **6** $\frac{140}{x}$ cm
7 $\frac{n}{3}$ or $\frac{1}{3}n$ **8** $\frac{x}{5}$ cm

Exercise 10e (page 83)
1 $(x + 20)$ min **2** $(6 - n)$ blue pens
3 $20a$ **4** $\frac{x}{1000}$ kg
5 ₦200x **6** ₦$\frac{380\,000}{d}$
7 $(20 - x)$ oranges **8** $(5x + 12)$ km
9 Team A, $\frac{n}{3}$ pts **10** $9x$ m²

Exercise 10f (page 83)
1 $93x$ cm
2 $6d$ cm
3 $(3x + y)$ matches
4 a $4x$ years **b** $(x + y)$ years
  c $(4x + y)$ years
5 $2005x$ grammes **6** ₦$\frac{c}{5}$
7 $(\frac{1}{2}n - 8)$ cattle **8** $\frac{x}{150}$
9 $(7x - 13)$ days **10** ₦$\left(\frac{5000}{x} - 360\right)$

Exercise 11a (page 85)
1 here are some rectangular shapes you may find in your classroom: door, door frame, window pane, window frame, ceiling, floor, wall, blackboard, desk top, book cover, pencil box top (there will be many more)
2 4
3 4
4 a opposite sides are equal in length
  b all the angles are right angles
5 360°
6 a the diagonals are the same length
  b the centre is the same distance from each corner
7 a 2 acute angles **b** 2 obtuse angles
8 yes, opposite sides of a rectangle are parallel to each other
9 a yes
  b a rectangle generally has two lines of symmetry

Exercise 11b (page 86)
3 both diagonals of a square are the same length
4 the angles at the centre are all right angles
5 each diagonal makes an angle of 45° with the sides of the square
6 a square has 4 lines of symmetry
7 opposite sides equal; opposite sides parallel; diagonals of equal length; four angles of 90°; four sides
8 in a square, all four sides are the same length;
in a square, the diagonals cross at right angles;
in a square, there are 4 lines of symmetry;
in a square the diagonals meet the sides at an angle of 45°;
none of these is true for a rectangle

Exercise 11c (page 87)
3 two of the angles should be equal in size
4 a AĈM = BĈM; AM̂C = BM̂C = 90°; CÂB = CB̂A
  b AM = BM
  c an isosceles triangle has only one line of symmetry
5 your sketch should show that BĈM = 20° and AM = 4 cm; you may also have found that CM̂A = CM̂B = 90° and that CÂM = CB̂M = 70°
6 in isosceles △ACB, the equal angles are A and B; the order of the letters helps to show the symmetry of the triangle

213

Exercise 11d (page 88)

2. each angle is 60°
3. an equilateral triangle has three equal sides, an isosceles triangle has only two equal sides; similarly for angles; an equilateral triangle has three lines of symmetry, an isosceles triangle has only one line of symmetry; all equilateral triangles have the same shape but isosceles triangles can have different shapes.

4.

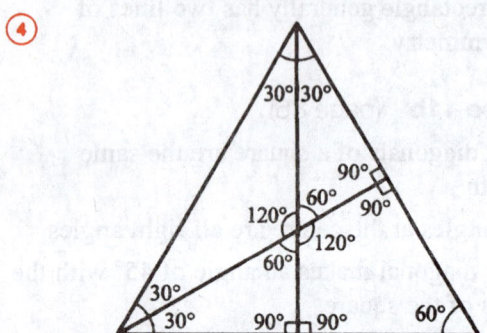

Fig. A1

5. a there are three lines of symmetry
   b all lines of symmetry pass through the same point
6. a 5   b 13   c 8   d 14

Exercise 11e (page 90)

2. a circle can have as many lines of symmetry as you like; every diameter is a line of symmetry

Exercise 12a (page 92)

2. a 6   b 6   c 6   d 4   e 7   f 7
3. 3, 2, 1, 0, −1, −2, −3

Exercise 12b (page 93)

1. a i (+3)   ii (−2)   iii (−1)   iv (+5)
   b i Omo   ii Ado   iii Ben   iv Sam
      v Olu
2. a +2m   b −5m   c +4m   d +3m
   e −3m   f −4m   g −1m   h +5m
   i 0   j +1m

Exercise 12c (page 95)

1. a +7m, −2m   b 9m
2. a +200m, −15m   b 215m

3. −15°C
4. 22°C
5. a i −8km   ii +9km   iii +15km
      iv −11km
   b i 17km   ii 6km   iii 26km
      iv 3km
6. a i +330m   ii −60m   iii +52m
      iv −128m
   b i 390m   ii 112m   iii 180m
      iv 458m
7. a −5h   b +7h   c +1½h
   d −¾h   e +3h   f −2h
   g +9h   h −3½h   i +4¾h
8. 13 min
9. 24 years
10. watch: 11·39, clock: 11·24
11. −210m
12. 8mm
13. −12°C
14. 2¼h
15. Fani: ₦5 800,
    Sola: ₦8 900 (1 900 + 6 400 + 600)
16. ₦40, ₦(−140)
17. a ₦800   b ₦2 500
18. ₦(−852 500)

Exercise 12d (page 96)

1. a +12   b +5   c −3
   d +15   e +4   f 0

2.
	start	move	finish
a	+2	5 units to the left	−3
b	+5	7 units to the left	−2
c	−1	7 units to the left	−8
d	+2	4 units to the right	+6
e	−3	5 units to the right	+2
f	−10	10 units to the right	0
g	+12	9 units to the left	+3
h	+14	30 units to the left	−16
i	−20	28 units to the right	+8
j	+1	2 units to the left	−1
k	+2	6 units to the left	−4
l	+5	2 units to the left	+3
m	+6	12 units to the left	−6
n	−2	2 units to the right	0

214

o	−15	30 units to the right	+15
p	+15	30 units to the left	−15
q	−11	24 units to the right	+13
r	+12	14 units to the left	−2
s	0	6 units to the right	+6
t	0	17 units to the left	−17
u	+3	2 units to the right	+5
v	+10	8 units to the left	+2
w	+6	10 units to the left	−4
x	−15	35 units to the right	+20
y	−4	11 units to the right	+7
z	+8	13 units to the left	−5

③ a −8, −3, −2, 0, +1, +5
b −5, −4, −2, +5, +7, +9
c −20, −14, −8, 0, +5, +6
d −18, −11, −6, 16, +11, +18
e −14, −10, −5, −3, −1, 0
f −11, −10, −9, +1, +16, +17

④ b −15, +8   c +4 > −13
d +18 > +1   e −18, −1
f 0 > −2   g −1, +1
h −7 > −17   i −13, +13
j 0 > −4   k +5 > −5
l −9, 0

Exercise 12e (page 98)

① a +10   d +13
  b +11   e +14
  c +12   f +15

② a +2   d −1
  b +1   e −2
  c 0   f −3

③ a −2   d +1
  b −1   e +2
  c 0   f +3

④ a −10   d −13
  b −11   e −14
  c −12   f −15

⑤ +19 ⑥ +9   ⑦ +13 ⑧ −7
⑨ +5   ⑩ −13 ⑪ −2   ⑫ +2
⑬ +18 ⑭ −18 ⑮ 0   ⑯ 0
⑰ −6   ⑱ +9   ⑲ −3   ⑳ +1

Exercise 12f (page 98)

① a 4   ② a 2   ③ a −2   ④ a −4

b 5	b 1	b −1	b −5
c 6	c 0	c 0	c −6
d 7	d −1	d 1	d −7
e 8	e −2	e 2	e −8

⑤ 4   ⑥ −4   ⑦ −8   ⑧ −7
⑨ −10 ⑩ 7   ⑪ −9   ⑫ −5
⑬ 7   ⑭ −11 ⑮ −1   ⑯ 8
⑰ 2   ⑱ −6   ⑲ 3   ⑳ −2

Exercise 12g (page 99)

① 8   ② −5   ③ −13   ④ −9
⑤ −1   ⑥ −30   ⑦ −34   ⑧ 15
⑨ −8   ⑩ −24   ⑪ −43   ⑫ −37
⑬ −45 ⑭ −122 ⑮ −26   ⑯ 34
⑰ −63 ⑱ −36   ⑲ −74   ⑳ −174

Exercise 12h (page 99)

① a +5   b 0   c +8
  +4   −1   +6
  +3   −2   +4
  +2   −3   +2
  +1   −4   0
  0   −5   −2

② a −3   b +2   c −8   d −14
  e 0   f +3   g −18 h −21
  i −5   j +20 k −20 l +20
  m −39 n −44 o −89 p −3
  q +6

Exercise 12i (page 100)

① a +3   b −6   c −3
  +4   −5   −2
  +5   −4   −1
  +6   −3   0
  +7   −2   +1

② a 11   b −5   c 11   d 5
  e 28   f 0   g 7   h 1
  i −1   j 50   k 30   l 20
  m −15 n −22 o 150 p 10
  q 0

Exercise 12j (page 100)

① a 4   b −4   c 3
  d 0   e 2   f −7

215

② 24°C
③ ₦900
④ a +5　b +3　c −12
　 d −11　e +8　f −30
⑤ a +4　b +16　c +5
　 d −4　e −7　f −7
⑥ ₦16 033
⑦ 13 BC
⑧ a

+	−3	−2	−1	0	+1	+2	+3
−3	−6	−5	−4	−3	−2	−1	0
−2	−5	−4	−3	−2	−1	0	+1
−1	−4	−3	−2	−1	0	+1	+2
0	−3	−2	−1	0	+1	+2	+3
+1	−2	−1	0	+1	+2	+3	+4
+2	−1	0	+1	+2	+3	+4	+5
+3	−0	+1	+2	+3	+4	+5	+6

b

−	−3	−2	−1	0	+1	+2	+3
−3	0	−1	−2	−3	−4	−5	−6
−2	+1	0	−1	−2	−3	−4	−5
−1	+2	+1	0	−1	−2	−3	−4
0	+3	+2	+1	0	−1	−2	−3
+1	+4	+3	+2	+1	0	−1	−2
+2	+5	+4	+3	+2	+1	0	−1
+3	+6	+5	+4	+3	+2	+1	0

⑨ a +6　b 0　c +450
　 d −120　e +2x　f +18y
⑩ a $-\frac{1}{2}$　b +3.5　c +8.7
　 d $+2\frac{1}{6}$　e −2.4°C　f +3.2°C

Exercise 13a (page 103)

① a 5.5 cm　b 5.5 cm　c 7.6 cm
　 d 12.2 cm　e 7.3 cm　f 9.3 cm
② a 6 cm　b 6 cm　c 5.7 cm
　 d 8.4 cm　e 8.5 cm　f 8.4 cm
③ The following measurements are only approximate:
　 a 7.5 cm　b 7.2 cm　c 6.3 cm
　 d 12.6 cm

Exercise 13b (page 106)

① a 3 cm　2 cm　10 cm
　 b 5 m　4 m　18 m
　 c 16 cm　10 cm　52 cm
　 d $2\frac{1}{2}$ m　1 m　7 m
　 e 6 m　$2\frac{1}{2}$ m　17 m
　 f $8\frac{1}{4}$ cm　$4\frac{1}{2}$ cm　$25\frac{1}{2}$ cm
　 g 5.1 cm　3.2 cm　16.6 cm
　 h 4.3 cm　0.8 cm　10.2 cm
　 i 7.35 cm　7.15 cm　29 cm
　 j 9 m　0.9 m　19.8 m
　 k 10 m　8 m　36 m
　 l 14 cm　12 cm　52 cm
　 m 17 cm　13 cm　60 cm
　 n 15 m　7.5 m　45 m
　 o 10.5 m　6 m　33 m
② a 6 m　24 m
　 b 14 cm　56 cm
　 c $2\frac{1}{4}$ m　9 m
　 d 8.3 cm　33.2 cm
　 e 7.25 cm　29 cm
　 f 9.6 cm　38.4 cm
　 g 10 cm　40 cm
　 h 90 cm　360 cm
　 i 4.5 m　18 m
　 j 3.6 m　14.4 m
　 k 13 cm　52 cm
　 l 12.3 m　49.2 m
③ a 1900 m　b 1.9 km
④ 300 m
⑤ ₦2 800
⑥ a 12.8 cm　b ₦640　c ₦12 800
⑦ a 20 m　b 25 m　c 18 m
⑧ a length = 9 m; breadth = 4 m; perimeter = 26 m;
　 b although each rectangle is made from the same number of tiles, it will be found that their perimeters are all different
⑨ a 22 cm　b 28 cm　c 34 cm
　 d 42 m　e 40 cm　f 11.2 km
⑩ 26 cm
⑪ 14 cm, 5 cm, 5 cm
⑫ 30 cm

Exercise 13c (page 108)

② a the circumference is greater than the diameter

b just over three times as great
c it should be true for all three objects
d if everyone has worked carefully, you should all get similar results

Exercise 13d (page 109)

① **a** 7 m   14 m   44 m
   b 3·5 cm   7 cm   22 cm
   c 14 cm   28 cm   88 cm
   d 21 m   42 m   132 m
   e 35 cm   70 cm   220 cm
   f 31·5 cm   63 cm   198 cm
   g 2·8 m   5·6 m   17·6 m
   h 4·9 m   9·8 m   30·8 m
   i 4·2 m   8·4 m   26·4 m
   j 3·85 m   7·7 m   24·2 m
② 440 m   ③ 62·8 cm   ④ 44 m
⑤ 66 cm   ⑥ 31·4 m
⑦ **a** 28 cm   **b** 22 cm   **c** 50 cm
⑧ 7 850 cm (78·5 m)
⑨ 198 m   ⑩ 31 m   ⑪ 11 m
⑫ **a** 88 m   **b** 37·5 g
⑬ 13·2 m or 1320 cm   ⑭ 568   ⑮ ₦94 200

Exercise 13e (page 110)

① 36 cm   ② 40 cm   ③ 32 cm
④ 44 cm   ⑤ 38 cm   ⑥ 32·9 cm

Exercise 14a (page 112)

① **a** 12 cm²   **b** 7½ cm²
   c 15 cm²   **d** 4 cm²
   e approx. 28 cm²   **f** 10 cm²
   g 6 cm²   **h** 10 cm²
   i 6 cm²   **j** approx. 3 cm²

Exercise 14b (page 114)

① **a** 3 cm   2 cm   6 cm²
   b 5 m   4 m   20 m²
   c 5 m   3 m   15 m²
   d 4 m   3 m   12 m²
   e 6 m   2½ m   15 m²
   f 5·2 m   3 m   15·6 m²
   g 2·1 m   3·4 m   7·14 m²
   h 4 m   4·5 m   18 m²
   i 12 cm   9 cm   108 cm²
   j 8 m   6 m   48 m²
   k 11 cm   8 cm   88 cm²
   l 6·3 m   5 m   31·5 m²
   m 13 cm   7 cm   91 cm²
   n 7·5 m   4 m   30 m²
   o 14 cm   6 cm   84 cm²

② **a** 6 cm   36 cm²
   b 9 m   81 m²
   c 7 m   49 m²
   d 4 cm   16 cm²
   e 1·2 m   1·44 m²
   f 2½ cm   6¼ cm²
   g 8 cm   64 cm²
   h 12 cm   144 cm²
   i 14 cm   196 cm²
   j 10 m   100 m²
   k 15 cm   225 cm²
   l 2·4 cm   5·76 cm²

③ **a** 60 m²   **b** 72 m²   **c** 16 m²
   d 28 m²   **e** 26 m²   **f** 13 m²
④ **a** 18 m²   **b** 25 m²   **c** 21 m²
   d 36 m²   **e** 63 m²   **f** 19 m²
⑤ **a** 14 m²   **b** ₦33 600
⑥ 36 m²   ⑦ 3·44 m²
⑧ 236 m²   ⑨ 132 m²
⑩ 752 cm²
⑪ **a** 1 008 cm²   **b** 256 cm²
⑫ 45 m²   ⑬ 3 litres
⑭ **a** 20 m²   **b** 8 boards
⑮ 112 m
⑯ **a** 250 cm²   **b** 18   **c** 4 500 cm²
⑰ 720 g   ⑱ ₦240
⑲ **a** perimeter = 16 units, area = 12 units²
   b the boy can also make rectangles 1 × 7, 3 × 5 and 4 × 4
   c all the perimeters are 16 units; the areas are 7, 15 and 16 units²
   d this shows that shapes can have the same perimeters but different areas

Exercise 14c (page 117)

① **a** 35 cm²   **b** 48 cm²   **c** 33 cm²
   d 15 cm²   **e** 63 cm²   **f** 40 cm²
   g 10 cm²   **h** 24 cm²   **i** 3 cm

    j 5 cm   k 4 m   l 4·5 cm
    m 12 cm

(2) a 5 cm   b 6 cm   c 7 m
    d 1·6 m   e 4·4 cm

(3) a i 40 cm²   ii height = 5 cm
    b i 30 cm²   ii base = 5 cm
    c i 36 cm²   ii height = 4 cm
    d i 12 cm²   ii base = 6 cm

Exercise 14d (page 120)

(1) a 16 cm²   b 9 cm²   c 35 cm²
    d 1·8 cm²   e 12·5 cm²   f 7 cm²
    g 6 cm²   h 15 cm²   i 3·75 cm²
    j 24 cm²   k 30 cm²   l 16 cm²

(2) a 30 cm²   b 16 cm²   c 18 cm²
    d 20 cm²   e 15 cm²   f 26 cm²
    g 40 cm²   h 37·5 cm²   i 26 cm²

Exercise 14e (page 122)

(1) a 7 m   14 m   154 m²
    b $3\frac{1}{2}$ cm   7 cm $38\frac{1}{2}$ cm²
    c 140 mm   280 mm   61 600 mm²
    d 14 m   28 m   616 m²
    e $1\frac{3}{4}$ cm $3\frac{1}{2}$ cm $9\frac{5}{8}$ cm²
    f 2·1 cm   4·2 cm   13·86 cm²

(2) a $19\frac{1}{4}$ cm²   b $38\frac{1}{2}$ cm²
    c $7\frac{7}{32}$ cm² (7·2 cm² approx.)   d 70 cm²
    e 5·88 cm²   f 504 cm²

(3) a $61\frac{1}{2}$ cm²   b $115\frac{1}{2}$ cm²   c 56 cm²
    d $38\frac{1}{2}$ cm²   e 126 cm²   f $25\frac{3}{4}$ cm²

(4) radius = 10 cm; area = 314 cm²

(5) 27·9 m²   (6) 39·25 cm²

(7) $\frac{1}{9}$ (8) ₦200

(9) a 15 cm   b 5 cm   c 157 cm²

(10) a 10 150 m²   b 400 m

Exercise 15a (page 124)

(1) $5a$ (2) $4x$ (3) xy (4) xy
(5) a^2 (6) x^2 (7) $6a$ (8) $6a$
(9) $6a$ (10) $6a$ (11) $28x$ (12) $40n$
(13) $2x^2$ (14) $12y^2$ (15) $32x^2$ (16) $20ab$
(17) $35pq$ (18) $27ab$ (19) $6x^2$ (20) $8y^2$
(21) $3x^2$ (22) $2pq$ (23) $6ab$ (24) $7mn$
(25) $12a^2$ (26) $35n^2$ (27) $30x^2$ (28) $36n^2$
(29) $50pq$ (30) $20ab$ (31) $28a^2b$ (32) $33ab^2$
(33) $18xy^2$ (34) $30xy^2$ (35) $14p^2q$ (36) $24a^2b$

Exercise 15b (page 125)

(1) $2a$ (2) $6a$ (3) $6x$ (4) $3y$
(5) $3x$ (6) $4c$ (7) $4x$ (8) $7y$
(9) $5y$ (10) $\frac{x}{9}$ (11) $\frac{d}{4}$ (12) $\frac{x}{2}$
(13) $7ab$ (14) $16y$ (15) $5pq$ (16) $17m$
(17) $2kl$ (18) $6a$ (19) d (20) $\frac{1}{a}$
(21) z (22) $3x$ (23) $6x$ (24) $5c$
(25) $7x^2$ (26) $2x^2$ (27) $5x$ (28) $4x$
(29) $6a^2$ (30) $13x$ (31) $11n$ (32) $6x$
(33) $6a$ (34) $9ab$ (35) $4x$ (36) $5q$

Exercise 15c (page 126)

(1) 6   (2) 5   (3) 0   (4) 22
(5) 2   (6) 24   (7) 23   (8) 35
(9) 20   (10) 10   (11) 1   (12) 0

Exercise 15d (page 126)

(1) $11x$ (2) $17p$ (3) $34n$
(4) $14b - 3$ (5) $6 + 10m$ (6) $12a + 5$
(7) $7y$ (8) $7a$ (9) $7x$
(10) $4n$ (11) $3 + 6y$ (12) 12
(13) $8a$ (14) $4x - 2$ (15) 1
(16) $10a$ (17) $17x$ (18) $53x$
(19) $16u$ (20) $10x$ (21) $5x$
(22) $5v$ (23) 0 (24) $2x$

Exercise 15e (page 127)

(2) a $3 + (7 + 2) = 3 + 9 = 12$
    b $3 + (7 + 2) = 3 + 7 + 2 = 10 + 2$
        $= 12$

(3) a $13 + (6 - 4) = 13 + 2 = 15$
    b $13 + (6 - 4) = 13 + 6 - 4 = 19 - 4$
        $= 15$

(4) a $3 + (9 - 4) = 3 + 5 = 8$
    b $3 + (9 - 4) = 3 + 9 - 4 = 12 - 4 = 8$

(5) a $6 + (4 - 2) = 6 + 2 = 8$
b $6 + (4 - 2) = 6 + 4 - 2 = 10 - 2 = 8$
(6) a $7 + (13 + 9) = 7 + 22 = 29$
b $7 + (13 + 9) = 7 + 13 + 9 = 20 + 9$
$= 29$
(7) a $3 + (8 - 2) = 3 + 6 = 9$
b $3 + (8 - 2) = 3 + 8 - 2 = 11 - 2 = 9$
(8) a $3 + (2 - 8) = 3 + (-6) = 23$
b $3 + (2 - 8) = 3 + 2 - 8 = 5 - 8 = -3$
(9) a $4 + (3 - 11) = 4 + (-8) = -4$
b $4 + (3 - 11) = 4 + 3 - 11 = 7 - 11$
$= -4$
(10) a $5 + (2 - 10) = 5 + (-8) = -3$
b $5 + (2 - 10) = 5 + 2 - 10 = 7 - 10$
$= -3$

(6) a $15 - (10 + 2) = 15 - 12 = 3$
b $15 - (10 + 2) = 15 - 10 - 2 = 5 - 2$
$= 3$
(7) a $11 - (2 - 1) = 11 - 1 = 10$
b $11 - (2 - 1) = 11 - 2 + 1 = 9 + 1$
$= 10$
(8) a $4 - (6 + 3) = 4 - 9 = -5$
b $4 - (6 + 3) = 4 - 6 - 3 = -2 - 3$
$= -5$
(9) a $5 - (14 - 5) = 5 - 9 = -4$
b $5 - (14 - 5) = 5 - 14 + 5 = -9 + 5$
$= -4$
(10) a $8 - (2 + 6) = 8 - 8 = 0$
b $8 - (2 + 6) = 8 - 2 - 6 = 6 - 6 = 0$

Exercise 15i (page 128)
(1) $a - b - c$ (2) $a - b + c$
(3) $a - b - c$ (4) $2a - 3b + c$
(5) $-5a - b + 2c$ (6) $5x - 3y - z$
(7) $a + b - c - d$ (8) $a - b - c + d$
(9) $a - b - c - d$ (10) $3a - 5b + 2c + 4d$
(11) $8a - b - 5c - 2d$ (12) $-2a - b + 4c - 3d$

Exercise 15f (page 127)
(1) $a + b + c$ (2) $a + b + c$
(3) $a + b - c$ (4) $a + 3b - 2c$
(5) $2a + b - 4c$ (6) $a - 5b - 5c$
(7) $a + b + c + d$ (8) $a - b + c - d$
(9) $a + b - c - d$ (10) $7a + -b - c - 3d$
(11) $5a + b + 3c - 3d$ (12) $6a - b + c - 4d$

Exercise 15j (page 128)
(1) $2a - 5$ (2) $6x - 2$
(3) $5x - 11y$ (4) $7 - 4n$
(5) $6n - m$ (6) $5a - 3$
(7) $4x + 2y$ (8) $5 - 5a$
(9) $7x + 11y$ (10) $2x + 4y$
(11) $6x - 5$ (12) $24a - 5b$

Exercise 15g (page 127)
(1) $2a - b$ (2) $a + 12$ (3) $5x + 3$
(4) $4m + 2n$ (5) $9a - 2b$ (6) $11a + 8b$
(7) $5a - 7$ (8) $4x + 6y$ (9) $2p - 7q$
(10) $8a + 11$ (11) $8 + 2n$ (12) $x + 5$
(13) $2x - 6y$ (14) $7a - 3$ (15) $8x - 12y$

Exercise 15k (page 129)
(1) a $(p - 15)$ naira   b $(2p - 15)$ naira
(2) a $(x + 40)$ naira   b $(2x + 40)$ naira
(3) $(2d + 20)$ naira   (4) ₦$(3x - y)$
(5) $2n + 1$ (6) $2m - 1$
(7) a $3x$ b $2x - 4$ c $(x + 4)$ sweets
(8) a $(m - n)$ naira
b $(m + 2n)$ naira
(9) a $b - 1$ and $b + 1$ b $3b$
(10) a $(2x + 300)$ naira
b they need $(700 - 2x)$ naira more

Exercise 15h (page 128)
(2) a $9 - (5 + 2) = 9 - 7 = 2$
b $9 - (5 + 2) = 9 - 5 - 2 = 4 - 2 = 2$
(3) a $16 - (4 - 1) = 16 - 3 = 13$
b $16 - (4 - 1) = 16 - 4 + 1 = 12 + 1$
$= 13$
(4) a $24 - (15 + 8) = 24 - 23 = 1$
b $24 - (15 + 8) = 24 - 15 - 8 = 9 - 8$
$= 1$
(5) a $12 - (9 - 5) = 12 - 4 = 8$
b $12 - (9 - 5) = 12 - 9 + 5 = 3 + 5$
$= 8$

Exercise 16a (page 131)

1. the missing values are:
   a $30\,m^3$ b $60\,m^3$ c $48\,cm^3$
   d $25\,m^3$ e $27\,cm^3$ f $2\,cm$
   g $2\,m$ h $3\,m$ i $6\,cm$
   j $34\,m^3$
2. $8\,cm^3$
3. $810\,cm^3$
4. $3\,m$
5. $3\,m$
6. the cube (by $1\,cm^3$)
7. $150\,m^3$; 10 people
8. $20\,m^2$
9. $450\,cm^3$
10. $4\,cm$
11. a i $288\,000\,cm^3$ ii $0.288\,m^3$ b $201.6\,kg$
12. a i $360\,000\,cm^3$ ii $0.36\,m^3$ b $360\,kg$
13. a $20\,000\,cm^3$ b $54\,kg$
14. 2 500 blocks
15. 1 000 cubes

Exercise 16b (page 133)

1. 2 litres
2. 4 litres
3. 750 litres
4. $49.5\,kl$
5. a 24 000 litres b nearly 5 days

Exercise 16c (page 134)

1. $90\,cm^3$
2. $60\,cm^3$
3. $72\,cm^3$
4. $7\tfrac{1}{2}\,cm^3$
5. $35\,cm^3$
6. $63\,cm^3$

Revision exercise 5 (page 135)

1. a 15.74 b 2.34
2. a 3460 b 8000
   c 0.0515 d 0.247
3. a 4 b 0.024 c 0.0064
4. a 0.06 b $90\,000$ c 100
5. 2.625
6. a $\tfrac{11}{40}$ b $27\tfrac{1}{2}\%$
7. 54
8. ₦$5\,610$
9. 95
10. ₦$1\,674$

Revision exercise 6 (page 135)

1. $(b+5)$ wk
2. $a-8$
3. $60m\,s$
4. $\tfrac{x}{4}$ (or $\tfrac{1}{4}x$) g
5. $105n\,cm$
6. $360°$
7. $10\,cm$
8. $6.9\,cm$
9. see answer to question 8, Exercise 11b
10. a 2 b 4 c 3 d 1

Revision exercise 7 (page 136)

1. a $+5$ b -9 c -14
2. a -11 b $+8$ c -3
3. $3\,BC$
4. a $-1\tfrac{5}{6}$ b $-8.2°C$
5. a $20x$ b $8y$ c $4b$ d $4c$
6. a $12mn$ b $6a^2b$ c $\tfrac{3a}{5b}$ d $7x$
7. a $5x$ b $-18x$
8. a $4a-4$ b $5x-5y$ c $5x-11y$
9. a $5x-3$ b $x-7y$ c $5b-4a$
10. ₦$(3x-a)$

Revision exercise 8 (page 137)

1. a $1\,cm$ b $6\,cm$ c $9\,cm$
2. $3.14\,m$
3. $36\,cm$; $80\,cm^2$
4. $176\,cm$; $2\,464\,cm^2$
5. $54\,cm^2$
6. $14\,cm^2$
7. $1\,925\,cm^2$
8. $720\,cm^3$; 90
9. $100\,000$ litres
10. $12\,000\,cm^3$

Exercise 17a (page 140)

1. a Eagles b Falcons
   c yes d 79 e 58
   f 13 g 2 h $\tfrac{1}{4}$ i nearly 2
   j 3 (to the nearest whole number)
   k 33 pts l 11 pts
2. a 23%
   b Malaria/fever and Injury/accident
   c HIV & AIDS and TB d statement ii
   e Malaria is the biggest cause of death in three of the age groups. However, the 15–59 age group has the highest population and 59% of those deaths are caused by HIV & AIDS and TB. Perhaps HIV & AIDS/TB is actually the biggest killer. We need more data – about population.
   f Malaria is a big killer. Yet it has been eradicated in many countries. Therefore, in theory, this should be the easiest and cheapest to address and would save many lives, particularly young lives. HIV & AIDS requires a change of social

behaviour and retro-viral drugs, which are very expensive. These factors are difficult for governments to address. However, it is affecting the biggest and most productive sector of the population. Perhaps this should be the biggest priority. Who would be a Minister of Health!?

3 a yes, from 361 students in 1995 to 506 students in 2000
   b 145
   c 10 classes in 1995; 10 classes in 1996
   d 1997   e 2001   f about 540
4 a bicycles
   b 63 (bicycles and motor bikes)
   c 4   d motor bike   e 0
   f no; all that can be said is that the boy did not see any buses among the 100 vehicles which passed him; some buses may travel on the road at other times
   g possibly in a small village; we would expect more buses and taxis in a city
5 a rent   b food   c ₦19 200
   d ₦13 900   e ₦35 000   f week 3
   g week 2
   h $\frac{1}{8}$ (in four weeks ₦13 900 is spent on entertainment out of ₦112 000 earned; ₦$\frac{13\,900}{112\,000} \simeq$ ₦$\frac{14\,000}{112\,000} = \frac{1}{8}$)

Exercise 18a (page 145)

1 a 15 students   b 87   c 41
   d 70   e 4th   f 9th equal
   g 12th (although he has the 10th best mark, there are 11 students in front of him)
   h 10 students   i 14 students
   j 1 student   k 64
2 a car: 5; lorry: 9; bus: 1; taxi: 2; others: 2
   b lorry   c 19
   d motor bikes, bicycles, army vehicles such as tanks
   e yes: 14 accidents to cars and lorries; only 5 accidents to all other vehicles.
3 a ships   b army   c navy
   d no   e 60 000   f 40 000
   g $2\frac{1}{2}$ approximately   h 25 000
4 a August   b 35 cm

c January, February, November, December
d January, February, March, April, May, October, November, December
e August, July, June, September, May, October
f June, July, August
g January, February, March, April, November, December
h 108 cm
i yes, in August and July 59 cm of rain fell
5 a no
   b Universities
   c Primary Schools
   d there are far more students and teachers in Primary Schools than in Universities; there are many more Primary Schools than Universities
   e $\frac{1}{2}$ f $\frac{1}{4}$ g $\frac{1}{6}$
6 a 10°   b 16   c 20
   d Yes (Although FCT is not a State, its schools receive the same educational benefits as those in the States.)

Exercise 18b (page 147)

1 a A, A, B, B, B, B, C, C, C, D
   b grade B
   c 6 students
   d

grade	A	B	C	D
frequency	2	4	3	1

Table A4

e

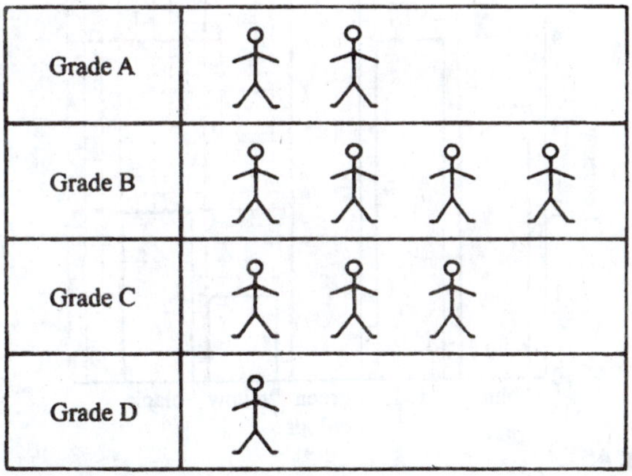

Grade A	👤 👤
Grade B	👤 👤 👤 👤
Grade C	👤 👤 👤
Grade D	👤

Fig. A2

221

② a

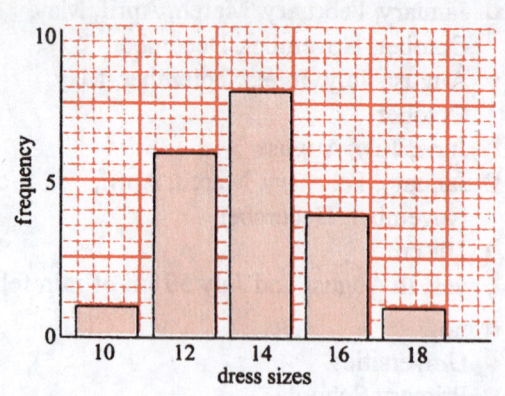

Fig. A3

b sizes 12, 14 and 16

③ a 12 vehicles
b

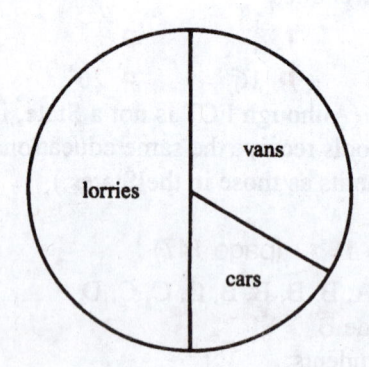

Fig. A4

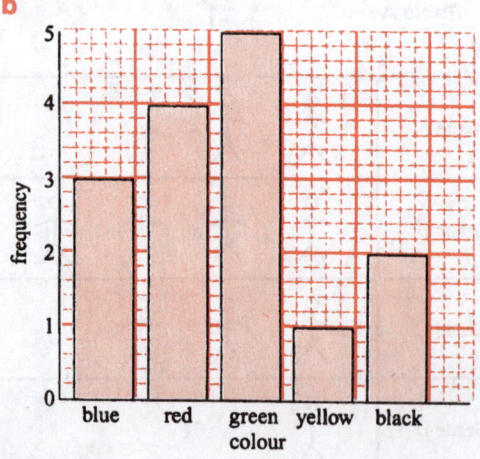

④ a green
b

Fig. A5

⑤ a $\frac{1}{8}$ b $\frac{3}{8}$ c 45°   d 135°

e

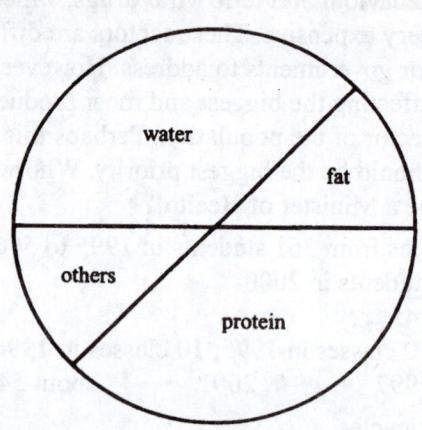

Fig. A6

⑪ a 360 animals
b

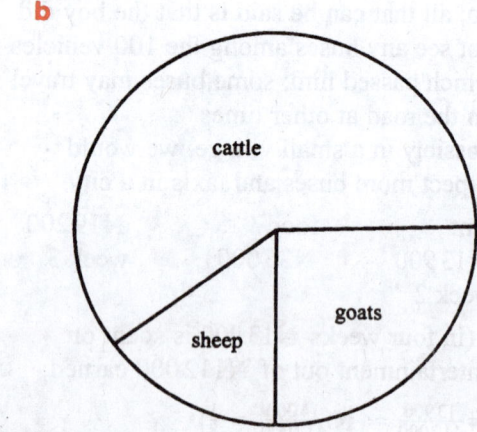

Fig. A7

⑫ a Table A.5

size	6	7	8	9	10	11
frequency	2	4	6	5	2	1

Table A5

b

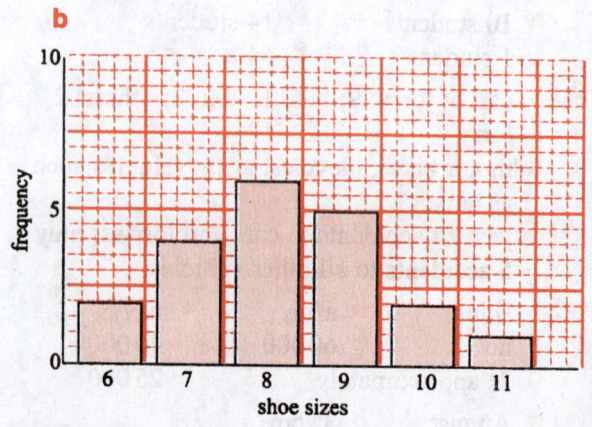

Fig. A8

222

c sizes 7, 8 and 9

13 a

score	frequency
5	4
6	3
7	6
8	8
9	7
10	5

Table A6

b 33 **c** 7 **d** 8

14 a

age (in years)	frequency
9	5
10	11
11	4
12	3
13	2

Table A7

b 25 **c** 4 years

15 a

number	1	2	3	4	5	6
frequency	2	3	7	5	7	1

Table A8

b 3 and 5

Exercise 19a (page 150)
(1) true (2) true (3) false (4) false
(5) true (6) false (7) true (8) true
(9) false (10) true (11) true (12) true
(13) false (14) true (15) false (16) false
(17) true (18) false (19) true (20) false

Exercise 19b (page 151)
(1) $x = 4$ (2) $x = 5$ (3) $x = 8$
(4) $x = 6$ (5) $x = 3$ (6) $x = 3$
(7) $x = 17$ (8) $x = 11$ (9) $x = 5$
(10) $x = 25$ (11) $x = 4$ (12) $x = 8$
(13) $x = 10$ (14) $x = 36$ (15) $x = 4$
(16) $x = 8$ (17) $x = 6$ (18) $x = 1$
(19) $x = 11$ (20) $x = 24$ (21) $x = 1$
(22) $x = 6$ (23) $x = 0$ (24) $x = 3$
(25) $x = 7$ (26) $x = 6$ (27) $x = 4$
(28) $x = 24$ (29) $x = 5$ (30) $x = 0$

Exercise 19c (page 152)
(1) $x = 7$ (2) $x = 4$ (3) $x = 4$
(4) $x = 3$ (5) $x = 5$ (6) $x = 6$
(7) $x = 10$ (8) $x = 6$ (9) $x = 10$
(10) $x = 36$ (11) $x = 6$ (12) $x = 30$
(13) $x = 21$ (14) $x = 4$ (15) $x = 20$
(16) $x = 6$ (17) $x = 7$ (18) $x = 6$
(19) $x = 2$ (20) $x = 6$ (21) $x = 1$
(22) $x = 10$ (23) $x = 20$ (24) $x = 17$
(25) $x = 7$ (26) $x = 9$ (27) $x = 0$
(28) $x = 5$ (29) $x = 48$ (30) $x = 35$

Exercise 19d (page 154)
(1) $y = 3$ (2) $a = 3$ (3) $x = 4$
(4) $p = 3$ (5) $n = 4$ (6) $m = 10$
(7) $t = 4$ (8) $x = 2$ (9) $a = 6$
(10) $y = 3$ (11) $d = 7$ (12) $q = 3$
(13) $b = 2$ (14) $a = 10$ (15) $a = 1$
(16) $x = 2$ (17) $a = 6$ (18) $x = 3$
(19) $x = 3$ (20) $x = 2$ (21) $x = 2$
(22) $x = 5$ (23) $x = 3$ (24) $x = 0$
(25) $a = 4$ (26) $x = 3$ (27) $b = 3$
(28) $y = 7$ (29) $p = 6$ (30) $w = 0$

Exercise 19e (page 154)
(1) $x = 4\frac{1}{3}$ (2) $x = 1\frac{5}{6}$ (3) $x = \frac{3}{5}$
(4) $x = \frac{3}{4}$ (5) $x = 3\frac{1}{2}$ (6) $x = \frac{6}{7}$
(7) $x = 1\frac{4}{9}$ (8) $x = \frac{1}{8}$ (9) $x = \frac{4}{5}$
(10) $x = 1\frac{1}{2}$ (11) $x = 2\frac{1}{3}$ (12) $x = 2\frac{1}{2}$
(13) $a = 3\frac{1}{4}$ (14) $x = 2\frac{1}{2}$ (15) $p = 3\frac{6}{7}$
(16) $y = 3\frac{1}{8}$ (17) $m = 2\frac{3}{10}$ (18) $n = 1\frac{8}{9}$
(19) $s = 3\frac{1}{2}$ (20) $x = 13\frac{1}{3}$

Exercise 19f (page 155)
(1) $n = 4$ (2) $y = 11$ (3) $c = 6$
(4) $b = 3$ (5) $x = 12$ (6) $s = 4$

⑦ $u = 11$ ⑧ $m = 4$ ⑨ $p = 6$ $v = 23°$ ($v + 35°$ vertically opposite to $58°$)
⑩ $a = 1$ ⑪ $t = 2$ ⑫ $f = 5$
⑬ $h = 8$ ⑭ $y = 5$ ⑮ $d = 7$ $w = 122°$ (vertically opposite to t)
⑯ $k = 2$ ⑰ $q = 3$ ⑱ $n = 8$ ⑫ $x = 90°$ (angles on a straight line)
⑲ $t = 5\frac{1}{2}$ ⑳ $a = 1\frac{3}{5}$ ㉑ $z = 2\frac{1}{3}$ $y = 62°$ ($y + 28°$ vertically opposite to right angle)
㉒ $x = 2\frac{1}{2}$ ㉓ $y = \frac{4}{9}$ ㉔ $b = 10\frac{1}{3}$ $z = 49°$ ($z + 41°$ vertically opposite to x)
㉕ $h = \frac{2}{3}$ ㉖ $k = \frac{7}{10}$ ㉗ $m = \frac{1}{4}$

Exercise 20c (page 159)

㉘ $z = 1\frac{5}{6}$ ㉙ $y = 1\frac{5}{11}$ ㉚ $y = 2\frac{1}{2}$

① $\hat{SOQ} = 37°$ (vertically opposite to $\hat{POR}$)
$\hat{POS} = 143°$ (adjacent on straight line to $\hat{POR}$)

Exercise 20a (page 156)

$\hat{ROQ} = 143°$ (vertically opposite to $\hat{POS}$)

① a $\hat{ACD} = 60°$, $\hat{BCD} = 120°$
b $\hat{ACD} + \hat{BCD} = 180°$

② $\hat{QXR} = 35°$ ③ $\hat{RXS} = 47°$

c the sum of the two angles should be $180°$

④ $\hat{PXQ} = 22°$

② a $\hat{AOC} = \hat{DOB}$ b $\hat{AOC} + \hat{AOD} = 180°$

⑤ a $\hat{CXD} = 54°$, $\hat{AXB} = 144°$
b $\hat{AXC} = 180°$
c AXC is a straight line

c COB is the same size as AOD
d $\hat{COB} = \hat{AOD}$ e $360°$

⑥ $2x + 2y = 180$, $x + y = \hat{MON} = 90°$

③ b the sum of the angles should be $360°$
c the sum of the angles at a point is $360°$

⑦ $x + 2x + 3x + 4x = 360$, $x = 36$; $\hat{EKF} = 36°$, $\hat{FKG} = 72°$, $\hat{GKH} = 108°$, $\hat{HKE} = 144°$

Exercise 20b (page 158)

⑧ $x + 2x + 6x = 180$, $x = 20$; $\hat{UXV} = 20°$

① $a = 130°$ (angles on a straight line)
② $b = 40°$ (angles on a straight line)

Exercise 20d (page 160)

③ $c = 115°$ (angles on a straight line)
$d = 65°$ (vertically opposite angles)
$e = 115°$ (vertically opposite angles)

① a WX, ZY, EF
b XY, WE, DE, or PS, QR, HG
c FG (this includes the segments, FS, FR, SR, SG, RG)
d yes, AD   e no

④ $f = 120°$ (angles at a point)
⑤ $g = 140°$ (angles at a point)
⑥ $h = 150°$ (adjacent angles on a straight line)

② a 8 angles
b corresponding angles are equal
c

⑦ $j = 142°$ (angles on a straight line)
$i = 55°$ (angles on a straight line)

⑧ $k = 45°$ (angles on a straight line)
$l = 135°$ (vertically opposite to $100°$ and $35°$ given)
$m = 45°$ (vertically opposite to k found)

⑨ $n = 34°$ (vertically opposite angles)
$p = 56°$ (angles on a straight line)
$q = 56°$ (vertically opposite to p)
$r = 90°$ (vertically opposite to given right angle)

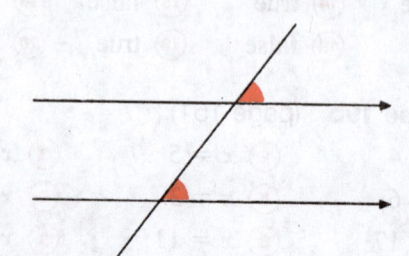

Fig. A9

d alternate angles are equal
e alternate angles are equal

⑩ $s = 25°$ (angles at a point; $2s = 50°$)

③ a $\hat{CYX}$, $\hat{DYQ}$, $\hat{YXB}$, $\hat{AXY}$ b $\hat{XYC}$, $\hat{YXA}$

⑪ $t = 122°$ (angles on a straight line)

224

④ a ŵ   b k̂   c û   d n̂
  e ŵ   f k̂   g t̂   h n̂

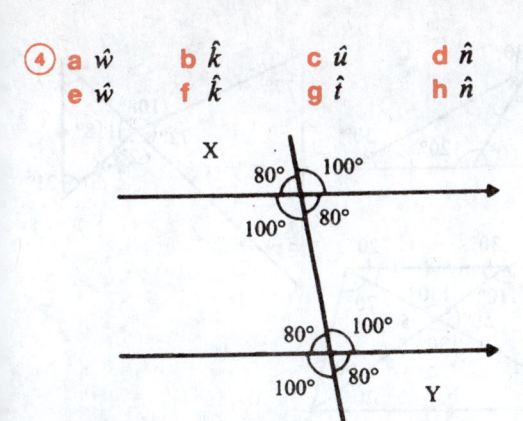

Fig. A10

Exercise 20e (page 162)
(It is possible that you may have different but correct reasons.)

① a = 110° (angles on a straight line)
  b = 70°   (vertically opposite angles)
  c = 110° (vertically opposite to a)
  d = 110° (alternate to c)
  e = 70°   (corresponding to b)
  f = 110° (corresponding to c)
  g = 70°   (corresponding angles)
② h = 40°   (alternate angles)
  i = 140° (angles on a straight line)
③ j = 75°   (angles on a straight line)
  k = 75°   (corresponding angles)
④ l = 45°   (alternate angles)
  m = 30°   (alternate angles)
⑤ n = 68°   (angles on a straight line)
  p = 68°   (alternate angles)
  q = 112° (alternate angles)
⑥ r = 113° (angles on a straight line)
  s = 67°   (corresponding angles)
  t = 67°   (alternate angles)
  u = 113° (alternate to r)
  v = 113° (corresponding to u)
⑦ w = 42°   (alternate angles)
  x = 138° (angles on a straight line)
  y = 63°   (angles on a straight line)
  z = 63°   (alternate angles)

Exercise 20f (page 162)

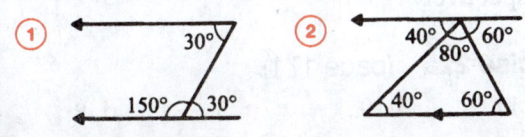

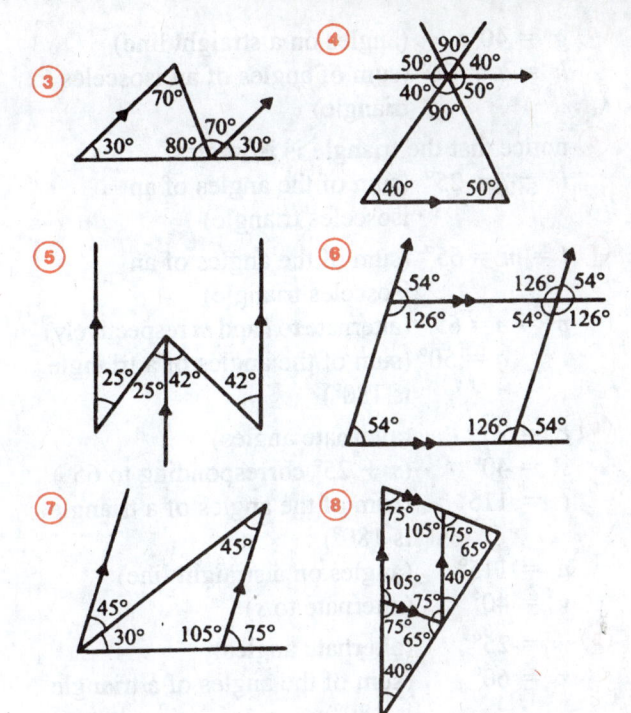

Fig. A11

Exercise 20g (page 162)
① a In △ABC, Â = 70°, B̂ = 70°, Ĉ = 40°
     In △PQR, P̂ = 42°, Q̂ = 63°, R̂ = 75°
  b 180°   c 180°
  d in both cases the sum of the angles of the triangles was 180°
② c thesum of the angles of both triangles was 180°
③ d thethree angles should form a straight line along one edge; the sum of adjacent angles on a straight line is 180°

Exercise 20h (page 164)
① a = 90°   (sum of the angles of a triangle is 180°)
② b = 130° (sum of the angles of a triangle is 180°)
③ c = 60°   (angles on a straight line)
  d = 80°   (sum of the angles of a triangle is 180°)
④ e = 75°   (base angles of an isosceles triangle)
  f = 30°   (sum of the angles of a triangle is 180°)

225

⑤ g = 40°   (angles on a straight line)
  h = k = 70° (sum of angles of an isosceles triangle)
⑥ notice that the triangle is isosceles
  i = j = 25° (sum of the angles of an isosceles triangle)
⑦ l = m = 65° (sum of the angles of an isosceles triangle)
  p = n = 65° (alternate to l and m respectively)
  q = 50°   (sum of the angles of a triangle is 180°)
⑧ r = 25°   (alternate angles)
  s = 40°   (s + 25° corresponding to 65°)
  t = 115°   (sum of the angles of a triangle is 180°)
  u = 115°   (angles on a straight line)
  v = 40°   (alternate to s)
⑨ w = 25°   (alternate angles)
  x = 60°   (sum of the angles of a triangle is 180°)
  y = 110°   (angles on a straight line)
  z = 45°   (sum of the angles of a triangle is 180°)

Exercise 20i (page 164)
① a 68°   b 79°   c 106°
  d 120°   e 64°   f 35°
  g 65°   h 71°   i 43°
  j 60°   k 90°   l 97°

②

	AB̂C	BÂC	AĈB	AĈD
a	58°	47°	75°	105°
b	65°	53°	62°	118°
c	67°	19°	94°	86°
d	46°	99°	35°	145°

Table A9

③ x + 2x + 3x = 180°, x = 30°; the angles are 30°, 60°, 90°
④ a 72°   b isosceles
  c the angles are 54°, 54°, 72°
⑤

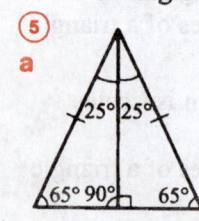

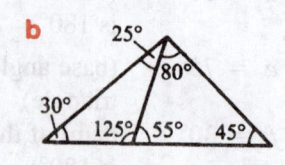

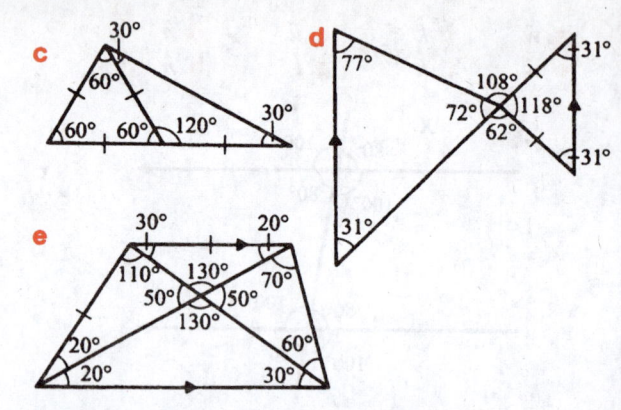

Fig. A12

Exercise 21a (page 167)
④ d there are two sides of 5 cm opposite to each other,
    there are two sides of 3 cm opposite to each other
  e there are two angles of 70° opposite to each other,
    there are two angles of 110° opposite to each other
⑤ the obtuse angles are equal; the acute angles are equal
⑥ c to the nearest mm, XA = XB = 2·2 cm and XB = XD = 2·8 cm
  d X is the mid-point of both diagonals of the parallelogram
⑦ c it is true that the diagonals of a parallelogram bisect each other
⑧ b 90°
⑨ b DC = 4·1 cm to the nearest mm, BÂD = 110°; BĈD = 66½ and AD̂C = 113½° to the nearest half-degree
⑩ AC = 6·2 cm, AD = 4·2 cm, DC = 3·1 cm, BD = 5·7 cm (all to the nearest mm)

Exercise 21b (page 169)
① c they are parallel to each other
⑥ the areas of the parallelograms are approximately 14·1 cm² and 11·6 cm² respectively

Exercise 22a (page 171)
① a 11   b 9   c 5   d 8

226

e 6   **f** 4   **g** 7   **h** 12
i 4   **j** 4·3

(2) **a** 4·5 cm   **b** ₦82   **c** 4·8 kg
d $3\frac{1}{4}$ **e** 0·63

(3) ₦1 277   (4) 3   (5) 36   (6) 25 °C

(7) **a** 15 mm   **b** 3 mm

(8) 27 goals   (9) 28 years

(10) approximately 13 men

(11) **a** 22 marks   **b** 55%

(12) **a** 10·7(3) hours
b advertisement ii) is accurate; advertisement i) is not accurate since some batteries do not last 10 hours

Exercise 22b (page 173)

(1) **a** 4   **b** 6   **c** 4   **d** $3\frac{1}{2}$ **e** 17
(2) **a** 4   **b** $5\frac{1}{2}$ **c** 6
d $3\frac{1}{2}$ **e** $26\frac{1}{2}$ **f** 15

Exercise 22c (page 173)

(1) **a** 9   **b** 4   **c** 14
d 36, 38 (bimodal)   **e** 3, 5 (bimodal)

(2) **a**

grade	A	B	C	D	E	F
frequency	3	5	2	4	5	1

Table A10

b B, E (bimodal)

(3) 7

Exercise 22d (page 174)

1	a	b	c	d	e
mode	7	5	12	7	10
median	9	6	11	7	10
mean	10	$6\frac{1}{2}$	10	6·3	10·4
2	a	b	c	d	e
mode	4	5	0	7	6
median	$3\frac{1}{2}$	6	3	7	$4\frac{1}{2}$
mean	$3\frac{1}{4}$	6	5	8	$4\frac{1}{2}$

Table A11

(3) **a** 17 students   **b** grade B   **c** grade C
(4) **a** size 7   **b** size $7\frac{1}{2}$

(5) **a** mode is 1 km   **b** median is 2 km
c mean is 2·3 km

(6) **a** 15 girls
b modal age is 16 years and median age is 16 years
c mean is $15\frac{8}{15}$ years

(7) **a** 20 students
b mode = 14 marks, median = 14 marks, mean = 14 marks

Exercise 23a (page 176)

(1) **a** cm   **b** cm   **c** mm   **d** km
e mm   **f** m   **g** mm   **h** mm
i km   **j** cm

(2) **a** g or kg   **b** t   **c** g
d g or kg   **e** kg   **f** g
g kg   **h** g   **i** kg   **j** kg

(3) **a** mℓ   **b** litres   **c** mℓ
d mℓ   **e** litres   **f** kℓ
g mℓ   **h** kℓ   **i** litres
j kℓ or litres

Exercise 23c (page 178)

the following are *not* sensible:
a), b), e), g), i), j), l), n), o), p), q), s), u), v), w), y)

Exercise 23d (page 179)

(1) **a** i 19 000   ii 18 600   iii 18 620
b i 25 000   ii 25 200   iii 25 250
c i 33 000   ii 32 800   iii 32 780
d i 7 000   ii 7 200   iii 7 160
e i 3 000   ii 3 000   iii 2 970
f i 9 000   ii 9 500   iii 9 480
g i 15 000   ii 14 900   iii 14 940
h i 27 000   ii 26 900   iii 26 890
i i 45 000   ii 45 100   iii 45 070
j i 6 000   ii 5 600   iii 5 620
k i 16 000   ii 16 100   iii 16 070
l i 13 000   ii 12 500   iii 12 510
m i 10 000   ii 9 900   iii 9 900
n i 30 000   ii 30 100   iii 30 100
o i 8 000   ii 8 400   iii 8 350

(2) **a** 350   **b** 380   **c** 700
d 710   **e** 720

(3) **a** 7   **b** 12   **c** 79
d 30   **e** 10

④ a 0.7 b 0.1 c 0.2
   d 0.5 e 1.0
⑤ a 0.16 b 0.17 c 0.71
   d 0.70 e 0.30
⑥ a i 1 ii 1.4
   b i 4 ii 4.1
   c i 10 ii 9.7
⑦ a i 0.4 ii 0.37
   b i 0.6 ii 0.63
   c i 0.2 ii 0.16
⑧ a i 30 ii 26 iii 26.5
   b i 10 ii 8 iii 8.4
   c i 10 ii 6 iii 5.8
⑨ a 1 b 0.8 c 0.80
⑩ a 100 b 70 c 70 d 69.7

Exercise 23e (page 180)
rough answers from rounded numbers:
① a $20 + 20 = 40$ b $70 - 50 = 20$
   c $20 \times 40 = 800$ d $600 \div 20 = 30$
   e $20 + 60 = 80$ f $90 - 30 = 60$
   g $70 \times 50 = 3500$ h $800 \div 20 = 40$
   i $40 + 50 = 90$ j $700 - 300 = 400$
   k $100 \times 100 = 10000$
   l $200 \div 20 = 10$
   m ₦500 + ₦600 = ₦1100
   n ₦500 − ₦200 = ₦300
   o $10 \times 6 = 60$ p $40 \div 8 = 5$
   q $100g + 500g = 600g$
   r $900m - 500m = 400m$
   s ₦500 × 20 = ₦10000
   t ₦7000 ÷ 20 = ₦350
② a $6 + 4 = 10$ b $12 + 9 = 21$
   c $3 \times 6 = 18$ d $14 \div 7 = 2$
   e $3 + 13 = 16$ f $6 - 3 = 3$
   g $17 \times 1 = 17$ h $16 \div 4 = 4$
   i $7 + 5 = 12$ j $8 - 3 = 5$
   k $8 \times 8 = 64$ l $10 \div 4 = 21\text{–}2$
   m $1 + 2 = 3$ n $10 \times 3 = 30$
   o $18 - 7 = 11$ p $12 \div 8 = 11\text{–}2$
   q $5m + 1m = 6m$ r $\$13 - \$5 = \$8$
   s $3kg \times 5 = 15kg$ t $20 \div 5 = 4$
③ a $0.4 \times 0.9 = 0.36$
   b $0.08 \times 0.03 = 0.0024$
   c $0.3 \times 0.7 = 0.21$
   d $0.05 \times 0.02 = 0.001$

e $0.09 \times 0.1 = 0.009$
f $0.8 \cdot 4 \, 0.2 = 4$
g $0.6 \div 0.03 = 20$
h $0.5 \div 0.1 = 5$
i $0.07 \div 0.3 = 0.23$
j $0.1 \div 0.03 = 3\frac{1}{3}$

Exercise 23f (page 181)
① compare the following accurate answers with the estimates to the corresponding questions in Exercise 23e:
   (1) e 75 j 366 o 55.68 t ₦280
   (2) e 16.22 j 4.1 o $10\frac{7}{8}$ t $3\frac{11}{16}$
   (3) e 0.0108 j 4
② ₦262 000 ③ 33 (approx.)
④ ₦33 500 ⑤ 204 000
⑥ estimate: $40 \times 10 = 400$
   accurate: $36 \times 12 = 432$
⑦ e
⑧ ₦1 677; the student forget to put in the decimal point correctly
⑨ estimate: ₦200 × 300 = ₦60 000
⑩ estimate: $3000 \div 6$ km per hour = 500 km per hour; accurate: 484 km per hour

Exercise 23g (page 181)
① 2.1 km ② 18 litres ③ 180 cm
④ 40 mangoes ⑤ 30 kg ⑥ 12 t
⑦ ₦4000 ⑧ 5 mm ⑨ 7 g ⑩ 8 m

Exercise 24a (page 183)
① $2 \times 10^3 + 3 \times 10^2 + 8 \times 10^1 + 9 \times 1$
② $6 \times 8^2 + 4 \times 8^1 + 7 \times 1$
③ $3 \times 6^4 + 5 \times 6^3 + 1 \times 6^2 + 5 \times 6^1 + 4 \times 1$
④ $4 \times 5^3 + 1 \times 5^2 + 0 \times 5^1 + 2 \times 1$
⑤ $1 \times 2^3 + 0 \times 2^2 + 1 \times 2^1 + 1 \times 1$
⑥ $3 \times 4^4 + 3 \times 4^3 + 0 \times 4^2 + 1 \times 4^1 + 0 \times 1$
⑦ $2 \times 7^4 + 6 \times 7^3 + 5 \times 7^2 + 2 \times 7^1 + 3 \times 1$
⑧ $1 \times 2^3 + 1 \times 2^2 + 0 \times 2^1 + 0 \times 1$
⑨ $2 \times 3^3 + 1 \times 3^2 + 0 \times 3^1 + 2 \times 1$
⑩ $8 \times 9^4 + 1 \times 9^3 + 0 \times 9^2 + 6 \times 9^1 + 2 \times 1$
⑪ $1 \times 2^4 + 0 \times 2^3 + 1 \times 2^2 + 1 \times 2^1 + 0 \times 1$

12. $1 \times 2^5 + 0 \times 2^4 + 1 \times 2^3 + 1 \times 2^2 + 0 \times 2^1 + 1 \times 1$

Exercise 24b (page 184)

3.

base ten	binary	base ten	binary
1	1	11	1011
2	10	12	1100
3	11	13	1101
4	100	14	1110
5	101	15	1111
6	110	16	10000
7	111	17	10001
8	1000	18	10010
9	1001	19	10011
10	1010	20	10100

Table A12

Exercise 24c (page 185)

1. 1, 10, 11, 100, 101, 110, 111, 1000, 1001, 1010, 1011, 1100, 1101, 1110, 1111, 10000, 10001, 10010, 10011, 10100

2.

2^1	2^2	2^3	2^4	2^5	2^6	2^7	2^8	2^9
2	4	8	16	32	64	128	256	512

3. a A(000), B(001), C(010), E(100), F(101), G(110), H(111)
   b The numbers in boxes A to H are the binary numbers from 0 to 7 in numerical order.

4. 1010001, 7 digits

5. a 3 b 8 c 32

6. a 11010 b 100000 c 100111
   d 101111 e 110100 f 111100
   g 1000001 h 1000111

7. a 13 b 14 c 16
   d 18 e 21 f 25
   g 41 h 56

8. a 0 b 1

9. a 100100 b 1000000

10. a 101 b 1001

Exercise 24d (page 187)

1. a 1000 b 1000 c 1011 d 1010
   e 100 f 100 g 1 h 1
   i 1001 j 100 k 110 l 1011

2. a 10111 b 11100 c 10001
   d 1101 e 1000 f 0
   g 110111 h 100001 i 1110
   j 10001 k 1010100 l 11001011

5. 1011010

Revision exercise 9 (page 189)

1. a 15 km, 10 km, 9 km, 8 km, 6 km, 5 km, 4 km, 2 km, 1 km
   b 6 km

2.

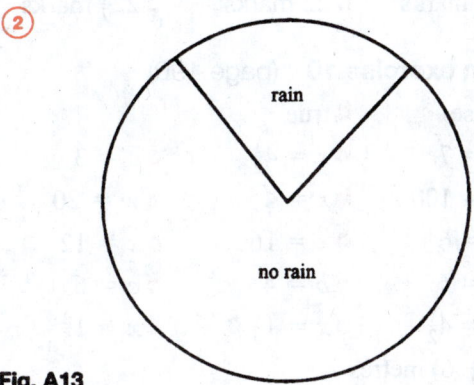

Fig. A13

3. 22 years

4. a 30 b $22\frac{1}{2}$ years

5. $22 \cdot 6\dot{3}$ ($22\frac{19}{30}$) years

6.

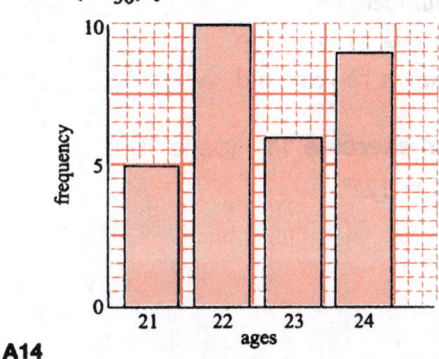

Fig. A14

7.

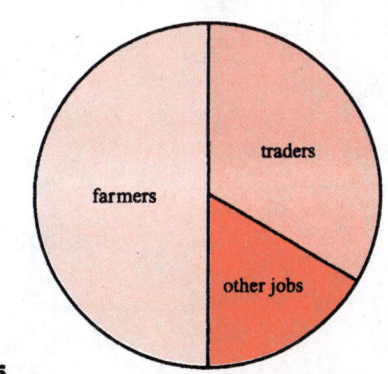

Fig. A15

229

8

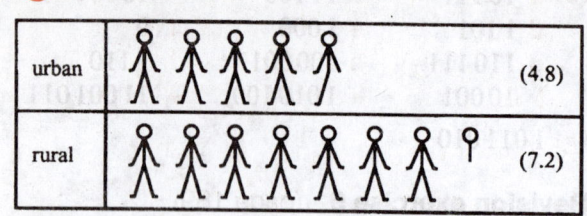

urban	👤👤👤👤	(4.8)
rural	👤👤👤👤👤👤👤	(7.2)

Fig. A16

9 2

10 a 23 marks **b** 22 marks **c** $22\frac{4}{7}$ marks

Revision exercise 10 (page 190)

1 a false **b** true
2 a $x = 7$ **b** $x = 4\frac{1}{2}$ **c** $c = 3$
3 a $x = 100$ **b** $x = 4$ **c** $w = 20$
4 a $x = 6$ **b** $x = 16$ **c** $x = 12$
5 a $a = 6$ **b** $b = 4$ **c** $c = 6$
6 a $x = 4\frac{1}{2}$ **b** $x = 1\frac{1}{3}$ **c** $x = 1\frac{2}{5}$
7 $(2b + 6)$ metres
8 $2b + 6 = 11$, $b = 2\frac{1}{2}$; the breadth is $2\frac{1}{2}$ m
9 $4n + 17 = 41$, $n = 6$; the number is 6
10 $3x - x = 24$, $x = 12$; the son is 12 years old

Revision exercise 11 (page 190)

1 $B\hat{O}C = 127°$
2 160°, 20° and 20°
3 72° **4** 148° **5** 57°
6 perpendicular distance of A from BC = 3·5 cm (approx.); area = 7·9 cm² (approx.)
7 $a = 125°$ $b = 125°$
  $c = 125°$ $d = 55°$
8 $a = 60°$ $b = 44°$ $c = 136°$
9 diagonal = 6·5 cm
10 $a = 62°$ $b = 62°$ $c = 35°$
  $d = 35°$ $e = 118°$

Revision exercise 12 (page 192)

1 a $1 \times 2^4 + 1 \times 2^3 + 1 \times 2^2 + 0 \times 2 + 1$
  b 2^9
2 11 011, 11 100
3 a 30 000 **b** 29 800 **c** 29 840
4 a 0·8 **b** 0·85 **c** 1
5 an even binary number ends with 0; an odd one ends with 1
6 a 1 110 **b** 11
7 100 100
8 a $9 \times 5 = 45$
  b $10 \times 6 = 60$
  c $0·8 \div 0·4 = 2$
9 ₦200 000 × 400 = ₦80 000 000
10 100 kg ÷ 8 = $12\frac{1}{2}$ kg

Index

Note: Page numbers in italic type refer to chapter summaries.

a^2 129
abacus 16
acute angles 63, *68*
addition 1, *3*
   approximation 180
   binary numbers 186, *188*
   decimal fractions 73–74, *80*
   fractions 32–33, *38–39*
   negative numbers 99, *101*
   positive numbers 97, *101*
algebra 41, *43*
   brackets 127–129, *129*
   coefficients 56, *60*
   division 124–125
   equations 150–155, *155*
   grouping like and unlike terms 58, *60*
   grouping positive and negative terms 57
   multiplication 124
   order of operations (BODMAS) 126, *129*
   simplification 57–58, *60*, 124–129
   terms in x 57, *60*
   from words 81–82
algebraic expressions 56, *60*, *84*
algebraic sentences 41, *43*, *84*
   equations 150–155, *155*
   true or false *43*
alternate angles 161–162, *165*
angles 61, *68*
   acute angles 63, *68*
   adjacent angles on a straight line 157, *165*
   alternate angles 161–162, *165*
   anticlockwise 64
   between lines 61–62, 156
   calculating sizes 157–158
   clockwise 64
   constructing angles 67
   corresponding angles 160–161, 162, *165*
   degrees 61

F angles 161, *165*
half turns 63
measuring angles 64–65
naming angles 63–64
non-parallel lines 160, *165*
obtuse angles 63, *68*
parallel lines 160–162, *165*
at a point 157, *165*
protractors 64, *68*
quarter turns 63
reflex angles 63, *68*
revolutions 61, *68*
right angles 63–64, *68*
as rotation 61
straight angles 63, *68*
transversals 160, *165*
in a triangle 162, *165*
turns 61
vertically opposite angles 157, *165*
Z angles 161, *165*
anticlockwise 64
approximation 179–180, *182*
Arabic numerals 17
arcs 89, 90
area 112–122, *123*, 194
   circles 121–122, *123*, 195
   cubes 195
   formulae for calculation 195
   parallelograms 116–117, *123*, 195
   rectangles 113–114, *123*, 195
   square centimetres (cm^2) 112
   square metres (m^2) 112, 194
   squares 113–114, *123*, 195
   trapeziums 120, *123*
   triangles 118–120, *123*, 195
arithmetic mean 171–172
averages 171–174, *175*
   bimodal distribution 175
   mean 171, *175*
   median 172, *175*
   mode 173–174, *175*

balance method of solving equations 152–154, *155*
bar charts 145, *149*
base eight 183
base five 11
base seven 12
base sixty 12
base ten 11, *18*, 183, *188*
base two 184–187, *188*
billion 19, *22*
bimodal distribution 175
binary system 184–187, *188*
   addition 186, *188*
   binary numbers 184
   converting between bases 185, *188*
   multiplication 186, 187, *188*
   subtraction 187, *188*
BODMAS (order of algebraic operations) 126, *129*
body measures 177, *182*
brackets 127–129, *129*

calendar 195
capacity 8, 132, *134*, 176, *182*, 195
   and volume 132
centigrammes (cg) 194
centimetres (cm) 8, 194
chords 89, 90
circles 89–90
   arcs 89, 90
   area 121–122, *123*, 195
   centre 89, 90
   chords 89, 90
   circumference 89, 90, 107–108, *111*
   diameter 89, 90
   lines 89–90
   perimeter 107–108, *111*, 195
   radius (radii) 89, 90
   regions 90
   sectors 90

segments 90
semi-circles 90
circumference 89, 90, *111*
   formulae for calculation 107–110
   measuring 107–108
clockwise 64
cm (centimetres) 8, 194
cm^2 (square centimetres) 112, 194
cm^3 (cubic centimetres) 130, 194
codes 14
coefficients 56, *60*
common denominator *38*
common factors 25, *28*
common multiples 26–27, *28*
cones 51
construction 166, *170*
   angles 67
   parallel lines 166–167
   perpendiculars 167–169
corresponding angles 160–161, 162, *165*
counting 11–12
counting boards 15–16
cubed numbers 24, *28*
cubes 47
   area 195
   volume 131, *134*, 195
cubic centimetres (cm^3) 130, 194
cubic metres (m^3) 130, 131, 194
cubic millimetres (mm^3) 194
cuboids 46–47, 50
   volume 131, *134*, 195
currencies 9, 195
cylinders 49, 50

data 139, *143*
   collection 141
   presentation 144–145, *149*
decagrammes (dag) 194
decametres (dam) 8, 194
decigrammes (dg) 194
decimal point 18, *18*
decimals 2, 7, 9, *80*
   addition 73–74, *80*
   changing decimals to fractions 79
   changing fractions to decimals 78–79, *80*
   division by powers of 10 75

division of decimals 77
   fractions 18, 21–22, 73
   multiplication by powers of 10 74–75
   multiplication of decimals 76, *80*
   and percentages 79, *80*
   recurring decimal 79, *80*
   subtraction 73–74, *80*
   terminating decimal 78, *80*
decimetres (dm) 8, 194
degrees 61
denominator 29, *38*
dg (decigrammes) 194
diameter 89, 90
digits 17, *18*
   grouping 20, *22*
   and words 21, *22*
directed numbers 96, *101*
distance 176, *182*
divisibility tests 195
division 6
   algebra 124–125
   approximation 180
   decimals 77
   fractions 35–36, *39*
   by powers of 10 75
dm (decimetres) 8, 194

edges 46, 54, *55*
equations 150–155, *155*
   balance method of solving 152–154, *155*
   checking the solution 153–154, *155*
   solutions 151
   solving an equation 151–155, *155*
   true and false open sentences 150, *155*
   unknown 150, *155*
equilateral triangles 87, 88, 89, *91*
equivalent fractions 30–31, *38*
Eratosthenes' sieve 24
estimation 176–177
   body measures 177, *182*
   common measures 176, *182*

F angles 161, *165*
faces 46, 54, *55*
factors 23–25, *28*
   common factors 25, *28*

highest common factor (HCF) 25–26, *28*
   index form 24–25, *28*
   prime factors 24, *28*
   prime numbers 23–24, *28*
formulae (perimeter, area, volume) 195
fractions 2, 7, 29–36, *38–39*
   addition 32–33, *38–39*
   changing decimals to fractions 79
   changing fractions to decimals 78–79, *80*
   common denominator *38*
   decimal fractions 18, 21–22, 73
   denominator 29, *38*
   division 35–36, *39*
   equivalent fractions 30–31, *38*
   improper fractions 30, *38*
   lowest common denominator 31, *38*
   lowest terms 32, *38*
   mixed numbers 30, *38*
   multiplication 34–35, *39*
   numerator 29, *38*
   as percentages 37–38, *39*
   proper fractions 30, *38*
   reciprocal 35, *39*
   simplest form 32, *38*
   subtraction 32–33, *38–39*
freehand sketches *170*
frequency tables 144, *149*

g (grammes) 8, 194
gases 44, *134*
generalised arithmetic 41
geometrical solids 44–55, *55*
   cones 51
   cubes 47, 131, *135*, 195
   cuboids 46–47, 50, 131, *135*, 195
   cylinders 49, 50
   edges 46, 54, *55*
   faces 46, 54, *55*
   nets 47, *55*
   planes 46
   prisms 49–50, *135*
   pyramids 51
   skeleton views 46–47, *55*
   spheres 53
   vertex (vertices) 46, 54, *55*

grammes (g) 8, 194
graphs 144–145
greater than 96

h (hours) 9, 194
ha (hectares) 194
half turns 63
hand-spans 177
HCF (highest common factor) 25–26, 28
hectares (ha) 194
hectogrammes (hg) 194
hectometres (hm) 194
hemispheres 53
hexagons 89
hg (hectogrammes) 194
highest common factor (HCF) 25–26, 28
Hindu–Arabic place-value system 17, *18*
hm (hectometres) 194
hours (h) 9, 194

improper fractions 30, *38*
index (indices) 24–25, *28*
information: statistics 139
isosceles triangles 87, *91*

kilogrammes (kg) 8, 194
kilolitres (kl) 8, 195
kilometres (km) 8, 194
km² (square kilometres) 194
kobo 9, 100–101

l (litres) 8, 132, *134*, 195
LCM (lowest common multiple) 27, *28*
Leap Years 195
length 8, 176, *182*, 194
less than 96
letters for numbers 41, *43*
line of symmetry 86, *91*
liquids 44, *134*
lists 144
litres (l) 8, 132, *134*, 195
lowest common denominator 31, *38*
lowest common multiple (LCM) 27, *28*

m (metres) 8, 194
m² (square metres) 112

m³ (cubic metres) 130, 131, 194
mass 8, 176, *182*, 194
mean 171, *175*
median 172, *175*
mensuration formulae 195
metres (m) 8, 194
milligrammes (mg) 8, 194
millilitres (ml) 8, *134*, 195
millimetres (mm) 8, 194
million 19, *22*
minutes (min) 9, 194
mixed numbers 30, *38*
ml (millilitres) 8, *134*, 195
mm (millimetres) 8, 194
mm³ (cubic millimetres) 194
mode 173–174, *175*
money 9, 195
multiples 26–27, *28*
    common multiples 26–27, *28*
    lowest common multiple (LCM) 27, *28*
multiplication 2, 5
    algebra 124
    approximation 180
    binary numbers 186, 187, *188*
    decimals 76, *80*
    fractions 34–35, *39*
    by powers of 10 74–75
multiplication table 195

naira 9
negative numbers 93–95, *101*
    addition 99, *101*
    directed numbers 96, *101*
    subtraction 100, *101*
nets 47, *55*
number bases 11, 183–184, *188*
    converting between bases 185, *188*
number lines 92–93, *101*
number systems
    counting 11–12
    place-value system 17–18, *18*
    symbols 13–14
numbers
    large numbers 19–20, *22*
    mixed numbers 30, *38*
    positive and negative 93–95, *101*
    small numbers 21–22
numerals 13
    Arabic 17

Hindu–Arabic (international) 17, *18*
    Roman system 13–14, 15, 17
numerator 29, *38*

obtuse angles 63, *68*
obtuse-angled triangles 87
octagons 89
open sentences 40, 150

paces 177
parallel lines 86
    angles 160–162, *165*
    construction 166–167
parallelograms 89
    area 116–117, *123*, 195
    perimeter 105
pentagons 89
per cent 36, *39*
percentages 2, 36–38, *39*
    and decimals 79, *80*
perimeter 102–110, *111*
    circles 107–108, *111*, 195
    formulae for calculation 104–110, 195
    measuring perimeters 102–104
    parallelograms 105
    rectangles 104–105, *111*, 195
    regular and irregular shapes 102–103
    squares 105, *111*, 195
perpendicular distance 169
perpendicular lines: construction 167–169
pi 108
pictograms 145, *149*
pie charts 145, *149*
place-value system 17–18, *18*
    decimal fractions 18
    Hindu–Arabic system 17, *18*
plane shapes 85–91
    area 112–122, *123*, 194
    circles 89–90
    perimeter 102–110, *111*
    polygons 88–89, *91*
    rectangles 85–86, *91*
    squares 86, 89, *91*
    triangles 86–88, *91*
planes 46
polygons 88–89, *91*
    quadrilaterals 68, 89, *91*
    regular polygons 88–89, *91*

positive numbers 93–95, *101*
  addition 97, *101*
  directed numbers 96, *101*
  subtraction 97, *101*
power 24, *28*
prime factors 24, *28*
prime numbers 23–24, *28*
prisms 49–50
  volume 133, *134*, 195
proper fractions 30, *38*
protractors 64, *68*
pyramids 51

quadrilaterals 68, 89, *91*
quarter turns 63
questionnaires 143

radius (radii) 89, 90
rank order 144, *149*
reciprocal 35, *39*
rectangles 85–86, *91*
  area 113–114, *123*, 195
  breadth 104
  centre 85
  diagonal 85, *91*
  length 104
  line of symmetry 86
  perimeter 104–105, *111*, 195
recurring decimal 79, *80*
reflex angles 63, *68*
regions of a circle 90
revolutions 61, *68*
right angles 63–64, *68*
right-angled triangles 87, *91*
  area 118
right-angled triangular prisms:
  volume 133, *134*, 195
Roman numerals 13–14, 15, *17*
rough sketches 166, *170*
rounding off numbers 178–179, *182*

scalene triangles 87, *91*
seconds (s) 9, 194
sectors 90
segments 90
semi-circles 90
SI system of units 8–9, 194–195

sieve of Eratosthenes 24
skeleton views 46–47, *55*
solids
  properties 44–55
  three-dimensional shapes 44–45
  volume 130–133, *134*, 194
  see also geometrical solids
spheres 53
square centimetres (cm²) 112, 194
square kilometres (km²) 194
square metres (m²) 112, 194
square millimetres (mm²) 194
squared numbers 24, *28*
squares 86, 89, *91*
  area 113–114, *123*, 195
  perimeter 105, *111*, 195
statistics 139–143, *143*
  averages 171–174, *175*
  bar charts 145, *149*
  data 139
  data collection 141
  frequency tables 144, *149*
  graphs 144–145
  lists 144
  pictograms 145, *149*
  pie charts 145, *149*
  presentation of data 144–145, *149*
  purpose 139
  questionnaires 143
  rank order 144, *149*
  tables *143*, 144
  tallies 141–143
straight angles 63, *68*
subtraction 1, 4
  approximation 180
  binary numbers 187, *188*
  decimal fractions 73–74, *80*
  fractions 32–33, *38–39*
  negative numbers 100, *101*
  positive numbers 97, *101*
symbols 196
  letters for numbers 41, *43*
  for numbers 13–14
  see also algebra
symmetry: line of symmetry 86, *91*

t (tonnes) 8, 194
tables
  data *143*, 144
  multiplication 195
  SI units 194–195
tally system 13, 141–143
terminating decimal 78, *80*
terms in x 57, *60*
thousand 19
three-dimensional shapes 44–45;
  see also geometrical solids
time 9, 194
tonnes (t) 8, 194
transversals 160, *165*
trapeziums 89
  area 120, *123*
triangles 86–88, *91*
  angles 162, *165*
  area 118–120, *123*, 195
  equilateral triangles 87, 88, 89, *91*
  isosceles triangles 87, *91*
  obtuse-angled triangles 87
  right-angled triangles 87, *91*, 118
  scalene triangles 87, *91*
trillion 19, *22*

unknown 150, *155*

vertex (vertices) 46, 54, *55*
volume 130–133, *134*, 194
  and capacity 132
  cubes 131, *134*, 195
  cubic centimetres (cm³) 130, 194
  cubic metres (m³) 130, 131, 194
  cuboids 131, *134*, 195
  formulae for calculation 195
  right-angled triangular prisms 133, *134*, 195

word problems 81–82

Z angles 161, *165*
zero 17, 96, *101*